Annual Editions: Criminal Justice, 40/e

**Joanne Naughton**

http://create.mheducation.com

ISBN-10: 1259658848     ISBN-13: 9781259658846

# Contents

# Detailed Table of Contents

# Preface

In publishing ANNUAL EDITIONS, we recognize the enormous role played by the public press in providing current, first-rate information about a broad spectrum of criminal justice issues. Many of the articles in various magazines, newspapers, and journals are appropriate for students, researchers, and professionals seeking accurate, current material to help bridge the gap between principles and theories, and the real world. These articles, however, become more useful for study when those of lasting value are carefully collected, organized, indexed, and reproduced in a low-cost format, providing easy and permanent access when the material is needed. That is the role played by *Annual Editions*.

**D**uring the 1970s, criminal justice emerged as an appealing, vital, and unique academic discipline. It emphasizes the professional development of students who plan careers in the field, and attracts those who want to know more about a complex social problem and how the United States deals with it. Criminal justice incorporates a vast range of knowledge from a number of different specialties, including law, history, and the behavioral and social sciences. Each specialty contributes to our fuller understanding of criminal behavior and of society's attitudes toward deviance.

In view of the fact that the criminal justice system is in a constant state of flux, and because the study of criminal justice covers such a broad spectrum, today's students must be aware of a variety of subjects and disciplines. Standard textbooks and traditional anthologies cannot keep pace with the changes as quickly as they occur. In fact, many such sources are already out of date the day they are published. *Annual Editions: Criminal Justice 40th Edition* strives to maintain currency in matters of concern by providing up-to-date information from the most recent literature in the criminal justice field.

This volume contains six units that treat Crime and Justice in America, Victimology, The Police, The Judicial System, Juvenile Justice, and Punishment and Corrections. The articles in these units were selected because they are informative as well as provocative. The selections are timely and useful in their treatment of ethics, punishment, juveniles, courts, police, prosecutors, and other related topics.

Also incorporated are a number of features designed to be useful to students, researchers, and professionals in the criminal justice field. They include the table of contents, setting out the titles of the articles and the units in which they can be found, and a list of relevant Internet sites. In addition, each unit is preceded by an overview that provides a background for informed reading of the articles, and each article is preceded by Learning Outcomes—a listing of goals for the reader to achieve by reading the article.

Finally, each article is followed by a section called Critical Thinking, containing questions designed to spur thoughtful consideration of the ideas raised in the article.

## Editor

Joanne Naughton is a former member of the NYPD, where she encountered most aspects of police work as a police officer, detective, sergeant, and lieutenant. She is also a former staff attorney with The Legal Aid Society, where she represented indigent criminal defendants. In addition to her hands-on experience in criminal justice, she was an adjunct professor at John Jay College of Criminal Justice and has retired from Mercy College where she was an assistant professor. She received her BA and JD at Fordham University.

## Academic Advisory Board

Members of the Academic Advisory Board are instrumental in the final selection of articles for each edition of *Annual Editions*. Their review of the articles for content, level, and appropriateness provides critical direction to the editors and staff. We think that you will find their careful consideration well reflected in this volume.

## Academic Advisory Board Members

**Harry N. Babb**
*Farmingdale State University of New York*

**Richard Baranzini**
*Liberty University*

**Joseph A. Bobak IV**
*Mount Aloysius College*

**Alton Braddock**
*University of Louisiana, Monroe*

**Frank Butler**
*La Salle University*

**James Byrne**
*University of Massachusetts, Lowell*

**Kelli Callahan**
*Park University*

**Terry Campbell**
*Kaplan University*

**Peter D. Chimbos**
*Brescia College at The University of Western Ontario*

**David Coffey**
*Thomas Nelson Community College*

**Bernard Cohen**
*Queens College*

**James Cunningham**
*State Fair Community College*

**Roger Cunningham**
*Eastern Illinois University*

**Michael T. Eskey**
*Park University*

**Bonnie Fisher**
*University of Cincinnati*

**David Forristal**
*Brown Mackie College*

**Paul Frankenhauser**
*Allied American University*

**Paul Fuller**
*Knoxville College*

**Peter Galante**
*Farmingdale State College*

**Alan Garcia**
*Bristol Community College*

**Arnett Gaston**
*University of Maryland*

**Barry Goodson**
*Columbia Southern University*

**Lisa Grey Whitaker**
*Arizona State University*

**Ken Haas**
*University of Delaware*

**Julia Hall**
*Drexel University*

**Bridget A. Hepner-Williamson**
*Sam Houston State University*

**Rick Herbert**
*South Plains College*

**Rosalee Hodges**
*Glendale Community College*

**Michael K. Hooper**
*Sonoma State University*

**Richard Hough**
*University of West Florida*

**Amanda Humphrey**
*Mount Mercy College*

**Larry Jablecki**
*Rice University*

**Gayle Jentz**
*North Hennepin Community College*

**Rachel Jung**
*Mesa Community College*

**Kim Kamins**
*Brown Mackie College*

**Scott Kelly**
*Penn State Altoona*

**William E. Kelly**
*Auburn University*

**Chandrika Kelso**
*National University*

**Steven Kempisty**
*Bryant & Stratton College*

**Lloyd Klein**
*St. Francis College/Hostos Community College*

**Kevin Kolbe**
*Solano Junior College*

**Jordan Land**
*Southwest Florida College*

**Michael A. Langer**
*Loyola University, Chicago*

**Barney Ledford**
*Mid-Michigan Community College*

**Matthew C. Leone**
*University of Nevada*

**Xiangdong Li**
*New York City College of Technology*

**Celia Lo**
*University of Alabama, Tuscaloosa*

**Jennelle London Joset**
*Sanford-Brown College*

**Mark Marsolais**
*Northern Kentucky University*

**Vertel Martin**
*Northampton Community College*

**Jon Maskaly**
*University of South Florida, Tampa*

**Suzanne Montiel**
*Nash Community College*

**Derek Mosley**
*Meridian Community College*

**James Murphy**
*College of Western Idaho*

**Bonnie O. Neher**
*Harrisburg Area Community College*

**Gary Neumeyer**
*Arizona Western College, Yuma*

**Michael Palmiotto**
*Wichita State University*

**Gary Prawel**
*Keuka College*

**Jeffrey Ian Ross**
*University of Baltimore*

**Michael P. Roy**
*Alpena Community College*

**Vincent M. Russo**
*Richard J. Daley College*

**Leslie Samuelson**
*University of Saskatchewan*

**Clifford L. Sanders Jr.**
*Clayton State University*

**Robin Sawyer**
*University of Maryland, College Park*

**Gary A. Sokolow**
*College of the Redwoods*

**Joseph A. Spadaro**
*Goodwin College*

**Darren Stocker**
*Cumberland County College*

**Michael Such**
*Hudson Valley Community College*

**Candace Tabenanika**
*Sam Houston State University*

**Amy Thistlethwaite**
*Northern Kentucky University*

**Al Trego**
*McCann School*

**Joseph L. Victor**
*Mercy College*

**Jason Weber**
*Rasmussen College, Bloomington*

**Larry Woods**
*Tennessee State University*

**Laura Woods Fidelie**
*Midwestern State University*

# Unit 1

# UNIT

Prepared by: Joanne Naughton

# Crime and Justice in America

The American justice system is comprised of three traditional components: Police, Courts, and Corrections. In addition, special attention is also given to crime victims and juveniles. Criminal justice issues continue to be a major problem in the United States. Court dockets are full, our prisons are overcrowded, probation and parole caseloads are overwhelming, our police are being urged to do more, and the bulging prison population places a heavy strain on the economy of the country.

Clearly, crime is a complex problem that defies simple explanations or solutions. While the more familiar crimes of murder, rape, assault, and drug law violations are still with us, international terrorism has become a pressing worry. The debate also continues about how to best handle juvenile offenders, sex offenders, and those who commit acts of domestic violence. The increasing prevalence of Internet crime also demands attention from the criminal justice system.

*Article*

Prepared by: Joanne Naughton

# What Is the Sequence of Events in the Criminal Justice System?

## Learning Outcomes

*After reading this article, you will be able to:*

- Name the agencies that make up the criminal justice system.
- State the various steps from the time someone is arrested for a crime.

## The Private Sector Initiates the Response to Crime

This first response may come from individuals, families, neighborhood associations, business, industry, agriculture, educational institutions, the news media, or any other private service to the public.

It involves crime prevention as well as participation in the criminal justice process once a crime has been committed. Private crime prevention is more than providing private security or burglar alarms or participating in neighborhood watch. It also includes a commitment to stop criminal behavior by not engaging in it or condoning it when it is committed by others.

Citizens take part directly in the criminal justice process by reporting crime to the police, by being a reliable participant (for example, a witness or a juror) in a criminal proceeding and by accepting the disposition of the system as just or reasonable. As voters and taxpayers, citizens also participate in criminal justice through the policymaking process that affects how the criminal justice process operates, the resources available to it, and its goals and objectives. At every stage of the process from the original formulation of objectives to the decision about where to locate jails and prisons to the reintegration of inmates into society, the private sector has a role to play. Without such involvement, the criminal justice process cannot serve the citizens it is intended to protect.

## The Response to Crime and Public Safety Involves Many Agencies and Services

Many of the services needed to prevent crime and make neighborhoods safe are supplied by noncriminal justice agencies, including agencies with primary concern for public health, education, welfare, public works, and housing. Individual citizens as well as public and private sector organizations have joined with criminal justice agencies to prevent crime and make neighborhoods safe.

## Criminal Cases Are Brought by the Government Through the Criminal Justice System

We apprehend, try, and punish offenders by means of a loose confederation of agencies at all levels of government. Our American system of justice has evolved from the English common law into a complex series of procedures and decisions. Founded on the concept that crimes against an individual are crimes against the State, our justice system prosecutes individuals as though they victimized all of society. However, crime victims are involved throughout the process and many justice agencies have programs that focus on helping victims.

There is no single criminal justice system in this country. We have many similar systems that are individually unique. Criminal cases may be handled differently in different jurisdictions, but court decisions based on the due process guarantees of the U.S. Constitution require that specific steps be taken in the administration of criminal justice so that the individual will be protected from undue intervention from the State.

The description of the criminal and juvenile justice systems that follows portrays the most common sequence of events in response to serious criminal behavior.

## Entry into the System

The justice system does not respond to most crime because so much crime is not discovered or reported to the police. Law enforcement agencies learn about crime from the reports of victims or other citizens, from discovery by a police officer in the field, from informants, or from investigative and intelligence work.

Once a law enforcement agency has established that a crime has been committed, a suspect must be identified and apprehended for the case to proceed through the system. Sometimes, a suspect is apprehended at the scene; however, identification of a suspect sometimes requires an extensive investigation. Often, no one is identified or apprehended. In some instances, a suspect is arrested and later the police determine that no crime was committed and the suspect is released.

## Prosecution and Pretrial Services

After an arrest, law enforcement agencies present information about the case and about the accused to the prosecutor, who will decide if formal charges will be filed with the court. If no charges are filed, the accused must be released. The prosecutor can also drop charges after making efforts to prosecute (*nolle prosequi*).

A suspect charged with a crime must be taken before a judge or magistrate without unnecessary delay. At the initial appearance, the judge or magistrate informs the accused of the charges and decides whether there is probable cause to detain the accused person. If the offense is not very serious, the determination of guilt and assessment of a penalty may also occur at this stage.

Often, the defense counsel is also assigned at the initial appearance. All suspects prosecuted for serious crimes have a right to be represented by an attorney. If the court determines the suspect is indigent and cannot afford such representation, the court will assign counsel at the public's expense.

A pretrial-release decision may be made at the initial appearance, but may occur at other hearings or may be changed at another time during the process. Pretrial release and bail were traditionally intended to ensure appearance at trial. However, many jurisdictions permit pretrial detention of defendants accused of serious offenses and deemed to be dangerous to prevent them from committing crimes prior to trial.

The court often bases its pretrial decision on information about the defendant's drug use, as well as residence, employment, and family ties. The court may decide to release the accused on his/her own recognizance or into the custody of a third party after the posting of a financial bond or on the promise of satisfying certain conditions such as taking periodic drug tests to ensure drug abstinence.

In many jurisdictions, the initial appearance may be followed by a preliminary hearing. The main function of this hearing is to discover if there is probable cause to believe that the accused committed a known crime within the jurisdiction of the court. If the judge does not find probable cause, the case is dismissed; however, if the judge or magistrate finds probable cause for such a belief, or the accused waives his or her right to a preliminary hearing, the case may be bound over to a grand jury.

A grand jury hears evidence against the accused presented by the prosecutor and decides if there is sufficient evidence to cause the accused to be brought to trial. If the grand jury finds sufficient evidence, it submits to the court an indictment, a written statement of the essential facts of the offense charged against the accused.

Where the grand jury system is used, the grand jury may also investigate criminal activity generally and issue indictments called grand jury originals that initiate criminal cases. These investigations and indictments are often used in drug and conspiracy cases that involve complex organizations. After such an indictment, law enforcement tries to apprehend and arrest the suspects named in the indictment.

Misdemeanor cases and some felony cases proceed by the issuance of an information, a formal, written accusation submitted to the court by a prosecutor. In some jurisdictions, indictments may be required in felony cases. However, the accused may choose to waive a grand jury indictment and, instead, accept service of an information for the crime.

In some jurisdictions, defendants, often those without prior criminal records, may be eligible for diversion from prosecution subject to the completion of specific conditions such as drug treatment. Successful completion of the conditions may result in the dropping of charges or the expunging of the criminal record where the defendant is required to plead guilty prior to the diversion.

## Adjudication

Once an indictment or information has been filed with the trial court, the accused is scheduled for arraignment. At the arraignment, the accused is informed of the charges, advised of the rights of criminal defendants, and asked to enter a plea to the charges. Sometimes, a plea of guilty is the result of negotiations between the prosecutor and the defendant.

If the accused pleads guilty or pleads *nolo contendere* (accepts penalty without admitting guilt), the judge may accept or reject the plea. If the plea is accepted, no trial is held and the offender is sentenced at this proceeding or at a later date. The plea may be rejected and proceed to trial if, for example, the judge believes that the accused may have been coerced.

If the accused pleads not guilty or not guilty by reason of insanity, a date is set for the trial. A person accused of a serious crime is guaranteed a trial by jury. However, the accused may ask for a bench trial where the judge, rather than a jury, serves as the finder of fact. In both instances the prosecution and defense present evidence by questioning witnesses while the judge decides on issues of law. The trial results in acquittal or conviction on the original charges or on lesser included offenses.

After the trial a defendant may request appellate review of the conviction or sentence. In some cases, appeals of convictions are a matter of right; all States with the death penalty provide for automatic appeal of cases involving a death sentence. Appeals may be subject to the discretion of the appellate court and may be granted only on acceptance of a defendant's petition for a *writ of certiorari*. Prisoners may also appeal their sentences through civil rights petitions and *writs of habeas corpus* where they claim unlawful detention.

## Sentencing and Sanctions

After a conviction, sentence is imposed. In most cases the judge decides on the sentence, but in some jurisdictions the sentence is decided by the jury, particularly for capital offenses.

In arriving at an appropriate sentence, a sentencing hearing may be held at which evidence of aggravating or mitigating circumstances is considered. In assessing the circumstances surrounding a convicted person's criminal behavior, courts often rely on presentence investigations by probation agencies or other designated authorities. Courts may also consider victim impact statements.

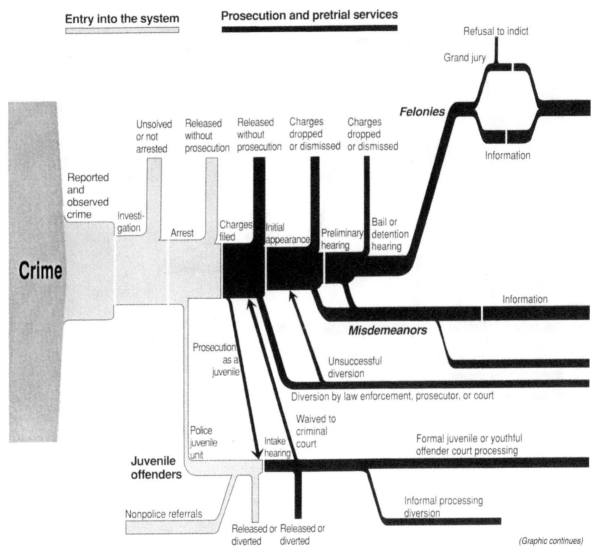

**Entry into the system**  **Prosecution and pretrial services**

*Felonies*

Refusal to indict

Grand jury

Information

**Crime**

Reported and observed crime

Unsolved or not arrested

Released without prosecution

Released without prosecution

Charges dropped or dismissed

Charges dropped or dismissed

Investigation

Arrest

Charges filed

Initial appearance

Preliminary hearing

Bail or detention hearing

Information

*Misdemeanors*

Prosecution as a juvenile

Unsuccessful diversion

Diversion by law enforcement, prosecutor, or court

Police juvenile unit

Intake hearing

Waived to criminal court

Formal juvenile or youthful offender court processing

**Juvenile offenders**

Nonpolice referrals

Released or diverted

Released or diverted

Informal processing diversion

*(Graphic continues)*

**Figure 1**

Note: This chart gives a simplified view of caseflow through the criminal justice system. Procedures vary among jurisdictions. The weights of the lines are not intended to show the actual size of caseloads.

The sentencing choices that may be available to judges and juries include one or more of the following:

- the death penalty
- incarceration in a prison, jail, or other confinement facility
- probation—allowing the convicted person to remain at liberty but subject to certain conditions and restrictions such as drug testing or drug restrictions such as drug testing or drug treatment
- fines—primarily applied as penalties in minor offenses
- restitution—requiring the offender to pay compensation to the victim. In some jurisdictions, offenders may be

sentenced to alternatives to incarceration that are considered more severe than straight probation but less severe than a prison term. Examples of such sanctions include boot camps, intense supervision often with drug treatment and testing, house arrest and electronic monitoring, denial of Federal benefits, and community service.

In many jurisdictions, the law mandates that persons convicted of certain types of offenses serve a prison term. Most jurisdictions permit the judge to set the sentence length within certain limits, but some have determinate sentencing laws that stipulate a specific sentence length that must be served and cannot be altered by a parole board.

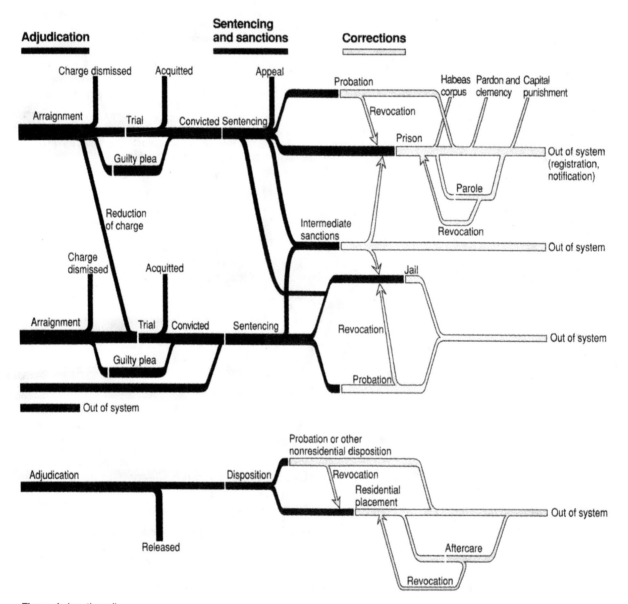

**Figure 1** *(continued)*

Source: Adapted from *The challenge of crime in a free society*. President's Commission on Law Enforcement and Administration of Justice, 1967. This revision, a result of the Symposium on the 30th Anniversary of the President's Commission, was prepared by the Bureau of Justice Statistics in 1997.

## Corrections

Offenders sentenced to incarceration usually serve time in a local jail or a State prison. Offenders sentenced to less than 1 year generally go to jail; those sentenced to more than 1 year go to prison. Persons admitted to the Federal system or a State prison system may be held in prison with varying levels of custody or in a community correctional facility.

A prisoner may become eligible for parole after serving a specific part of his or her sentence. Parole is the conditional release of a prisoner before the prisoner's full sentence has been served. The decision to grant parole is made by an authority such as a parole board, which has power to grant or revoke parole or to discharge a parolee altogether. The way parole decisions are made varies widely among jurisdictions.

Offenders may also be required to serve out their full sentences prior to release (expiration of term). Those sentenced under determinate sentencing laws can be released only after they have served their full sentence (mandatory release) less any "goodtime" received while in prison. Inmates get goodtime

# Discretion Is Exercised throughout the Criminal Justice System

Discretion is "an authority conferred by law to act in certain conditions or situations in accordance with an official's or an official agency's own considered judgment and conscience."[1] Discretion is exercised throughout the government. It is a part of decision making in all government systems from mental health to education, as well as criminal justice. The limits of discretion vary from jurisdiction to jurisdiction.

Concerning crime and justice, legislative bodies have recognized that they cannot anticipate the range of circumstances surrounding each crime, anticipate local mores, and enact laws that clearly encompass all conduct that is criminal and all that is not.[2]

Therefore, persons charged with the day-to-day response to crime are expected to exercise their own judgment within limits set by law. Basically, they must decide—

- whether to take action
- where the situation fits in the scheme of law, rules, and precedent
- which official response is appropriate.[3]

To ensure that discretion is exercised responsibly, government authority is often delegated to professionals. Professionalism requires a minimum level of training and orientation, which guide officials in making decisions. The professionalism of policing is due largely to the desire to ensure the proper exercise of police discretion.

The limits of discretion vary from State to State and locality to locality. For example, some State judges have wide discretion in the type of sentence they may impose. In recent years, other states have sought to limit the judge's discretion in sentencing by passing mandatory sentencing laws that require prison sentences for certain offenses.

## Notes

1. Roscoe Pound, "Discretion, dispensation and mitigation: The problem of the individual special case," *New York University Law Review* (1960) 35:925, 926.
2. Wayne R. LaFave, *Arrest: The decision to take a suspect into custody* (Boston: Little, Brown & Co., 1964), pp. 63–184.
3. Memorandum of June 21, 1977, from Mark Moore to James Vorenberg, "Some abstract notes on the issue of discretion."

Bureau of Justice Statistics (www.ojp.usdoj.gov/bjs/). January 1998. NCJ 167894. To order: 1-800-732-3277.

# Who Exercises Discretion?

| These criminal justice officials . . . | must often decide whether or not or how to— |
| --- | --- |
| Police | Enforce specific laws<br>Investigate specific crimes; Search people |
| Prosecutors | File charges or petitions for adjudication<br>Seek indictments<br>Drop cases<br>Reduce charges |
| Judges or magistrates | Set bail or conditions for release<br>Accept pleas<br>Determine delinquency<br>Dismiss charges<br>Impose sentence<br>Revoke probation |
| Correctional officials | Assign to type of correctional facility<br>Award privileges<br>Punish for disciplinary infractions |
| Paroling authorities | Determine date and conditions of parole<br>Revoke parole |

credits against their sentences automatically or by earning them through participation in programs.

If released by a parole board decision or by mandatory release, the releasee will be under the supervision of a parole officer in the community for the balance of his or her unexpired sentence. This supervision is governed by specific conditions of release, and the releasee may be returned to prison for violations of such conditions.

## Recidivism

Once the suspects, defendants, or offenders are released from the jurisdiction of a criminal justice agency, they may be processed through the criminal justice system again for a new crime. Long term studies show that many suspects who are arrested have prior criminal histories and those with a greater number of prior arrests were more likely to be arrested again. As the courts take prior criminal history into account at sentencing, most prison inmates have a prior criminal history and many have been incarcerated before. Nationally, about half the inmates released from State prison will return to prison.

## The Juvenile Justice System

Juvenile courts usually have jurisdiction over matters concerning children, including delinquency, neglect, and adoption. They also handle "status offenses" such as truancy and running away, which are not applicable to adults. State statutes define which persons are under the original jurisdiction of the juvenile court. The upper age of juvenile court jurisdiction in delinquency matters is 17 in most States.

The processing of juvenile offenders is not entirely dissimilar to adult criminal processing, but there are crucial differences. Many juveniles are referred to juvenile courts by law enforcement officers, but many others are referred by school officials, social services agencies, neighbors, and even parents, for behavior or conditions that are determined to require intervention by the formal system for social control.

At arrest, a decision is made either to send the matter further into the justice system or to divert the case out of the system, often to alternative programs. Examples of alternative programs include drug treatment, individual or group counseling, or referral to educational and recreational programs.

When juveniles are referred to the juvenile courts, the court's intake department or the prosecuting attorney determines whether sufficient grounds exist to warrant filing a petition that requests an adjudicatory hearing or a request to transfer jurisdiction to criminal court. At this point, many juveniles are released or diverted to alternative programs.

All States allow juveniles to be tried as adults in criminal court under certain circumstances. In many States, the legislature *statutorily excludes* certain (usually serious) offenses from the jurisdiction of the juvenile court regardless of the age of the accused. In some States and at the Federal level under certain circumstances, prosecutors have the *discretion* to either file criminal charges against juveniles directly in criminal courts or proceed through the juvenile justice process. The juvenile court's intake department or the prosecutor may petition the juvenile court to *waive* jurisdiction to criminal court. The juvenile court also may order *referral* to criminal court for trial as adults. In some jurisdictions, juveniles processed as adults may upon conviction be sentenced to either an adult or a juvenile facility.

In those cases where the juvenile court retains jurisdiction, the case may be handled formally by filing a delinquency petition or informally by diverting the juvenile to other agencies or programs in lieu of further court processing.

If a petition for an adjudicatory hearing is accepted, the juvenile may be brought before a court quite unlike the court with jurisdiction over adult offenders. Despite the considerable discretion associated with juvenile court proceedings, juveniles are afforded many of the due-process safeguards associated with adult criminal trials. Several States permit the use of juries in juvenile courts; however, in light of the U.S. Supreme Court holding that juries are not essential to juvenile hearings, most States do not make provisions for juries in juvenile courts.

In disposing of cases, juvenile courts usually have far more discretion than adult courts. In addition to such options as probation, commitment to a residential facility, restitution, or fines, State laws grant juvenile courts the power to order removal of children from their homes to foster homes or treatment facilities. Juvenile courts also may order participation in special programs aimed at shoplifting prevention, drug counseling, or driver education.

Once a juvenile is under juvenile court disposition, the court may retain jurisdiction until the juvenile legally becomes an adult (at age 21 in most States). In some jurisdictions, juvenile offenders may be classified as youthful offenders, which can lead to extended sentences.

Following release from an institution, juveniles are often ordered to a period of aftercare that is similar to parole supervision for adult offenders. Juvenile offenders who violate the conditions of aftercare may have their aftercare revoked, resulting in being recommitted to a facility. Juveniles who are classified as youthful offenders and violate the conditions of aftercare may be subject to adult sanctions.

## The Governmental Response to Crime Is Founded in the Intergovernmental Structure of the United States

Under our form of government, each State and the Federal Government has its own criminal justice system. All systems must respect the rights of individuals set forth in court interpretation of the U.S. Constitution and defined in case law.

State constitutions and laws define the criminal justice system within each State and delegate the authority and responsibility for criminal justice to various jurisdictions, officials, and institutions. State laws also define criminal behavior and groups of children or acts under jurisdiction of the juvenile courts.

Municipalities and counties further define their criminal justice systems through local ordinances that proscribe the local agencies responsible for criminal justice processing that were not established by the State.

Congress has also established a criminal justice system at the Federal level to respond to Federal crimes such as bank robbery, kidnaping, and transporting stolen goods across State lines.

## The Response to Crime Is Mainly a State and Local Function

Very few crimes are under exclusive Federal jurisdiction. The responsibility to respond to most crime rests with State and local governments. Police protection is primarily a function of cities and towns. Corrections is primarily a function of State governments. Most justice personnel are employed at the local level.

## Critical Thinking

1. Explain discretion and how it is exercised in the criminal justice system.
2. What are the steps that follow once a suspect is arrested by police and charged with a crime?
3. How are young people who violate the law treated?

## Create Central

www.mhhe.com/createcentral

## Internet References

**Bureau of Justice Statistics**
www.bjs.gov/content/justsys.cfm

**The National Center for Victims of Crime**
www.victimsofcrime.org/help-for-crime-victims/get-help-bulletins-for-crime-victims/the-criminal-justice-system

U.S. Department of Justice, 1998.

*Article* Prepared by: Joanne Naughton

# Can a Jury Believe What It Sees?

## *Videotaped Confessions Can Be Misleading*

JENNIFER L. MNOOKIN

## Learning Outcomes

*After reading this article, you will be able to:*

- Discuss the advantages of videotaping confessions of criminal suspects.

- Explain what recent research shows about such recordings.

L os Angeles—Last week the FBI, the Drug Enforcement Administration and other federal law enforcement agencies instituted a policy of recording interrogations of criminal suspects held in custody. Only a minority of states and local governments have a similar requirement, but the new rule, which applies to nearly every federal interrogation, will most likely spur more jurisdictions to follow suit. It's not far-fetched to think that such recordings may soon become standard police practice nationwide.

Supporters of the practice present recordings as a solution for a host of problems, from police misconduct to false confessions. But while there are lots of good reasons to require them, they are hardly a panacea; in fact, the very same qualities that make them useful—their seeming vividness and objectivity—also risk making them misleading, and possibly even an inadvertent tool for injustice.

Support for electronic recording has been accelerating in recent years, and its backers now come from all sides of the criminal-justice process. Though some in law enforcement remain critical of the idea, firsthand experience with recording tends to turn law enforcers into supporters—it eliminates uncertainty about police conduct and lets investigators focus on the interrogation rather than taking detailed notes.

Likewise, criminal prosecutors find that when a defendant confesses or provides incriminating information, the video offers vivid and powerful evidence. At the same time, it aids defendants because the very presence of the camera is likely to reduce the use of coercive or unfair tactics in interrogation, and documents illegitimate behavior if and when it does occur. And a recording provides judges and juries with information about what took place in a more objective form.

Given this chorus of support, what's not to like?

The short answer is that, according to recent research, interrogation recording may in fact be too vivid and persuasive. Even seemingly neutral recordings still require interpretation. As advertisers and Hollywood directors know well, camera angles, close-ups, lenses, and dozens of other techniques shape our perception of what we see without our being aware of it.

In a series of experiments led by the psychologist G. Daniel Lassiter of Ohio University, mock juries were shown exactly the same interrogation, but some saw only the defendant, while others had a wider-angle view that included the interrogator. When the interrogator isn't shown on camera, jurors are significantly less likely to find an interrogation coercive, and more likely to believe in the truth and accuracy of the confession that they hear—even when the interrogator explicitly threatens the defendant.

Professor Lassiter and other psychologists have consistently shown this "camera perspective bias" across a substantial series of experiments, finding in one study that even professionals like judges and police interrogators are not immune.

Experiments like these feed a larger concern: whether the police, prosecutors, defense lawyers, judges, or jurors can actually tell the difference between true and false confessions, even with the more complete record of interactions that recorded interrogations provide.

We know that false confessions really do occur, even in very serious crimes, and probably more frequently than most people expect. But why? We know something about certain interrogation techniques, as well as defendant vulnerabilities like youth or mental disability, that may create heightened risks for false confessions. But we don't yet know enough about the psychology of false confessions to be able to accurately "diagnose" the reliability of a given confession just by watching it.

The problem is that many of the red flags that frequently occur in false confessions—like unusually long interrogations, the inclusion of inaccurate details, or the police "feeding" some crime-related information to the suspect—can also occur in the confessions of the guilty. This means there's no surefire way to tell false confessions and true confessions apart by viewing a recording, except in extreme cases.

And yet by making confessions so vivid to juries, recording could paper over such complications, and sometimes even make the problem worse. The emotional impact of a suspect declaring his guilt out loud, on video, is powerful and hard to dislodge, even if the defense attorney points out reasons to doubt its accuracy.

This doesn't mean that mandating recording of interrogations is a bad idea. Routine recording will serve to make them fairer and less coercive—and this might well help reduce the number of false confessions.

But we need to recognize that by itself, video recording cannot stop all the problems with interrogations, prevent false confessions or guarantee that we will spot them when they do occur.

We are still a long way from fully understanding why the innocent confess during interrogations, and why we believe them when they do—regardless of what we see on camera.

## Critical Thinking

1. What are some factors that may create heightened risks for false confessions?

2. Describe Lassiter's work regarding confessions.

3. How can false confessions be distinguished from valid ones?

## Internet References

**IZA**
ftp.iza.org
**U.S. Department of Justice**
www.justice.gov

---

**JENNIFER L. MNOOKIN** is a professor of law at the University of California, Los Angeles.

---

*Article*

Prepared by: Joanne Naughton

# Maze of Gun Laws in U.S. Hurts Gun Control Efforts

EILEEN SULLIVAN

## Learning Outcomes

*After reading this article, you will be able to:*

- Appreciate the difficulty of regulating guns in the United States.

- Describe the roadblock created by Congressional opposition to new gun laws.

There is a legal avenue to try to get any gun you want somewhere in the U.S., thanks to the maze of gun statutes across the country and the lack of certain federal laws.

That undermines gun-control efforts in communities with tougher gun laws—and pushes advocates of tighter controls to seek a federal standard. Gun rights proponents say enforcing all existing laws makes more sense than passing new ones.

An Associated Press analysis found that there are thousands of laws, rules and regulations at the local, county, state and federal levels. The laws and rules vary by state, and even within states, according to a 2011 compilation of state gun laws by the Bureau of Alcohol, Tobacco, Firearms and Explosives.

These laws and regulations govern who can carry a firearm, what kind of firearm is legal, the size of ammunition magazines, and more. In some places, a person can buy as many guns as desired.

Not only can people acquire military-style assault weapons, they can also get gangster-style Tommy guns, World War II-era bazookas and even sawed-off shotguns.

"If you regulate something on the local or state level, you are still a victim to guns coming into other localities or states," said Laura Cutilletta, a senior staff attorney at the California-based Law Center to Prevent Gun Violence.

In California, most guns come from Nevada, where there is almost no regulation of firearms, Cutilletta said, and in Arizona, gun owners don't need a permit.

President Barack Obama earlier this month announced a $500 million plan to tighten federal gun laws. The December shooting massacre in Newtown, Conn., that killed 20 children and six adults at an elementary school launched the issue of gun control policy to a national focus not seen in decades.

Obama is urging Congress to pass new laws, some of which would set a minimum standard for the types of firearms and ammunition that are commercially available. Sen. Dianne Feinstein, D-Calif., on Thursday said she was introducing a new assault weapons ban.

The powerful gun lobby says the problem lies in enforcement of existing laws.

"Which begs the question: Why are we putting more laws on the books if we're not enforcing the laws we already have on the books?" said Andrew Arulanandam, spokesman for the National Rifle Association.

New gun laws will face tough opposition in Congress, particularly from members who rely on the NRA during election campaigns. The NRA contributed more than $700,000 to members of Congress during the 2012 election cycle, according to the Center for Responsive Politics.

Recognizing the opposition in Congress, states already are passing their own new gun laws while officials from some states are promising to ignore any new federal mandates. As the national debate on gun control and Second Amendment rights escalates, the terms being used won't mean the same thing everywhere, due to the thousands of laws, rules and regulations across the country.

"The patchwork of laws in many ways means that the laws are only as effective as the weakest law there is," said Gene Voegtlin of the International Association of Chiefs of Police. "Those that are trying to acquire firearms and may not be able to do that by walking into their local gun shop will try to find a way to do that. This patchwork of laws allows them to seek out the weak links and acquire weapons."

Obama wants to address this, in part, by passing federal gun-trafficking laws that carry heavy penalties. It's difficult to crack down on trafficking because the penalties are too low to serve as a deterrent, and federal prosecutors decline many cases because of a lack of evidence. For instance, in order to charge someone with willfully participating in a business of selling firearms without a license, the ATF needs to prove that the guns were not sold out of the suspect's private collection, the Justice Department inspector general has said.

Obama has also called for a new federal law banning magazines that carry more than 10 rounds of ammunition—a measure that was in effect during the previous assault weapons ban, between 1994 and 2004. High-capacity magazines have been used in recent deadly mass shootings, including those in Newtown, and in the suburban Denver movie theater attack last summer.

A high-capacity ammunition magazine means different things in different places.

In California, considered by many to have some of the strongest gun laws in the country, a large-capacity magazine is one that holds more than 10 rounds. In Illinois there is no state law regarding magazines. Yet, there are laws regarding magazines in Chicago where the threshold is more than 12 rounds. But about 40 miles away in Aurora, Ill., this type of magazine is called a large-capacity ammunition feeding device and means anything more than 15 rounds.

In 44 states, including Arizona, Colorado, Connecticut, Texas and Virginia where these magazines have been used in deadly mass shootings, there are no laws against using them, according to a 2012 analysis by the Law Center to Prevent Gun Violence. If a federal law banned magazines that hold more than 10 rounds, it would become the minimum standard.

The definition of "assault weapon" also varies. There is no federal definition of an assault weapon, and the meaning of the term is inconsistent even within the gun industry. California defines an assault weapon as a "firearm (that) has such a high rate of fire and capacity for fire-power that its function as a legitimate sports or recreational firearm is substantially outweighed by the danger that it can be used to kill and injure human beings." The law specifically lists 60 rifles, 14 pistols and five shotguns. Neighboring states Nevada and Arizona have no assault weapon restrictions.

Federal law does not prohibit the ownership of any weapon, said Ginger Colbrun, a Bureau of Alcohol, Tobacco, Firearms and Explosives spokeswoman in Washington. In order to buy or own certain firearms, including automatic weapons, machine guns and bazookas, people do have to apply for permission from the federal government. But as long as the application for a restricted firearm is approved, and there is no state law barring ownership of that type of gun, it's legal.

"There is such a variation in the number of laws that regulate the distribution of guns that there is no adequate minimum standard," said Richard Aborn, president of the New York-based Citizens Crime Commission. "The federal government has an obligation to establish at least minimum standards that have to be complied with before a gun can be sold anywhere in America."

## Critical Thinking

1. What kind of gun laws would be most effective at controlling gun violence?
2. Would federal definitions be beneficial?

## Create Central

www.mhhe.com/createcentral

## Internet References

**Bureau of Alcohol, Tobacco, Firearms and Explorsives**
   www.atf.gov
**Law Center to Prevent Gun Violence**
   http://smartgunlaws.org

*Article* Prepared by: Joanne Naughton

# Record Number of Exonerations Driven by Texas Drug Cases

Juan A. Lozano

## Learning Outcomes

*After reading this article, you will be able to:*

- Show why the statistics on false convictions in 2014 differed from the year before.

- Describe how the procedure in Harris County regarding the testing of drug evidence differs from many jurisdictions around the country.

Houston—The U.S. saw a record number of exonerations in 2014, and it was due in part to 33 cases in Texas in which individuals had their drug convictions dismissed after lab tests determined they never had illegal substances, a report released Tuesday shows.

The National Registry of Exonerations said 125 people falsely convicted of crimes were exonerated last year. That's 34 more than in 2013, the year with the previous highest total. The registry is a project of the University of Michigan and Northwestern University law schools and has documented more than 1,500 such cases in the U.S. since 1989.

The breakdown in 2014 was typical of previous years, with homicides and sex crimes making up more than half with 65 cases. Texas had the most exonerations with 39. New York was second with 17.

But the big difference in 2014 was an increase in cases where individuals convicted of drug-related charges were exonerated by lab tests that showed they didn't have controlled substances, said Samuel Gross, a Michigan law professor and registry editor.

Of the 39 drug cases in the U.S. in 2014, Harris County in Texas—home to Houston—had 33 of them. In 2013, there were only 11 such exonerations in the U.S.

Inger Chandler, chief of the conviction review section with the Harris County District Attorney's Office, said there were inconsistent practices regarding how her office handled reviews of drug convictions.

Most of the 33 drug cases in Harris County in 2014 were ones where individuals pleaded guilty before a lab test was completed. There were often delays in completing tests and even when they were finished, there could be additional delays in getting the results to prosecutors or defense attorneys.

Chandler said her office has since streamlined its procedures so that all reviews of these cases now go through her section.

When asked why someone would plead guilty to a crime they did not commit, Chandler replied, "That is the question of the day."

Chandler said she believes some of the individuals thought they did have drugs and "got a plea deal early in the process and wanted to move on."

There were also many individuals who because of their criminal history, faced higher punishment ranges if convicted at trial, she said.

"We are reviewing our internal processes . . . taking a look at whether we need to wait for lab reports before allowing defendants to plead guilty," Chandler said.

Gross said it's unclear if the drug cases in Harris County are a reflection of a similar problem across the country. While Harris County still tests drug evidence in cases after a guilty plea, many jurisdictions around the country don't.

"Behind this is a much bigger question and one much harder to address," he said. "One of the reasons people plead guilty for a crime they have not committed is they can't make bail and have to wait in jail while waiting for trial. If they are convicted, they might get decades in prison. They plead guilty if they are offered a deal that is too good to resist."

Those pleading guilty in Harris County ended up getting sentences ranging from probation to two years in prison.

Chandler said she hopes people see that her office realized there was a problem with these cases and is now working to fix it.

"Everyone deserves for the process to be fair," she said.

Gross said the registry's report should be seen as a positive, as it highlights the work being done to address wrongful convictions.

He also pointed to the work of the Brooklyn District Attorney's Conviction Review Unit, which in 2014 exonerated 10 individuals in murder cases that were more than 20 years old.

"We will learn from these cases how to prevent false convictions in the future," he said. "That is the most important thing that could come out of this work."

## Critical Thinking

1. Why would an innocent person ever plead guilty?
2. Should drug use be criminal?

## Internet References

**Innocence Project**
www.innocenceproject.org/

**Innocence Project**
www.innocenceproject.org/cases-false-imprisonment

**University of Michigan Law School**
www.law.umich.edu/

## Article

Prepared by: Joanne Naughton

# Stop and Seize

## Aggressive Police Take Hundreds of Millions of Dollars from Motorists not Charged with Crimes.

MICHAEL SALLAH, ROBERT O'HARROW, JR., AND STEVEN RICH

### Learning Outcomes

*After reading this article, you will be able to:*

- Explain Equitable Sharing.
- Describe the script that highway interdictors seemed to follow.
- Compare civil asset forfeiture with criminal forfeiture.

After the terror attacks on Sept. 11, 2001, the government called on police to become the eyes and ears of homeland security on America's highways.

Local officers, county deputies and state troopers were encouraged to act more aggressively in searching for suspicious people, drugs and other contraband. The departments of Homeland Security and Justice spent millions on police training.

The effort succeeded, but it had an impact that has been largely hidden from public view: the spread of an aggressive brand of policing that has spurred the seizure of hundreds of millions of dollars in cash from motorists and others not charged with crimes, a *Washington Post* investigation found. Thousands of people have been forced to fight legal battles that can last more than a year to get their money back.

Behind the rise in seizures is a little-known cottage industry of private police-training firms that teach the techniques of "highway interdiction" to departments across the country.

One of those firms created a private intelligence network known as Black Asphalt Electronic Networking & Notification System that enabled police nationwide to share detailed reports about American motorists—criminals and the innocent alike—including their Social Security numbers, addresses and identifying tattoos, as well as hunches about which drivers to stop.

Many of the reports have been funneled to federal agencies and fusion centers as part of the government's burgeoning law enforcement intelligence systems—despite warnings from state and federal authorities that the information could violate privacy and constitutional protections.

A thriving subculture of road officers on the network now competes to see who can seize the most cash and contraband, describing their exploits in the network's chat rooms and sharing "trophy shots" of money and drugs. Some police advocate highway interdiction as a way of raising revenue for cash-strapped municipalities.

"All of our home towns are sitting on a tax-liberating gold mine," Deputy Ron Hain of Kane County, Ill., wrote in a self-published book under a pseudonym. Hain is a marketing specialist for Desert Snow, a leading interdiction training firm based in Guthrie, Okla., whose founders also created Black Asphalt.

Hain's book calls for "turning our police forces into present-day Robin Hoods."

Cash seizures can be made under state or federal civil law. One of the primary ways police departments are able to seize money and share in the proceeds at the federal level is through a long-standing Justice Department civil asset forfeiture program known as Equitable Sharing. Asset forfeiture is an extraordinarily powerful law enforcement tool that allows the government to take cash and property without pressing criminal charges and then requires the owners to prove their possessions were legally acquired.

The practice has been controversial since its inception at the height of the drug war more than three decades ago, and its abuses have been the subject of journalistic exposés and congressional hearings. But unexplored until now is the role of the federal government and the private police trainers in encouraging officers to target cash on the nation's highways since 9/11.

"Those laws were meant to take a guy out for selling $1 million in cocaine or who was trying to launder large amounts of money," said Mark Overton, the police chief in Bal Harbour, Fla., who once oversaw a federal drug task force in South Florida. "It was never meant for a street cop to take a few thousand dollars from a driver by the side of the road."

To examine the scope of asset forfeiture since the terror attacks, *The Post* analyzed a database of hundreds of thousands of seizure records at the Justice Department, reviewed hundreds of federal court cases, obtained internal records from training firms and interviewed scores of police officers, prosecutors and motorists.

*The Post* found:

- There have been 61,998 cash seizures made on highways and elsewhere since 9/11 without search warrants or indictments through the Equitable Sharing Program, totaling more than $2.5 billion. State and local authorities kept more than $1.7 billion of that while Justice, Homeland Security and other federal agencies received $800 million. Half of the seizures were below $8,800.

- Only a sixth of the seizures were legally challenged, in part because of the costs of legal action against the government. But in 41 percent of cases—4,455—where there was a challenge, the government agreed to return money. The appeals process took more than a year in 40 percent of those cases and often required owners of the cash to sign agreements not to sue police over the seizures.

- Hundreds of state and local departments and drug task forces appear to rely on seized cash, despite a federal ban on the money to pay salaries or otherwise support budgets. *The Post* found that 298 departments and 210 task forces have seized the equivalent of 20 percent or more of their annual budgets since 2008.

- Agencies with police known to be participating in the Black Asphalt intelligence network have seen a 32 percent jump in seizures beginning in 2005, three times the rate of other police departments. Desert Snow-trained officers reported more than $427 million in cash seizures during highway stops in just one five-year period, according to company officials. More than 25,000 police have belonged to Black Asphalt, company officials said.

- State law enforcement officials in Iowa and Kansas prohibited the use of the Black Asphalt network because of concerns that it might not be a legal law enforcement tool. A federal prosecutor in Nebraska warned that Black Asphalt reports could violate laws governing civil liberties, the handling of sensitive law enforcement information and the disclosure of pretrial information to defendants. But officials at Justice and Homeland Security continued to use it.

Justice spokesman Peter Carr said the department had no comment on *The Post*'s overall findings. But he said the department has a compliance review process in place for the Equitable Sharing Program and attorneys for federal agencies must review the seizures before they are "adopted" for inclusion in the program.

"Adoptions of state and local seizures—when a state and local law enforcement agency requests a federal seizing agency to adopt a state and local seizure for federal forfeiture— represent an average of only 3 percent of the total forfeiture amount since 2007," Carr said.

The Justice Department data released to *The Post* does not contain information about race. Carr said the department prohibits racial profiling. But in 400 federal court cases examined by *The Post* where people who challenged seizures and received some money back, the majority were black, Hispanic or another minority.

A 55-year-old Chinese American restaurateur from Georgia was pulled over for minor speeding on Interstate 10 in Alabama and detained for nearly two hours. He was carrying $75,000 raised from relatives to buy a Chinese restaurant in Lake Charles, La. He got back his money 10 months later but only after spending thousands of dollars on a lawyer and losing out on the restaurant deal.

A 40-year-old Hispanic carpenter from New Jersey was stopped on Interstate 95 in Virginia for having tinted windows. Police said he appeared nervous and consented to a search. They took $18,000 that he said was meant to buy a used car. He had to hire a lawyer to get back his money.

Mandrel Stuart, a 35-year-old African American owner of a small barbecue restaurant in Staunton, Va., was stunned when police took $17,550 from him during a stop in 2012 for a minor traffic infraction on Interstate 66 in Fairfax. He rejected a settlement with the government for half of his money and demanded a jury trial. He eventually got his money back but lost his business because he didn't have the cash to pay his overhead.

"I paid taxes on that money. I worked for that money," Stuart said. "Why should I give them my money?"

## In Defense of Seizures

Steven Peterson, a former U.S. Drug Enforcement Administration agent who arranged highway interdiction training through a company called the 4:20 Group, said that patrol officers used to try to make their names with large drug busts. He said he saw that change when agency leaders realized that cash seizures could help their departments during lean times.

"They saw this as a way to provide equipment and training for their guys," Peterson said. "If you seized large amounts of cash, that's the gift that keeps on giving."

There is no question that state and federal forfeiture programs have crippled powerful drug-trafficking organizations, thwarted an assortment of criminals and brought millions of dollars to financially stressed police departments.

Advocates of highway interdiction say it plays an important role in protecting the public and that officers take care to respect the rights of citizens.

"We don't go hunting for money in general," said Sandy Springs, Ga., Officer Mike DeWald, who has served as a trainer for 4:20. "I never have been pressured to go after money. We are in pursuit of the criminal element."

Police trainers said that their work has helped make the country safer by teaching police to be more vigilant in identifying drug smugglers and terrorists.

"9/11 caused a lot of officers to realize they should be out there looking for those kind of people," said David Frye, a part-time Nebraska county deputy sheriff who serves as chief instructor at Desert Snow and was operations director of Black Asphalt. "When money is taken from an organization, it hurts them more than when they lose the drugs."

Frye and Desert Snow's founder, a former California highway patrolman named Joe David, defended Black Asphalt, which David started in 2004. They said they have taken steps in recent years to ensure that the informal police network complies with state and federal laws. David declined to speak to *The Post*.

"The Black Asphalt is not flawless, however the intent behind it is," David and Frye wrote in a letter in 2012 sent to police and obtained by *The Post*. "The information being moved through the system has proven itself reliable on hundreds of occasions. Much more reliable than any criminal informant. The results have been staggering. It has proven itself an extremely valuable tool for law enforcement."

Hain, Desert Snow's marketing official, said "the operational and software platforms of the Desert Snow site and Black Asphalt site are completely separate." He said Black Asphalt is "a secure system for intelligence sharing" and does not store information.

"No personal identifying information from seizure reports have ever been collected or stored by the Black Asphalt," Hain said. "The Black Asphalt software is simply a pass-through system that allows the user to input data, which is then sent directly, via e-mail, to a select group of law enforcement (i.e. local investigators, ICE Bulk Cash Smuggling Center, DEA agents, etc.). Again, none of the personal information is held within the system, only the summary of the seizure. And then the seizure narratives are only maintained for 21 days before they get purged."

*The Post* obtained hundreds of Black Asphalt records from law enforcement sources with access to the system.

Among Black Asphalt's features is a section called BOLO, or "be on the lookout," where police who join the network can post tips and hunches. In April, Aurora, Colo., police Officer James Waselkow pulled over a white Ford pickup for tinted windows. Waselkow said he thought the driver, a Mexican national, was suspicious in part because he wore a University of Wyoming cap.

"He had no idea where he was going, what hotel he was staying in or who with," Waselkow wrote. The officer searched the vehicle with the driver's consent but found no contraband. But he was still suspicious, so he posted the driver's license plate on Black Asphalt. "Released so someone else can locate the contraband," he wrote. "Happy hunting!"

Waselkow's department did not respond to a request for an interview.

*The Post*'s review of 400 court cases, which encompassed seizures in 17 states, provided insights into stops and seizures.

In case after case, highway interdictors appeared to follow a similar script. Police set up what amounted to rolling checkpoints on busy highways and pulled over motorists for minor violations, such as following too closely or improper signaling. They quickly issued warnings or tickets. They studied drivers for signs of nervousness, including pulsing carotid arteries, clenched jaws and perspiration. They also looked for supposed "indicators" of criminal activity, which can include such things as trash on the floor of a vehicle, abundant energy drinks or air fresheners hanging from rearview mirrors.

One recent stop shows how the process can work in the field.

In December 2012, Frye was working in his capacity as a part-time deputy in Seward County, Neb. He pulled over John Anderson of San Clemente, Calif., who was driving a BMW on Interstate 80 near Lincoln. Frye issued a warning ticket within 13 minutes for failing to signal promptly when changing lanes.

He told Anderson he was finished with the stop. But Frye later noted in court papers that he found several indicators of possible suspicious activity: an air freshener, a radar detector and inconsistencies in the driver's description of his travels.

The officer then asked whether the driver had any cocaine, methamphetamine, heroin or large amounts of cash and sought permission to search the BMW, according to a video of the stop. Anderson denied having drugs or large amounts of cash in his car. He declined to give permission for a search. Frye then radioed for a drug-sniffing dog, and the driver had to wait another 36 minutes for the dog to arrive.

"I'm just going to, basically, have you wait here," Frye told Anderson.

The dog arrived and the handler said it indicated the presence of drugs. But when they searched the car, none was found. They did find money: $25,180.

Frye handcuffed Anderson and told him he was placing him under arrest.

"In Nebraska, drug currency is illegal," Frye said. "Let me tell you something, I've seized millions out here. When I say that, I mean millions. . . . This is what I do."

Frye suggested to Anderson that he might not have been aware of the money in his vehicle and began pressing him to sign a waiver relinquishing the cash, mentioning it at least five times over the next hour, the video shows.

"You're going to be given an opportunity to disclaim the currency," Frye told Anderson. "To sign a form that says, 'That is not my money. I don't know anything about it. I don't want to know anything about it. I don't want to come back to court.' "

Frye said that unless the driver agreed to give up the money, a prosecutor would "want to charge" him with a crime, "so that means you'll go to jail."

An hour and six minutes into the stop, Frye read Anderson his Miranda rights.

Anderson, who told Frye he worked as a self-employed debt counselor, said the money was not illicit and he was carrying it to pay off a gambling debt. He would later say it was from investors and meant to buy silver bullion and coins. More than two hours after the stop had begun, he finally agreed to give up the cash and Frye let him go. Now Anderson has gone to court to get the money back, saying he signed the waiver and mentioned the gambling debt only because he felt intimidated by Frye.

A magistrate has ruled at a preliminary step in the case that Frye had reasonable suspicion to detain Anderson. Frye said he always follows the law and has never had a seizure overturned.

Legal scholars who viewed the video of the stop told *The Post* that such practices push constitutional limits. Officers often are taught not to tell the driver they have a right to leave at any time after a traffic stop is concluded. But extended stops in which the officer uses psychological pressure on the driver without charges or Miranda warnings can cross the line.

"Encouraging police to initiate searches for the purpose of seizing cash or other assets, rather than to seize evidence to be used in a prosecution, is a dangerous development," said Clifford Fishman, a law professor at Catholic University and former New York City prosecutor. "It is particularly troubling if police officers are trained to manipulate the suspect into forfeiting the assets or waiving the right to contest the search."

David A. Harris, a University of Pittsburgh law professor, said Frye's stop crossed the line when he detained the driver while summoning a canine.

"You cannot elongate the stop to bring in the dogs," he said. "In doing that, you're detaining the person without probable cause. That ain't kosher."

# A Tool in the Drug War

Civil asset forfeiture law is among the more unusual areas of American jurisprudence. It does not involve evidence of a crime or criminal charges. It is a civil action against an object, such as currency or a boat, rather than a person. It has its basis in British admiralty law, which allowed the taking of a ship to recover damages.

In 1970, Congress turned the federal civil asset forfeiture law into a weapon against the illegal drug trade, allowing for the seizure of aircraft, boats and vehicles used to transport drugs. The federal law was eventually expanded to include cash tied to drug trafficking and to allow the money to be shared with local and state police, who could keep up to 80 percent of the seized assets. When police make a seizure, a federal agency must approve or "adopt" it for inclusion in Justice's Equitable Sharing Program.

It was a much more effective tool for federal prosecutors than criminal forfeiture, which required the conviction of a defendant with proof beyond a reasonable doubt. Most significantly, the law places the burden of proof on the property owner to demonstrate that an object is not tied to criminal activity.

As the drug trade ramped up throughout the 1980s, money deposited into Justice's federal forfeitures fund increased from $27 million in 1985 to $556 million in 1993. (It reached $2.6 billion in 2007.) Some of that increase was driven by Operation Pipeline, a nationwide DEA program launched in 1986 that promoted highway interdiction training for state and local police.

Several newspapers later wrote exposés about innocent people being caught up in the forfeiture net and police spending on luxuries. *The Orlando Sentinel* won a Pulitzer Prize in 1993 for pointing out that the Volusia County Sheriff's Office had used state seizure laws to take $8 million from motorists, 9 out of 10 of them minorities.

The attention prompted Congress to reform federal seizure laws in 2000, allowing owners to be reimbursed for their legal fees after successful lawsuits. But a key reform was cut. It would have removed what some lawmakers called the "perverse incentive" to target cash—the sharing of money between the feds and locals. It died after police and Justice waged a "voracious lobbying" campaign, according to former representative Barney Frank (D-Mass.).

"We didn't have the votes," said Frank, who is still an ardent critic of asset forfeiture. "There is this terrible unfairness. It is about as fundamental a denial of their constitutional rights as I can think of."

After Sept. 11, 2001, civil forfeiture and the war on drugs became entwined with efforts to improve homeland security. Smugglers of all kinds turned away from airports because of the tightened security and took to the nation's interstate highway system. With federal encouragement, police from small towns, rural counties and big cities sought specialized training.

Among those that met the demand was Desert Snow, a family-owned company founded in 1989 by Joe David, a California highway patrolman. Other firms also stepped up, including the 4:20 Group, Caltraps, Hits, Diamondback Training and Global Counter-Smuggling Training Consultants. Soon more than a dozen companies were competing for millions in state and federal grants and contracts, along with fees from local departments across the country.

The training had an immediate effect in some areas.

After the Kansas Highway Patrol arranged sessions through Desert Snow for state and local police in 2005 and 2006, the amount of cash flowing into police budgets from seizures nearly doubled, from an average of $2.6 million a year between 2000 and 2006 to $4.9 million a year after 2007.

After 25 Wisconsin State Patrol officers received training from Desert Snow in 2010, the agency's cash seizures the following year more than doubled to $585,657. "It creates a surge period," said Sgt. Nate Clarke, a state patrol supervisor. "These guys get all fired up because they're seeing photo after photo of seizures on the PowerPoints."

The number of agencies participating yearly under Equitable Sharing went up 22 percent to 2,842 between 2003 and 2007, while cash seizures without search warrants or indictments during that period rose more than 50 percent, to $242 million. Under the Obama administration, police have made more than 22,000 such seizures worth about $1 billion through the Justice Department program.

Federal support helped drive the surge. In Florida, Indiana, Oklahoma, Tennessee and Wisconsin alone, police spent a total of at least $1 million during the last decade in Justice and Homeland Security grants for Desert Snow training. The DEA, Customs and Border Protection, Immigration and Customs Enforcement and others spent an additional $2.5 million in contracts on Desert Snow training for police, records show. The DEA also paid more than $2 million for training from the 4:20 Group. Individual local and state police forces across the country paid millions more for the training using seized cash, one of the uses permitted by Equitable Sharing rules.

The police trainers estimate they have taught more than 50,000 police officers in the more aggressive techniques during the last decade.

Some trainers say they worry that an overemphasis on seizing money has distorted policing.

"Over a period of a single decade, the culture was now totally changed," said Shawn Pardazi, a detective in Pearl, Miss., and owner of Global Counter-Smuggling Training Consultants and a former Desert Snow trainer.

As the demand for training grew, the competition among the firms for business became fierce.

"It's all about the money," said James Eagleson, owner of the 4:20 Group, who also once worked at Desert Snow.

## Getting the Money Back

Decisions that police make during brief roadway stops take motorists who challenge the seizures a year on average to resolve, according to a *Post* analysis. For 350 owners, it took more than two years to get their money back.

Last year, Ming Tong Liu, 55, a Chinese-born American from Newnan, Ga., was stopped on I-10 in Alabama for driving 10 miles over the speed limit while heading to Louisiana to buy the Hong Kong Chinese restaurant in Lake Charles for himself and his investors—two daughters and another relative.

A Mobile County sheriff's deputy gave Liu a ticket for speeding and asked for permission to search the car. The deputy found $75,195 in a suitcase in the back seat, neatly wrapped in white napkins and placed in a black plastic bag and then took the money after the deputy said Liu gave conflicting accounts of his travel plans.

The deputy took Liu to a sheriff's department office and called for an officer from U.S. Customs and Border Protection, which stood to share in the money.

Liu's attorney, Rebecca Ding-Lee, said the officers overstepped their authority, held Liu for nearly two hours and searched his car unlawfully without a warrant. "He cannot speak English," she said. "He didn't understand what the police said."

Ten months after the cash was seized, customs officials agreed to return the money, documents show.

Police often rely on drug-sniffing dogs to justify warrantless searches when a driver refuses to give consent. In 48 cases examined by *The Post*, dogs alerted to the presence of drugs but the officers found only money.

In October 2008, Benjamin Molina, 40, a permanent resident from El Salvador, was traveling through Virginia on I-95 when an Emporia police officer pulled him over for tinted windows. A carpenter, Molina was going from North Carolina to his home in Perth Amboy, N.J. The officer wrote him a warning ticket and began asking him questions, including whether he had cash in the car.

Molina told the officer that he was shopping for a used car and had $18,000 in his pockets. Molina's face began to tremble, which police said they took as a sign of possible wrongdoing. Molina said his cheek twitched from medication he was taking for a health condition that included kidney disease. Molina also had duct tape in his car, which police said is "commonly used by traffickers."

The officer asked Molina, who had no criminal history, to hand over the cash. The officer placed the money in an envelope, which he set down on the ground alongside two empty envelopes.

A dog called to the scene sat down next to the envelope with the cash, indicating the presence of drugs, according to police.

The police took the money, but Molina took steps to get it back.

He hired David Smith, an Alexandria attorney and former federal prosecutor who once headed the federal government's forfeiture program in the Eastern District of Virginia.

After Molina appealed, a federal prosecutor refunded the money. It took four months.

Smith said the Molina case is an example of the kind of overreach that the civil asset forfeiture reforms passed by Congress in 2000 were aimed at preventing.

"This type of police bounty hunting is antithetical to everything our criminal justice system is supposed to stand for," said Smith, who helped craft the reform legislation.

Among the indicators police look for are rental cars, which are often used by smugglers.

On Nov. 1, 2011, Jose Jeronimo Sorto and his brother-in-law, Victor Ramos Guzman, were driving a rented sedan on I-95 south of Richmond when a Virginia state trooper stopped them. Both were lay leaders of the Pentecostal Nuevo Renacer church in Baltimore. They were carrying $28,500 in church funds meant for the purchase of land to build a church in El Salvador and a trailer for a new congregation in North Carolina.

Their experience has been cited as a case study in civil forfeiture abuse by *The Post*'s editorial page, the *New Yorker* magazine and others. Unknown until now in the public debate is the fact that the trooper who made the stop, C.L. Murphy, is a top interdiction trainer for Virginia State Police and Desert Snow, as well as a member of Black Asphalt.

Murphy told Sorto and Guzman that they were speeding and following too closely. Murphy said Guzman told him about the cash and consented to a search of the car.

Guzman, 39, of Sterling, Va., said he showed the trooper documents indicating that he belonged to a tax-exempt church, and he said the cash had been collected from congregation members. But Murphy disregarded their explanations, saying they contained inconsistencies. He called Immigration and Customs Enforcement, which accepted the seizure for the Equitable Sharing Program, and he escorted the men to a nearby police station. He did not issue a ticket but seized the cash after Guzman signed a waiver.

Three lawyers agreed to represent the church members for free. Three months later, they received a check from ICE for $28,500.

Virginia State Police spokeswoman Corinne Geller would only say, "The facts of the stop speak for themselves."

ICE spokeswoman Marsha Catron defended the seizure, saying in a statement "the situation was indicative of bulk cash smuggling" and that Guzman consented by signing a waiver for the money.

"Both the male driver and passenger disclaimed ownership of the money and provided inconsistent and contradictory statements," Catron said. She added: "Money was ultimately returned to Mr. Ramos Guzman after he provided documentation that the cash belonged to his church."

Guzman told *The Post* he was truthful to the trooper the entire time. The experience left him shaken.

"They didn't give me a chance to explain," Guzman said. "There was no way out."

---

## About This Story

*The Washington Post* relied on an array of materials to explore the rise of civil seizures in recent years, with a particular focus on highway seizures made by state and local police. For details about seizures and the techniques employed by police, reporters reviewed more than 400 federal court cases in which owners of cash filed legal appeals to get it back. *The Post* also examined some seizures made under state forfeiture laws.

Through Freedom of Information Act requests, *The Post* obtained a database from the Justice Department containing details about 212,000 seizures since 1996 through the Equitable Sharing Program, the federal government's largest asset forfeiture effort.

Justice officials did not release data that pinpointed the geographic location of each seizure, so it is impossible to identify precisely how many seizures occur during traffic stops. To focus on roadside stops, *The Post* looked at cases that were not made at businesses and that occurred without warrants or indictments: 61,998 seizures have met those criteria since Sept. 11, 2001. That group of cases was then compared to a list obtained by *The Post* of 1,654 departments and agencies with officers who are members of an unofficial police intelligence network known as the Black Asphalt Electronic Networking & Notification System that is focused on highway stops and seizures.

*The Post* also obtained more than 43,000 Justice Department reports from state and local police departments across the country that participated in Equitable Sharing, along with records provided by the Institute for Justice, a nonprofit civil liberties group, to assess how seizures contribute to department budgets.

# Critical Thinking

1. What do you think of Officer Waselkow's stop of the motorist?

2. Do you agree with the legal scholars, cited in the article, discussing the stop of the motorist by Deputy Frye?

3. What did Ron Hain mean when he called for "turning our police forces into present-day Robin Hoods"?

# Internet References

**The Washington Post**
www.washingtonpost.com/

**US Department of Justice**
www.justice.gov/

**US Department of Justice**
www.justice.gov/copy

**ALICE CRITES** contributed to this report. Also contributing were Alexia Campbell, Cathaleen Chen, Hoai-Tran Bui, Nagwa Abdallah and Justin Warren, who were attached to *The Washington Post*'s Investigative Unit through a partnership with the Investigative Reporting Workshop at American University.

*Article*                                    Prepared by: Joanne Naughton

# The Fine Print in Holder's New Forfeiture Policy Leaves Room for Continued Abuses

An exception for joint task forces allows evasion of state property protections.

JACOB SULLUM

## Learning Outcomes

*After reading this article, you will be able to:*

- Report how the Attorney General scaled back the Equitable Sharing Program.

- State whether drug cases qualify for the "public safety" exception.

- Explain what the author means by "A more serious problem" with the new policy.

Last week Attorney General Eric Holder scaled back the Equitable Sharing Program, which enables local law enforcement agencies to evade state limits on civil asset forfeiture. But he did not end that program, and the fine print in the new policy seems to leave a lot of leeway for continued abuses.

In the order describing the new policy, Holder says "federal adoption of property seized by state or local law enforcement under state law is prohibited, except for property that directly relates to public safety concerns, including firearms, ammunition, explosives, and property associated with child pornography." Although that exception sounds like it could be a pretty big loophole, the Justice Department seems to be construing it narrowly. A newly posted form says "Federal Adoptions of state or local seizures are limited to firearms, ammunitions, explosives, and child pornography instrumentalities." In other

words, drug cases do not qualify for the "public safety" exception, a point confirmed by a DOJ notice published on Friday.

A more serious problem with the new policy is that adoption, where a state or local agency seizes property and then asks the Justice Department to pursue forfeiture under federal law, is just one part of the Equitable Sharing Program. Holder's policy explicitly exempts "seizures by state and local authorities working together with federal authorities in a joint task force," "seizures by state and local authorities that are the result of joint federal-state investigations or that are coordinated with federal authorities as part of ongoing federal investigations," and "seizures pursuant to federal seizure warrants, obtained from federal courts to take custody of assets originally seized under state law."

Since there are hundreds of federally funded "multijurisdictional task forces" across the country, that first exception could prove to be very significant. Holder's order "does not prohibit the worst uses of the equitable sharing asset forfeiture program, particularly excepting seizures in which there is federal task force participation or direction," says Eapen Thampy, executive director of Americans for Forfeiture Reform. "As virtually every drug task force I know of has a federal liaison on call, this means business as usual by local law enforcement using civil asset forfeiture through the Equitable Sharing Program to enforce the Controlled Substances Act and other federal statutes. In other words, the exception swallows the rule."

On his *Washington Post* blog, my former *Reason* colleague Radley Balko highlights the same exception. "If it only applies to those investigations in which federal law enforcement personnel are actively involved," he says, "that's less troubling." Thampy is not sanguine on that point. "I do not read the Holder memo as requiring active participation," he says, "and if such a determination were to be made, it is hard to see the government defining 'active participation' narrowly." Thampy adds that "a substantial amount of equitable sharing is related to task force activity," since "most departments that receive a substantial amount of equitable sharing proceeds already do so through task force activity" that is overseen, assisted, or funded by the federal government.

The ban on forfeiture adoptions in drug cases nevertheless does some good. It puts an end to egregious abuses such as the slush fund created by police in Bal Harbour, Florida, with the proceeds of federally adopted forfeitures. *The Miami Herald* reported that the little town's cops raked in $19.3 million over three years, which they used for parties, trips, and fancy equipment such as "a 35-foot boat powered by three Mercury outboards" and "a mobile command truck equipped with satellite and flat-screen TVs."

The *Omaha World-Herald* reports that Douglas County, Nebraska, Sheriff Tim Dunning is fuming about the Justice Department's new forfeiture policy. "This benefits nobody but drug dealers," Dunning said. "Federal law is a tremendously bigger hammer. I don't see what hammer we are going to have over these people now." Dunning will sorely miss that hammer, because his state requires proof beyond a reasonable doubt to seize property allegedly linked to crime, while federal law requires only "a preponderance of the evidence"—i.e., any probability greater than 50 percent.

That low standard allowed Nebraska state troopers to take $124,700 in cash from a motorist named Emiliano Gonzolez in 2003. Gonzolez claimed the money was intended to buy a refrigerated produce truck, and there was no real evidence that he was involved in drug trafficking. In 2006 a federal appeals court nevertheless upheld the forfeiture, which would not have been possible under Nebraska law. The main impact of Holder's directive will be seen in cases like this one, where a single law enforcement agency seeks federal adoption because it makes highway robbery easier or more lucrative.

**Addendum:** In a statement posted on Friday, the Institute for Justice expresses a concern similar to Thampy's: "Today's announced policy would stop the process of adoption, where state and local officials use federal law to forfeit property without charging owners with a crime and then profit from those forfeitures, regardless of whether those forfeitures are permitted under state law. But the new policy leaves open a significant loophole, as state and local law enforcement can still partner with federal agents through joint task forces for forfeitures not permitted under state law, and state and local law enforcement can use such task forces to claim forfeiture proceeds they would not be entitled to under state law."

**Addendum II:** According to a 2012 report from the Government Accountability Office, "adoptions made up about 17 percent of all equitable sharing payments" in 2010, which suggests that Holder's new policy will affect less than one-fifth of cases in which state or local agencies profit from federal forfeitures. An estimate in the press release issued by the Justice Department on Friday suggests the share is even lower when measured by revenue. "Over the last six years," the DOJ says, "adoptions accounted for roughly three percent of the value of forfeitures in the Department of Justice Asset Forfeiture Program." By comparison, the DOJ's reports to Congress indicate that equitable sharing payments to state and local agencies accounted for about 22 percent of total deposits during those six years. That suggests adoptions, which the DOJ says represented about 3 percent of deposits, accounted for less than 14 percent of equitable sharing.

**Note:** An earlier calculation, based on data for fiscal year 2013, put the share at less than 10 percent. The six-year average is different because of variations in total federal forfeitures and the percentage going to the states.

## Critical Thinking

1. How does the Attorney General's order allow abuses to continue?
2. What is Eapen Thampy's objection?
3. Why does Sheriff Tim Dunning object to the Justice Department's new forfeiture policy?

## Internet References

**Reason.com**
http://reason.com/blog/2012/10/29/feds-investigate-asset-forfeiture-slush

**The Washington Post**
https://www.washingtonpost.com/news/the-watch/wp/2015/01/16/breaking-down-holders-move-to-limit-civil-asset-forfeiture-abuse/

**US Department of Justice**
http://www.justice.gov/afp/reports-congress

**US Department of Justice**
http://www.justice.gov/sites/default/files/opa/press-releases/attachments/2015/01/16/attorney_general_order_prohibiting_adoptions.pdf

**US Department of Justice**
http://www.justice.gov/sites/default/files/criminal-afmls/legacy/2015/01/16/request-for-adoption-form.pdf

*Article*                                            Prepared by: Joanne Naughton

# FBI Admits Flaws in Hair Analysis over Decades

SPENCER S. HSU

## Learning Outcomes

*After reading this article, you will be able to:*

- State which two organizations are assisting the government with the review of questioned forensic evidence.

- Describe the problem and show how the investigation came about.

- Discuss what Professor Garrett says about why the problem with faulty forensic evidence has gone on for so long.

The Justice Department and FBI have formally acknowledged that nearly every examiner in an elite FBI forensic unit gave flawed testimony in almost all trials in which they offered evidence against criminal defendants over more than a two-decade period before 2000.

Of 28 examiners with the FBI Laboratory's microscopic hair comparison unit, 26 overstated forensic matches in ways that favored prosecutors in more than 95 percent of the 268 trials reviewed so far, according to the National Association of Criminal Defense Lawyers (NACDL) and the Innocence Project, which are assisting the government with the country's largest post-conviction review of questioned forensic evidence.

The cases include those of 32 defendants sentenced to death. Of those, 14 have been executed or died in prison, the groups said under an agreement with the government to release results after the review of the first 200 convictions.

The FBI errors alone do not mean there was not other evidence of a convict's guilt. Defendants and federal and state prosecutors in 46 states and the District are being notified to determine whether there are grounds for appeals. Four defendants were previously exonerated.

The admissions mark a watershed in one of the country's largest forensic scandals, highlighting the failure of the nation's courts for decades to keep bogus scientific information from juries, legal analysts said. The question now, they said, is how state authorities and the courts will respond to findings that confirm long-suspected problems with subjective, pattern-based forensic techniques—like hair and bite-mark comparisons—that have contributed to wrongful convictions in more than one-quarter of 329 DNA-exoneration cases since 1989.

---

## Flawed Forensic Hair Testimony from the FBI Lab

The FBI has identified for review roughly **2,500 cases** in which the FBI Lab reported a hair match.

- Reviews of **342 defendants' cases** have been completed. About 1,200 cases remain, including 700 in which police or prosecutors have not responded to requests for trial transcripts or other information.
- **268 trials** in which hair evidence was used against defendants.
- **268 trials** in which hair evidence was used against criminal defendants.
- FBI examiners gave flawed forensic testimony in **257 of those 268 trials,** or more than **95 percent.**
- **257 trials** with flawed forensic testimony.
- **32 death-penalty cases** with flawed forensic testimony.

*NOTE*: The FBI is completing reviews of about 900 lab reports.

*Source*: National Association of Criminal Defense Lawyers and Innocence Project analysis of FBI and Justice Department data as of March 2015, *The Washington Post*.

In a statement, the FBI and Justice Department vowed to continue to devote resources to address all cases and said they "are committed to ensuring that affected defendants are notified of past errors and that justice is done in every instance. The Department and the FBI are also committed to ensuring the accuracy of future hair analysis testimony, as well as the application of all disciplines of forensic science."

Peter Neufeld, co-founder of the Innocence Project, commended the FBI and department for the collaboration but said, "The FBI's three-decade use of microscopic hair analysis to incriminate defendants was a complete disaster."

"We need an exhaustive investigation that looks at how the FBI, state governments that relied on examiners trained by the FBI and the courts allowed this to happen and why it wasn't stopped much sooner," Neufeld said.

Norman L. Reimer, the NACDL's executive director, said, "Hopefully, this project establishes a precedent so that in future situations it will not take years to remediate the injustice."

While unnamed federal officials previously acknowledged widespread problems, the FBI until now has withheld comment because findings might not be representative.

Sen. Richard Blumenthal (D-Conn.), a former prosecutor, called on the FBI and Justice Department to notify defendants in all 2,500 targeted cases involving an FBI hair match about the problem even if their case has not been completed, and to redouble efforts in the three-year-old review to retrieve information on each case.

"These findings are appalling and chilling in their indictment of our criminal justice system, not only for potentially innocent defendants who have been wrongly imprisoned and even executed, but for prosecutors who have relied on fabricated and false evidence despite their intentions to faithfully enforce the law," Blumenthal said.

Senate Judiciary Committee Chairman Charles E. Grassley (R-Iowa) and the panel's ranking Democrat, Patrick J. Leahy (Vt.), urged the bureau to conduct "a root-cause analysis" to prevent future breakdowns.

"It is critical that the Bureau identify and address the systemic factors that allowed this far-reaching problem to occur and continue for more than a decade," the lawmakers wrote FBI Director James B. Comey on March 27, as findings were being finalized.

The FBI is waiting to complete all reviews to assess causes but has acknowledged that hair examiners until 2012 lacked written standards defining scientifically appropriate and erroneous ways to explain results in court. The bureau expects this year to complete similar standards for testimony and lab reports for 19 forensic disciplines.

Federal authorities launched the investigation in 2012 after *The Washington Post* reported that flawed forensic hair matches might have led to the convictions of hundreds of potentially innocent people since at least the 1970s, typically for murder, rape and other violent crimes nationwide.

The review confirmed that FBI experts systematically testified to the near-certainty of "matches" of crime-scene hairs to defendants, backing their claims by citing incomplete or misleading statistics drawn from their case work.

In reality, there is no accepted research on how often hair from different people may appear the same. Since 2000, the lab has used visual hair comparison to rule out someone as a possible source of hair or in combination with more accurate DNA testing.

Warnings about the problem have been mounting. In 2002, the FBI reported that its own DNA testing found that examiners reported false hair matches more than 11 percent of the time. In the District, the only jurisdiction where defenders and prosecutors have re-investigated all FBI hair convictions, three of seven defendants whose trials included flawed FBI testimony have been exonerated through DNA testing since 2009, and courts have exonerated two more men. All five served 20 to 30 years in prison for rape or murder.

University of Virginia law professor Brandon L. Garrett said the results reveal a "mass disaster" inside the criminal justice system, one that it has been unable to self-correct because courts rely on outdated precedents admitting scientifically invalid testimony at trial and, under the legal doctrine of finality, make it difficult for convicts to challenge old evidence.

"The tools don't exist to handle systematic errors in our criminal justice system," Garrett said. "The FBI deserves every recognition for doing something really remarkable here. The problem is there may be few judges, prosecutors or defense lawyers who are able or willing to do anything about it."

Federal authorities are offering new DNA testing in cases with errors, if sought by a judge or prosecutor, and agreeing to drop procedural objections to appeals in federal cases.

However, biological evidence in the cases often is lost or unavailable. Among states, only California and Texas specifically allow appeals when experts recant or scientific advances undermine forensic evidence at trial.

Defense attorneys say scientifically invalid forensic testimony should be considered as violations of due process, as courts have held with false or misleading testimony.

The FBI searched more than 21,000 federal and state requests to its hair comparison unit from 1972 through 1999, identifying for review roughly 2,500 cases where examiners declared hair matches.

Reviews of 342 defendants' convictions were completed as of early March, the NACDL and Innocence Project reported. In addition to the 268 trials in which FBI hair evidence was used against defendants, the review found cases in which defendants pleaded guilty, FBI examiners did not testify, did not assert a match or gave exculpatory testimony.

When such cases are included, by the FBI's count examiners made statements exceeding the limits of science in about 90 percent of testimonies, including 34 death-penalty cases.

The findings likely scratch the surface. The FBI said as of mid-April that reviews of about 350 trial testimonies and 900 lab reports are nearly complete, with about 1,200 cases remaining.

The bureau said it is difficult to check cases before 1985, when files were computerized. It has been unable to review 700 cases because police or prosecutors did not respond to requests for information.

Also, the same FBI examiners whose work is under review taught 500 to 1,000 state and local crime lab analysts to testify in the same ways.

Texas, New York and North Carolina authorities are reviewing their hair examiner cases, with ad hoc efforts underway in about 15 other states.

## Critical Thinking

1. Do you believe the "flawed testimony" given by FBI witnesses rises to the level of misconduct?
2. What does Peter Neufeld mean when he says "complete disaster" to describe the problem?

## Internet References

**The Washington Post**
www.washingtonpost.com/

**The Washington Post**
www.washingtonpost.com/2

**Urban Institute**
www.urban.org

SPENCER S. HSU is an investigative reporter, two-time Pulitzer finalist and national Emmy award nominee.

*Article*

Prepared by: Joanne Naughton

# Eric Holder Warns About America's Disturbing Attempts at Precrime

PETER SUDERMAN

## Learning Outcomes

*After reading this article, you will be able to:*

- Illustrate the concept of precrime.

- Explain Holder's position on programs that attempt to offer risk assessments of offenders.

- Show that, although race could not be an explicit factor, it could be built into a system implicitly.

The premise of the 2002 science fiction movie *Minority Report* was that police in a near-future Washington, DC had developed an innovative system to stop crime before it happens. The system, called precrime, was based on the visions of a trio of psychics who could sense criminal activity shortly before it happened. That allowed cops to arrive on the scene and preemptively arrest offenders. It was the end of crime in the District, with criminals apprehended just before they could offend.

America doesn't quite practice precrime yet, but in several states it's edging closer. One difference between the reality and the movie is that instead of psychics we use actuaries.

States such as Pennsylvania, Virginia, and Missouri have developed programs that attempt to offer risk assessments of offenders. Those risk assessments, which are based on a variety of factors including age, education level, and neighborhood of residence as well as past criminality, are meant to guide judges in sentencing. The explicit goal is to reduce future instances of criminality, which means that instead of sentencing people for crime already committed, sentences based on these risk assessments are instead sentencing people for crimes that they, or people like them, might commit.

In a speech last week to the National Association of Criminal Defense Lawyers (which *Reason*'s Jacob Sullum previously noted here), Attorney General Eric Holder warned against the use of such risk assessments:

> When it comes to front-end applications—such as sentencing decisions, where a handful of states are now attempting to employ this methodology—we need to be sure the use of aggregate data analysis won't have unintended consequences.

> Here in Pennsylvania and elsewhere, legislators have introduced the concept of "risk assessments" that seek to assign a probability to an individual's likelihood of committing future crimes and, based on those risk assessments, make sentencing determinations. Although these measures were crafted with the best of intentions, I am concerned that they may inadvertently undermine our efforts to ensure individualized and equal justice. By basing sentencing decisions on static factors and immutable characteristics—like the defendant's education level, socioeconomic background, or neighborhood—they may exacerbate unwarranted and unjust disparities that are already far too common in our criminal justice system and in our society.

> Criminal sentences must be based on the facts, the law, the actual crimes committed, the circumstances surrounding each individual case, and the defendant's history of criminal conduct. They should not be based on unchangeable factors that a person cannot control, or on the possibility of a future crime that has not taken place. Equal justice can only mean individualized justice, with charges, convictions, and sentences befitting the conduct of each defendant and the particular crime he or she commits.

It's not hard to understand the surface appeal of such tools to policymakers. It looks reasonable. It feels scientific. The goal is to identify likely reoffenders and prevent them from committing a second crime. As a 2011 article in the *Federal Sentencing Reporter* put it, it's a shift away from the traditional "backward-looking retributive approach" toward a "formalized, forward-looking, utilitarian" goal.

But Holder is right to be concerned about what is, in effect, a kind of actuarial profiling.

It's a troubling approach. Individuals should be sentenced based on what they have done, not what they might do, and especially not what other members of some group they belong to are likely, on average, to do.

The latter issue is particularly worrying. If a risk assessment recommends longer sentences for people from a particular neighborhood, and a judge follows that recommendation, then the result is effectively to sentence an individual for what his or her neighbors have done.

Even if this approach can be shown to prevent some types or instances of crime, that's not how a criminal justice system is supposed to work. By a roughly similar logic, we could lock up everyone—or even just everyone with the right risk profile, regardless of what crimes they have or have not already committed—from a high crime neighborhood, and call it a success when crime goes down.

Indeed, the same reasoning could lead to support for explicitly race-based sentencing. As a report on Virginia's risk assessment model notes, the state sentencing commission settled on 11 different identifiers to use in determining an offender's risk profile. In the end, race was explicitly excluded from the model, but in the initial analysis, it was "strongly significant" as a factor.

If you follow the "forward-looking utilitarian" logic of the idea to its ugly end, then it's all too easy to imagine a system that explicitly singles out certain races for harsher sentences, not because of the individual particulars of the crime in question, but because of the aggregate actions of other people who share that person's race.

Now, as Virginia's guidelines also suggest, it's unlikely that any state would ever decide to make race an explicit factor. And if that did happen, it's virtually certain that the courts wouldn't let it stand. But even if race is never made an explicit factor, it could be built into the system implicitly, with nonrace identifiers that have the practical effect of singling out certain races. (It's worth noting that there's already some evidence that, intentionally or not, prosecutors end up offering harsher plea deals to minorities.)

If anything, then, it's a system that could lead to something worse than the psychic-powered precrime of *Minority Report*. In the movie, cops targeted specific individuals who were just hours or minutes from committing a crime. Under a system that relied heavily on the sort of data-driven sentencing that Holder describes in his speech, we'd be targeting not individuals so much as large groups of people, and punishing them for what other people who they resemble have done, or might possibly do, months or years in the future.

## Critical Thinking

1. What's wrong with programs that seek to determine who is likely to commit crimes, if they can be shown to prevent some types of crimes?

2. Do you believe it makes good sense for a judge to be able to sentence a guilty person from a high crime neighborhood to a longer sentence than someone from another neighborhood?

## Internet References

**Reason.com**
   reason.com/blog/2014/08/01/eric-holder-says-mandatory- minimums-are

**The National Center for State Courts**
   www.vcsc.virginia.gov/risk_off_rept.pdf

**U.S. Department of Justice**
   www.justice.gov/opa/speech/attorney-general-eric-holder-speaks-national-association-criminal-defense-lawyers-57th

**Vera Institute of Justice**
   www.vera.org/pubs/special/race-and-prosecution-manhattan

# Unit 2

# UNIT

Prepared by: Joanne Naughton

# Victimology

For many years, crime victims were not considered to be an important topic for criminological study. Now, however, criminologists consider that focusing on victims and victimization is essential to understanding the phenomenon of crime. The popularity of this area of study can be attributed to the early work of several criminologists such as Hans von Hentig and, later, Stephen Schafer, who examined victim-offender interactions and stressed reciprocal influences and role reversals.

Victimology focuses on the relationship of the victim to the criminal offender: whether they were strangers, mere acquaintances, friends, family members, or even intimates; and why a particular person or place was targeted.

The victim's role in the criminal justice process has received increasing attention from a growing number of criminologists in recent years, and as more criminologists focus their attention on the victim's role in the process, victimology will take on even greater importance.

*Article*                                                    Prepared by: Joanne Naughton

# Telling the Truth about Damned Lies and Statistics

Joel Best

## Learning Outcomes

*After reading this article, you will be able to:*

- Evaluate statistics more critically.

- Understand how statistics can be misinterpreted.

The dissertation prospectus began by quoting a statistic—a "grabber" meant to capture the reader's attention. The graduate student who wrote this prospectus undoubtedly wanted to seem scholarly to the professors who would read it; they would be supervising the proposed research. And what could be more scholarly than a nice, authoritative statistic, quoted from a professional journal in the student's field?

So the prospectus began with this (carefully footnoted) quotation: "Every year since 1950, the number of American children gunned down has doubled." I had been invited to serve on the student's dissertation committee. When I read the quotation, I assumed the student had made an error in copying it. I went to the library and looked up the article the student had cited. There, in the journal's 1995 volume, was exactly the same sentence: "Every year since 1950, the number of American children gunned down has doubled."

This quotation is my nomination for a dubious distinction: I think it may be the worst—that is, the most inaccurate—social statistic ever.

What makes this statistic so bad? Just for the sake of argument, let's assume that "the number of American children gunned down" in 1950 was one. If the number doubled each year, there must have been two children gunned down in 1951, four in 1952, eight in 1953, and so on. By 1960, the number would have been 1,024. By 1965, it would have been 32,768 (in 1965, the F.B.I. identified only 9,960 criminal homicides in the entire country, including adult as well as child victims). By 1970, the number would have passed one million; by 1980, one billion (more than four times the total U.S. population in that year). Only three years later, in 1983, the number of American children gunned down would have been 8.6 billion (nearly twice the earth's population at the time). Another milestone would have been passed in 1987, when the number of gunned-down American children (137 billion) would have surpassed the best estimates for the total human population throughout history (110 billion). By 1995, when the article was published, the annual number of victims would have been over 35 trillion—a really big number, of a magnitude you rarely encounter outside economics or astronomy.

Thus my nomination: estimating the number of American child gunshot victims in 1995 at 35 trillion must be as far off—as hilariously, wildly wrong—as a social statistic can be. (If anyone spots a more inaccurate social statistic, I'd love to hear about it.)

Where did the article's author get this statistic? I wrote the author, who responded that the statistic came from the Children's Defense Fund, a well-known advocacy group for children. The C.D.F.'s *The State of America's Children Yearbook 1994* does state: "The number of American children killed each year by guns has doubled since 1950." Note the difference in the wording—the C.D.F. claimed there were twice as many deaths in 1994 as in 1950; the article's author reworded that claim and created a very different meaning.

It is worth examining the history of this statistic. It began with the C.D.F. noting that child gunshot deaths had doubled from 1950 to 1994. This is not quite as dramatic an increase as it might seem. Remember that the U.S. population also rose throughout this period; in fact, it grew about 73 percent—or nearly double. Therefore, we might expect all sorts of things—including the number of child gunshot deaths—to increase, to nearly double, just because the population grew. Before we can decide whether twice as many deaths indicate that things are getting worse, we'd have to know more. The C.D.F. statistic raises other issues as well: Where did the statistic come from? Who counts child gunshot deaths, and how? What is meant by a "child" (some C.D.F. statistics about violence include everyone under age 25)? What is meant by "killed by guns" (gunshot-death statistics often include suicides and accidents, as well as homicides)? But people rarely ask questions of this sort when they encounter statistics. Most of the time, most people simply accept statistics without question.

Certainly, the article's author didn't ask many probing, critical questions about the C.D.F.'s claim. Impressed by the statistic, the author repeated it—well, meant to repeat it. Instead, by rewording the C.D.F.'s claim, the author created a mutant statistic, one garbled almost beyond recognition.

But people treat mutant statistics just as they do other statistics—that is, they usually accept even the most implausible claims without question. For example, the journal editor who accepted the author's article for publication did not bother to consider the implications of child victims doubling each year. And people repeat bad statistics: The graduate student copied the garbled statistic and inserted it into the dissertation prospectus. Who knows whether still other readers were impressed by the author's statistic and remembered it or repeated it? The article remains on the shelf in hundreds of libraries, available to anyone who needs a dramatic quote. The lesson should be clear: Bad statistics live on; they take on lives of their own.

Some statistics are born bad—they aren't much good from the start, because they are based on nothing more than guesses or dubious data. Other statistics mutate; they become bad after being mangled (as in the case of the author's creative rewording). Either way, bad statistics are potentially important: They can be used to stir up public outrage or fear; they can distort our understanding of our world; and they can lead us to make poor policy choices.

The notion that we need to watch out for bad statistics isn't new. We've all heard people say, "You can prove anything with statistics." The title of my book, *Damned Lies and Statistics*, comes from a famous aphorism (usually attributed to Mark Twain or Benjamin Disraeli): "There are three kinds of lies: lies, damned lies, and statistics." There is even a useful little book, still in print after more than 40 years, called *How to Lie With Statistics*.

## We shouldn't ignore all statistics, or assume that every number is false. Some statistics are bad, but others are pretty good. And we need good statistics to talk sensibly about social problems.

Statistics, then, have a bad reputation. We suspect that statistics may be wrong, that people who use statistics may be "lying"—trying to manipulate us by using numbers to somehow distort the truth. Yet, at the same time, we need statistics; we depend upon them to summarize and clarify the nature of our complex society. This is particularly true when we talk about social problems. Debates about social problems routinely raise questions that demand statistical answers: Is the problem widespread? How many people—and which people—does it affect? Is it getting worse? What does it cost society? What will it cost to deal with it? Convincing answers to such questions demand evidence, and that usually means numbers, measurements, statistics.

But can't you prove anything with statistics? It depends on what "prove" means. If we want to know, say, how many children are "gunned down" each year, we can't simply guess—pluck a number from thin air: 100, 1,000, 10,000, 35 trillion,

whatever. Obviously, there's no reason to consider an arbitrary guess "proof" of anything. However, it might be possible for someone—using records kept by police departments or hospital emergency rooms or coroners—to keep track of children who have been shot; compiling careful, complete records might give us a fairly accurate idea of the number of gunned-down children. If that number seems accurate enough, we might consider it very strong evidence—or proof.

The solution to the problem of bad statistics is not to ignore all statistics, or to assume that every number is false. Some statistics are bad, but others are pretty good, and we need statistics—good statistics—to talk sensibly about social problems. The solution, then, is not to give up on statistics, but to become better judges of the numbers we encounter. We need to think critically about statistics—at least critically enough to suspect that the number of children gunned down hasn't been doubling each year since 1950.

A few years ago, the mathematician John Allen Paulos wrote *Innumeracy*, a short, readable book about "mathematical illiteracy." Too few people, he argued, are comfortable with basic mathematical principles, and this makes them poor judges of the numbers they encounter. No doubt this is one reason we have so many bad statistics. But there are other reasons, as well.

Social statistics describe society, but they are also products of our social arrangements. The people who bring social statistics to our attention have reasons for doing so; they inevitably want something, just as reporters and the other media figures who repeat and publicize statistics have their own goals. Statistics are tools, used for particular purposes. Thinking critically about statistics requires understanding their place in society.

While we may be more suspicious of statistics presented by people with whom we disagree—people who favor different political parties or have different beliefs—bad statistics are used to promote all sorts of causes. Bad statistics come from conservatives on the political right and liberals on the left, from wealthy corporations and powerful government agencies, and from advocates of the poor and the powerless.

In order to interpret statistics, we need more than a checklist of common errors. We need a general approach, an orientation, a mind-set that we can use to think about new statistics that we encounter. We ought to approach statistics thoughtfully. This can be hard to do, precisely because so many people in our society treat statistics as fetishes. We might call this the mind-set of the awestruck—the people who don't think critically, who act as though statistics have magical powers. The awestruck know they don't always understand the statistics they hear, but this doesn't bother them. After all, who can expect to understand magical numbers? The reverential fatalism of the awestruck is not thoughtful—it is a way of avoiding thought. We need a different approach.

One choice is to approach statistics critically. Being critical does not mean being negative or hostile—it is not cynicism. The critical approach statistics thoughtfully; they avoid the extremes of both naïve acceptance and cynical rejection of the numbers they encounter. Instead, the critical attempt to evaluate numbers, to distinguish between good statistics and bad statistics.

The critical understand that, while some social statistics may be pretty good, they are never perfect. Every statistic is a way of summarizing complex information into relatively simple numbers. Inevitably, some information, some of the complexity, is lost whenever we use statistics. The critical recognize that this is an inevitable limitation of statistics. Moreover, they realize that every statistic is the product of choices—the choice between defining a category broadly or narrowly, the choice of one measurement over another, the choice of a sample. People choose definitions, measurements, and samples for all sorts of reasons: Perhaps they want to emphasize some aspect of a problem; perhaps it is easier or cheaper to gather data in a particular way—many considerations can come into play. Every statistic is a compromise among choices. This means that every definition—and every measurement and every sample—probably has limitations and can be criticized.

Being critical means more than simply pointing to the flaws in a statistic. Again, every statistic has flaws. The issue is whether a particular statistic's flaws are severe enough to damage its usefulness. Is the definition so broad that it encompasses too many false positives (or so narrow that it excludes too many false negatives)? How would changing the definition alter the statistic? Similarly, how do the choices of measurements and samples affect the statistic? What would happen if different measures or samples were chosen? And how is the statistic used? Is it being interpreted appropriately, or has its meaning been mangled to create a mutant statistic? Are the comparisons that are being made appropriate, or are apples being confused with oranges? How do different choices produce the conflicting numbers found in stat wars? These are the sorts of questions the critical ask.

As a practical matter, it is virtually impossible for citizens in contemporary society to avoid statistics about social problems. Statistics arise in all sorts of ways, and in almost every case the people promoting statistics want to persuade us. Activists use statistics to convince us that social problems are serious and deserve our attention and concern. Charities use statistics to encourage donations. Politicians use statistics to persuade us that they understand society's problems and that they deserve our support. The media use statistics to make their reporting more dramatic, more convincing, more compelling. Corporations use statistics to promote and improve their products. Researchers use statistics to document their findings and support their conclusions. Those with whom we agree use statistics to reassure us that we're on the right side, while our opponents use statistics to try and convince us that we are wrong. Statistics are one of the standard types of evidence used by people in our society.

It is not possible simply to ignore statistics, to pretend they don't exist. That sort of head-in-the-sand approach would be too costly. Without statistics, we limit our ability to think thoughtfully about our society; without statistics, we have no accurate ways of judging how big a problem may be, whether it is getting worse, or how well the policies designed to address that problem actually work. And awestruck or naïve attitudes toward statistics are no better than ignoring statistics; statistics have no magical properties, and it is foolish to assume that all statistics are equally valid. Nor is a cynical approach the answer; statistics are too widespread and too useful to be automatically discounted.

It would be nice to have a checklist, a set of items we could consider in evaluating any statistic. The list might detail potential problems with definitions, measurements, sampling, mutation, and so on. These are, in fact, common sorts of flaws found in many statistics, but they should not be considered a formal, complete checklist. It is probably impossible to produce a complete list of statistical flaws—no matter how long the list, there will be other possible problems that could affect statistics.

The goal is not to memorize a list, but to develop a thoughtful approach. Becoming critical about statistics requires being prepared to ask questions about numbers. When encountering a new statistic in, say, a news report, the critical try to assess it. What might be the sources for this number? How could one go about producing the figure? Who produced the number, and what interests might they have? What are the different ways key terms might have been defined, and which definitions have been chosen? How might the phenomena be measured, and which measurement choices have been made? What sort of sample was gathered, and how might that sample affect the result? Is the statistic being properly interpreted? Are comparisons being made, and if so, are the comparisons appropriate? Are there competing statistics? If so, what stakes do the opponents have in the issue, and how are those stakes likely to affect their use of statistics? And is it possible to figure out why the statistics seem to disagree, what the differences are in the ways the competing sides are using figures?

At first, this list of questions may seem overwhelming. How can an ordinary person—someone who reads a statistic in a magazine article or hears it on a news broadcast—determine the answers to such questions? Certainly news reports rarely give detailed information on the processes by which statistics are created. And few of us have time to drop everything and investigate the background of some new number we encounter. Being critical, it seems, involves an impossible amount of work.

In practice, however, the critical need not investigate the origin of every statistic. Rather, being critical means appreciating the inevitable limitations that affect all statistics, rather than being awestruck in the presence of numbers. It means not being too credulous, not accepting every statistic at face value. But it also means appreciating that statistics, while always imperfect, can be useful. Instead of automatically discounting every statistic, the critical reserve judgment. When confronted with an interesting number, they may try to learn more, to evaluate, to weigh the figure's strengths and weaknesses.

Of course, this critical approach need not—and should not—be limited to statistics. It ought to apply to all the evidence we encounter when we scan a news report, or listen to a speech—whenever we learn about social problems.

Claims about social problems often feature dramatic, compelling examples; the critical might ask whether an example is likely to be a typical case or an extreme, exceptional instance. Claims about social problems often include quotations from different sources, and the critical might wonder why those sources have spoken and why they have been quoted: Do they have particular expertise? Do they stand to benefit if they influence others? Claims about social problems usually involve arguments about the problem's causes and potential solutions. The critical might ask whether these arguments are convincing. Are they logical? Does the proposed solution seem feasible and appropriate? And so on. Being critical—adopting a skeptical, analytical stance when confronted with claims—is an approach that goes far beyond simply dealing with statistics.

Statistics are not magical. Nor are they always true—or always false. Nor need they be incomprehensible. Adopting a critical approach offers an effective way of responding to the numbers we are sure to encounter. Being critical requires more thought, but failing to adopt a critical mind-set makes us powerless to evaluate what others tell us. When we fail to think critically, the statistics we hear might just as well be magical.

## Critical Thinking

1. Why are there bad statistics?
2. How can one approach statistics critically?
3. What was wrong with the following statement made in 1995: "Every year since 1950 the number of American children gunned down has doubled"?

## Create Central

www.mhhe.com/createcentral

## Internet References

**Bureau of Justice Statistics**
www.bjs.gov

**Federal Bureau of Investigation (F.B.I.)**
www.fbi.gov/about-us/cjis/ucr/ucr-statistics-their-proper-use

JOEL BEST is a professor of sociology and criminal justice at the University of Delaware. This essay is excerpted from *Damned Lies and Statistics: Untangling Numbers from the Media, Politicians, and Activists*, published by the University of California Press and reprinted by permission. Copyright © 2001 by the Regents of the University of California.

*Article*                                                      Prepared by: Joanne Naughton

# AP IMPACT: Abused Kids Die as Authorities Fail to Protect

HOLBROOK MOHR AND GARANCE BURKE

## Learning Outcomes

*After reading this article, you will be able to:*

- Describe some of the reasons that child protection agencies are failing to protect many children.

- Explain the reasons comprehensive, publicly available data is necessary.

- Show how states submit information to the federal government, and how unreliable that information can be.

Butte, Montana (AP)—At least 786 children died of abuse or neglect in the U.S. in a six-year span in plain view of child protection authorities—many of them beaten, starved or left alone to drown while agencies had good reason to know they were in danger, The Associated Press has found.

To determine that number, the AP canvassed the 50 states, the District of Columbia and all branches of the military—circumventing a system that does a terrible job of accounting for child deaths. Many states struggled to provide numbers. Secrecy often prevailed.

Most of the 786 children whose cases were compiled by the AP were under the age of 4. They lost their lives even as authorities were investigating their families or providing some form of protective services because of previous instances of neglect, violence or other troubles in the home.

Take Mattisyn Blaz, a 2-month-old from Montana who died when her father spiked her "like a football," in the words of a prosecutor.

Matthew Blaz was well-known to child services personnel and police. Just two weeks after Mattisyn was born on June 25, 2013, he came home drunk, grabbed his wife by her hair and threw her to the kitchen floor while she clung to the newborn. He snatched the baby from her arms, giving her back only when Jennifer Blaz called police.

Jennifer Blaz said a child protective services worker visited the day after her husband's attack, spoke with her briefly and left. Her husband pleaded guilty to assault and was ordered by a judge to take anger management classes and stay away from his wife.

She said the next official contact between the family and Montana child services came more than six weeks later—the day of Mattisyn's funeral.

The system also failed Ethan Henderson, who was only 10 weeks old but already had been treated for a broken arm when his father hurled him into a recliner so hard that it caused a fatal brain injury.

Maine hotline workers had received at least 13 calls warning that Ethan or his siblings were suffering abuse—including assertions that an older sister had been found covered in bruises, was possibly being sexually abused and had been burned by a stove because she was left unsupervised.

Ethan himself had arrived at daycare with deep red bruises dappling his arm.

Still, the caseworker who inspected the family's cramped trailer six days before Ethan died on May 8, 2012, wrote that the baby appeared "well cared for and safe in the care of his parents."

## Lack of Government Data

Because no single, complete set of data exists for the deaths of children who already were being overseen by child protective services workers, the information compiled over the course of AP's eight-month investigation represents the most comprehensive statistics publicly available.

The AP reviewed thousands of pages of official reports, child fatality records and police documents for the period in question, which ran from fiscal year 2008 through 2013.

And, even then, the number of abuse and neglect fatalities where a prior open case existed at the time of death is undoubtedly much higher than the tally of 760.

Seven states reported a total of 230 open-case child deaths over the six-year period, but those were not included in the AP count because the states could not make a distinction between investigations started due to the incident that ultimately led to a child's death and cases that already were open when the child received the fatal injury.

Some states did not provide data for all six years, not all branches of the military provided complete information, and no count of open-case deaths of any type was obtained from the Bureau of Indian Affairs or FBI, which investigate allegations of abuse on reservations.

The lack of comprehensive data makes it difficult to measure how well those responsible for keeping children safe are protecting their most vulnerable charges.

The data collection system on child deaths is so flawed that no one can even say with accuracy how many children overall die from abuse or neglect every year. The federal government estimates an average of about 1,650 deaths annually in recent years; many believe the actual number is twice as high.

Even more lacking is comprehensive, publicly available data about the number of children dying while the subject of an open case or while receiving assistance from the agencies that exist to keep them safe—the focus of AP's reporting.

When asked to explain why so many children with open cases have died at the hands of their caretakers, a spokeswoman for the U.S. Department of Health and Human Services, which oversees the nation's major child abuse prevention programs, said the agency had no immediate response.

But spokeswoman Laura Goulding said colleagues wanted to know more about how the AP derived its figures. "Are you willing to share your source for that?" she wrote in an email.

States submit information on child abuse deaths to the federal government on a voluntary basis—some of it comprehensive, some of it inaccurate.

For instance, a significant number of deaths were not reported to the South Carolina team reviewing child deaths in the state, said Perry Simpson, director of the South Carolina Legislative Audit Council. That meant the data the review team provided the federal government was wrong.

And a judge in Kentucky issued a scathing order last year against the state's Cabinet for Health and Family Services for willfully circumventing open records laws and failing to release full records on child abuse deaths, fining the agency $765,000.

"There can be no effective prevention when there is no public examination of the underlying facts," Franklin Circuit Judge Phillip Shepherd said.

In some cases, states withhold information about child deaths in violation of the terms of federal grants they receive.

HHS says all states receiving grants under a prevention and treatment program must "allow the public to access information when child abuse or neglect results in a child fatality," unless those details would put children, their families or those who report child abuse at risk, or jeopardize an investigation.

In addition, grants issued under a section of the Social Security Act are tied to a requirement that states describe how they calculate data on child maltreatment deaths submitted to the federal government.

Still, no state has ever been found to be in violation of disclosure requirements and federal grants have never been withheld, according to Catherine Nolan, who directs the Office on Child Abuse and Neglect, a sub-agency of HHS.

"Obviously, the overarching goal is always keeping the children safe from harm. It's a matter of how the states have decided they want to do it," Nolan said.

The information that states provide to the federal government through the voluntary system also is severely lacking. A 2013 report showed that 17 states did not provide the federal government with a key measure of performance: how many children had died of child abuse after being removed from their homes and then reunited with their families within a five-year period.

Withholding information about such fatalities allows child protective agencies to shroud their activities—and their failures. It also leaves a major void for researchers and policy makers looking for ways to identify and protect the children in risky situations.

"We all agree that we cannot solve a problem this complex until we agree it exists," said David Sanders, chairman of the federal Commission to Eliminate Child Abuse and Neglect Fatalities, whose members have been traveling the country studying child deaths under a congressional mandate.

"If, for example, you want to fix something like fatalities due to children being left alone, it seems that it would be important to know how often that is happening and what it looks like to come up with a solution," he said.

The child welfare system is fragmented, with hundreds of different agencies—from state governments to county offices, tribes and the military—operating by their own set of standards.

Some states, like New York and Ohio, have county-administered systems, with data collection and retention scattered. In others, a state agency provides child welfare services. And still others, such as Florida, have privatized some child welfare operations.

And because there is no single definition of what constitutes abuse or neglect, what is counted as maltreatment in one locality may not be in another.

## Montana Secrets

Nowhere was the AP's challenge steeper than Montana, where the state's confidentiality law allows the child protective services agency to operate with impunity. The AP discovered the Department of Public Health and Human Services' involvement in Mattisyn Blaz's short life, and her death, only by examining hundreds of pages of court files from the criminal trial of her father.

The state makes public only the number of children who died from maltreatment in a given year. Officials said state law prohibits them from releasing details on the number of children who died after having a prior history with child protective services.

Department spokesman Jon Ebelt acknowledged Montana law conflicts with federal disclosure requirements and said officials would seek a change in state law to allow for the disclosure of more information.

As part of the blanket secrecy, it is not clear what, if anything, child welfare authorities did to help Mattisyn Blaz.

Based on information obtained from the court file, it is clear that Matthew Blaz's violent streak was known to authorities. His former girlfriend had accused him of assaulting her while she cradled their 9-week-old son in 2011. He attacked his wife, Jennifer, at least twice in 2012, on one occasion dragging her around the house by her hair. She told authorities he regularly threatened to kill her.

Mattisyn's older half-sister—10 at the time—cowered under a bed after Blaz threatened to come after her and was so afraid she began sleeping with a knife nearby, the children's grandmother said.

The protective order issued in July 2013 should have prevented Matthew Blaz from remaining in the home, but soon he was back with the family. "I honestly thought after I bailed him out and we talked, and with the no alcohol, you know, and him going to AA, I really thought things were going to change," his wife said.

When Jennifer Blaz went to work on Aug. 16, 2013, she left her husband to care for the girls. For reasons still unknown, he became enraged and threw the baby, fracturing her skull and causing other devastating injuries, according to prosecutor Samm Cox.

Later that day, he loaded the children into his car and drove across town to pick up a chain saw that had been repaired and then stopped for some sandwiches. He dropped one off to his wife at work, but never mentioned anything was wrong with the baby.

When Matthew picked his wife up that afternoon, he calmly told her that a 12-year-old neighborhood boy had dropped Mattisyn earlier in the day. Jennifer noticed the baby didn't look right and called for an ambulance.

By then, it was too late for little Mattisyn.

Last month, Matthew Blaz was sentenced to life in prison, with no possibility of parole.

## A System Still Failing

When President Richard Nixon signed the Child Abuse Prevention and Treatment Act into law in 1974, it was seen as a sign of federal commitment to preventing child abuse through state-level monitoring.

But in 1995, a board reviewing the progress that had been made issued a scathing report headlined "A Nation's Shame: Fatal Child Abuse and Neglect in the United States."

The report called for better information and transparency, and flagged "serious gaps in data collection." "Until we develop more comprehensive and sophisticated data, our efforts to understand and prevent child maltreatment-related deaths will be severely handicapped," it said.

Nearly 20 years later, the AP found that many such problems persist.

Michael Petit, who was appointed by President Barack Obama to serve on the federal Commission to Eliminate Child Abuse and Neglect Fatalities, said meetings have been fruitful but will bring no substantive change unless Congress requires states to do more.

"The child safety net in this country is not equal to the size of the problem that's coming at it," said Petit, the former head of Maine's child protective services agency and founder of the advocacy group Every Child Matters. "The system overall is in crisis."

That system is plagued with worker shortages and a serious overload of cases. For instance, a caseworker in Texas who investigated abuse reports about a 2-year-old who eventually died in the care of his mother was juggling 37 cases a few weeks before he died.

In addition:

- Budgets are tight, and some experts say funding shortages lead to more deaths. Conditions improved when Alabama spent more money on child welfare as part of a 15-year federal consent decree. But since 2007, when the decree ended, funding has shrunk nearly every year—and the number of open-case deaths has started to climb, from one in 2009 to five in 2013.

- Insufficient training for those who answer child abuse hotlines leads to reports being misclassified, sometimes with deadly consequences. In Arizona, a June 2013 call about an 8-month-old with a suspicious broken arm was logged incorrectly and not investigated. The girl died of a brain injury about a month later, after being burned on the face with a cigarette lighter and shaken violently.

- The lack of a comprehensive national child welfare database that would allow caseworkers to keep track of individual cases, child by child, means some abusive caregivers known to authorities can slip through the cracks by crossing state lines.

- A policy that promotes keeping families intact plays a major role in the number of deaths, because children remain in abusive situations. According to Vermont police, 2-year-old Dezirae Sheldon was left in her home even after suffering two broken legs under suspicious circumstances. Caseworkers said they'd felt "an overwhelming push" to keep the family together, based on their general training. Dezirae died in February from blunt force trauma to the head; her stepfather is charged with second-degree murder. A police detective wrote: "This focus on reunification very often puts the needs of the parents often above the needs and interest of the child or victim."

- Worst of all, nearly 40 percent of the 3 million child abuse and neglect complaints made annually to child protective services hotlines in the U.S. are "screened out" and never investigated.

## Failure at Its Extreme

The case of 10-week-old Ethan Henderson—whose family in Arundel, Maine, had been the subject of at least 13 calls to child protective services—presents a particularly telling example of a repeated systemic failure.

Only two of those calls were investigated—one involving Ethan and his twin brother, and the other, their sister. In addition, more than a half-dozen physicians, nurses and other care-givers failed to report signs that the blue-eyed boy with wispy blond hair was being terribly hurt. Some have escaped scrutiny and punishment to this day.

Maine child welfare officials said the state's confidentiality law prohibited them from discussing details about their involvement in Ethan's case. Records obtained by AP, however, suggest the state missed numerous opportunities to properly assess the safety of Ethan and his siblings, neglecting to follow up promptly even after identifying warning signs.

According to evidence produced as part of the criminal case against Ethan's father, Gordon Collins-Faunce, the police made two of those calls but hotline workers decided that neither merited a response.

Ethan's grandmother, Jan Collins, said she called the hotline just before the twins were born because she feared her son and another man who frequented the family's mobile home could hurt the children.

"I said I thought Gordon was delusional. They just dismissed that," she said. "I kept thinking that tomorrow I will find out that the state has gotten involved."

The twins were born a few weeks premature on Feb. 21, 2012—and just four weeks later, Ethan's mother took him to a nearby hospital with a broken left arm. She told his pediatrician that Ethan's father had accidentally twisted it lifting the baby from his crib. The doctor never reported the injury, even though Maine law requires physicians to immediately report possible child abuse.

About a month later, Ethan arrived at daycare unable to move his neck and with dark bruises on his right arm. Workers took photos of the bruises, but never reported them, said Maine Police Det. Lauren Edstrom, who investigated Ethan's death. The next week, Ethan arrived at daycare with such a high fever that workers called his mother to take him to the hospital, evidence shows.

When Ethan was nearly 10 weeks old, a family friend finally called the hotline to report bruises on the twins and a white, blistering burn on their sister's hand. Edstrom said the friend decided to tell hotline workers she was a daycare volunteer so that they would take the report seriously. That represented the second report worthy of investigation.

Melissa Guillerault, the child welfare agency worker dispatched to the gray double-wide trailer on May 2, called ahead to let the family know she was coming. Still, she found Collins-Faunce and his wife had five bags of trash on the porch.

Though the state later acknowledged Guillerault learned of Ethan's earlier broken arm during that visit, records show she found the couple to be "cooperative and engaging." She said the children "appeared clean, healthy and comfortable," although she didn't inspect them for bruises. In a section of her report designated for the listing of "signs of danger," the worker wrote: "None at this time."

Three days later, according to Collins-Faunce's confession to police, he grew so frustrated by Ethan's cries that he picked up his son by the head and threw him into a chair, causing severe brain damage. Before calling 911, evidence shows he went outside to smoke and play the video game "Police Pursuit."

Ethan died three days later, on May 8, 2012. His father was convicted of manslaughter last year; his siblings were placed in foster care and adopted.

Virginia McNamara, a pediatric nurse who visited Ethan at his home and never reported the signs of possible abuse, lost her license to practice in Maine. Ethan's pediatrician, Dr. Lisa Gouldsbrough, was never disciplined, although she received a letter of guidance from the Maine board that licenses osteopathic doctors aimed at helping her "in avoiding complaints of this nature in the future." Guillerault was promoted to a supervisory role within the department, a position she still holds.

None of them responded to AP's requests for comment, and neither did the Maine Department of Health and Human Services.

The records that spell out the state's involvement with the family remain secret.

# Critical Thinking

1. What are some ways child protection agencies can improve?
2. What did Judge Phillip Shepherd mean by his statement about effective prevention?
3. What do you think about Catherine Nolan's statement regarding federal grants to states?

# Internet References

**Children's Justice Act**
http://nrccps.org/wp-content/uploads/CJA-FAQs-DEC-2013.pdf

**Child Trends Data Bank**
http://www.childtrends.org/wp-content/uploads/2014/07/40_Child_Maltreatment.pdf

**Lexington Herald Leader**
http://www.kentucky.com/2013/12/23/3002988_judge-fines-ky-cabinet-756000.html?rh=1

**US Advisory Board on Child Abuse and Neglect**
http://files.eric.ed.gov/fulltext/ED393570.pdf

**West Hawaii Today**
http://westhawaiitoday.com/community-bulletin/abused-kids-die-authorities-fail-protect?qt-popular_quick_tab=1

*Article*                                        Prepared by: Joanne Naughton

# This Is How a Domestic Violence Victim Falls Through the Cracks

Melissa Jeltsen

## Learning Outcomes

*After reading this article, you will be able to:*

- Explain the ways a victim can be controlled by an abuser.
- Understand why a victim will stay with an abuser instead of just leaving.
- Show the effect of guns on domestic violence in Arkansas.

Berryville, Arkansas—Two days before she died, Laura Aceves stood on the side of the road and frantically dialed the police for the last time.

It was early afternoon and the 21-year-old had finished her shift at the Berryville Tyson Foods plant, where she worked on an assembly line deboning chicken. Moments after pulling out of the parking lot, her car broke down. At the nearest service station, a mechanic identified the problem: Someone had poured bleach in her gas tank.

Laura knew who was responsible. Her abusive ex-boyfriend, Victor Acuna-Sanchez, was out on bail and had a history of destroying her stuff. "No one else would have done this," she told police.

According to family members and court records, Laura spent the last year of her life being terrorized by Acuna-Sanchez. He allegedly beat her with a baseball bat, dragged her behind a car, strangled her until she blacked out on the floor and told her over and over how he would kill her if she ever left him.

At the time, Acuna-Sanchez, 18, was awaiting trial for charges stemming from two prior attacks on Laura, including a felony for aggravated assault. He was out on bail, under court order to have no contact with Laura and to check in with probation by phone each week.

At the gas station, Laura told police where she thought Acuna-Sanchez might be staying and pleaded for their help. An officer said he'd search for him, but came up empty-handed. That evening, Laura, who had three young children, posted a vague message on Facebook hinting at her troubles: *It is gonna be a long night.*

Less than 48 hours later, she was found in her apartment with a gunshot wound to the head. Her four-month-old son was crying by her side, coated in so much blood that EMTs thought he'd been shot too. Laura had an open casket funeral. No amount of makeup could conceal her black eyes.

A year and a half has passed since her murder. On a clear day in April, her mother, Laura Ponce, drives to her last apartment and stands in the driveway, holding back tears.

The apartment complex is on the outskirts of town, on a steep, twisting ridge in the Ozarks. In the spring, the shrubs lining the road flush with tiny purple flowers. It's the road that leaves town, the path out of Carroll County.

"She was trying to get as far away as she could," Ponce says. "It wasn't enough."

As with many women who are killed in domestic violence homicides, Laura's death was foreshadowed by a documented trail of warning signs. But in this small town in rural Arkansas, those red flags went unheeded. Despite Acuna-Sanchez's history of brutal attacks and repeated violations of his bail conditions, the justice system failed to keep him away from the woman he vowed to kill.

"Everybody knew she was in danger," Ponce says. "A police officer came to my house and I told him everything in detail: How Victor beat her up, how he told us we were all going to be murdered, and that he had guns. Why couldn't anyone stop him?"

Robert Hancock, a neighbor, spots Ponce through his window and comes outside to talk. He was home the night Laura died. His mother owns the 12-unit apartment complex, which is now for sale. They haven't been able to rent Laura's unit since her death. Everyone knows what happened there.

"You have to trust that God will take care of it, one way or another," he says. "Are you a Christian—do you believe in God?"

"I do," Ponce says, her voice strained. "But I don't believe in the justice of Berryville."

Sheriff Bob Grudek, 71, sits in his office at the jail where Acuna-Sanchez is being held on capital murder charges and rattles off a list of small-town problems facing Carroll County.

Theft, mostly of farm equipment. People stripping copper wire off the chicken houses and selling it. Kids stealing their parents' prescription drugs. DUIs. Some methamphetamine. And a lot of domestic violence.

In the last decade, Arkansas has frequently been ranked as one of the 10 worst states in the nation when it comes to men killing women, according to annual reports by the Violence Policy Center. The ranking is based on FBI data on incidents in which a sole male offender kills a single female victim, a typical indicator of domestic homicide.

In Arkansas, the combination of lots and lots of guns and lax firearm laws contributes to the problem. Research has shown if a batterer has access to a gun, the victim is eight times more likely to be killed. According to an analysis by the Center for American Progress, in 2010 Arkansas had the third-worst gun murder rate for women in the nation.

In the aftermath of Laura's gruesome murder, a blame game between the sheriff and prosecutor's office played out in the local press.

Acuna-Sanchez was out on bail at the time of Laura's death, awaiting trial for earlier assaults against her. In the month leading up to her death, he repeatedly broke the conditions of his pretrial release, but faced few consequences.

Just three weeks before she was killed, police arrested him for violating a no-contact order. Despite a record of escalating violence against Laura, he was released without bail the following day.

In a local newspaper, Grudek blamed Acuna-Sanchez's release on gaps in communication between the prosecutor and the judge. Since he had violated the no-contact order, prosecutors could have asked the judge to hold him pending trial, but they didn't.

Deputy prosecuting attorney Devon Closser said that was because they didn't know about his most recent arrest. She told The Lovely County Citizen that there was no procedure in place to inform prosecutors when protective orders had been violated—and that the system could use "fine-tuning."

In an interview with *The Huffington Post,* Closser declined to discuss the case, but said it was "not unusual" for offenders to be released quickly if they were arrested simply for violating a no-contact order.

Records also show that Acuna-Sanchez wasn't checking in with a probation officer, as he was ordered to do as a condition of bail, but no one noticed.

Grudek said he couldn't comment on Acuna-Sanchez's case specifically. But he shared his perspective on the problem of domestic violence, which he said he formulated by watching Dr. Phil.

"This is a very serious social problem," he said, speculating that the crime was related to the breakdown of the traditional family structure. "Maybe if our culture goes back to when we had different values . . . I don't remember when I was a kid hearing about any domestic violence."

In fact, the opposite is true. Domestic violence has been on a steady decline in the U.S. for the past 20 years. Since the landmark Violence Against Women Act was passed in 1994, annual rates of domestic violence have plummeted by 64 percent. But the U.S. still has the highest rate of domestic violence homicide of any industrialized country.

Each day on average, three women are murdered by intimate partners—husbands and ex-husbands, boyfriends, and estranged lovers. Compared to men, women are far more often murdered by someone they know. In 2010, 39 percent of U.S. female homicide victims were killed by an intimate partner. Just 3 percent of men suffered the same fate.

When asked how Carroll County could improve its handling of domestic violence cases, Grudek said he was unconvinced that a more proactive response—like setting high bail for serial abusers, or requiring GPS tracking for offenders who violate restraining orders—would make a substantial difference.

"The question you're asking me is what's wrong with the courts," he said. "I'm asking you, what's wrong with the women?"

Grudek said domestic violence prevention should focus on why women return to their abusers, and that it wasn't "logical or responsible" to think the criminal justice system could solve the problem.

But across the country, many people are hopeful that it can play a pivotal role to help reduce domestic violence deaths.

While one in four women will be victims of domestic violence at some point in their lives, only a small fraction of cases turn lethal. The trick, many experts now believe, is identifying which women are at highest risk of death so they can be targeted for intervention.

Twenty-five years ago, Jacquelyn Campbell, now viewed as the country's leading expert on domestic homicide, created a screening tool that helps police, court personnel and victim advocates identify the women who are at the greatest risk of being killed.

Victims of domestic abuse are asked 20 questions, including: Do you believe he is capable of killing you? Does he own a gun? Is he violently and constantly jealous of you?

"We now know enough about the risk factors that we need to assess perpetrators for risk of homicide," Campbell said in an interview.

At the time of her death, Laura would have scored an 18—in "extreme danger"—on Campbell's lethality screening test, according to calculations by *The Huffington Post*. "The system might have worked best together to identify that perpetrator as high-risk and manage that case in a more proactive way," Campbell said.

Jurisdictions in at least 33 states are now screening domestic violence victims, in a process dubbed "lethality assessment." A number of different screening tools are in use, all stemming from Campbell's seminal research in the 80s.

States that have adopted some form of lethality assessment are showing impressive progress. Over the past 6 years, an ambitious lethality assessment program in Maryland reduced its domestic violence homicide rate by 25 percent. A team in Newburyport, Massachusetts, has intervened in 129 high-risk cases since 2005 and has had zero homicides.

Last year, encouraged by these success stories, the U.S. Justice Department began funding 12 pilot programs across the country to train police in lethality assessment. In a speech announcing the initiative, Vice President Joe Biden hailed the approach.

"Lives are being saved—we know how to do it," Biden said. "We know what risk factors put someone in greater danger of being killed by the person they love—and that also means we have the opportunity to step in and try to prevent these murders."

Legislators in Oklahoma recently passed a bill requiring police to screen victims with an 11-question checklist to determine if they are at high risk of being killed or severely assaulted. Once a woman is determined to be at high risk, police inform her about the danger she is in, encourage her to seek help and connect her with key resources.

In neighboring Arkansas, police are not currently being trained to screen women using lethality assessment. When asked about the value of identifying high-risk victims, Grudek said he would use a screening tool if the state introduced it, but expressed skepticism.

"It doesn't make any difference what kind of training officers get. You can tell that person they are at risk. But they will keep going back," he said. "Women continue to live in that environment. Why don't you do a study on why victims go back to these abusers? Why do they do that?"

There are many complex reasons why women stay with abusive partners. Leaving can be economically impossible, as well as dangerous. Research has shown that women are at greatest risk of homicide at the point of separation or after leaving a violent partner.

Fixating on that question—why doesn't the woman just leave—reveals a fundamental misunderstanding about the realities of domestic abuse, said Kim Gandy, president of the National Network to End Domestic Violence.

"So often, when people say, 'Why didn't she just leave?' the reality is that she did leave, or tried to," Gandy said. "Often she has reached out for help repeatedly, to the police, to the courts, sometimes to friends or family. Often she has a protective order and he assaults her anyway."

Blaming the victim for not leaving indicates ignorance about the power and control that is an integral part of domestic abuse, she said.

"If these kinds of police attitudes are common—the idea that it's really the victim's fault for being in that situation—then it would certainly deter a victim from seeking police help or protection," she said. "These kinds of attitudes are one of the reasons that abusers feel they can do whatever they want, and not have to answer for their violence."

Linda Tyler, a former state representative who fought to strengthen domestic violence laws in Arkansas, said that police, prosecutors and judges across the state aren't adequately educated about domestic violence and don't do a good enough job protecting victims from abusers.

"We consistently have no-contact orders violated, and victims subsequently assaulted or killed," she said in an interview.

In 2009, she spearheaded a bill that gives judges the power to put GPS tracking on offenders who violate restraining orders. Keeping tabs on domestic abusers during the pretrial period has shown to be effective—a 2012 study found that when offenders out on bail are made to wear GPS trackers, they rarely try to contact their victims.

As Tyler traveled the state seeking support for the bill, she was dismayed by what she found.

"There were so many cases, over and over, where law enforcement just didn't believe the victim," she said. "I had prosecutors tell me that women made this stuff up. It's unfortunately still an environment of—I'm a husband and I think I have the right to beat my wife, if that's what I feel like I need to do. That goes with marital privileges."

Her bill passed but has not been embraced by Arkansas' judges. She said she knew of only three counties out of 75 that have used GPS tracking in response to the bill.

"I'm frustrated that it's not used more often," she said. "It may not be the only tool to use to curb domestic violence, but it is at least a tool and we seem to have so few of them, so we should really consider using it more than we do."

Tyler said more training is urgently needed for police, prosecutors and judges, as is increased data gathering on domestic violence.

"We don't effectively collect data on a statewide basis that allows us to compare performance from one jurisdiction to the other," she said. "We should identify the areas where we have significant issues of violations of protective orders and hold those jurisdictions accountable, or at the very least make the information public so that the voters are informed. As you know, we do elect our county prosecutors, judges and sheriff."

Laura was 2 years older than Acuna-Sanchez, and the two didn't move in the same circles. But Berryville is a small place. In 2011, at a friend's birthday party, they connected and started dating.

She was 19 and had two kids from a previous relationship. He was just 17. Within days, they were a couple.

From the very beginning, Ponce said, Acuna-Sanchez was violent. As is often the case with batterers, his methods of abuse went far beyond physical beatings. Ponce described a harrowing cycle of harassment, where he would brutally assault Laura, steal or destroy her belongings—a form of economic abuse—and threaten to kill her and her kids if she left him.

"He beat her on a weekly basis," Ponce said. "She suffered like you wouldn't imagine. Daytime, nighttime. It was a living hell."

Acuna-Sanchez had a reputation around town for violent behavior.

According to a woman who went to high school with him, he "wasn't ever afraid to fight." In a court-ordered mental health evaluation, he told a psychiatrist that he fought in school constantly, starting in elementary school, where he was eventually expelled. At 11, he said he was ordered to receive mental health treatment due to "anger problems." He said his father hit him a lot, "hard enough to where you're bleeding," and his mother married a string of violent men who beat her in front of him.

A woman who witnessed the relationship and who asked to remain anonymous said Acuna-Sanchez was deeply controlling. "Laura acted like she always had to do what he wanted and if she didn't, there'd be hell to pay," she said. "Sometimes they were happy but most of the time she was scared of him."

In one case, Laura fled to her mother after an assault and asked her for a copy of her passport. Acuna-Sanchez had destroyed the original by burning it in the kitchen sink, along with her social security card and birth certificate.

"She had her hair over her eyes. I grabbed her, tipped her face up—all purple," Ponce said. "I screamed and said I was going to call the cops. She said, 'Please, no mama, he will kill us all.'"

In March 2012, less than a year after they started dating, Laura became pregnant with Acuna-Sanchez's child. She filed a restraining order soon after.

"I have tried to leave him before, but he always finds me and makes my life miserable by taking my things or my mom's things until I get back with him," she wrote in the restraining order. "He told me he wouldn't leave me alone."

Researchers are split on how effective restraining orders are at protecting victims. At the most basic level, they serve as documentation of misbehavior that can be used to arrest offenders. But they are often ignored—abusers violate restraining orders an estimated 40 percent of the time—and there's no way to track how many domestic abuse homicide victims had restraining orders against their killers at their time of death.

Even after filing a restraining order, Laura struggled to separate from Acuna-Sanchez. The two briefly rekindled their relationship, though Ponce describes Laura's participation as involuntary.

"I don't like to call it 'dating,'" she said. "Laura did not want to continue the relationship. He was forcing her to be with him. If she didn't do what he said, she had to pay."

Each time she tried to leave him, he would intimidate her with threats, beat her and destroy her belongings. "She was so exhausted," Ponce said. "Every time he would ruin her things, and she had to start over. She didn't have much money."

At the court hearing to make the restraining order permanent, Laura declined to pursue it and the petition was dismissed.

But after Laura gave birth to their baby boy, Jordan, the abuse accelerated.

A week after Jordan was born, on Sept. 1, police responded to a 911 call at Laura's house. She told police that Acuna-Sanchez had hit her in the face, then smashed her car with a hammer and destroyed the baby's car seat by tearing all the stuffing out.

He was arrested for domestic battery that day. On Sept. 4, he was released on bail with a protective order to have no contact with Laura. But two days later, Acuna-Sanchez returned to her apartment.

In the police report, Laura said she heard a noise outside and opened the door to peek out. Acuna-Sanchez pushed his way in and tried to kiss her. When she refused, she told police, he tackled her to the ground and strangled her. She blacked out. When she regained consciousness, she said, her newborn baby was lying by her side and Acuna-Sanchez had fled, stealing her cell phone and car keys. When police arrived, "she was crying and holding her two-week-old child," the officer wrote.

It took over a month for Acuna-Sanchez to be arrested. It is not clear why police did not apprehend him earlier.

On Oct. 3, he was arrested and charged with aggravated assault on a family member, a felony, and with violating the no-contact order. This time he was held in jail for a month. On November 15, he was granted bail, and told he wasn't allowed to contact Laura. He was also ordered to call the probation office two times a week.

But due to an apparent error at the courthouse, the probation office was never notified that Acuna-Sanchez was on probation and therefore required to stay in close contact with an officer. He never once called in.

In a letter sent to prosecutors, Kent Villines, assistant area manager of the Arkansas Department of Community Correction, confirmed the Berryville office had been unaware of the order. "I checked with all the personnel . . . and no one knew anything about this situation," he wrote, "therefore Victor Acuna has not been checking in with this office at any time."

Villines told *The Huffington Post* that it was the prosecutor's responsibility to send over the order, and that it was "rare" for an order to fall through the cracks. "Usually, with this system we have set up, things don't disappear, but sometimes they do," he said.

In early December, Acuna-Sanchez was arrested for violating the no-contact order once more, after police spotted him in a car with Laura. The next day, Berryville District Judge Scott Jackson released him on his personal recognizance; no bail. That was the last time he was in police custody while Laura was still alive.

At Christmas, Ponce said, Laura told Acuna-Sanchez that she was leaving town. She had been saving money and was planning to rent an apartment in Missouri with her best friend.

"That was her biggest mistake, telling him," Ponce said. "He wasn't going to just let her go."

Laura didn't make it to the New Year.

On New Year's Eve, 2011, police found her dying on the floor of her apartment. Hours later, they arrested Acuna-Sanchez at his mother's house. He was found hiding in the shower, armed with a 22-caliber handgun. In the pocket of his overalls were 39 bullets and the key to Laura's apartment.

He is now awaiting trial on capital murder charges. If convicted, he will face death or life imprisonment without parole.

On a Saturday night in early April, locals gather outside the courthouse for a memorial for Laura.

Little has changed in Carroll County since her death. As far as Ponce can tell, there's been no real effort to reform how domestic violence cases are handled. And there's been no acknowledgement that anything went wrong.

"The only thing I've been told is the system needs 'fine-tuning,'" Ponce says. "Nothing is different."

She's dejected by the lack of progress and alarmed that no steps have been taken to prevent this kind of tragedy from happening again. That's her biggest fear. Ponce organized the memorial—plastering the town with posters and posting an ad in the local newspaper—hoping to raise awareness about domestic violence in the community. She doesn't want Laura's death to be for nothing. It has to mean something.

At dusk, she pulls up in a minivan with Laura's three kids in tow. After Laura's death, she abruptly became the caretaker of a newborn, as well as Laura's two school-aged children.

"I had no baby clothes," Ponce recalls. Now, her life revolves around the kiddos, as she calls them.

Jordan, who will be 2 in August, still wakes up screaming most nights. Christopher, Laura's other son, is 6. And then there's Josie, her only daughter, who is 8.

All three are in therapy over their mother's brutal death. Research has shown that kids who grow up witnessing domestic violence suffer lasting emotional effects and are more likely to have behavioral problems.

The kids sit on the ground and wait quietly for the memorial to start. The crowd is mostly Latino, but there are at least a dozen Caucasians in the crowd of around 40. Kids outnumber adults two to one.

Someone hands out purple ribbons. An oversized sketch of Laura, donated by a local artist, is displayed on an easel. Pamphlets about domestic violence support are scattered across a table.

There is no shelter for battered women in all of Carroll County. The director of the closest shelter, The Sanctuary, located 30 miles away in Harrison, speaks to the crowd about their services: temporary accommodation, a 24-hour crisis line, support groups and assistance with protective orders and court advocacy. The director of community outreach translates afterwards in Spanish.

Ponce chokes up when it's her turn to take the microphone.

"I want to turn Laura's tragedy into a way to help other people," she says. "If anyone is in that situation, do not wait. A restraining order is just a piece of paper. Leave, get into a shelter, move out, don't wait."

Her point is clear—Women won't get help here. The only recourse is to flee. She offers to drive them.

Ponce directs her harshest words toward the local justice system, which she says failed her family.

"They have to do their jobs more seriously and they need to communicate," she says. "I'm just going to keep fighting and fighting until I see justice served."

Josie, Laura's firstborn, tries not to cry. She prefers to remember the good times with her mom. They used to bake cookies together and play in the park. And whenever her mom got sad, she'd play "Don't Worry, Be Happy," and the two would dance around and everything would be better.

She stays very still while her grandmother talks. She listens.

When the 21 balloons are released—one for each year of Laura's life—Josie cranes her head upward and watches the purple spheres become smaller and smaller in the distance, until they are just little dots and then nothing at all.

*Need help? In the U.S., call 1-800-799-SAFE (7233) for the National Domestic Violence Hotline.*

## Critical Thinking

1. Could any one in the criminal justice system have done anything that might have prevented Laura's death?

2. What do you think of Jacquelyn Campbell's screening tool?

3. Based on what Linda Tyler learned, should GPS tracking devices be used on violators of restraining orders?

## Internet References

**Center for American Progress**

cdn.americanprogress.org/wp-content/uploads/2013/04/americaUnderTheGun-2.pdf

**Violence Policy Center**

www.vpc.org/domesticviolence.htm

*Article*

Prepared by: Joanne Naughton

# Human Sex Trafficking

AMANDA WALKER-RODRIGUEZ AND RODNEY HILL

## Learning Outcomes

*After reading this article, you will be able to:*

- Outline the scope of human sex trafficking.
- Describe how victims are recruited into the business of human sex trafficking.

Human sex trafficking is the most common form of modern-day slavery. Estimates place the number of its domestic and international victims in the millions, mostly females and children enslaved in the commercial sex industry for little or no money.[1] The terms *human trafficking* and *sex slavery* usually conjure up images of young girls beaten and abused in faraway places, like Eastern Europe, Asia, or Africa. Actually, human sex trafficking and sex slavery happen locally in cities and towns, both large and small, throughout the United States, right in citizens' backyards.

Appreciating the magnitude of the problem requires first understanding what the issue is and what it is not. Additionally, people must be able to identify the victim in common trafficking situations.

## Human Sex Trafficking

Many people probably remember popular movies and television shows depicting pimps as dressing flashy and driving large fancy cars. More important, the women—adults—consensually and voluntarily engaged in the business of prostitution without complaint. This characterization is extremely inaccurate, nothing more than fiction. In reality, the pimp *traffics* young women (and sometimes men) completely against their will by force or threat of force; this is human sex trafficking.

## The Scope

Not only is human sex trafficking slavery but it is big business. It is the fastest-growing business of organized crime and the third-largest criminal enterprise in the world.[2] The majority of sex trafficking is international, with victims taken from such places as South and Southeast Asia, the former Soviet Union, Central and South America, and other less developed areas and moved to more developed ones, including Asia, the Middle East, Western Europe, and North America.[3]

Unfortunately, however, sex trafficking also occurs domestically.[4] The United States not only faces an influx of international victims but also has its own homegrown problem of interstate sex trafficking of minors.[5]

> **The United States not only faces an influx of international victims but also has its own homegrown problem of interstate sex trafficking of minors.**

Although comprehensive research to document the number of children engaged in prostitution in the United States is lacking, an estimated 293,000 American youths currently are at risk of becoming victims of commercial sexual exploitation.[6] The majority of these victims are runaway or thrown-away youths who live on the streets and become victims of prostitution.[7] These children generally come from homes where they have been abused or from families who have abandoned them. Often, they become involved in prostitution to support themselves financially or to get the things they feel they need or want (like drugs).

Other young people are recruited into prostitution through forced abduction, pressure from parents, or through deceptive agreements between parents and traffickers. Once these children become involved in prostitution, they often are forced to travel far from their homes and, as a result, are isolated from their friends and family. Few children in this situation can develop new relationships with peers or adults other than the person victimizing them. The lifestyle of such youths revolves around violence, forced drug use, and constant threats.[8]

Among children and teens living on the streets in the United States, involvement in commercial sex activity is a problem of epidemic proportion. Many girls living on the street engage in formal prostitution, and some become entangled in nationwide organized crime networks where they are trafficked nationally. Criminal networks transport these children around the United States by a variety of means—cars, buses, vans, trucks, or planes—and often provide them counterfeit identification to use in the event of arrest. The average age at which girls first become victims of prostitution is 12 to 14. It is not only the girls on the streets who are affected; boys and transgender youth enter into prostitution between the ages of 11 and 13 on average.[9]

## The Operation

Today, the business of human sex trafficking is much more organized and violent. These women and young girls are sold to traffickers, locked up in rooms or brothels for weeks or months, drugged, terrorized, and raped repeatedly.[10] These continual abuses make it easier for the traffickers to control their victims. The captives are so afraid and intimidated that they rarely speak out against their traffickers, even when faced with an opportunity to escape.

## Today, the business of human sex trafficking is much more organized and violent.

Generally, the traffickers are very organized. Many have a hierarchy system similar to that of other criminal organizations. Traffickers who have more than one victim often have a "bottom," who sits atop the hierarchy of prostitutes. The bottom, a victim herself, has been with the trafficker the longest and has earned his trust. Bottoms collect the money from the other girls, discipline them, seduce unwitting youths into trafficking, and handle the day-to-day business for the trafficker.

Traffickers represent every social, ethnic, and racial group. Various organizational types exist in trafficking. Some perpetrators are involved with local street and motorcycle gangs, others are members of larger nationwide gangs and criminal organizations, and some have no affiliation with any one group or organization. Traffickers are not only men—women run many established rings.

## Traffickers represent every social, ethnic, and racial group.

Traffickers use force, drugs, emotional tactics, and financial methods to control their victims. They have an especially easy time establishing a strong bond with young girls. These perpetrators may promise marriage and a lifestyle the youths often did not have in their previous familial relationships. They claim they "love" and "need" the victim and that any sex acts are for their future together. In cases where the children have few or no positive male role models in their lives, the traffickers take advantage of this fact and, in many cases, demand that the victims refer to them as "daddy," making it tougher for the youths to break the hold the perpetrator has on them.

Sometimes, the traffickers use violence, such as gang rape and other forms of abuse, to force the youths to work for them and remain under their control. One victim, a runaway from Baltimore County, Maryland, was gang raped by a group of men associated with the trafficker, who subsequently staged a "rescue." He then demanded that she repay him by working for him as one of his prostitutes. In many cases, however, the victims simply are beaten until they submit to the trafficker's demands.

In some situations, the youths have become addicted to drugs. The traffickers simply can use their ability to supply them with drugs as a means of control.

Traffickers often take their victims' identity forms, including birth certificates, passports, and drivers' licenses. In these cases, even if youths do leave they would have no ability to support themselves and often will return to the trafficker.

These abusive methods of control impact the victims both physically and mentally. Similar to cases involving Stockholm Syndrome, these victims, who have been abused over an extended period of time, begin to feel an attachment to the perpetrator.[11] This paradoxical psychological phenomenon makes it difficult for law enforcement to breach the bond of control, albeit abusive, the trafficker holds over the victim.

# National Problem with Local Ties

## The Federal Level

In 2000, Congress passed the Trafficking Victims Protection Act (TVPA), which created the first comprehensive federal law to address trafficking, with a significant focus on the international dimension of the problem. The law provides a three-pronged approach: *prevention* through public awareness programs overseas and a State Department-led monitoring and sanctions program; *protection* through a new T Visa and services for foreign national victims; and *prosecution* through new federal crimes and severe penalties.[12]

As a result of the passing of the TVPA, the Office to Monitor and Combat Trafficking in Persons was established in October 2001. This enabling legislation led to the creation of a bureau within the State Department to specifically address human trafficking and exploitation on all levels and to take legal action against perpetrators.[13] Additionally, this act was designed to enforce all laws within the 13th Amendment to the U.S. Constitution that apply.[14]

U.S. Immigration and Customs Enforcement (ICE) is one of the lead federal agencies charged with enforcing the TVPA. Human trafficking represents significant risks to homeland security. Would-be terrorists and criminals often can access the same routes and use the same methods as human traffickers. ICE's Human Smuggling and Trafficking Unit works to identify criminals and organizations involved in these illicit activities.

The FBI also enforces the TVPA. In June 2003, the FBI, in conjunction with the Department of Justice Child Exploitation and Obscenity Section and the National Center for Missing and Exploited Children, launched the Innocence Lost National Initiative. The agencies' combined efforts address the growing problem of domestic sex trafficking of children in the United States. To date, these groups have worked successfully to rescue nearly 900 children. Investigations successfully have led to the conviction of more than 500 pimps, madams, and their associates who exploit children through prostitution. These convictions have resulted in lengthy sentences, including multiple 25-year-to-life sentences and the seizure of real property, vehicles, and monetary assets.[15]

Both ICE and the FBI, along with other local, state, and federal law enforcement agencies and national victim-based advocacy groups in joint task forces, have combined resources and expertise on the issue. Today, the FBI participates in approximately 30 law enforcement task forces and about 42 Bureau of Justice Assistance (BJA)-sponsored task forces around the nation.[16]

In July 2004, the Human Smuggling Trafficking Center (HSTC) was created. The HSTC serves as a fusion center for information on human smuggling and trafficking, bringing together analysts, officers, and investigators from such agencies as the CIA, FBI, ICE, Department of State, and Department of Homeland Security.

## The Local Level

With DOJ funding assistance, many jurisdictions have created human trafficking task forces to combat the problem. BJA's 42 such task forces can be demonstrated by several examples.[17]

- In 2004, the FBI's Washington field office and the D.C. Metropolitan Police Department joined with a variety of nongovernment organizations and service providers to combat the growing problem of human trafficking within Washington, D.C.

- In January 2005, the Massachusetts Human Trafficking Task Force was formed, with the Boston Police Department serving as the lead law enforcement entity. It uses a two-pronged approach, addressing investigations focusing on international victims and those focusing on the commercial sexual exploitation of children.

- The New Jersey Human Trafficking Task Force attacks the problem by training law enforcement in the methods of identifying victims and signs of trafficking, coordinating statewide efforts in the identification and provision of services to victims of human trafficking, and increasing the successful interdiction and prosecution of trafficking of human persons.

- Since 2006, the Louisiana Human Trafficking Task Force, which has law enforcement, training, and victim services components, has focused its law enforcement and victim rescue efforts on the Interstate 10 corridor from the Texas border on the west to the Mississippi border on the east. This corridor, the basic northern border of the hurricane-ravaged areas of Louisiana, long has served as a major avenue of illegal immigration efforts. The I-10 corridor also is the main avenue for individuals participating in human trafficking to supply the labor needs in the hurricane-damaged areas of the state.

- In 2007, the Maryland Human Trafficking Task Force was formed. It aims to create a heightened law enforcement and victim service presence in the community. Its law enforcement efforts include establishing roving operations to identify victims and traffickers, deputizing local law enforcement to assist in federal human trafficking investigations, and providing training for law enforcement officers.

## Anytown, USA

In December 2008, Corey Davis, the ringleader of a sex-trafficking ring that spanned at least three states, was sentenced in federal court in Bridgeport, Connecticut, on federal civil rights charges for organizing and leading the sex-trafficking operation that exploited as many as 20 females, including minors. Davis received a sentence of 293 months in prison followed by a lifetime term of supervised release. He pleaded guilty to multiple sex-trafficking charges, including recruiting a girl under the age of 18 to engage in prostitution. Davis admitted that he recruited a minor to engage in prostitution; that he was the organizer of a sex-trafficking venture; and that he used force, fraud, and coercion to compel the victim to commit commercial sex acts from which he obtained the proceeds.

According to the indictment, Davis lured victims to his operation with promises of modeling contracts and a glamorous lifestyle. He then forced them into a grueling schedule of dancing and performing at strip clubs in Connecticut, New York, and New Jersey. When the clubs closed, Davis forced the victims to walk the streets until 4 or 5 A.M. propositioning customers. The indictment also alleged that he beat many of the victims to force them to work for him and that he also used physical abuse as punishment for disobeying the stringent rules he imposed to isolate and control them.[18]

As this and other examples show, human trafficking cases happen all over the United States. A few instances would represent just the "tip of the iceberg" in a growing criminal enterprise. Local and state criminal justice officials must understand that these cases are not isolated incidents that occur infrequently. They must remain alert for signs of trafficking in their jurisdictions and aggressively follow through on the smallest clue. Numerous websites openly (though they try to mask their actions) advertise for prostitution. Many of these sites involve young girls victimized by sex trafficking. Many of the pictures are altered to give the impression of older girls engaged in this activity freely and voluntarily. However, as prosecutors, the authors both have encountered numerous cases of suspected human trafficking involving underage girls.

> **Local and state criminal justice officials must understand that these cases are not isolated incidents that occur infrequently.**

The article "The Girls Next Door" describes a conventional midcentury home in Plainfield, New Jersey, that sat in a nice middle-class neighborhood. Unbeknownst to the neighbors, the house was part of a network of stash houses in the New York area where underage girls and young women from dozens of countries were trafficked and held captive. Acting on a tip, police raided the house in February 2002, expecting to find an underground brothel. Instead, they found four girls between the ages of 14 and 17, all Mexican nationals without documentation.

However, they were not prostitutes; they were sex slaves. These girls did not work for profit or a paycheck. They were captives to the traffickers and keepers who controlled their every move. The police found a squalid, land-based equivalent of a 19th-century slave ship. They encountered rancid, doorless bathrooms; bare, putrid mattresses; and a stash of penicillin, "morning after" pills, and an antiulcer medication that can induce abortion. The girls were pale, exhausted, and malnourished.[19]

Human sex trafficking warning signs include, among other indicators, streetwalkers and strip clubs. However, a jurisdiction's lack of streetwalkers or strip clubs does not mean that it is immune to the problem of trafficking. Because human trafficking involves big money, if money can be made, sex slaves can be sold. Sex trafficking can happen anywhere, however unlikely a place. Investigators should be attuned to reading the signs of trafficking and looking closely for them.

# Investigation of Human Sex Trafficking

ICE aggressively targets the global criminal infrastructure, including the people, money, and materials that support human trafficking networks. The agency strives to prevent human trafficking in the United States by prosecuting the traffickers and rescuing and protecting the victims. However, most human trafficking cases start at the local level.

## Strategies

Local and state law enforcement officers may unknowingly encounter sex trafficking when they deal with homeless and runaway juveniles; criminal gang activity; crimes involving immigrant children who have no guardians; domestic violence calls; and investigations at truck stops, motels, massage parlors, spas, and strip clubs. To this end, the authors offer various suggestions and indicators to help patrol officers identify victims of sex trafficking, as well as tips for detectives who investigate these crimes.

### Patrol Officers

- Document suspicious calls and complaints on a police information report, even if the details seem trivial.
- Be aware of trafficking when responding to certain call types, such as reports of foot traffic in and out of a house. Consider situations that seem similar to drug complaints.
- Look closely at calls for assaults, domestic situations, verbal disputes, or thefts. These could involve a trafficking victim being abused and disciplined by a trafficker, a customer having a dispute with a victim, or a client who had money taken during a sex act.
- Locations, such as truck stops, strip clubs, massage parlors, and cheap motels, are havens for prostitutes forced into sex trafficking. Many massage parlors and strip clubs that engage in sex trafficking will have cramped living quarters where the victims are forced to stay.
- When encountering prostitutes and other victims of trafficking, do not display judgment or talk down to them. Understand the violent nature in how they are forced into trafficking, which explains their lack of cooperation. Speak with them in a location completely safe and away from other people, including potential victims.

- Check for identification. Traffickers take the victims' identification and, in cases of foreign nationals, their travel information. The lack of either item should raise concern.

### Detectives/Investigators

- Monitor websites that advertise for dating and hooking up. Most vice units are familiar with the common sites used by sex traffickers as a means of advertisement.
- Conduct surveillance at motels, truck stops, strip clubs, and massage parlors. Look to see if the girls arrive alone or with someone else. Girls being transported to these locations should raise concerns of trafficking.
- Upon an arrest, check cell phone records, motel receipts, computer printouts of advertisements, and tollbooth receipts. Look for phone calls from the jailed prostitute to the pimp. Check surveillance cameras at motels and toll facilities as evidence to indicate the trafficking of the victim.
- Obtain written statements from the customers; get them to work for you.
- Seek assistance from nongovernmental organizations involved in fighting sex trafficking. Many of these entities have workers who will interview these victims on behalf of the police.
- After executing a search warrant, photograph everything. Remember that in court, a picture may be worth a thousand words: nothing else can more effectively describe a cramped living quarter a victim is forced to reside in.
- Look for advertisements in local newspapers, specifically the sports sections, that advertise massage parlors. These businesses should be checked out to ensure they are legitimate and not fronts for trafficking.
- Contact your local U.S. Attorney's Office, FBI field office, or ICE for assistance. Explore what federal resources exist to help address this problem.

## Other Considerations

Patrol officers and investigators can look for many other human trafficking indicators as well.[20] These certainly warrant closer attention.

### General Indicators

- People who live on or near work premises
- Individuals with restricted or controlled communication and transportation
- Persons frequently moved by traffickers
- A living space with a large number of occupants
- People lacking private space, personal possessions, or financial records
- Someone with limited knowledge about how to get around in a community

### Physical Indicators

- Injuries from beatings or weapons
- Signs of torture (e.g., cigarette burns)
- Brands or scarring, indicating ownership
- Signs of malnourishment

### Financial/Legal Indicators

- Someone else has possession of an individual's legal/travel documents
- Existing debt issues
- One attorney claiming to represent multiple illegal aliens detained at different locations
- Third party who insists on interpreting. Did the victim sign a contract?

### Brothel Indicators

- Large amounts of cash and condoms
- Customer logbook or receipt book ("trick book")
- Sparse rooms
- Men come and go frequently

## Conclusion

This form of cruel modern-day slavery occurs more often than many people might think. And, it is not just an international or a national problem—it also is a local one. It is big business, and it involves a lot of perpetrators and victims.

Agencies at all levels must remain alert to this issue and address it vigilantly. Even local officers must understand the problem and know how to recognize it in their jurisdictions. Coordinated and aggressive efforts from all law enforcement organizations can put an end to these perpetrators' operations and free the victims.

## Notes

1. www.routledgesociology.com/books/Human-Sex-Trafficking-isbn9780415576789 (accessed July 19, 2010).
2. www.unodc.org/unodc/en/human-trafficking/what-is-human-trafficking.html (accessed July 19, 2010).
3. www.justice.gov/criminal/ceos/trafficking.html (accessed July 19, 2010).
4. Ibid.
5. www.justice.gov/criminal/ceos/prostitution.html (accessed July 19, 2010).
6. Richard J. Estes and Neil Alan Weiner, *Commercial Sexual Exploitation of Children in the U.S., Canada, and Mexico* (University of Pennsylvania, Executive Summary, 2001).
7. Ibid.
8. http://fpc.state.gov/documents/organization/9107.pdf (accessed July 19, 2010).
9. Estes and Weiner.
10. www.womenshealth.gov/violence/types/human-trafficking.cfm (accessed July 19, 2010).
11. For additional information, see Nathalie De Fabrique, Stephen J. Romano, Gregory M. Vecchi, and Vincent B. Van Hasselt, "Understanding Stockholm Syndrome," *FBI Law Enforcement Bulletin*, July 2007, 10–15.
12. Trafficking Victims Protection Act, Pub. L. No. 106–386 (2000), codified at 22 U.S.C. § 7101, et seq.
13. Ibid.
14. U.S. CONST. amend. XIII, § 1: "Neither slavery nor involuntary servitude, except as a punishment for crime whereof the party shall have been duly convicted, shall exist within the United States, or any place subject to their jurisdiction."
15. U.S. Department of Justice, "U.S. Army Soldier Sentenced to Over 17 Years in Prison for Operating a Brothel from Millersville Apartment and to Drug Trafficking," www.justice.gov/usao/md/Public-Affairs/press_releases/press10a.htm (accessed September 30, 2010).
16. www.fbi.gov/hq/cid/civilrights/trafficking_initiatives.htm (accessed September 30, 2010).
17. www.ojp.usdoj.gov/BJA/grant/42HTTF.pdf (accessed September 30, 2010).
18. http://actioncenter.polarisproject.org/the-frontlines/recent-federal-cases/435-leader-of-expansive-multi-state-sex-trafficking-ring-sentenced (accessed July 19, 2010).
19. www.nytimes.com/2004/01/25/magazine/25SEXTRAFFIC.html (accessed July 19, 2010).
20. http://httf.wordpress.com/indicators/ (accessed July 19, 2010).

## Critical Thinking

1. Do you believe prostitutes are victims of human sex traffickers?
2. How can sex traffickers compel anyone to become a sex worker against his or her will?
3. What laws have been enacted to deal with sex trafficking?

## Create Central

www.mhhe.com/createcentral

## Internet References

**Polaris Project**
  www.polarisproject.org/human-trafficking/sex-trafficking-in-the-us
**Science Daily**
  www.sciencedaily.com/releases/2013/09/130925132333.htm

From *FBI Law Enforcement Bulletin* by Amanda Walker-Rodriguez and Rodney Hill, March 2011. Published by Federal Bureau of Investigation. www.fbi.gov.

*Article*　　　　　　　　　　　　　　　Prepared by: Joanne Naughton

# Upon Further Review: Inside the Police Failure to Stop Darren Sharper's Rape Spree

T. Christian Miller et al.

## Learning Outcomes

*After reading this article, you will be able to:*

- Relate some of the problems that still exist in the prosecution of sexual assaults, more than 20 years after Congress and states reformed rape laws.

- Describe the deep-seated societal attitudes that make rape uniquely difficult to prosecute in this country.

- Show how the way that rape kits are handled is a longstanding national problem.

This story was co-published with the New Orleans Advocate and Sports Illustrated.

New Orleans—It was 5:06 A.M. on a Tuesday in September 2013 when sex crimes Detective Derrick Williams caught the call. It came from the hospital. It was a distraught woman. She was saying she had been raped.

She told Williams a familiar story of French Quarter trespass: She'd hit the clubs the night before, she said. Drank a lot. Met a man. Went to his house. And awoke the next morning to find him on top of her, naked. But she told Williams she had never said yes to sex.

Williams typed up a brief report. He labeled the incident a rape. But Case No. I-31494-13 wasn't quite ordinary. The accuser was a former cheerleader for the New Orleans Saints. And the alleged rapist was Darren Sharper, a hero of the Saints' 2009 Super Bowl team, former Pro Bowl player and broadcast analyst for the league's television network.

News of the Sept. 23, 2013 incident quickly shot up the ranks. New Orleans' police superintendent and top prosecutor were briefed. In the weeks that followed, police records show that Williams gathered evidence. He got a warrant to collect a sample of Sharper's DNA. It matched a swab taken from the woman's body. Witnesses told of seeing Sharper with the intoxicated woman at a club, and later at his condo. Video footage confirmed Sharper and the woman had been together.

It wasn't enough for the district attorney's office. This was a "heater"—police shorthand for a high profile case. Prosecutors were hesitant to move too quickly on a local football hero with deep pockets and savvy lawyers, according to two individuals with knowledge of the investigation. They held off on an arrest warrant.

"If his name was John Brown, he would have been in jail," one criminal justice official with knowledge of the case said. "If a woman says, 'He's the guy that raped me,' and you have corroborating evidence to show they were together and she went to the hospital and she can identify him, that guy goes to jail."

Sharper did not—and continued an unchecked crime spree that ended only with his arrest in Los Angeles last year after sexually assaulting four women in 24 hours. In March, Sharper owned up to his savagery. He agreed to plead guilty or no contest to raping or attempting to rape nine women in four states. The pending deal allows his possible release after serving half of a 20-year sentence—a strikingly light punishment that has drawn widespread criticism.

Sharper's rampage of druggings and rapes could have been prevented, according to a two-month investigation by *ProPublica* and *The New Orleans Advocate* based on police records in five states, hundreds of pages of court documents and dozens of interviews across the country.

Nine women reported being raped or drugged by Sharper to four different agencies before his January 2014 capture. But police and prosecutors along the way failed to investigate fully the women's allegations. They made no arrests. Some victims and eyewitnesses felt their claims were downplayed. Corroborating evidence, including DNA matches and video surveillance, was minimized or put on hold.

Perhaps most critically, police did not inquire into Sharper's history. Had they done so, they would have detected a chilling predatory pattern that strongly bolstered the women's accounts.

Sharper typically chose victims who were white women in their early 20s, records show. He picked them up in pairs at nightclubs, and took them home to his hotel or residence. Sharper had drinks with them, sometimes lacing drinks he gave the women with drugs that rendered them unconscious.

The *ProPublica* and *Advocate* investigation thus reveals wider problems in the prosecution of sexual assaults in America. More than 20 years after Congress and state legislatures reformed laws to put more rapists in prison, police and prosecutors do not take full advantage of the tools at their disposal.

One key part of the change was to make it easier to use a suspect's history of sexual assaults at trial. But prosecutors and police often do not seek out other possible victims. One recent assessment called the reform effort "a failure."

The FBI also created a database to contain detailed case descriptions to help police capture serial rapists who operate across state lines. But it is seldom used. Of 79,770 rapes reported to police in 2013, only 240 cases were entered into the database—0.3 percent.

Today, studies show that only about one in three victims report sexual assaults in the first place. Of those reports, Department of Justice statistics show, less than 40 percent result in an arrest, a far lower figure than for other major crimes such as murder or aggravated assault.

"We do an abysmal job of investigating and prosecuting rape," said Kim Lonsway, the research director for End Violence Against Women International, a leading police training organization. "There are failures at all levels."

To be sure, deep-seated societal attitudes make rape uniquely difficult to prosecute. Victims are ashamed or afraid to report it. Police and prosecutors can be reluctant to pursue it. Cases involving drugs and alcohol can turn on whether victims consented to sex, adding to the complexity.

And each of the cases involving Sharper, taken in isolation, presented prosecutors with hurdles. In secretly recorded phone calls with his victims, Sharper didn't make incriminating statements. He moved fast, in one city one day and in another the next. He drugged many of his victims with powerful amnesiacs, resulting in cloudy or even non-existent memories.

But taken as a whole, the Sharper case underscores American law enforcement's trouble with solving rape cases: Investigations are often cursory, sometimes incompetent, frequently done in ignorance of the suspect's past sex assault history.

Sharper's victims suffered the failures most. With Sharper, they encountered a man practiced in defense and deception. With police and prosecutors, they found deference toward the accused, and what often felt like disbelief concerning their claims.

*ProPublica* and *The New Orleans Advocate* contacted five of Sharper's alleged victims. Except for brief interviews with two women, none wanted to discuss the allegations. And none wanted their names used.

"It's pretty black and white," one woman said about the police. "They didn't do their job."

# A Football Career of 'Calculated Risks'

Sharper worked hard to become "Sharp," the football player, ladies' man and on-air analyst.

He and his brother, Jamie, also a future NFL player, were raised in a middle-class family in Richmond, Va. They were football stars at suburban Hermitage High School.

Jamie wound up at the University of Virginia. Darren decided to go to the College of William and Mary—a school known more for academics. Its football team competed in a second tier football conference.

Sharper chose the school because he wanted to play quarterback. But when he got there, the head coach made a fateful decision. He wanted Darren Sharper on defense. At 6 feet 2, 210 pounds, Sharper excelled as a safety. By his junior year, he was drawing interest from NFL scouts who coveted his rare ability to get his hands on passes he either batted away or intercepted.

The Green Bay Packers chose him with the 60th pick in the 1997 draft. The first year, he didn't start. But he had an impact, running back two interceptions and a fumble recovery for touchdowns. The Packers made it to the Super Bowl, but lost to the Broncos.

Sharper broke out during the 2000 season. That year, he led the NFL with nine interceptions and earned his first of two selections to the Associated Press All-Pro First Team. The next year, he signed a six-year, $30 million contract extension.

Over eight years with the Packers, and four more with the Minnesota Vikings, Sharper never lost his nose for the ball. His ability to break up plays was Hall of Fame-caliber.

"He was just really good at being able to read what the receivers and quarterbacks were doing, and he would jump routes," said Scott McGarrahan, a retired NFL safety and one of Sharper's teammates on the Packers. "It was calculated risks."

He also flattened wide receivers. He earned a reputation as one of the hardest-hitting safeties in football. He once acknowledged that his early tackles would be deemed illegal under later NFL rules designed to prevent concussions.

"Guys are now getting flagged and fined for hits that were legal when I first came into the league," Sharper said in a 2012 interview with *Ebony* magazine.

Despite the on-field ferocity, Sharper was invariably described by fellow players and friends as polite, courteous and kind. He had a charity for kids. He took an interest in women's issues. He briefly dated actress and former model Gabrielle Union, a rape victim who became an outspoken advocate. He raised money for breast cancer. The NFL as an institution embraced him, and he was selected to appear in a league book, *NFL Dads Dedicated to Daughters,* designed to raise awareness of battered women. In the book's photo, he draped an arm around his daughter.

"My daughter makes me mindful of how women are treated: undervalued and exploited," he wrote. "Which is why I feel compelled to take advantage of this opportunity to speak up about domestic violence."

Sharper remained guarded about his personal life. He was close to his family, especially his brother, Jamie. But he seemed to have few close friends.

"Be courteous to all, but intimate with few; and let those be well-tried before you give them your confidence," he said in one tweet.

What Sharper did have over the years was women—lots of them. He sponsored parties and charity events with suggestive names, such as "One Night Stand." He and his friends were regulars at night clubs in Miami, with 5 to 10 women sitting at their table.

By 2009, Sharper's career looked to be winding down. The Saints signed him to a one-year, $1.2 million contract.

It turned out to be a miracle year—for both Sharper and the Saints. Sharper stormed through the season, his best ever, tying for the NFL lead with nine interceptions. He broke the NFL's single-season record for most yards in interception returns, and he scored three of the Saints defense's five touchdowns that regular season.

His performance helped lift the Saints to their first Super Bowl victory—less than five years after Hurricane Katrina had decimated New Orleans. The Saints beat the Indianapolis Colts, 31-17. After 13 years in the NFL, Sharper finally got his Super Bowl ring.

He had also found a new home. New Orleans fans loved the "Sharper Shake," the bombastic, shoulder-wriggling shuffle he performed after a big play. They loved how he hit. And they loved his looks.

On Twitter, Instagram and elsewhere online, female fans gushed about his dimples and speculated about his bedroom prowess. One page on an anonymous blog called Kiss 'n Tale drew more than 5,000 comments about Sharper and his purported sexual talents.

"DARREN SHARPER IS THE HOTTEST, SEXIEST, FINEST, MOST BEAUTIFUL MAN I'VE EVER SEEN IN MY LIFE," read one of the tamer remarks.

On a squad later plagued by scandals involving Vicodin pills that went missing from the team's medical supplies and allegations of bounties for on-field hits, Sharper was considered one of the good guys.

"He was a perfect gentleman. He was an older player. He never gave us any trouble," one former Saints official said.

Sharper's football career essentially ended after the Super Bowl. He injured himself during the offseason and played nine lackluster games in the Saints' 2010 campaign.

He played his last game for the Saints on January 8, 2011.

## 'In Rape, the Victim Is the Case'

Two months later, at 10:12 A.M. on March 18, 2011, Miami Beach police got a call from the rape crisis unit in Miami's sprawling Jackson Memorial Hospital. Two women had arrived that morning asking for rape examinations. Officer Alejandro Fernandez was dispatched to interview them.

Fernandez was new to the job: he'd been sworn in as a probationary police officer a month earlier. When he arrived, Fernandez interviewed two college students from the University of Georgia in Athens. They told the following story, according to police records.

The two girls had spent spring break in Miami. The night before, they had wound up at Mansion, a 40,000-square foot nightclub in south Miami Beach that pulsed nightly. A glitterati capital—neon, urgent—Mansion drew Jay-Z and Prince, Britney Spears and P. Diddy.

There, they met Wascar Payano, a promoter who knew a mutual friend. After a night at the club, Payano suggested that the three women accompany him to visit another friend: Darren Sharper.

The women agreed, and stepped into the world of NFL off-season parties.

The NFL season ends in February with the Super Bowl. Afterwards, many players head to condos and homes in party cities accustomed to accommodating the rich and famous—Miami Beach, Los Angeles and Las Vegas.

There, at popping, gleaming nightclubs, pro players take up seats at VIP tables, dropping $15,000 to $25,000 a night to buy drinks, food and exclusive access. Women in search of a sexual encounter with an NFL player make their way to the same clubs.

For the players, the arrangement offers easy access to women. And for some women, it offers the chance of thrill sex, bragging rights, maybe long-term romance.

Darren Sharper was a regular on the scene. Beginning in the late 2000s, Sharper met a lot of women through Payano, who was well connected in Miami Beach. In an interview, Payano said it was not difficult work.

"He was handsome and famous," Payano said. "He liked women."

Sharper was also a gambler who bet on baseball and basketball games. Sharper wagered as much as $25,000 a week placing offshore bets. Sharper needed the money, Payano said. His retirement from the NFL had seen his salary drop from more than $1 million a year to hundreds of thousands of dollars a year. Sharper, who had flown friends on vacations to Europe and the Caribbean, now insisted on splitting checks.

He saw gambling as a way to try to maintain his nightclub lifestyle.

"He was afraid he'd go broke," Payano said. "He'd seen it happen to other NFL players."

As detailed in a 2014 *Sports Illustrated* article, Payano had his own history of allegations of trouble with women. While attending the University of Miami in 2009, he had been arrested after allegedly spitting on a woman during a confrontation. Police dropped the case, and no charges were filed. Payano, a wounded Iraq veteran, maintained his innocence.

The experience of being accused gave Payano an appreciation for the danger that faced an NFL player: A woman with an axe to grind, or a desire to extort money, could make life difficult for the player, his reputation and his team.

"A lot of women don't tell the truth," Payano said.

After a night of drinking and dancing, Payano and the women went back to Sharper's condo.

The women and Payano met Sharper at his $6.7 million, 3,500 square-foot apartment. Its 20th floor windows were filled with stunning views of the Atlantic and the surrounding city. Two heavyset men were in the back, along with Jamie Sharper, the records show.

Payano and one of the women went into a nearby room. The other two women, exhausted from their night of partying, fell asleep on couches in the living room, the police records show.

Later that evening, according to police reports, one of the women in the living room awoke to find a man attempting to put his penis into her mouth. She pushed the man away, but awoke later to find the man trying to lift up her dress.

Upset, the woman woke her friend. She then woke Payano and her other friend from the bedroom. The women told Payano and their friend what had happened. Both women said they discovered that their underwear had been removed during the night.

Payano took the two women to the hospital on the morning of March 18, records show.

There, the two women underwent a rape kit—a forensic examination that typically lasts from two to four hours. The exam includes a full body inspection where a nurse searches for bodily fluids that may contain samples of an attacker's DNA. There is a toxicological exam, which attempts to determine whether drugs are present. And there is an examination for evidence of bruising or other damage that may indicate assault.

It can be an emotionally draining procedure—but not one that can ultimately determine whether a rape has occurred. At best, the rape kit can add evidence to a case.

The women decided to contact Miami Beach police. When Fernandez, the young officer, arrived at the hospital, he spoke with the nurse. The nurse, he wrote in his police report, told him that she "did not find any evidence" of a sexual assault. But in an interview with CBS News last year, the nurse said that she "would never say that, that's not my role."

Fernandez also reported that the victim identified the man who assaulted her as either "Darren or Jamie" Sharper—perhaps an indication of confusion.

But Payano said that Jamie was never mentioned by either victim, nor involved in the case.

Fernandez's report contains no mention of an effort to contact Darren Sharper. Nor are there signs that he attempted to collect evidence from Sharper's apartment. He never referred the case to Miami Beach's criminal investigations unit for further investigation. He never contacted prosecutors to determine whether probable cause existed.

Perhaps most important, there is no sign that Fernandez sent the women's rape kits to a lab for a more detailed examination. The failure to promptly test rape kits is a longstanding national problem that has hampered investigations for years. The federal government estimates there is a current backlog of hundreds of thousands of such kits sitting unexamined in police stations and testing labs.

Fernandez did consult with his superiors. And five days after the incident, he closed the case, records show. It was not labeled a crime. It sits in Miami Beach records as a "miscellaneous incident."

Miami Beach police would not be interviewed or respond to written questions. In a brief email, Detective Ernesto Rodriguez, a department spokesman, defended the agency's actions. Efforts to reach Fernandez through the Miami Beach police union were unsuccessful.

"The women involved never said that they were sexually assaulted, nor was there any physical evidence," Rodriguez wrote. "The officers consulted with a detective, and based on the lack of evidence of a crime, they all concluded that no further action could be taken by the department."

Anne Munch, a former prosecutor who worked on the Kobe Bryant rape trial in Colorado, is one of the country's leading experts in the investigation of sexual assaults, providing advice to the Department of Defense, the Department of Justice and police departments interested in improving their investigative techniques.

At *ProPublica*'s request, Munch agreed to review the public records released by law enforcement agencies in conjunction with the Sharper investigation. While not complete, the files provide a glimpse into police activity in some jurisdictions.

In general, the cases displayed many of the characteristics that make rape investigations so confounding, she said. Women who are assaulted often have fragmentary or conflicting memories—a direct result of the trauma of the event. Police must take special care in interviewing victims by understanding that uncertain recollections are common. Investigating officers need to seek corroboration from witnesses and confidants, not just rape kits.

"In rape, the victim is the case," Munch said.

Munch, as a result, questioned whether the Miami Beach department did a complete investigation. She noted that investigators should always attempt to contact the suspect before closing the investigation. There is no sign of such an attempt by the Miami Beach police. The rape kits performed were put to no immediate use. And records show no efforts to speak with witnesses from the night in the condo.

"One of the priorities in these cases, given what we know about sex offenders, is that it's typically not a he said, she said situation," she said.

"It's he said, they said."

## 'She's On the Potion'

It was after midnight on Sept. 23, 2013, and Tony Stafford was relaxing at a club inside Jax Brewery, an imposing, crenellated building overlooking the Mississippi, once the South's largest brewery. It had been a good night for Stafford, who was managing partner at a bar on nearby Bourbon Street. The Saints had beaten the Arizona Cardinals earlier in the day. Stafford had decided to treat his staff to drinks.

It was around 2 A.M. when he saw a woman he knew stumbling through the crowded club in a daze. To Stafford, the woman, a former Saints cheerleader, looked like she was sleepwalking.

Stafford became alarmed. He saw Sharper, whom he also knew, sitting in a corner with a hat pulled low, eying the woman. Stafford went up to him and asked about the woman.

Stafford said Sharper told him the woman was okay. He was taking her back to his apartment about a mile away. "She's on the potion. She's ready," he told Stafford. Sharper then took the woman's hand and walked out.

The remark chilled Stafford.

He wasn't going home with a woman, Stafford said in a recent interview, "he was going home with a zombie."

Concerned, Stafford called another old friend: a deputy sheriff, Brandon Licciardi, who hung out with Sharper. He convinced Licciardi to check on the woman's welfare. Licciardi

told Stafford that he'd gone to Sharper's condo. He'd caught a glimpse of the woman lying flat in Sharper's bed.

Another woman was in the apartment as well, along with a Sharper friend, according to an account Licciardi later gave authorities.

Sharper had pushed him back. "Dude, I got this," Sharper told Licciardi, according to the transcript of Licciardi's interview with investigators. "Y'all go home. Everything's fine. . . . I'mma bring her home."

Licciardi said he heard the deadbolt click behind him as he left.

The next morning, the woman called Stafford in tears. She had awoken to find Sharper on top of her, naked, records show. She didn't know what had happened. Stafford said he convinced her to go to the hospital for a rape kit exam.

A short while later, Stafford got a call from Detective Williams. The sex crimes unit detective wanted to interview him.

The unit was not held in high esteem. In the wake of killings by police after Hurricane Katrina, the U.S. Department of Justice had investigated the New Orleans police department for civil rights violations. Among the problems uncovered: "under-enforcement and under-investigation of violence against women." In 2013, a federal judge signed a consent decree ordering widespread reforms. They included 17 specific mandates to fix the department's shoddy handling of sexual-assault reports.

But later investigations would not show much progress. One report by the New Orleans inspector general found that police had mis-categorized nearly half of forcible rapes as "miscellaneous incidents" or "unfounded." The effect was to lower the rate of sexual assaults reported to the FBI.

Another investigation found that five detectives had failed to document follow-up investigation in the vast majority of reported sex crimes assigned to them.

One of those detectives: Derrick Williams.

Williams joined the New Orleans police department in 1996, spending some of his time in the juvenile division. He transferred to the sex crimes unit on a temporary basis, but wound up staying, said Eric Hessler, a police union lawyer representing the detective.

Stafford had doubts about Williams. He found the detective hostile. Williams, he said in an interview, emphasized that the woman had retained a civil lawyer—which Stafford took as a slur meaning that his friend was just seeking money.

Stafford grew angry and upset. He got up to leave. He told Williams that he had more information about the case. But months would pass before he felt comfortable disclosing more details to investigators outside the department.

"It didn't feel like they were really investigating a crime," Stafford said of the initial police response. "(It felt) like they were only going through the motions."

Williams also questioned the second woman who had been in Sharper's condo. The woman had been raped by Sharper. But she found Williams rude, and decided not to tell him anything, she later told authorities. She revealed details about the attack to district attorney's investigators only after Sharper's arrest in Los Angeles.

Williams did pursue the trail, at least at first,. He tried to interview Sharper, but was blocked by Sharper's attorney. He got a warrant allowing police to obtain a DNA sample from the former Saint. Sharper came to police headquarters with his attorney for a mouth swab. And on Nov. 4, six weeks after the night at Jax, the Louisiana State Police lab reported that Sharper's DNA matched DNA found on the woman.

Hessler, the lawyer for Williams, denied that the detective ever insinuated the former cheerleader was seeking money. Hessler said Williams had done his best to build a case.

By early November, Williams had a victim willing to testify; eyewitness accounts confirming parts of her story; video tracking her wobbly entrance into the condo; and physical evidence implicating Sharper.

What he didn't have was police brass or a prosecutor willing to approve an arrest warrant. Not that they weren't interested in the case. Hessler said that New Orleans District Attorney Leon Cannizzaro and former New Orleans Police Superintendent Ronal Serpas received regular briefings and monitored the investigation.

The high-level input did not help, Hessler said.

"It would help if they would dedicate the resources to you. It would help if they would dedicate support, time and everything else that's needed to solve it," Hessler said. "It doesn't help to have 10 people screaming in your ear, telling different things for you to do every day of the week."

Hessler said that Williams was not detached to investigate Sharper full time until after Los Angeles police made their arrest.

"This detective should've been allowed to focus solely and primarily on these allegations, and he was not," Hessler said.

Another criminal justice official with knowledge of the case said top officials were micromanaging Williams, demanding a bulletproof case before they would sign off on Sharper's arrest.

"The D.A.'s position and the administration's position was, because this was a high-profile case, we want to make sure we do this the right way. It was mainly because of the celebrityness," the official said. "You can't go in there half-cocked hoping you can scare them into pleading guilty or something. You only get one bite at the apple."

A New Orleans police spokesman declined to discuss the case, saying that Cannizzaro's office had asked to handle all questions pertaining to the case. Cannizzaro declined to be interviewed or respond to written questions from *ProPublica* and the *New Orleans Advocate*. Serpas, now retired, also declined requests for an interview.

Studies have shown that both police and prosecutors tend to look "downstream" in rape cases. That means their decisions are strongly influenced by whether they believe that a jury is likely to convict the suspect.

Jurors are more likely to convict in a case where a stranger uses force to rape a victim with a spotless background—sometimes referred to as a "righteous victim."

But such cases are the exception. Most rapes are between acquaintances. Most do not involve violence. And many involve victims perceived to have put themselves at risk: drinking at a bar or going home with strangers.

Many rapes come down to a single, difficult-to-prove issue: consent. Jurors are traditionally hesitant to convict when one person testifies to hearing yes, while the other person swears to saying no.

"There's a reluctance to label someone a rapist without very compelling evidence that the person is, in fact, a rapist," said Cassia Spohn, an Arizona State University professor who has studied the prosecution of rape cases for decades.

Still, Williams might have strengthened his case if he had taken one additional step. A call to police in Miami Beach, which Sharper listed as his permanent address, would have turned up Sharper's name in connection with the 2011 spring break incident.

Munch, the rape expert, said such inquiries are among the most important aspects of any investigation. Studies have shown that rapists have frequently committed prior sexual assault offenses. Such history can help support a new victim's case.

The details of the New Orleans case were eerily similar to the Miami incident. Women in both cases who were young, white and blond. Women who had passed out at Sharper's residence—either from alcohol or drugs. Women in both cases who woke to a sexual assault.

But Williams never made the call.

And Sharper was already on the move.

## More Women, More Drugs, Little Action

A month after allegedly raping the former cheerleader in New Orleans, Sharper was in Los Angeles to appear as an analyst for an NFL Network broadcast.

On the night of Oct. 30, 2013, he walked into Bootsy Bellows, a small nightclub that marks the end of the sprawl of bars along the Sunset Strip. There, a friend introduced him to two women. After the club closed, Sharper invited the women to an afterparty.

On the way, Sharper told the women he had to stop by his hotel to "pick up something," according to court records. He invited the women to his suite, where he gave both shots of Patron XO Cafe, a coffee-flavored tequila.

Both women blacked out within minutes of consuming the shots. Police said the drinks were spiked with zolpidem, the generic name for popular sleep aid Ambien, as well as morphine.

One woman awoke at 8:30 A.M. She was naked, and Sharper was astride her. The second woman woke up on a couch, and interrupted the pair in Sharper's bedroom. The women fled. They took a cab home.

Some eight days later, at 5:30 P.M., one of the women and her mother walked into the North Hollywood substation of the Los Angeles Police Department. The intake officer dutifully checked off the criteria that the department uses to screen cases. No serious injury. No specific modus operandi. No fingerprints or other evidence.

The check boxes combined to make the case a low priority.

Detective John Macchiarella didn't begin his investigation until two weeks after the woman filed the complaint, according to court documents. Once engaged, Macchiarella had the victim place a "pretext call" in hopes of eliciting incriminating information from Sharper. Police monitored the call, but did not issue an arrest warrant.

After that, there is little sign of action. Macchiarella did not attempt to interview Sharper. Nor did he obtain a sample of his DNA.

Most crucially, there is no indication that he tried to contact agencies in the other places where Sharper had lived.

If he had, of course, he might have learned of Miami Beach's closed case. Or more importantly, that Sharper was under active investigation in New Orleans. By the time Macchiarella started his investigation, Williams had already received the report matching Sharper's DNA to a sample found on the woman's body.

Without other evidence to corroborate the women's stories, Macchiarella's investigation stalled out.

Macchiarella did not respond to requests for comment. The Los Angeles Police Department would not comment.

The backgrounds of the accuser and the accused in rape cases were central in the grassroots movement to improve sexual assault laws two decades ago. In 1991, William Kennedy Smith, nephew of former Sen. Ted Kennedy, was accused of raping a young woman in Palm Beach. After his arrest, three women alleged that Smith had raped them in previously unreported cases. A judge forbade the women's testimony. Smith was acquitted.

In response to public anger over rape cases that appeared to favor the accused, then-Rep. Susan Molinari pushed a new law through Congress in 1994 that made it easier for prosecutors to introduce a defendant's history of sexual assault in cases involving sexual assault and child molestation.

The law was unusual. In American jurisprudence, a suspect's criminal history is not ordinarily allowed as evidence. The logic is simple: Jurors are supposed to weigh the evidence of a specific incident. Introducing a pattern of conduct might bias jurors to find the accused guilty.

Over time, research has emerged that supports the idea that in rape, the criminal history of the accused is relevant. One oft-cited study showed that rapists had committed a median of three rapes.

The International Association of Police Chiefs, the country's most influential police organization, recommends that detectives try to find previous victims. Police training organizations emphasize the importance of seeking such information in every case.

Nonetheless, the federal law, and similar versions adopted by states, remains controversial. Scholars decry it as an overreach that deprives the accused of the right to a fair trial. Some state top courts have overturned such laws as being unconstitutional. A 2013 review of the reform effort called it "a failure."

Another investigative tool sits largely unused. In the 1970s, a Los Angeles police detective trying to solve a case involving a serial killer had found himself reduced to looking through newspaper clippings. He proposed a solution to the FBI in the form of a database, the Violent Criminal Apprehension Program, or ViCAP.

Police agencies can enter detailed case information into the database allowing other law enforcement officials the ability to search for similarities to their own case.

But police departments and prosecutors have been slow to adapt, thus the 0.3 percent of case that ever get entered into the database.

Yet another underused option in rape investigations is the FBI's Combined DNA Index System, or CoDIS. Famed for its utility in solving cold cases, the database allows police to enter DNA from criminal suspects in search of a match to other crimes. Women's advocates say that police do not use the system enough in rape cases.

In the absence of any communication with each other, the New Orleans and Los Angeles investigations continued on parallel tracks. Neither produced any results. And neither stopped Sharper.

He had moved on to a new hunt.

## 'You Know I Was Passed Out!'

On Nov. 20, 2013, Sharper flew into Sky Harbor International Airport in Phoenix at about 9 P.M. to meet a friend: a 21-year-old, dark-haired senior at Arizona State University with whom he had previously been intimate.

The woman took Sharper home to her apartment, where she lived with another female Arizona State student. Sharper, the young woman and a girlfriend who lived down the hall, decided to hit the nightclub scene.

Police records detail what ensued: At one bar, Sharper's friend got sick and vomited on the table. Sharper, the woman, and her friend returned to the apartment. The group had to carry her inside. Her roommate helped carry the stricken woman to her room, changed her into her pajamas and left her passed out in bed.

By the apartment's kitchen, Sharper was still ready to party. He'd stripped down to his boxers and had prepared what he called "Frat Shots" for the women. He insisted they drink. One woman downed a shot. Another drank half, and put the drink aside.

The effects were unexpected. The young woman who took the full shot was unconscious within minutes. The roommate and Sharper arranged her on a nearby couch. The sole remaining conscious woman then retired to her bedroom and locked the door. She called her boyfriend in Louisiana. Upon lying down, she "was dizzy and had lost control of her motor functions and her muscles felt weak," according to the police report.

Her boyfriend suggested she open a window for fresh air, but she couldn't muster enough force to slide the glass. The boyfriend said splashing water on her face might help. She walked out of her bedroom, heading to a sink in a shared bathroom. Then she stopped. She saw Sharper naked, thrusting into the body of the woman who had passed out on the couch. She would tell police she couldn't see whether her friend was conscious, or if she was witnessing a sex act.

The woman continued to the sink, wetted her face and hurried back to her bedroom. She remained on the phone with her boyfriend and relayed what she'd just witnessed. Suddenly, there was a knock on the door she had left open upon returning.

Sharper stood in front of her in his boxer shorts. He wanted to explain that he and the woman he'd been assaulting had "something going on," records show. Sharper said he'd talk about it in the morning.

The next morning, all three women confronted Sharper, who told them he had no memory of the previous night. By noon, he had left the apartment.

The three women then went to a local hospital, where two of them received rape kit examinations. One exam showed minor injuries to the victim consistent with intercourse. Detective Kevin Mace, who had served on the sex crimes unit for just over a year, was called in.

At 1:28 A.M. on Friday, November 22, 10 Tempe police officers searched the apartment. They collected drink bottles, used plastic cups from a trash can, a rug, couch cushions and clothing, the case file shows. One of the discarded cups still held remnants of a drink that Sharper mixed. Officers also found a broken pink pill.

Mace called the victims later that day to find out if any took prescription drugs; all said no.

Detectives received the rape kit evidence and exam report on November 25. The examiner's diagnosis was as follows: sexual assault by history, minor physical injuries by exam, crime lab results pending, Mace wrote. Results did not conflict with the victims' statements. Nor did they seal a conviction.

Mace did not document how he interpreted the results, or if they had any effect on the investigation. The detective declined interview requests for this story.

Tempe police continued to move. Seven officers worked the case. They got clothing and DNA samples from the women. They interviewed the boyfriend who had received the call during the alleged rape.

One victim met Detective Brad Breckow at Tempe Police Department headquarters four days after the assault, a little after 6:30 P.M. on the Monday before Thanksgiving 2013.

She'd been corresponding with Sharper by voicemail and text message. They were supposed to talk on the phone that evening.

Breckow prepared the victim for the conversation, one he now would be recording. Police have a script for these exchanges, named pretext calls, which have become common in sex assault investigations. The aim is to see if the accused will admit to misconduct.

Several different statements were printed out and placed before the victim. Among them: "Why did you take my clothes off? You know I was passed out."

She dialed Sharper at 6:48 P.M., and he picked up. But he complained his phone battery was low and said he'd call back. Which he did, from a blocked number.

The victim set out to press Sharper on details. Sharper had already vaguely apologized without acknowledging what he had done. "Apologize for what?" is scrawled across the top of Breckow's handwritten notes.

Once on the phone, the woman was angry. But Sharper was nimble, never discussing specifics. He said they needed to move forward as friends. He'd been "fucked up," as intoxicated as anyone that night. The victim struggled to direct the conversation.

Perhaps exasperated, she told Sharper "he had probably done something like this before," according to Breckow's notes describing the call.

"That (is) ridiculous," Sharper replied.

Actually, it was dead on. By the time of the Tempe rape, Sharper had refined his technique of drugging and raping women.

Date rape drugs have long been a popular topic in media reports. But far and away the most common drug used in sexual assaults is alcohol—and it's astonishingly effective.

Alcohol can cause blackouts, rendering victims unable to remember. It's easy to get. And it can devastate a victim's credibility. A woman may tell police she had two beers at a party. But if her attacker spiked the drink with additional alcohol, and tests come back showing a high blood alcohol level, it's difficult to convince a jury that the woman isn't lying.

"Not only do perpetrators get what they wanted, but they discredit the witness, too," said Robert Hoffman, a New York toxicologist. "The whole thing is planned, thought out and executed, like any other crime."

Sharper, however, had crossed into the more rarefied world of prescription drugs. Only about 4 percent of rapes involve such pharmacological agents, according to one study. Among the more exotic ones are Rohypnol, or roofies, which are banned in the U.S., and GHB, which is tightly controlled. Both drugs cause amnesia, and they are quickly expelled from the body, making them difficult to detect.

Sharper's drugs of choice were more familiar. Police charged that he used some combination of zolpidem, the active ingredient in Ambien; benzodiazepines such as Valium and Xanax; and drugs like Quaaludes and MDMA, or molly, both illegal party drugs.

Experts are not sure what motivates sex offenders to use such drugs. Some believe that such rapists are more like serial killers—interested in the thrill of the chase, and the capture of their prey. Whatever the motive or the satisfactions, the calculation is simple: Women with no memory make poor witnesses.

"The lack of memory is a huge barrier to coming forward and a huge barrier to getting a proper police response," said Trinka Porrata, a former Los Angeles Police Department street narcotics squad supervisor who is now president of Project GHB, a national date rape drug awareness group. "There's also a problem at the prosecution phase."

Tempe police had strong suspicions that Sharper had used drugs on the victims. They sent away samples of the victims' hair for testing—Ambien can be detected there long after it has been flushed from the body.

Munch, the rape investigations expert, praised the work done by Tempe police in the initial stages. "They do a good job on focusing on the perpetrator's conduct. They are focusing on what he did," she said.

But despite the evidence they gathered in the initial weeks, the investigation slowed. Between Dec. 13, 2013 and Jan. 17, 2014, the Tempe case log contains only two entries. Crucial evidence—such as the pill found in the room and samples from the drink mixed by Sharper—sat untested in a Tempe police storage locker.

And once again, the Arizona detectives did not look into Sharper's background in other cities. In fact, the department deemed that such evidence was not worth gathering—despite a state law designed to make it easier to use a suspect's history in rape cases.

"In a trial setting, it is highly unlikely that a 'series' of events in different jurisdictions would be made known to a jury that is deciding guilt or innocence on a single event," said department spokesman Lt. Michael Pooley.

The delays and decisions gave Sharper the freedom to return to California—and his stalking ground.

## An Arrest Warrant At Last

Sharper's spree of sexual violence peaked in January 2014, according to police and court records.

After attending a party on Jan. 14, 2014 at the Roosevelt Hotel to commemorate the 50th anniversary of *Sports Illustrated* Magazine's Swimsuit Edition, two women decided to go to Bootsy Bellows—the club on the Sunset Strip where Sharper had met his previous victims.

There, one woman started talking to Sharper. When the two realized they were headed to the same afterparty, Sharper and the women decided to share a ride. Sharper said he first had to pick up something from his hotel, the landmark Century Plaza in Century City.

Once inside the lobby of the gleaming, curved hotel, they went to Sharper's room. Both women crowded into the bathroom. When they exited, Sharper greeted them with two mixed drinks he described as vodka and cranberry juice.

The women said they didn't want anything. Sharper insisted. The drinks tasted strange to both women. Within 10 minutes, they were both unconscious.

The women woke up the next morning at 9 A.M. One felt pain and burning in her vagina. They left without seeing Sharper. After talking later that day, the women decided to go to the Santa Monica Rape Crisis Center. They walked into the center at midnight.

The next day, they made their report to the Los Angeles Police Department's Westside police station. This time, the officer taking the report noted that Sharper's attacks featured a modus operandi.

Macchiarella, the detective who caught the first Los Angeles case, also got the second. Alarm bells went off. A judge issued an arrest warrant.

It was too late. After Sharper raped the women in Los Angeles, he flew into Las Vegas on Jan. 15, 2014. There, he met up with two women and a male companion. All went to Sharper's room. Sharper mixed drinks for them, and they all blacked out.

When the women woke up, one remembered that she had woken during the night to find Sharper naked on top of her. The other felt as though she had had sex, but had no memory of it.

The man awoke in the hotel lobby, with no memory of how he arrived there. Both women went to a local hospital and received rape kit examinations, reports show.

Sharper had now drugged and raped four women within 24 hours. He flew back to Los Angeles.

He was arrested at his hotel at 3 P.M. on Jan. 17, 2014.

A few hours later, the news dropped: At 1 A.M. Pacific Time, Jan. 18, 2014, TMZ reported that Sharper had been arrested in Los Angeles on rape charges.

Law enforcement agencies across the country began scrambling.

## 'Guilty'

Over the next year, police and prosecutors finally started talking to each other. They turned up new victims. They got arrest warrants for previous ones. And a portrait of Sharper emerged from the investigations as a calculated and methodical serial rapist.

In Miami, a woman came forward after the news broke to report that Sharper had raped her in 2012. She told police she needed to "clear her conscience." Prosecutors said there was "no reason to doubt the credibility of the victim in this matter, especially given the apparent conduct of the subject as documented by other police agencies," records show. But the Miami Dade State Attorney's office decided not to file charges.

Miami Beach police also decided not to re-open the 2011 case involving the two University of Georgia women. The women's rape kits had been destroyed.

Rodriguez, the agency's spokesman, said the department had recently contacted the victim in the 2011 case. She told the agency that she did not consider herself to have been sexually assaulted, Rodriguez said.

"We have no crime to investigate," Rodriguez said.

In Arizona, Tempe stepped up the pace of their investigation. For the next two months, investigators recorded a new development every two days on average. They collected victim medical records, got a warrant for Sharper's cell phone records, and obtained lab results which showed Sharper's DNA on one victim's leggings. On March 11, an Arizona grand jury returned an arrest warrant for Sharper.

It was served to him in the Los Angeles County jail.

Tempe police officials said their investigation was "both comprehensive and complex."

In New Orleans, the case exploded. Within days of Sharper's arrest, the New Orleans District Attorney's office assigned one of their crack investigators to the case. The FBI threw two agents into the mix to chase a multi-state drug angle.

Investigators soon discovered that Williams had been duped during the initial investigation.

In the fall, Williams had interviewed Licciardi, the man who had gone to Sharper's home to check on the cheerleader's welfare. At the time, Licciardi portrayed himself as a fellow cop who had tried to help out.

But Licciardi was not what he seemed, authorities concluded. James O'Hern, the newly assigned investigator, and the FBI found evidence suggesting that Licciardi was actually Sharper's connection to New Orleans' seamy side.

Licciardi had befriended Sharper in 2010, when the two met at the opening of a Bourbon Street bar. Sharper was the celebrity guest. Licciardi provided security. Over the next several years, the two grew close.

Licciardi allegedly trafficked in drugs, worked for a gambling operation collecting marks, and sent out text messages bragging about beating his girlfriend until she was unable to walk, according to court testimony. Licciardi grew so out of control that his estranged mother confided to a friend, "We have raised a monster," according to court testimony.

Sharper gambled heavily in Louisiana, as he had in Florida. Licciardi helped Sharper place bets with an offshore gambling outfit.

Licciardi also served as Sharper's source for women and drugs, according to court documents. He is accused of delivering some victims to Sharper after drugging them first with Ambien, Xanax, Valium, MDMA or some combination.

In fact, Licciardi left out a crucial detail in describing his valorous efforts to check up on the cheerleader. He had actually delivered the woman to Sharper and had helped Sharper drug her, authorities charged in court documents.

"Licciardi treats women as if they are nothing or of no value," one former girlfriend told investigators, according to court testimony.

Licciardi has denied all charges. He remains in jail awaiting trial.

Investigators got a better understanding of Licciardi's role once they examined his phone. There, they found a video and a photo sent by Sharper of the former cheerleader that he allegedly assaulted, naked and passed out.

When police later showed her the video, she identified herself and broke down in tears.

Over the course of the next several months, New Orleans used the contents of Licciardi's phone, as well as testimony from eyewitnesses, to track down other alleged victims.

In one case, Sharper and Licciardi had teamed up to drug a woman at the Super Bowl festivities held in New Orleans in February 2013, according to court documents and people with knowledge of the case. Licciardi allegedly raped the woman at Sharper's condo after meeting her at a pre-Super Bowl party at Jax.

In another case, Licciardi had sex with a woman, then turned her over to Sharper, according to interviews and official documents. The two men had rented adjacent rooms at a New Orleans hotel, across the street from Sharper's condo. Sharper sent Licciardi a text message: "We need an hour in here."

In December 2014, the New Orleans District Attorney's office and federal prosecutors indicted Sharper, Licciardi and another alleged accomplice, Erik Nuñez.

Sharper was charged with drugging women and then raping three of them. Nuñez was accused of raping two of the same women. Licciardi was charged with rape, drugging and sex trafficking. A federal indictment charged Sharper and Licciardi in a conspiracy to drug women for rape, dating back to 2010.

Nuñez, who only faces state charges, has pleaded innocent to the allegations made against him.

News of the additional victims left Williams, the original detective on the Sharper case, sputtering with anger. After Licciardi spilled details of Sharper's attacks to the New Orleans District Attorney's investigator O'Hern, Williams scolded him for not revealing more during their initial interview.

"I'm a cop, and I'm pissed off, cause you knew a lot of this information the first time you came and spoke to me. We could have gotten a lot of this out of the way," Williams said, according to a transcript of the interview.

"Whatever truths that need to come out, shit done hit the fan at this point," Williams told Licciardi.

Williams was right. The case moved into the battleground of courtrooms in four states.

Sharper hired top-flight Los Angeles attorneys Blair Berk and Leonard Levine to lead the defense. During pre-trial hearings, Sharper's legal team attacked the women's stories.

One victim in Los Angeles had initially lied about the presence of another witness, defense documents said. In Arizona, one woman had prior consensual sex with Sharper. In Nevada, one of the victims told friends about her sexual encounter with Sharper, making no mention of sexual assault.

But in the end, as evidence mounted, the Sharper team decided to cut a deal. Sharper agreed to plead guilty or no contest to charges in Louisiana, Arizona, California and Nevada, as well as federal drug charges.

In exchange, he would receive a 20 year prison sentence, but be eligible for release in nine years. He would register as a sex offender. And he would be on probation for life.

The deal provoked widespread anger. Sharper had been facing life in prison if convicted of aggravated rape charges.

"I was definitely shocked," said Ebony Tucker, executive director of the Louisiana Foundation Against Sexual Assault. "It's hard to excuse how someone who's raped nine women that we know of in four states is only going to serve nine years in prison."

On the morning of March 23, Darren Sharper walked into a windowless courtroom in downtown Los Angeles in a gray, pinstripe suit. Judge Michael Pastor reviewed the deal with Sharper.

Looking down, Pastor asked: "Are you entering each plea freely and voluntarily?"

"Yes sir," Sharper responded.

"Do you realize that this is a final answer?" Pastor asked.

"Yes sir," Sharper answered.

Suddenly, it was easy to see.

The women had been right.

Sharper was a rapist.

## Critical Thinking

1. What do you think about the way Miami Beach Officer Fernandez managed the rape case he received?

2. What is meant by the statement: "In rape, the victim is the case"?

3. Are rape cases typically "he said, she said" situations?

## Internet References

**Office of Inspector General, City of New Orleans**

http://www.nolaoig.org/uploads/File/Public%20Letters/2014/ROI%20%20Sex%20Crimes%20FINAL%2020141111.pdf

**Pro Publica**

http://www.propublica.org/documents/item/1719911-2011-03-18-miami-beach-police-report-redacted-copy.html

**Pro Publica**

http://www.propublica.org/documents/item/1686601-tempe-police-report03122015.html

**Pro Publica**

http://www.propublica.org/documents/item/1699822-2002-lisak-repeatrapeinundetectedrapists.html

**Social Science Research Network**

http://papers.ssrn.com/sol3/papers.cfm?abstract_id=2382749

*Article*                                                                    Prepared by: Joanne Naughton

# He Was Abused by a Female Teacher, but He Was Treated Like the Perpetrator

SIMONE SEBASTIAN

## Learning Outcomes

*After reading this article, you will be able to:*

- Consider the effects on young men of sexual abuse by older female authority figures.

- Show what usually happens when such cases get to court.

- Discuss the research regarding male suffering as a result of sexual abuse.

Cameron Clarkson was a 16-year-old football player when he suddenly landed in the middle of a sex crime investigation at his St. Paul, Minn., high school. Lawyers grilled him on the details of his sexual history. School officials, in a statement to the press, cited him for not invoking the school's sexual harassment policy and said he "bragged to fellow students about what had happened." His car was vandalized with red-dyed tampons and smeared with peanut butter, to which he is fatally allergic, by an unknown assailant. The shape of a penis was burned into his front lawn with bleach.

"People kept reminding me that I ruined that poor girl's life," Clarkson says.

The "poor girl" was a teacher at his school. Gail Gagne, a 25-year-old basketball and lacrosse coach, was a full-time substitute teacher at Cretin-Derham Hall High School and a couple of months away from becoming a regular physical education instructor. One day, she offered to give Clarkson a ride home after he left the school gym, leading to what he describes as the first of a series of sexual encounters between them in 2008—in Gagne's car, in their homes, in hotels. He says their relationship ended two months later; another student told school officials about it the next spring.

Gagne was fired and charged with two felony counts of criminal sexual conduct with a student. But in the investigations that followed, Clarkson was treated more like the perpetrator than the victim. Gagne, meanwhile, faced an easier path in some ways. She denied any sexual contact with Clarkson but entered an Alford plea, in which a defendant does not admit guilt but recognizes that prosecutors have enough evidence to convict her. The deal reduced her charges to a fifth-degree gross misdemeanor with a one-year sentence, which was suspended—a far lighter punishment than the possible four-year prison sentence for the felony charges she faced. (Gagne's lawyer still says there was no sexual contact.)

For male victims of sexual abuse, this is how it goes. Growing evidence shows that boys who are sexually preyed upon by older female authority figures suffer psychologically in much the same way that girls do when victimized by older men. But in schools, courts and law offices, male victims are treated openly with a double standard, according to interviews with a dozen experts in law, psychology and social work. Some say boys should get the same protective care that girls do; other people who work with these cases argue that male teens are driven by raging hormones and are only too happy to explore their new sexuality with older women. But all of the experts agree that the discrepancy in the treatment of victims of nonviolent sexual abuse by their high school teachers is real. And it shows: Male victims typically receive lower awards in civil cases, the experts say, and female perpetrators get lighter sentences.

There is a clear hierarchy in courtrooms, lawyers say. Cases involving a male teacher and a female student result in the most severe punishments and the highest damages. Los Angeles-based lawyer David Ring, whose firm Taylor & Ring represents plaintiffs in sexual abuse suits, has worked on hundreds of teacher–student cases and says it's not unusual for those against male teachers to end with judgments of more than $1 million. In one example, a jury awarded $5.6 million to a high school girl in a sexual abuse case involving her 40-year-old teacher. The teacher was convicted of a felony, sentenced to a year in jail and ordered to pay 40 percent of the civil damages to the student, who was 14 at the time of the encounters. (Chino Valley High School was ordered to pay the other 60 percent.)

But jurors and prosecutors don't have nearly the same outrage for abusive female teachers, Ring says: " 'So what? Good for him.' That's how society looks at it." Male students, in his experience, rarely collect damages of more than $200,000. In November, Clarkson settled his case against Cretin-Durham Hall High School for $75,000. The case against Gagne settled for just $1.

Clarkson's attorney, Sarah Odegaard, says her team made a strategic choice: They stood to win a larger award from the school, so they agreed to a token gesture from Gagne in lieu of a trial in which she would have denied the sexual relationship. In cases like this—with "an attractive, young female" defendant—jury bias doesn't work in favor of the victim, Odegaard says. "It's not a bias we want to acknowledge, but we have to," she says. "There have been some successes involving female teachers and coaches, but more often, you see lower verdicts."

Exact comparisons between cases are difficult to make; every case is unique. Sentences and monetary damages are shaped by the number and type of sexual encounters, the age of the victim relative to the state's age of consent, and—rightly or wrongly—the level of suffering the victim displayed during the investigation, among other factors. But while there's no data tracking the nationwide disparity in how male and female sexual abuse victims are treated (one possible reason: male abusers tend to be significantly older than their female victims, which leads to larger penalties, according to several lawyers who work on these cases), everybody seems to agree that the disparity exists.

The problem, rather, is that not everyone sees a problem with it. "I think they *should* be treated different," says Minneapolis-based defense lawyer Joe Friedberg. "Every high school boy had some kind of fantasy about some female teacher. I walk away from these cases and say, 'That would have been my finest hour.' I don't know that I see the damage to the victim in those cases."

Many more studies track female victims than male ones, but the research matches experts' anecdotal observations about the severity of male suffering. In a 2004 study, researchers in Australia reviewed the psychiatric histories of more than 1,600 people who had been sexually abused as children. They found that both male and female victims had higher rates of psychiatric treatment for personality, anxiety and other disorders compared with the general population. Nearly one in four male victims had received treatment, compared with 10 percent of female victims.

In another 2004 study, researcher Myriam Denov, then at the University of Ottawa, conducted in-depth interviews with 14 victims of sexual abuse by females. Both male and female victims reported experiencing damaging long-term effects, including depression, substance abuse, self-injury, dysfunctional relationships with women and even suicide attempts.

"I'm sick of life and how I'm lying / I'm sick of this earth and what I'm trying to do," a 16-year-old boy wrote in a seemingly suicidal poem to Denise Keesee, then a 32-year-old teacher at Sherwood High School in Oregon with whom he had sex, according to news reports. Last April, a judge sentenced Keesee to just one month in jail for sexual abuse of the student. Her lawyer declined to comment.

Girls are four times more likely to be victims of sexual abuse than boys, according to the National Center for Victims of Crime. That imbalance has meant that sexual assault policies are not applied to the 1 in 20 abused boys with the same urgency they are applied to female victims. "You are laughed at and not believed," says Denov, the researcher who conducted the 2004 study.

The victims are disbelieved precisely because they are so rare, and the failure to be heard adds another layer of trauma. "Because of our views of mothering and nurturing," Denov adds, people wonder: "'How is it possible that a woman can commit a sexual offense?' People can't get their head around what that means."

Evidence of arousal is often used against boys, too. Clarkson says, "I was asked [by lawyers] how something that ended in me ejaculating could possibly be abuse," he recalls.

That's a common mistake, says psychiatrist Brian Jacks. Even if a boy cooperates in the sexual encounter—and brags about it to friends—that doesn't mean the experience won't have long-term, negative effects. "They are swaggering around at this point," Jacks says. "You don't realize the consequences until later in life. You realize that you were taken advantage of. . . . I promise you, it's going to mess up your life."

Clarkson said the psychological effects of his relationship with Gagne caught up with him soon after it ended. He started skipping school, spending the day sitting in his bedroom in the dark. He lost interest in the activities most important to him and gave up on his dream of playing football in college. In his first year of college at Howard University, he smoked marijuana heavily, drank copiously and struggled to engage in social activities. Psychiatrist Raymond Patterson diagnosed Clarkson with depression, saying it was "directly related to the sexual abuse he suffered," according to court documents.

"There are people who believe that I cannot possibly be a victim of abuse because of my appearance," says Clarkson. Gagne's lawyer struggled with exactly this point during an interview. "He looks like he is 35. And Gail looks 20," he says.

Clarkson believes that race compounded the discrimination against him. He is black; Gagne is white. Society views black men as sexual predators rather than as victims, he wrote in a summary of his experience. "I was referred to as simply a physical body, with no regard for the development of my mind or soul."

## Critical Thinking

1. Why do you think Cameron Clarkson wasn't treated the way a victim of sexual abuse is usually treated?

2. Do you agree with attorney Joe Friedberg's statement about every high school boy?

3. What are some of the reasons male victims are often disbelieved?

## Internet References

**Administration for Children & Families**
Child Abuse & Neglect | Children's Bureau | Administration for Children and Families

**Sage Publications**
http://jiv.sagepub.com/content/19/10/1137.short

**The National Center for Victims of Crime**
http://www.victimsofcrime.org/media/reporting-on-child-sexual-abuse/child-sexual-abuse-statistics

**SIMONE SEBASTIAN** works for *The Washington Post* as deputy editor for PostEverything and is an assistant editor of *Outlook*.

*Article*

Prepared by: Joanne Naughton

# Male Victims of Campus Sexual Assault Speak Out

Emily Kassie

## Learning Outcomes

*After reading this article, you will be able to:*

- Relate how likely it is that rape victims will attempt suicide.
- Report what studies show about victims of sexual violence.

Note: The following story contains descriptions of sexual assault that some readers might find upsetting.

It was Andrew's sixth night of freshman year at Brown University when he was assaulted by a male student in his dorm bathroom. When Andrew brought on-campus charges, his assailant was expelled.

Unlike myriad students who report mishandled cases in the burgeoning national campaign against sexual assault, Andrew initially believed his case was handled appropriately.

But after *The Huffington Post* discovered Andrew's assailant had previously been found responsible for assaulting two other students and had not been expelled, Andrew was devastated.

Andrew has decided to share his story in hopes that victims of assault—and specifically male victims—be taken more seriously.

"It's time to include male survivors' voices," he said. "We are up against a system that's not designed to help us."

In the early hours of Sept. 5, 2011, Andrew, who asked that his last name be withheld, was up late excitedly chatting with his hallmates in Keeney Quad, one of two main freshman housing units. Jumping from room to room, Andrew admired the varied displays his classmates had on their walls. In his room, Andrew had put up Art Deco travel posters and a screen print of neighborhoods in his hometown of Washington, D.C.

Around 5 A.M., his classmates returned to their rooms while Andrew headed to the communal bathrooms to brush his teeth. Halfway down the hall, a male student he didn't recognize passed him. Not thinking much of it, Andrew entered the bathroom and began to wash his hands.

A knock on the door surprised him. The bathroom required a dorm key, so anyone who lived in the building should have been able to get inside. Andrew opened the door. It was the same student he had seen in the hall.

Andrew went back to the sink, and the student approached him. "You're hot," Andrew remembers him saying. The student propositioned him but Andrew politely declined.

"Nobody has to know," the student said.

He came up behind Andrew, grabbed his crotch and moved him into the bathroom stall. Frozen, Andrew protested but did not fight back, scared of what would happen if he did.

For 15 minutes the stranger assaulted him.

Andrew has a hard time articulating what he felt during the assault. All he remembers is being unable to speak or act. "I just remember focusing on the stall door, knowing that he was between me and my escape."

When the assault was over, the assailant "just left." Andrew remembers resting his head against the bathroom stall and listening to the buzz of the fluorescent lights as he tried to reconcile what had just happened to him.

"I didn't even know his name," Andrew said. "I didn't know who he was. Nobody saw anything."

Andrew later found out the assailant's name through a mutual friend. During the hearing process he also learned that his assailant was a sophomore who had been visiting a residential adviser in the dorm earlier that night.

The day after the assault, Andrew told his friends what happened, but joked that it was a "5 A.M. hookup in the bathroom." It was easier to deal with the shame if he felt control over the situation. At 8 P.M. Andrew and his classmates were required to attend a mandatory orientation meeting entitled "Understanding Sexual Assault."

Andrew remembers feeling isolated in the auditorium populated by his peers. "It was a sad twist of irony," he said.

At first, Andrew berated himself, wondering if he could have done more to stop it. But after a couple months he started feeling like himself again, excelling in his introductory course on Urban Studies and joining groups like the Queer Alliance, the Brown University Chorus and a coed literary fraternity.

Things took a turn in the spring when Andrew was cast in a campus production of "Don Pasquale" and attended rehearsals nightly on the north side of campus, where his assailant lived—and seeing him "almost every single time" he was there.

On the morning of Feb. 29, 2012, he had a panic attack. "I got in the shower and suddenly started shaking and could only see in front of me and probably couldn't have told you where or who I was."

Andrew started meeting regularly with a counselor, but initially chose not to share the assailant's name, as he was not ready to pursue a campus hearing. But in May, after a couple months of counseling, he decided to file a formal complaint with the university. The hearing was held the following November.

Andrew's assailant participated via phone as, unbeknownst to Andrew, he was on suspension for two other cases of sexual assault.

The two other victims, Brenton (who would only give his first name), and another student who requested to remain anonymous, said they filed a joint complaint in December 2011. They had hearings for their cases in March 2012; the university found the assailant responsible for sexual misconduct in both cases and suspended him until the following December.

"I was happy that he got suspended, but I didn't think it was enough. I knew there were even more people he had gotten to," Brenton said.

After Andrew's hearing in November, the university found the assailant responsible for a third case of sexual misconduct and expelled him. The assailant appealed all three sanctions and was rejected. He declined to comment for this article.

The timeline of all three assaults was as follows:

After this story was published, a fourth student came forward and told *HuffPost* that the same perpetrator had harassed him, stalked him and threatened his life after a sexual encounter. According to documents obtained by *HuffPost*, the encounter occurred in September 2011, and the harassment resulted in a university no-contact order between the two students. This means the university was aware of the perpetrator's history of harassment during the first two sexual misconduct hearings and still only imposed a one-semester suspension on the perpetrator.

Brown has recently been in the news for accusations of mishandled cases of sexual assault, notably that of Lena Sclove, which prompted a federal Title IX investigation.

In Sclove's case, the accused student was found responsible for two counts of sexual misconduct and suspended for two semesters. Similarly, the student who assaulted Brenton and the anonymous victim was merely suspended for just over one semester.

Brown's failure to impose a sufficient sanction was unsurprising to Andrew but upsetting nonetheless. "I wish they had taken it seriously the first one or two times," he said. "The process weighed on me from April to November. ... I could've had days of my sophomore year that I didn't have to drag myself out of bed every morning. ... To know that [the hearing process] could have been prevented if they had expelled him the first time is incredibly upsetting. My sophomore year could have been totally different."

Brown's president, Christina Paxson, recently sent a letter to the Brown community outlining revisions to Brown's sexual assault policy, including that a student given a sanction that includes separation from the university would be immediately removed from campus residences (though not necessarily barred from campus). The letter also included clearer guidelines on how the university determines a sanction, but it didn't determine specific sanctions for violations of sexual misconduct, leaving Andrew's concern unaddressed.

In a statement emailed to *The Huffington Post*, Brown University said it could not comment on the individual cases.

"The circumstances of each case are taken into account by the conduct board and adjudicated under our current sanctioning guidelines, which are reviewed regularly," the statement said. "We believe our process is the right one for our University and we remain committed to doing all we can to keep our community safe and to being a leader in establishing best practices."

For all the focus on campus sexual assault in recent years, male victims have been frequently absent from the news coverage, except for the most tragic cases, like that of Trey Malone, an Amherst College student who committed suicide after his assault.

One study shows rape victims are 13 times more likely than non-crime victims to have attempted suicide. Jennifer Marsh, vice president of victims services at Rape, Abuse & Incest National Network, the largest anti-sexual-assault organization in the nation, said both men and women who survive sexual assault face similar psychological effects—but there are some differences. "Male survivors who are suicidal tend to use more lethal means," Marsh said.

Studies show that one in five women has been the victim of attempted or completed rape in her lifetime, and that approximately 50 percent of transgender people experience sexual violence at some point in their lifetimes. But statistics vary on the incidence of sexual assault against men. According to a study by the Centers for Disease Control and Prevention, of 5,000 college students at over 130 colleges, one in 25 men answered "yes" to the question "In your lifetime have you been forced to submit to sexual intercourse against your will?" Other organizations, such as 1in6, an advocacy group for male survivors, put the estimate much higher, at one in six males before the age of 18.

Steve LaPore, founder and director of 1in6, believes male sexual assaults are underreported because the issue is still taboo. While women have "really moved the ball forward," resulting in a heightened awareness about sexual assault against women and children, it's an awareness that doesn't include men as victims, he said.

"Culturally we still don't want to see men as vulnerable or hurt," LaPore explained. "We tell little boys and men to pull themselves up by their bootstraps." Because of the stigma, he said, there are fewer resources available for male victims.

LaPore was not surprised by the fact that Andrew's assailant initially received a lighter punishment. "In many cases we find that it's more difficult for men to be believed, or to take their case seriously," he said. "I think we've done a pretty good job of seeing men's roles as bystanders and preventers, but we don't recognize men who are survivors of sexual assault and abuse."

Clayton Bullock, psychiatrist and co-author of *Male Victims of Sexual Assault: Phenomenology, Psychology, Physiology,* found that male victims are also less likely to come forward or be taken seriously because of their physiological response to assault.

"It is possible for men to get aroused and ejaculate when being assaulted," Bullock said. "What's particularly bewildering for the males is that if they ejaculated or were aroused during the assault, it adds a layer of shame or confusion in their culpability of their own victimization."

Men also have difficulty with the language of sexual assault, according to Jim Hopper, instructor of psychology at Harvard Medical School and a founding board member of 1in6.

"There are words like 'victim' and 'survivor' that are hard to identify with, especially for men," Hopper said. "For many men, they don't want to be a 'victim' because it's antithetical to what it means to be a real man."

A friend of Malone's at Amherst, who identified himself as Eric for this article, said he was raped by his freshman-year roommate. After feeling dissatisfied with the school's handling of his case, Eric attempted suicide by overdosing on Benadryl, but it didn't work.

"I remember waking up to [my roommate] kissing the back of my neck, and I feel his erect dick behind me," Eric recalled.

"I turn around and am like, 'What are you doing?' And he says, 'What are you doing in my room?' And I said, 'No, dude, you're in my bed.'"

Eric feels he was targeted because of his sexuality. "I was very open about being gay, so I think that's a big part of it; he assaulted me because he knew I was gay," Eric said. "After that I felt like I couldn't be as out as I was. He thought that was an invitation."

Andrew, who identifies as queer, believes it's more difficult for people to talk about queer victims of assault. "They don't want to think that queer people exist to begin with, so the idea that sexual assault happens in those communities is something people don't want to talk about," he said. "There are some people who also believe [sexual assault] is punishment or retribution for being queer."

The 2010 National Intimate Partner and Sexual Violence Survey from the Centers for Disease Control and Prevention found about 40 percent of gay men, 47 percent of bisexual men and 21 percent of heterosexual men in the U.S. "have experienced sexual violence other than rape at some point in their lives."

Bullock says gay men are often targets of sexual assault because of gay-bashing, or because of conflicted feelings about the assailant's own attraction to other men in which they are "exorcising their internalized homophobia."

And since the LGBTQ community is often perceived as promiscuous, it can be difficult for victims to come forward.

"The sentiment I hear the most and feel the most is that because we're being open about our sexuality, when someone assaults us it's not an assault," Eric said. "Like, 'Oh you were kind of asking for it,' or 'Are you surprised you got assaulted?'"

Eric struggled at Amherst in the immediate aftermath of his assault, eventually dropping out when the administration allowed his assailant to remain on campus. After leaving college, he joined the military and became an engineer. He's feeling optimistic about what's next, but he still feels the impact of what happened to him.

"You know 'Carry That Weight'?" he asked, referring to Columbia University student Emma Sulkowicz's campaign to raise awareness of college sexual assault by carrying a mattress around campus until her rapist is expelled. "How I imagine carrying my weight is physical weight. I actually gained a lot of weight, and part of that was intentional. It's comforting for me being heavier and less looked at as a sex object. In my life I want to be smart, I want to finish college, I want to be good at my job. But I don't want to be attractive."

According to Marsh, Eric's sentiment is typical of both male and female victims.

"The idea that they don't want any type of attention, or anything remotely resembling sexual advances," Marsh said. "I think there's a fear that this could happen again. And if they make themselves so unappealing, they won't get hurt the way they've been hurt before."

Like many other victims, Eric doesn't think the punishment for sexual assault at colleges is sufficient.

"If we treated rape the way we treated plagiarism on college campuses, there would be minimal rape," Eric insisted. "They expel people all the time for plagiarism."

However, punishment for rape is just one part of the solution. LaPore, founder of 1in6, believes resources need to be more easily accessible for men, including the way clinics and programs are named and advertised. "If we could become willing to be inclusive, we would see more men willing to come forward and say we would like some help," he said.

Michael Rose, who was in the same coed fraternity as Andrew at Brown, believes the role of bystanders is also integral. "Making sure every space is a safe space" is important, he said. "If more people can be trained as bystanders, and feel comfortable intervening. That's huge."

Rose was surprised when Andrew told him about the assault. Despite Rose's involvement in Brown's Sexual Assault Peer Education program, Andrew was the first male survivor he had met.

"We were just together in the lounge and we had been talking about consensual sex and life on campus, and he mentioned to me he'd been assaulted his first semester," Rose said. "I was shocked at first. You never want it to happen, but especially not to someone you know."

Rose was one of the first people Andrew told about his assault. He told his parents about it the following summer and came out as a survivor to his friends on Facebook during his junior year, when he participated in an online campaign for sexual assault survivors called Project Unbreakable.

He also participated in "Carry That Weight" in solidarity with Sulkowicz's campaign by carrying a stall door, since his assault occurred in a bathroom.

Both experiences helped Andrew in his healing process. Upon sharing his story, he received encouragement from his friends and family. "My parents were pretty supportive," he said. "They reiterated the points that I was still valuable and it had no impact on how they thought of me."

Andrew is now a senior at Brown. He's finishing his concentration in Urban Studies, writing a thesis on suburban poverty and completing an applied music program. A sign on his dorm door reads, "Hi! Come talk to me about sexual assault, consent, relationships or really anything."

Walking along the campus green, Andrew seems energized. He talks about the campus buildings and how they provide a great microcosm for exploring urban planning. Specifically, he likes to think about transportation and how it connects people.

As Andrew passes the auditorium where he had his freshman orientation on sexual assault, he says he wants to continue advocating for sexual assault victims. He believes telling his story could make a difference, especially for men. "There are a lot of male survivors who haven't found someone they can relate to," he said. "I want to break the silence, and I want other men to know that they're not alone."

This article has been updated with new information regarding an incident in 2011 involving a fourth student who had made a complaint to the university about the same perpetrator. The complaint resulted in the university issuing a no-contact order between the two students. Brown declined to comment on the incident.

## Critical Thinking

1. Why do you think schools like Brown don't simply expel students who have harmed other students?

2. Does it surprise you to read about male victims of sexual violence on college campuses?

3. Do you think it would be better to report all these incidents directly to the police?

## Internet References

**LA Times**

http://www.latimes.com/local/lanow/la-me-ln-california-teacher-sex-students-20150122-story.html

**NJ.com**

http://www.nj.com/news/index.ssf/2013/04/a_look_at_teacher-student_sex.html#incart_m-rpt-1

**S.E.S.A.M.E.**

http://www.sesamenet.org/survivors/male-survivors/12-survivors/male-survivors/1-male-victims

**TDCAA**

http://www.tdcaa.com/node/1277

# Unit 3

# UNIT

# The Police

Prepared by: Joanne Naughton

Police officers are the guardians of our rights under the Constitution and the law, and as such they have an awesome task which, in turn, requires furnishing police with immense powers. They are asked to maintain order, prevent crime, protect citizens, arrest wrongdoers, aid the sick, control juveniles, control traffic, and provide emergency services on a moment's notice. Sometimes in the service of these duties, police officers may sustain injuries or lose their lives.

In recent years, the job of the police officer has become even more complex and dangerous. Illegal drug use and trafficking are still major problems; racial tensions are explosive; and terrorism is now an alarming reality. As our population grows more numerous and diverse, the role of the police in America becomes ever more challenging, requiring skills that can only be obtained by greater training and professionalism. It is also vital that the public be aware of how their various police departments are carrying out their duties, providing citizen oversight.

*Article*

Prepared by: Joanne Naughton

# The Changing Environment for Policing, 1985–2008

DAVID H. BAYLEY AND CHRISTINE NIXON

## Learning Outcomes

*After reading this article, you will be able to:*

- State the differences between the policing environments in 1985 and 2008.
- Relate some of the challenges facing police executives today.
- Show how the growth of private security affects policing.

## Introduction

In 1967, the President's Commission on Law Enforcement and the Administration of Justice published *The Challenge of Crime in a Free Society*. This publication is generally regarded as inaugurating the scientific study of the police in America in particular but also in other countries. Almost 20 years later, the John F. Kennedy School of Government, Harvard University, convened an Executive Session on the police (1985–1991) to examine the state of policing and to make recommendations for its improvement. Its approximately 30 participants were police executives and academic experts. Now, 20 years further on, the Kennedy School has again organized an Executive Session. Its purpose, like the first, is to combine professional with scholarly appraisals of the police and their contribution to public safety.

So the question naturally arises, what are the differences in the environment for policing between these two time periods? Are the problems as well as the institution of the police similar or different from one period to the next? Our thesis is that policing in the mid-1980s was perceived to be in crisis and there was a strong sense that fundamental changes were needed in the way it was delivered. In contrast, police are considered to be performing well 20 years later by both practitioners and outside observers. Crime has been falling for almost 18 years and any new challenges, including terrorism, appear to be manageable without the invention of new strategies for the delivery of police services. Past experience contains the lessons needed for the future. In our view, this assessment may be mistaken, not because existing policies are defective in controlling crime but because the institutions that provide public safety are changing in profound ways that are not being recognized.

## The Policing Environment in 1985

Policing in the United States was under siege in the 1980s for two reasons: (1) crime had been rising from the early 1960s, and (2) research had shown that the traditional strategies of the police were ineffective at coping with it. In 1960, the serious crime rate was 1,887 per 100,000 people. In 1985 it was 5,224, almost a threefold increase. This trend peaked in 1990 at 5,803. Violent crime (i.e., murder, rape, robbery and aggravated assault) rose from 161 per 100,000 people in 1960 to 558 in 1985, on the way to quadrupling by 1991 (Maguire and Pastore, 2007). Crime was, understandably, a big issue, feeding what could properly be called a moral panic.

Prompted by the President's Commission on Law Enforcement and the Administration of Justice in 1967, researchers in universities and private think-tanks began to study the effectiveness of standard police strategies. In the ensuing two decades, studies were published showing that crime rates were not affected by:

- Hiring more police (Loftin and McDowell, 1982; Krahn and Kennedy, 1985; Koenig, 1991; Laurie, 1970; Gurr, 1979; Emsley, 1983; Silberman, 1978; Reiner, 1985; Lane, 1980).
- Random motorized patrolling (Kelling et al., 1974; Kelling, 1985; Morris and Heal, 1981).
- Foot patrols (Police Foundation, 1981).
- Rapid response to calls for service (Tien, Simon and Larson, 1978; Bieck and Kessler, 1977; Spelman and Brown, 1981).
- Routine criminal investigation (Laurie, 1970; Burrows, 1986; Greenwood, Petersilia and Chaiken, 1977; Eck, 1982; Royal Commission on Criminal Procedure, 1981).

These conclusions, despite challenges to some of them on methodological grounds, were considered authoritative. They were so well accepted, in fact, that Bayley could say in 1994 that "one of the best kept secrets of modern life" was that the police do not prevent crime. "Experts know it, the police know it, and the public does not know it" (Bayley, 1994:3).

No wonder, then, that the first Executive Session concluded that fundamental changes were needed in police strategies. The Session took the lead in developing and legitimating a new model for the delivery of police services—community policing. The key recommendation was that police needed to be reconnected to the public in order both to enhance their crime-control effectiveness and to increase public respect. The strategy for doing this was community policing, including problem-oriented policing (Trojanowicz and Bucqueroux, 1990; Goldstein, 1990). Of the 17 studies published by the first Executive Session as *Perspectives on Policing,* eight featured "community" or "community policing" in the title, and several others discussed the importance of community. George Kelling and Mark Moore, members of the session, argued that the evolution of American policing could be described as movement from a politicized system to professionalism, then to constitutionalism, and ultimately to community policing (Kelling and Moore, 1988).

The first Executive Session also encouraged a new management style for policing, namely, one based on the analysis of crime and disorder problems and the evaluation of remediation programs. This process of description and analysis was to be carried out jointly by police and outside experts, such as academic scholars and management consultants.

## The Policing Environment in 2008

When the second Executive Session met in January 2008, crime in the United States had declined dramatically since 1990. The serious crime rate (Part I crimes) had fallen to 3,808 per 100,000 people by 2006, a decline of 34 percent (Maguire and Pastore, 2007).[1] Even though the violent crime rate was still three times higher in 2006 than in 1960 (474 versus 161 per 100,000 people), it had declined by 37.5 percent since its peak in 1991, a huge change for the better. The police, in particular, feel that the decline vindicates their crime-control efforts, notably the strategy attributed to Bill Bratton of New York City, of the strict enforcement of laws against disorder and the management technique known as *zero tolerance,* managed through COMPSTAT (Bratton and Knobler, 1998; Eck and Maguire, 2000).

The decline has been so dramatic that it offset the continued questioning by analysts of the importance of police action in controlling crime (Eck and Maguire, 2000). Furthermore, there are now positive findings about the efficacy of certain police strategies. The most authoritative summary of this research comes from a panel of the National Research Council (Skogan and Frydl, 2004).

Reviewing all research conducted since the President's Commission (1967) and available in English, the panel reaffirmed the findings of the 1970s and 1980s that the standard practices of policing—employing more sworn officers, random motorized patrolling, rapid response and criminal investigation—failed to reduce crime when applied generally throughout a jurisdiction. It should be noted that most of the research on these topics, except for analysis of the effect of the number of

police employees on crime, dated from the earlier period. At the same time, the panel found that police could reduce crime when they focused operations on particular problems or places and when they supplemented law enforcement with other regulatory and abatement activities.

The strongest evidence for effectiveness was some form of problem solving, especially when focused on "hot spots," that is, locations accounting for a high volume of repeat calls for police service. Nonenforcement options included changing the physical design of buildings and public spaces, enforcing fire and safety codes, providing social services to dysfunctional families, reducing truancy and providing after-school programs for latch-key children.

By 2008, police executives could feel much happier about their efforts to control crime than they had 20 years before. Scholars, too, agreed that strategies used since the 1980s were efficacious, by and large.

This is not to say that police leaders currently feel that they can rest on their laurels nor that the environment for policing is entirely benign. Police executives understand that they are confronting several challenges, some new and some old:

- **Declining budgets and the rising cost of sworn police officers.** The cost of policing has quadrupled between 1985 and 2005, according to the Bureau of Justice Statistics (Gascón and Foglesong, 2009). The causes are rising labor costs for both sworn officers and civilian personnel, increased demand for police services and the growing complexity of police work. As a result, police budgets are increasingly at risk, with some cities reducing the number of police officers per capita.

- **Terrorism.** The primary impact of the Sept. 11 terrorist attack on state and local policing in the United States has been to improve their capacity for risk assessment of local vulnerabilities and first-responding in the event of terrorist incidents (Bayley and Weisburd, 2009). Although threat assessment and first-responding are understood to be core responsibilities of local police, their role with respect to counterterrorism intelligence gathering and analysis is more problematic. At the moment, most intelligence about terrorism comes from federal sources. Some observers take the view that local law enforcement, especially in the United States with its radically decentralized police system, does not have the personnel or skills to collect operational intelligence in a cost-effective way. Others argue, however, that local general-duties police who work among the population are essential for detecting precursor terrorist activities and building cooperative relations with the communities in which terrorists live (Bayley and Weisburd, 2009). Many police executives are critical of the federal government, therefore, for downgrading its law enforcement attention from nonterrorist crime and for reducing its support for local community-responsive and crime-prevention activities.

- **New immigrants, both legal and illegal.** Until recently, most American police departments took the view that enforcing immigration was a federal rather than a local responsibility. They took this view, in part, because they wanted illegal immigrants to feel free to approach police when they were victims of crime, particularly when they were exploited by employers. Police executives felt that even people who were in the country illegally deserved protection under the law. Recently, however, driven by growing anti-illegal immigration feelings in their jurisdictions, some police departments have begun to enforce immigration regulations. As anticipated, this has alienated these communities at the very moment when the importance of connecting with immigrants—legal as well as illegal—has become imperative as a response to terrorism. Not only may foreign terrorists take cover in immigrant communities but these communities, especially if they are disadvantaged and marginalized, may produce their own home-grown perpetrators. Great Britain and France have both experienced this phenomenon. Thus, the threat of terrorism raises difficult questions about the scope, intensity and methods of law enforcement in immigrant communities.

- **Racial discrimination.** Charges of unequal treatment on the basis of race have been a continual problem for police since the rise of civil rights consciousness in the 1960s. Concerns raised about the substantial amount of discretion possessed by frontline police was one of the first issues taken up by police researchers more than 40 years ago. Various aspects of policing have been implicated—arrests, use of force, shootings, street stops, search and seizure, offense charging and equality of coverage (Fridell et al., 2001; Skolnick and Fyfe, 1993; Walker, 2003). Not only is racial discrimination an enduring issue for police executives to manage but its potential for destroying the reputation of police agencies and the careers of officers is hard to exaggerate. It is the allegation that every police chief dreads.

- **Intensified accountability.** Oversight of police performance, with regard to effectiveness in controlling both crime and personal behavior, has grown steadily in the past few years. The monitoring of institutional performance has been part of a governmentwide movement to specify measurable performance indicators. External oversight of individual behavior has involved complaints commissions, citizen review panels and ombudsmen. Many would argue that the quality of policing with respect to crime control and personal behavior has improved over the last half of the 20th century as a result of these developments. The public, however, seems more skeptical, especially with respect to the behavior of individual officers. At least that would be a fair reading of the fact that in the United States as well as other English-speaking countries, the demand for greater oversight of police behavior continues to grow, fed by the media's insatiable appetite for stories about police misdeeds.

There are two aspects to what is being asked for: (1) holding the police to account for performing the services for which they were created—crime prevention and criminal investigation and (2) disciplining officers who behave improperly in the course of their duties.

Today, more than 100 of America's largest cities have some sort of civilian oversight of police behavior compared with only a handful in the early 1990s (Walker, 2003). Independent civilian review of complaints against the police has been established in the last three decades in Great Britain, New Zealand, Australia and Canada. But this is only the most visible tip of a larger iceberg. Oversight has also intensified in the form of tighter financial auditing, performance indicators mandated by governmental and quasi-governmental bodies, enactment of more stringent legal standards and federal consent decrees. This is in addition to what seems to police to be an unappeasable media appetite for revelations about police, and even ex-police, misbehavior.

- **Police unions.** While acknowledging the reasons that led to the growth of police unions, police executives complain about its impact on management. In particular, they criticize the reflexive defense of work rules that inhibit strategic innovation and organizational change, the elaborate procedures required to discipline poorly performing officers, and the inculcation of an occupational culture preoccupied with tangible rewards.

Although all of these current challenges certainly complicate their work, police executives do not view them as a crisis for policing as was the case in the mid-1980s. These challenges are complex and difficult but manageable within the competence of experienced executives. With the arguable exception of terrorism, they do not require a shift in the strategies of policing.

Embedded in this sense of achievement among police professionals is frustration with the gap between objective measures of public safety and public perceptions. Although crime may have declined, the public's fear has not. Police commonly attribute this discrepancy to the exaggeration of crime by the media and the failure to give credit where credit is due.

## The Looming Watershed

We believe that policing may be approaching, if not well into, a period of change that will significantly affect what police do and how they do it. It may be as significant as the period after 1829 when Sir Robert Peel created the London Metropolitan Police. The choice of 1829 as the reference point is not rhetorical. This year marked the beginning of the gradual monopolization of the police function by government. Starting in 1829, governments in Anglo-Saxon countries, much earlier in Europe, assumed responsibility for policing—for hiring, paying, training and supervising. What is happening now is the reverse of that: nation-states are losing their monopoly on policing.

The pressures eroding the monopoly of governments within national boundaries to create and manage policing come from three directions:

- The internationalization of policing.
- The devolution of policing to communities.
- The growth of private policing.

In short, policing is being pushed up, down and sideways from its traditional mooring in government.

## The Internationalization of Policing

Policing has shifted away from national governments because of the development of a genuinely international police capacity and increased international collaboration in law enforcement. The United Nations now has more than 11,000 police recruited from about 118 countries and deployed in 13 missions. The United States currently contributes 268 police to UNPOL (formerly CIVPOL). Although UNPOL's primary mission is "to build institutional police capacity in post-conflict environments" (Kroeker, 2007), its officers have been armed in Kosovo, Timor-Leste and Haiti and enforce laws alongside the local police. It is worth mentioning that this is part of a broader development of international institutions of justice, including the development of a portable international criminal code, courts and tribunals authorized to try individuals, and prisons for persons both convicted and under trial.

The United States now collaborates widely with law enforcement agencies abroad. As of February 2010, the FBI has offices in 70 cities overseas and the DEA has offices in almost 90 (see FBI and DEA home pages). The United States trains more than 10,000 police a year at its four International Law Enforcement Training Academies (located in Budapest, Bangkok, Gaborone and San Salvador) and brings many more trainees to the United States. The United States also participates in a host of international task forces and ad hoc law enforcement operations that focus on drugs, terrorism, trafficking in people and, more recently, cyber-crime, including pornography. The United States has also encouraged—some would say "pressured"—countries to bring their laws into conformity with American practice, for example, with respect to wiretapping, the use of informants, asset forfeiture, and the Racketeer Influenced and Corrupt Organizations Act (Nadelman, 1997; Snow, 1997). American influence, direct and indirect, has been so powerful that Chris Stone says there has been an "Americanization of global law enforcement" (Stone, 2003). The United States, furthermore, has begun to create a reserve force of police and other criminal justice experts that can be deployed at short notice to countries emerging from conflict.

If policing is a fundamental attribute of government, along with external defense, then the world has begun to create a world government of sorts. Although seeds of this movement preceded the first Executive Session, a major impetus was the fall of the Berlin Wall in 1989 and the subsequent implosion of the Soviet Union (Bayley, 2006).

## The Devolution of Policing to Communities

The attitude of police generally in the Western world, but especially in its English-speaking democracies, toward collaborating with members of the public who act voluntarily to improve public security has undergone a major change since the 1980s. No longer viewed as nuisances or dangerous vigilantes, these people are now seen as "co-producers" of public safety. This transformation of view is attributable in large part to the acceptance of community policing, which the first Executive Session was instrumental in promoting. Police in democratic countries now actively encourage citizen participation by sharing information, training volunteers, consulting the public about priorities, mobilizing collaborative crime-prevention programs, enlisting the public as informants in problem solving, and soliciting help from city planners, architects and the designers of products to minimize criminal opportunities. Neighborhood Watch is probably the best known police-citizen partnership. Others include Business Improvement Districts, mobile CB-radio patrols, and private-sector programs for providing equipment and professional skills to police departments.

It has become axiomatic in policing that the public should be encouraged to take responsibility for enhancing public safety. As police themselves now recognize, they cannot do the job alone. Public participation is seen by police and academics alike as a critical contributor to police effectiveness and thus to public safety.

## The Growth of Private Policing

Policing is being pushed sideways by the growth in the private security industry. Estimates of its strength are not exact because "private security" covers a wide range of activities— e.g., guarding, transporting valuables, investigating, installing protective technology and responding to alarms—and is supplied by companies commercially to others as well as by businesses to themselves. The U.S. Department of Labor estimated that there were slightly more than 1 million private security guards in 2005 (U.S. Bureau of Labor Statistics, 2005). That would be 49 percent more than the number of full-time sworn police officers in the same year (673,146). A report issued by the International Association of Chiefs of Police (IACP) and the Community Oriented Police Services (COPS) Office estimated, however, that in 2004, the number was about 2 million (IACP, 2005). If that were true, there would be almost three times as many private security personnel as full-time police officers. The discrepancy between figures of the Department of Labor and those of IACP-COPS may have arisen because the larger estimate includes in-house security provided by private organizations, whereas the Department of Labor figures only include the personnel of companies providing security services commercially. The larger figure is the one most often cited in commentaries on private policing (Cunningham and Taylor, 1985; Singer, 2003).

The growth of private security appears to be a phenomenon of the last quarter of the 20th century (Nalla and Newman, 1991). It was first documented in *The Hallcrest Report: Private Security and Police in America* (Cunningham and Taylor, 1985), which estimated the number at 1.5 million. This was more than twice the number of public police at that time. Although the use of private security was certainly visible to police officials in the 1980s, the number of *commercial* private security personnel has grown by as much as two-thirds. Their number rose sharply immediately after the Sept. 11 attack, fell in 2003 (although not to pre-Sept. 11 levels) and has continued to increase (U.S. Bureau of Labor Statistics, 2007). It is reasonable to assume that the number of *in-house* private security personnel has also increased, though perhaps not as much.

Worldwide, there are now more private police than government-run police: 348 versus 318 per 100,000, according to a survey by Jan Van Dijk (2008). The highest rates are in the United States, Canada and central Europe. Britain and Australia also have slightly more private security personnel than public police (Australian Bureau of Statistics, 2006; European Union, 2004). In the European Union, only Britain and Ireland have more private than public police (European Union, 2004). Statistics are not available for Latin America, Africa, and South and Southeast Asia, but private security is certainly very visible there.

The point to underscore is that worldwide, and dramatically in the United States, there has been a steady growth in the number of private "police." If visible guardians are a deterrent to crime, as the routine-activities theory of crime asserts and as police themselves strongly believe, then one reason for the decline in crime in the United States since the early 1990s might be the growth in private security. As far as we are aware, analyses of the crime drop in the United States have not tested for this possibility.

The effect of these three changes in the environment for policing is to diversify the providers of public safety. Governments, especially country-based governments, no longer direct or provide public safety exclusively. The domestic security function has spread to new levels of government but, more important, to nonstate actors, volunteers and commercial providers. The police role is now shared. This is not simply saying that there are now both public and private police. Public and private policing have blended and are often hard to distinguish. Governments hire private police to supplement their own police; private entrepreneurs hire public police. We are in an era of what Les Johnston refers to as hybrid policing (Johnston, 1992).

Until now, assessments of the police have focused on two questions: How can they be made more effective, and how can the behavior of individual officers be improved? Now, we suggest, a third question has arisen: Who is responsible for policing?

## Changes within Public Policing

Not only are changes occurring in the environment that may affect the structure of policing but police themselves are in the process of changing the way they work. The factors driving this are (1) the threat of terrorism, (2) intelligence-led policing and (3) DNA analysis. Each of these developments transfers initiative in directing operations to specialists who collect and analyze information and away from both general-duties police and the public. Ironically, these changes could undo the signature contribution of the 1980s—community policing.

### The Threat of Terrorism

Although many anti-terrorism experts understand the importance of working with communities, especially immigrant ones, counterterrorism centralizes decision making, shifting it upward in police organizations and making it less transparent. In the aftermath of Sept. 11, a new emphasis has been placed on the development of covert intelligence gathering, penetration and disruption. In the United States, the development of covert counterterrorism capacity has been unequally distributed, being more pronounced in larger police forces. Where it occurs, important questions arise about legal accountability as well as operational payoff. These issues are familiar to police, having arisen before in efforts to control illegal narcotics and organized crime.

### Intelligence-Led Policing

Intelligence-led policing[2] utilizes crime mapping, data mining and the widespread use of closed-circuit television monitoring, which all rely on analysis based on information collected from impersonal sources. It thereby empowers senior commanders to develop their own agendas for law enforcement rather than consulting with affected communities.

### DNA Analysis

DNA analysis allows crimes to be solved without witnesses or confessions. Research in the 1970s showed that the identification of suspects by victims and witnesses was essential to the solving of most crimes (Greenwood, Petersilia and Chaiken, 1977). Detectives, contrary to their fictional portrayals, work from the identification of suspects by the public back to the collection of evidence to prove guilt. DNA changes that, emphasizing forensic evidence over human testimony, promising a technological solution to criminal identification.

The effect of these developments—the threat of terrorism, intelligence-led policing and DNA analysis—impels the police to rely more on their own intellectual and physical resources and on centralized decision making for agendas and strategies. It lessens the importance of consulting with and mobilizing the disaggregate resources of communities. It also favors enforcement as the tool of choice over preventive strategies of regulation and abatement. These changes in orientation may be necessary and may raise police effectiveness, but they also represent a return to the sort of insular professionalism that characterized policing before the 1980s.

## The Challenges of Change

The changes described both inside and outside the established police structures and functions create issues that will have to be confronted. With the expansion of private policing, public safety may become more inequitably distributed on the basis of economic class. The affluent sectors of society, especially its commercial interests, may be more protected, and the poor sectors less protected (Bayley and Shearing, 2001). This trend could be exacerbated if the tax-paying public at the same time withdraws its support from the public police in favor of private security. There are indications that this has already occurred in public education, where people with the means to pay for private schools are increasingly reluctant to support public education. If this should occur in policing, a dualistic system could evolve—responsive private policing for the affluent, and increasingly underfunded public policing for the poor (Bayley and Shearing, 2001). The political consequences of this could be calamitous.

Furthermore, who is to hold private policing to legal and moral account? Public police in the United States and other democracies have been made accountable in many ways.

Public police executives themselves often argue that they are too accountable, meaning they are scrutinized too closely, too mechanically and at a substantial cost in reporting. Private policing, however, is imperfectly regulated and it is unclear whether existing law provides sufficient leverage (Joh, 2004; Prenzler and Sarre, 2006).

So, an ironic question arises: Is there a continuing role for government in ensuring an equitable and lawful distribution of security at the very time that government is losing its monopoly control? Should it accomplish by regulation what it no longer can by ownership? If so, how should this be done? In particular, what agency of government would be responsible for it?

The internationalization of policing also raises issues of control and legitimacy. Simply put, whose interests will be served by policing under international auspices? Will it be collective interests articulated by constituent states and powerful organized interests, or by the needs of disaggregate populations represented through participative institutions? Democratic nation-states emphasize the needs of individuals in directing police. It is not at all clear that international institutions will do the same, although they have taken impressive steps on paper to articulate comprehensive standards of police conduct (U.N. High Commissioner for Human Rights, 1996).

Finally, we submit that policing may be facing a clash of cultures as the public increasingly demands participation in the direction and operation of policing while at the same time police agencies become more self-directing and self-sufficient in their use of intelligence resources. This issue is not new. It is the same issue that policing faced in the 1980s and that was tackled in the first Executive Session. How important is public legitimacy for police effectiveness and public safety? How can the support of the public be maintained while police take advantage of powerful new technologies that may decrease interaction with them?

## Conclusion

In the United States and other developed democracies, changes are occurring that may undermine the monopoly of state-based policing as well as its community-based paradigm. In pointing out these changes between 1985 and 2008, we are not making value judgments about them. These changes may have made the police more effective at providing public safety without infringing human rights in unacceptable ways. We call attention to these changes because their potential effects are enormous and largely unappreciated. They constitute an invisible agenda as consequential as the problems discussed in the 1980s.

Twenty years ago, policing was in the throes of what is now regarded as a revolution in its operating approach. It shifted from a philosophy of "give us the resources and we can do the job" to realizing the importance of enlisting the public in the coproduction of public safety. Policing today faces much less obvious challenges. Current strategies and technologies seem to be sufficient to deal with foreseeable threats to public safety, with the possible exception of terrorism. If this is so, then policing will develop in an evolutionary way, fine-tuning operational techniques according to experience, particularly the findings of

evidence-based evaluations. If, however, changes in the environment are reshaping the structure and hence the governance of policing, and adaptations within the police are weakening the connection between police and public, then we may be entering a period of evolutionary discontinuity that could be greater than that of the 1980s, perhaps even of 1829. Both the role of police in relation to other security providers and the soul of the police in terms of how it goes about its work may be in play today in more profound ways than are being recognized.

## References

Australian Bureau of Statistics. "2006 Census of Population and Housing, Australia, Occupation by Sex (Based on Place of Employment)." Accessed February 11, 2010, at www.censusdata.abs.gov.au.

Bayley, David H. *Police for the Future.* New York: Oxford University Press, 1994.

Bayley, David H. *Changing the Guard: Developing Democratic Police Abroad.* New York: Oxford University Press, 2006.

Bayley, David H. and Clifford Shearing. *The New Structure of Policing: Description, Conceptualization, and Research Agenda.* Final report. Washington, D.C.: U.S. Department of Justice, National Institute of Justice, July 2001. NCJ 187083.

Bayley, David H. and David Weisburd. "Cops and Spooks: The Role of the Police in Counterterrorism." In *To Protect and Serve: Policing in an Age of Terrorism,* ed. David Weisburd, Thomas E. Feucht, Idit Hakimi, Lois Felson Mock and Simon Perry. New York: Springer, 2009:81–100.

Bieck, William and David A. Kessler. *Response Time Analysis.* Kansas City, Mo.: Board of Police Commissioners, 1977.

Bratton, William and Peter Knobler. *Turnaround: How America's Top Cop Reversed the Crime Epidemic.* New York: Random House, 1998.

Burrows, John. *Investigating Burglary: The Measurement of Police Performance.* Research Study 88. London: Home Office, 1986.

Cunningham, William C. and Todd H. Taylor. *The Hallcrest Report: Private Security and Police in America.* Portland, Ore.: Chancellor Press, 1985.

Eck, John E. *Solving Crimes: The Investigation of Burglary and Robbery.* Washington, D.C.: Police Executive Research Forum, 1982.

Eck, John E. and Edward Maguire. "Have Changes in Policing Reduced Violent Crime? An Assessment of the Evidence." In *The Crime Drop in America,* ed. Alfred Blumstein and Joel Wallman. New York: Cambridge University Press, 2000:207–265.

Emsley, Clive. *Policing and Its Context, 1750–1870.* London: Macmillan, 1983.

European Union. "Panoramic Overview of Private Security Industry in the 25 Member States of the European Union." Presentation at Fourth European Conference on Private Security Services, Brussels, Belgium. Confederation of European Security Services and UNI-Europa, 2004. Accessed February 11, 2010, at www.coess.org/pdf/ panormal.pdf.

Fridell, Lori, Robert Lunney, Drew Diamond and Bruce Kubu. *Racially Biased Policing: A Principled Response.* Washington, D.C.: Police Executive Research Forum, 2001.

Gascón, George and Todd Foglesong. "How to Make Policing More Affordable: A Case Study of the Rising Costs of Policing in the United States." Draft paper submitted to the Second Harvard

Executive Session on Policing and Public Safety, Cambridge, Mass., 2009.

Goldstein, Herman. *Problem Oriented Policing*. Philadelphia, Penn.: Temple University Press, 1990.

Greenwood, Peter W., Joan Petersilia and Jan Chaiken. *The Criminal Investigation Process*. Lexington, Mass.: D.C. Heath, 1977.

Gurr, Ted R. "On the History of Violent Crime in Europe and America." In *Violence in America: Historical and Comparative Perspectives,* ed. H.D. Graham and Ted R. Gurr. Beverly Hills, Calif.: Sage Publications, 1979:353–374.

International Association of Chiefs of Police. *Post 9-11 Policing: The Crime Control–Homeland Security Paradigm—Taking Command of New Realities*. Alexandria, Va.: IACP, 2005.

Joh, Elizabeth E. "The Paradox of Private Policing." *Journal of Criminal Law and Criminology* 95(1):(2004)49–131.

Johnston, Les. *The Rebirth of Private Policing*. London: Routledge, 1992.

Kelling, George L. "Order Maintenance, the Quality of Urban Life, and Police: A Different Line of Argument." *In Police Leadership in America,* ed. William A. Geller. New York: Praeger Publishers, 1985:309–321.

Kelling, George L. and Mark H. Moore. *The Evolving Strategy of Policing*. Harvard University, Kennedy School of Government, Perspectives on Policing Series, No. 4. Washington, D.C.: National Institute of Justice, November 1988. NCJ 114213.

Kelling, George L., Antony M. Pate, Duane Dieckman and Charles Brown. *The Kansas City Preventive Patrol Experiment: Summary Report*. Washington, D.C.: Police Foundation, 1974.

Koenig, Daniel J. *Do Police Cause Crime? Police Activity, Police Strength and Crime Rates*. Ottawa, Ontario: Canadian Police College, 1991.

Krahn, Harvey and Leslie Kennedy. "Producing Personal Safety: The Effects of Crime Rates, Police Force Size, and Fear of Crime." *Criminology* 23 (1985): 697–710.

Kroeker, Mark. Informal presentation to biannual meeting of the International Police Advisory Commission, Abuja, Nigeria, January 2007.

Lane, Roger. "Urban Police and Crime in Nineteenth-Century America." In *Crime and justice,* ed. N. Morris and Michael Tonry. Chicago: University of Chicago Press, 1980.

Laurie, Peter. *Scotland Yard*. New York: Holt, Rinehart & Winston, 1970.

Loftin, Colin and David McDowell. "The Police, Crime, and Economic Theory: An Assessment." *American Sociological Review* 47 (1982): 393–401.

Maguire, Kathleen and Ann L. Pastore, eds. *Sourcebook of Criminal Justice Statistics*. Years 2000–2007. Washington, D.C.: U.S. Department of Justice, Bureau of Justice Statistics. Accessed February 11, 2010, at www.albany.edu/sourcebook /about.html.

Morris, Pauline and Kevin Heal. *Crime Control and the Police: A Review of Research*. Research Study 67. London: Home Office, 1981.

Nadelman, Ethan A. "The Americanization of Global Law Enforcement: The Diffusion of American Tactics and Personnel." In *Crime and Law Enforcement in the Global Village,* ed. William F. McDonald. Cincinnati, Ohio: Anderson Publishing, 1997:123–138.

Nalla, Mahesh and Graeme Newman. "Public versus Private Control: A Reassessment." *Journal of Criminal Justice* 19 (1991): 537–549.

Police Foundation. *The Newark Foot Patrol Experiment*. Washington, D.C.: Police Foundation, 1981.

Prenzler, Tim and Rick Sarre. "Private and Public Security Agencies: Australia." In *Plural Policing: A Comparative Perspective,* ed. T. Jones and T. Newburn. London: Routledge, 2006:169–189.

President's Commission on Law Enforcement and the Administration of Justice. *The Challenge of Crime in a Free Society*. Washington, D.C.: U.S. Government Printing Office, 1967.

Reiner, Robert. *The Politics of the Police*. New York: St. Martin's Press, 1985.

Royal Commission on Criminal Procedure. Research Study 17. London: HMSO, 1981.

Shearing, Clifford D. "The Relation Between Public and Private Policing." In *Modern Policing,* ed. N. Morris and Michael Tonry. Chicago: University of Chicago Press, 1992.

Silberman, Charles. *Criminal Violence, Criminal Justice*. New York: Random House, 1978.

Singer, Peter W. *Corporate Warriors: The Rise of the Privatized Military Industry*. Cornell Studies in Security Affairs. Ithaca, N.Y.: Cornell University Press, 2003.

Skogan, Wesley and Kathleen Frydl. *Fairness and Effectiveness in Policing: The Evidence*. Washington, D.C.: National Academies Press, 2004.

Skolnick, Jerome H. and James Fyfe. *Beyond the Law*. New York: Free Press, 1993.

Snow, Thomas. "Competing National and Ethical Interests in the Fight Against Transnational Crime: A U.S. Practitioners Perspective." In *Crime and Law Enforcement in the Global Village,* ed. William F. McDonald. Cincinnati: Anderson Publishing, 1997:169–186.

Spelman, William and Dale K. Brown. *"Calling the Police": Citizen Reporting of Serious Crime*. Washington, D.C.: Police Executive Research Forum, 1981.

Stone, Christopher. "Strengthening Accountability in the New Global Police Culture." Presentation at conference on Crime and the Threat to Democratic Governance, Woodrow Wilson International Center for Scholars, Washington, D.C., 2003.

Tien, James M., James W. Simon and Richard C. Larson. *An Alternative Approach to Police Patrol: The Wilmington Split-Force Experiment*. Washington, D.C.: U.S. Government Printing Office, 1978.

Trojanowicz, Robert C. and Bonnie Bucqueroux. *Community Policing: A Contemporary Perspective*. Cincinnati: Anderson Publishing, 1990.

United Nations High Commissioner for Human Rights. *International Human Rights Standards for Law Enforcement: A Pocket Book on Human Rights for Police*. Geneva, Switzerland: UNHCHR, 1996.

U.S. Bureau of Labor Statistics, U.S. Department of Labor. "May 2005 Occupational Employment and Wage Estimates." Accessed February 11, 2010, at www.bls.gOv/oes/oes_dl/htm#2005_m.

U.S. Bureau of Labor Statistics, U.S. Department of Labor. "Security Guard Employment Before and After 2001." Summary 07–08 (August 2007). Accessed March 22, 2010, at www.bls.gov/opub /ils/pdf/opbils61.pdf.

Van Dijk, Jan. *The World of Crime*. Los Angeles: Sage Publications, 2008.

Walker, Samuel. "The New Paradigm of Police Accountability: The U.S. Justice Department 'Pattern or Practice' Suits in Context." *St. Louis University Public Law Review* 22(1) (2003):3–52.

## Notes

1. The FBI, which provides the statistics on crimes known to the police, stopped calculating a rate for the entire Part I index after 2001. It did, however, continue to publish rates for both violent and property crime, from which a total rate for all Part I crime can be calculated.

2. Intelligence-led policing may be confused with evidence-based policing. Intelligence-led policing refers to the targeting of operations on the basis of specific information, whereas evidence-based policing refers to shaping of operational strategies on the basis of evaluations of their efficacy.

## Critical Thinking

1. Why was community policing developed?
2. What factors are affecting the way policing is done today?
3. Does the increase of private policing present the possibility of problems?
4. What has been the public's reaction to the fact that crime has declined?

## Create Central

www.mhhe.com/createcentral

## Internet References

**Law Enforcement Guide to the World Wide Web**
http://leolinks.com

**National Institute of Justice/National Criminal Justice Reference Service**
www.ncjrs.gov/policing/man199.htm

**DAVID H. BAYLEY** is Distinguished Professor in the School of Criminal Justice at the State University of New York, Albany. **CHRISTINE NIXON** is APM Chair, Victorian Bushfire Reconstruction and Recovery Authority, and State Commissioner of Police, Victoria, Australia (Retired). The authors acknowledge valuable research assistance provided by Baillie Aaron, Research Assistant, in the Program in Criminal Justice and Police Management, John F. Kennedy School of Government, Harvard University.

From *New Perspectives in Policing*, http://goo.gl/dvnJ3 (September 2010). Copyright © by John F. Kennedy School of Government at Harvard University with funding by the National Institute of Justice. This article is available free of charge online at: http://cms.hks.harvard.edu/var/ezp_site/storage/fckeditor/file/pdfs/centers-programs/programs/criminal-justice/NPIP-The-Changing-Environment-for-Policing-1985–2008.pdf.

## *Article*

Prepared by: Joanne Naughton

# Judge Rejects New York's Stop-and-Frisk Policy

JOSEPH GOLDSTEIN

## Learning Outcomes

*After reading this article, you will be able to:*

- Understand the objections to "stop-and-frisk"
- Describe the remedies ordered by the judge in *Floyd v. City of New York*.

In a repudiation of a major element in the Bloomberg administration's crime-fighting legacy, a federal judge has found that the stop-and-frisk tactics of the New York Police Department violated the constitutional rights of minorities in New York, and called for a federal monitor to oversee broad reforms.

In a decision issued on Monday, the judge, Shira A. Scheindlin, ruled that police officers have for years been systematically stopping innocent people in the street without any objective reason to suspect them of wrongdoing. Officers often frisked these people, usually young minority men, for weapons or searched their pockets for contraband, like drugs, before letting them go, according to the 195-page decision.

These stop-and-frisk episodes, which soared in number over the last decade as crime continued to decline, demonstrated a widespread disregard for the Fourth Amendment, which protects against unreasonable searches and seizures by the government, according to the ruling. It also found violations with the 14th Amendment's equal protection clause.

Judge Scheindlin found that the city "adopted a policy of indirect racial profiling by targeting racially defined groups for stops based on local crime suspect data." She rejected the city's arguments that more stops happened in minority neighborhoods solely because those happened to have high-crime rates.

"I also conclude that the city's highest officials have turned a blind eye to the evidence that officers are conducting stops in a racially discriminatory manner," she wrote.

Noting that the Supreme Court had long ago ruled that stop-and-frisks were constitutionally permissible under certain conditions, the judge stressed that she was "not ordering an end to the practice of stop-and-frisk. The purpose of the remedies addressed in this opinion is to ensure that the practice is carried out in a manner that protects the rights and liberties of all New Yorkers, while still providing much needed police protection."

City officials did not immediately comment on the ruling, or on whether they planned to appeal. Mayor Michael R. Bloomberg scheduled a news conference at 1 p.m. to discuss the decision.

To fix the constitutional violations, the judge designated an outside lawyer, Peter L. Zimroth, to monitor the Police Department's compliance with the Constitution.

Judge Scheindlin also ordered a number of other remedies, including a pilot program in which officers in at least five precincts across the city will wear body-worn cameras in an effort to record street encounters. She also ordered a "joint remedial process"—in essence, a series of community meetings—to solicit public input on how to reform stop-and-frisk.

The decision to install Mr. Zimroth, a partner in the New York office of Arnold & Porter, LLP, and a former corporation counsel and prosecutor in the Manhattan district attorney's office, will leave the department under a degree of judicial control that is certain to shape the policing strategies under the next mayor.

Relying on a complex statistical analysis presented at trial, Judge Scheindlin found that the racial composition of a census tract played a role in predicting how many stops would occur.

She emphasized what she called the "human toll of unconstitutional stops," noting that some of the plaintiffs testified that their encounters with the police left them feeling that they did not belong in certain areas of the cities. She characterized each stop as "a demeaning and humiliating experience."

"No one should live in fear of being stopped whenever he leaves his home to go about the activities of daily life," the judge wrote. During police stops, she found, blacks and Hispanics "were more likely to be subjected to the use of force than whites, despite the fact that whites are more likely to be found with weapons or contraband."

The ruling, in *Floyd v. City of New York,* follows a two-month nonjury trial in Federal District Court in Manhattan earlier this year over the department's stop-and-frisk practices.

Judge Scheindlin heard testimony from about a dozen black or biracial men and a woman who described being stopped, and she heard from statistical experts who offered their conclusions based on police paperwork describing some 4.43 million stops between 2004 and mid-2012. Numerous police officers and commanders testified as well, typically defending the legality of stops and saying they were made only when officers reasonably suspected criminality was afoot.

While the Supreme Court has long recognized the right of police officers to briefly stop and investigate people who are behaving suspiciously, Judge Scheindlin found that the New York police had overstepped that authority. She found that officers were too quick to deem as suspicious behavior that was perfectly innocent, in effect watering down the legal standard required for a stop.

"Blacks are likely targeted for stops based on a lesser degree of objectively founded suspicion than whites," she wrote.

She noted that about 88 percent of the stops result in the police letting the person go without an arrest or ticket, a percentage so high, she said, that it suggests there was not a credible suspicion to suspect the person of criminality in the first place.

## Critical Thinking

1. Do you agree with the judge's ruling?
2. Despite the fact that the court's decision has been overturned on appeal, do you believe the incoming mayor should follow the judge's ruling, as he has said he will?

## Create Central

www.mhhe.com/createcentral

## Internet References

**American Civil Liberties Union**
www.aclu.org/racial-justice/racial-profiling
**Jurist**
http://jurist.org/paperchase/2013/11/federal-appeals-court-upholds-stop-and-frisk-ruling.php

*Article*                                                      Prepared by: Joanne Naughton

# Social Media: Legal Challenges and Pitfalls for Law Enforcement Agencies

MICHAEL T. PETTRY

## Learning Outcomes

*After reading this article, you will be able to:*

- Understand why police department employees should not "post first and think later."

- See how an attorney might use an officer's postings on social media in a criminal prosecution.

- Explain how the Supreme Court analyzes First Amendment cases involving public employees.

Current statistics regarding individuals' use of social media are staggering.[1] According to the International Association of Chiefs of Police's (IACP) Center for Social Media website, Facebook users share approximately 684,478 pieces of content every minute, and the average user creates 90 pieces of content each month, including links, news stories, blog posts, notes, photo albums, and videos.[2] Each day 1 million accounts are added to Twitter, and Instagram records approximately a billion "likes" for material posted on the site.[3]

Given the thorough integration of social media into peoples' lives and the ease with which users instantly share their thoughts, opinions, and "status" with family, friends, and strangers, not surprisingly, some users will post items that other people may find inappropriate. This becomes particularly problematic when an employee of a public safety agency posts or is depicted in such material. Because of the significant adverse effects public safety employees' misuse of social media can have on them as witnesses, on agency operations, and on the department's relationship with the community it serves, many police agencies have addressed their employees' use of social media, whether proactively in the form of policy, reactively

in the face of an incident, or both. A former chief of police in Smithfield, Virginia, and past president of the IACP stated, "This is something that all police chiefs around the country, if you're not dealing with it, you better deal with it."[4]

Some law enforcement employees, particularly those accustomed to using social media regularly to communicate with "friends" or "followers," often post material with little or no consideration as to who may have access to it or how it may be shared. Not surprisingly, there have been a number of recent examples of the perils for officers or other department employees who "post first and think later."

Perhaps, further complicating the issue for police agencies, because of evolving generational standards as to what constitutes private information, younger officers and other agency employees may be more inclined to share information publicly that in the past may have been communicated only to family members or close acquaintances. This may be particularly true for members of the generation known as millenials. "Accustomed to documenting their lives in real time on social-media forums like Facebook and Twitter, they are bringing their embrace of self-disclosure into the office with them."[5] Even employees who attempt to limit the type and amount of information placed into the public domain face challenges presented by social media sites' privacy policies that seem to be in constant flux and contain language undecipherable to the average user.[6]

## Pitfalls and the Need for Guidance

In what may be one of the first well-publicized cases of its kind, *New York v. Waters* highlights how an officer's off-duty musings can cause serious repercussions for the integrity of a criminal prosecution.[7] In *Waters* the attorneys assigned to represent the defendant, Gary Waters, in a felony gun possession case learned that the arresting officer had a MySpace account.[8]

During the course of their representation of Waters, the attorneys accessed the officer's MySpace account because much of the information contained on the page was visible to the general public.[9] In perusing the officer's postings, Waters' attorneys learned that he just recently had described his mood as "devious." Jurors also heard how just weeks before the trial the officer's Facebook page's status indicated he was watching the movie *Training Day* to brush up on proper police procedure.[10]

The defense attorneys delved further into the officer's online postings and located comments attributable to him concerning video clips of arrests made by other officers.[11] Commenting on a video of an officer who punched a handcuffed man, the officer opined that "[i]f he wanted to tune him up some, he should have delayed cuffing him."[12] Another comment suggested that "[i]f you were going to hit a cuffed suspect, at least get your money's worth...."[13] These comments played into the defense's theory of the case that the officer and his partner used excessive force against their client and then planted a gun on him to justify the force used in effecting the arrest.

When later asked about the comments he had posted on social media sites, the officer noted, "I'm not going to say it was the best of things to do in retrospect."[14] Referring to Waters' acquittal on the most serious charge of felony possession of a firearm, the officer said, "I feel it's partially my fault" and added, "It paints a picture of a person who could be overly aggressive. You put that together, it's reasonable doubt in anybody's mind."[15]

While the *Waters* case was one of the first where an officer's use of social media adversely affected a court case, there have been innumerable instances over the last several years where law enforcement officers' inappropriate uses of social media sites have garnered unwelcome public attention for both the officer and the agency. For example, in 2011 in Albuquerque, New Mexico, the media quickly learned that the officer involved in an on-duty shooting had listed his occupation on his Facebook page as "human waste disposal."[16] When later asked about the characterization of his job in these terms the officer acknowledged that it was "extremely inappropriate and a lapse in judgment on my part."[17] Another recent example that led to not only negative attention for the officer and his department but also the scrutiny of the U.S. Secret Service was an officer's posting on Facebook of a picture of seven teenagers—some holding guns—along with a bullet-riddled t-shirt bearing the likeness of President Barack Obama. The photograph, entitled "Another trip to the ranch," was taken after the police officer, his son, and several of the son's friends had spent the day shooting targets in the desert. The posting caught the attention of the local news media and prompted a visit from Secret Service agents.[18]

Upon learning of the officer's posting, the Peoria, Arizona, Police Department initiated an internal investigation.[19] Finding that the officer's actions violated the portion of the department's code of conduct that states that "all employees shall conduct themselves in a manner that shall never bring discredit or embarrassment to the city of Peoria or the Peoria Police Department," the department demoted the officer and imposed an 80-hour suspension.[20] The officer, a veteran with many years of distinguished service to the department, was quoted in a news article as saying, "I was an idiot for putting it (the photo) on Facebook, but to have all the pluses in my career forgotten over this one incident, which harmed no one, I think, is taking things too far."[21]

As the above examples illustrate, officers' postings on social media sites can have a negative impact on not only them personally but also their agencies. In addition to compromising their ability to serve as witnesses in criminal proceedings, public safety employees' inappropriate or careless postings on social media sites can impact an agency negatively in a variety of ways.[22] For example, an employee's statements about coworkers and departmental leadership can create dissension in the workplace, involve sexually explicit or inappropriate communication, jeopardize ongoing investigations by revealing sensitive information, or damage a law enforcement agency's relationship with the diverse community it serves.[23]

# First Amendment Issues for Public Employees

Because of the ever-increasing frequency of government employees' use of social media both on and off duty, many law enforcement agencies recently have begun to adopt policies and guidelines that specifically address this issue. These policies set forth the expectations and rules governing employees' use of social media, and violation of them can subject the employee to departmental discipline. Even in the absence of a specific policy regulating the use of social media, employees' use of social media in a manner detrimental to their agency can subject them to discipline for violating other departmental policies and guidelines.[24]

Because public employees' postings, comments, and likes on social media sites likely will be characterized as speech, the protections afforded all citizens under the First Amendment to the Constitution likely will be implicated.[25] "The U.S. Supreme Court long has recognized that individuals do not relinquish their constitutional rights by entering into public service."[26] Indeed, while all public employees retain the rights and protections afforded under the First and other Amendments to the Constitution, the courts have recognized that the government has considerably more ability as an employer to regulate its employees' speech than it would simply as a sovereign.[27] As the cases cited herein illustrate, existing case law provides law enforcement administrators with ample guidance as to the limits they can place on employees' use of social media and the discipline that properly can be imposed in the event an employee's speech violates these standards.

For courts considering whether a government employer has exceeded its ability to restrict employees' speech, the threshold issue to be addressed is whether employees made the statements or created the speech in their official capacity or as private citizens. While the legal standards to be applied in cases arising from an employee's on-duty or official-capacity speech are well-defined, police administrators sometimes are unsure of their ability to regulate speech made by their off-duty employees. Although a detailed analysis of the regulation of public employees' speech is beyond the scope of this article, an overview of the legal landscape governing public employees' First Amendment protections will be provided.

In a series of cases beginning in the late 1960s, the Supreme Court began defining the contours of First Amendment protections afforded public employees.[28] The legal standard used by courts to determine whether government employers had exceeded their ability to sanction employees for their speech required them to balance the employee's interests as private citizens commenting on matters of public concern against the government employer's interest in conducting its operations efficiently.[29] Under this standard the courts were required to begin their analysis by determining whether the speech in question, as a matter of law, touched on a matter of public concern.

According to the Supreme Court, speech on a matter of public concern is speech that is "a subject of legitimate news interest; that is, a subject of general interest of value and concern to the public at the time of publication."[30] If the speech in question does not touch on a matter of public concern, the courts will defer to the government employer's decision to discipline employees for their speech.[31] However, if it is determined that the speech does, in fact, relate to a matter of public concern, the court is required to apply a balancing test. In conducting its analysis of whether the employee's speech is that which warrants constitutional protection, the court will assess its value against the negative effect it has on the government entity's interest in ensuring efficient operations in the workplace.[32]

The Supreme Court first applied this analysis in its decision in *Pickering v. Board of Education,* when it considered whether a school board had improperly terminated a school teacher who had written a letter to a local newspaper critical of the school board's approach to raising revenue for the district.[33] In upholding the terminated employee's claim, the Court found that his speech did not negatively impact the school district's interests in maintaining operational efficiency because he did not have

regular contact with the school board members criticized in the letter.[34] The result might have been different had the employee's actions interfered with the employer's interest in maintaining discipline and a harmonious relationship among coworkers.[35]

Subsequent to its decision in *Pickering,* the Court decided *Connick v. Myers,* in which it considered the First Amendment claim of an assistant district attorney (ADA) who was fired after she prepared and circulated a questionnaire among her coworkers concerning office policies, morale, and their feelings regarding supervisors in the office.[36] In finding that the questionnaire circulated by the former ADA predominantly concerned a private concern versus one of a public nature, the Court rejected the claim.

Although one of the items contained in the questionnaire may have been considered a matter falling within the public concern as it asked whether employees had been pressured into working on political campaigns, the Court found that the employer's concerns about the negative effects associated with the circulation of the questionnaire outweighed the First Amendment value of that portion of the questionnaire.[37] Thus, the holding in *Connick* affirmed the Court's interest in granting government employers sufficient latitude and discretion to manage their internal operations. As the court noted in its opinion:

> When close working relationships are essential to fulfilling public responsibilities, a wide degree of deference to the employer's judgment is appropriate. Furthermore, we do not see the necessity for an employer to allow events to unfold to the extent that the disruption of the office and the destruction of working relationships is manifest before taking action.[38]

## Statements Made by Employees in Their Official Capacity

In 2006 the Supreme Court decided *Garcetti v. Ceballos,* which served to further clarify a government employer's ability to restrict speech made by its employees while serving in their official capacity. In *Garcetti* a deputy district attorney brought a First Amendment claim against his employer, the Los Angeles County District Attorney's Office, stating that it had retaliated against him for writing a memorandum expressing concerns about an affidavit in a criminal case.[39] In rejecting the deputy DA's claim, the Court held that:

> [when] public employees make statements pursuant to their official duties, the employees are not speaking as citizens for First Amendment purposes, and the Constitution does not insulate their communications from employer discipline.[40]

The Court further explained its reasoning by stating:

Restricting speech that owes its existence to a public employee's professional responsibilities does not infringe any liberties the employee might have enjoyed as a private citizen. It simply reflects the exercise of employer control over what the employer itself has commissioned or created.[41]

## Regulation of Public Employees' Off-Duty Speech

Deciding the proper legal analysis to apply when dealing with statements made by off-duty law enforcement officers can be problematic given that officers often are considered to be always on duty. And, indeed, few would argue that employees of public safety agencies are and should be held to a higher standard of conduct both on and off duty.[42] In recognition of the unique position police officers hold in society, the IACP's Code of Ethics states that an officer will "keep my private life unsullied as an example to all and will behave in a manner that does not bring discredit to me or my agency."[43] Police departments' codes of conduct that include language, such as that contained in the Code of Ethics, often impose constraints on employees' behavior as "part of their job is to safeguard the public's opinion of them."[44]

The Court's holding in *Garcetti* reaffirmed the principle that "when a citizen enters government service, the citizen, by necessity, must accept certain limitations on his or her freedom."[45] Thus, in the context of the regulation of employee use of social media, clearly, most statements made by public employees in their official capacity will have few of the First Amendment protections enjoyed by private citizens. However, because many [of] the missteps made by officers in their use of social media occur while off duty, the government employer will need to determine whether the employee was speaking as a private citizen and whether the speech concerned a matter of public concern.

In its decision in *City of San Diego v. Roe,* the Supreme Court used its existing "public concern" test to determine whether an officer's off-duty behavior warranted protection under the First Amendment.[46] Although not directly addressing the issue of an officer's inappropriate use of social media, the *Roe* decision, nonetheless, provides a government employer with considerable guidance as to how it can discipline employees for off-duty speech that it views as harmful to its mission.

*Roe* involved the case of a San Diego, California, police officer who was terminated after it was discovered that he had offered for sale on the adults-only section of eBay a video of himself stripping off a police uniform and masturbating.[47] Although the uniform worn by the officer in the video was not the specific uniform worn by members of the San Diego police force, it was clearly identifiable as a police uniform.[48] His eBay user name was *Code3stud@aol.com,* a reference to an emergency police radio call.[49]

A police department investigation into the officer's activities on the eBay site concluded that he had violated several departmental policies, including conduct unbecoming an officer, engaging in outside employment, and immoral conduct.[50] When confronted with the results of the internal investigation, the officer admitted to selling the videos and police paraphernalia.[51] The department ordered the officer to "cease displaying, manufacturing, distributing or selling any sexually explicit materials or engaging in any similar behaviors, via the internet, U.S. mail, commercial vendors or distributors, or any other medium available to the public."[52] Although the officer complied with several of the department's requirements, he failed to remove his seller's profile from the site. The department terminated the officer when it learned of his failure to follow its previous directive.[53]

Following his dismissal the officer brought suit in federal court claiming that the department's termination of his employment violated his First Amendment right to free speech.[54] In granting the city's motion to dismiss, the district court agreed that Roe's conduct in selling the official police uniforms and the production and sale of the sexually explicit material was not speech that related to a matter of "public concern" under the test set forth in *Connick.*[55] In its reversal of the district court's decision to grant the city's motion to dismiss the officer's suit, the Ninth Circuit Court of Appeals held the officer's "conduct fell within the protected category of citizen commentary on matters of public concern" due to the fact that the public expression did not relate to an internal workplace grievance, occurred while he was off duty and away from the workplace, and did not relate to his employment.[56]

The city appealed the decision to the Supreme Court, which began its analysis of the case by reaffirming the principle that "[a] government employee does not relinquish all First Amendment rights otherwise enjoyed by citizens just by reason of his or her employment."[57] According to the Court, "when government employees speak or write on their own time on topics unrelated to their employment, the speech can have First Amendment protection, absent some governmental justification 'far stronger than mere speculation' in regulating it."[58]

In determining whether the officer's off-duty expressive conduct warranted protection under the First Amendment, the Court relied upon the analytical framework it had adopted in *Connick,* which requires an examination of the "content, form, and context of a given statement, as revealed by the whole record," to determine whether the employee's speech involves a matter of public concern.[59] Applying that standard to the facts of *Roe,* the Court concluded that the officer's "expression does not qualify as a matter of public concern under any view of the public concern test."[60] In its opinion reversing the Ninth Circuit, the Court considered whether the San Diego Police Department had "legitimate and substantial interests of its own" that were compromised by the officer's speech.[61] As the Court noted:

> Roe took deliberate steps to link his videos and other wares to his police work, all in a way injurious to his employer. The use of the uniform, the law enforcement reference in the website, the listing of the speaker as 'in the field of law enforcement,' and the debased parody of an officer performing indecent acts while in the course of official duties brought the mission of the employer and the professionalism of its officers into serious disrepute.[62]

Because the officer's conduct clearly implicated his position as a police officer, the Court recognized that the government as an employer had substantial expressive interests of its own that were threatened by his speech, which, thereby, justified its decision to terminate his employment.

Another case that offers guidance to law enforcement agencies confronted with issues involving employees' off-duty speech is *Dible v. City of Chandler*.[63] This case involved an officer terminated from a local police department after it was learned he had been operating a website that featured sexually explicit material involving his wife. Approximately a year after the officer and his wife established the website, rumors about its existence began to circulate through the police department.[64] Thereafter, the officer was ordered to cease all activity involving the website and was placed on administrative leave.[65] Negative publicity for the police department ensued as the local media reported that the website had been operated by a police officer. An internal investigation conducted by the department found that the matter had adversely impacted working conditions at the department and that police officer morale "really hit bottom."[66]

Following his termination for violating the department's regulation against bringing discredit to the City service and for his less-than-candid answers during the internal investigation, the officer appealed to the City's merit board. Evidence was adduced at the hearing that showed officers had been subjected to ridicule because of the website and that one officer was referred to as a "porn whore" by an individual she was trying to arrest.[67] Other negative impacts to the department, such as its difficulty recruiting female police officers, also were considered by the merit board, which affirmed the department's decision to terminate Dible.

The officer and his wife then sued the City of Chandler in federal district court, claiming the City had violated the officer's First Amendment right to freedom of speech when it terminated him for his involvement in setting up and operating the website. The district court granted the City's motion to dismiss the claim, and the officer and his wife appealed to the Ninth Circuit Court of Appeals.

In its decision upholding the City's ability to terminate a police officer for engaging in off-duty expression that could harm the department, the Court questioned whether police officers ever can disassociate themselves from their powerful public position sufficiently to make their speech (and other activities) entirely unrelated to that position in the eyes of their supervisors and the public. Whether overt or temporarily hidden, Ronald Dible's activity had the same practical effect—"it brought the mission of the employer and the professionalism of its officers into serious disrepute."[68]

The U.S. District Court for the District of Oregon's recent decision in *Shepherd v. McGee* directly addresses the First Amendment issues raised by a government employer's imposition of discipline due to an employee's postings to a social media site.[69] In that case the plaintiff, a former employee of the Oregon Department of Human Services (DHS), brought a First Amendment claim alleging she had been wrongfully discharged on account of postings she had made to her personal Facebook page.

At the time of her termination from DHS, the employee served as a child protective services (CPS) caseworker. In that capacity she was responsible for investigating reports of child abuse and neglect and preparing the cases for review and disposition by the juvenile court. Although less than 10 percent of the cases she handled actually were heard by the court, every case could potentially be heard by the court and, therefore, needed to be prepared as if it would.[70] In investigating and preparing the cases for court, the employee worked closely with both the local district attorney's office and the Oregon Department of Justice.

While employed at the DHS the employee maintained a personal Facebook page on which she identified herself as a "Child Protective Services Case Worker at Department of Human Services."[71] The Facebook page contained no disclaimers that the information contained therein was her own personal opinion and not that of her employer. Moreover, none of her posts contained any such clarifying language. The employee's Facebook page's privacy settings made her postings and other content visible to any of her Facebook friends, which numbered in the hundreds, and included among them a local judge, deputy district attorneys, defense attorneys, and more than a dozen law enforcement officers.[72]

While employed at DHS the employee made a number of inflammatory and controversial posts on her personal Facebook page in which, among other things, she criticized her clients' purchases, advocated forced sterilization of certain clients, and suggested that child abusers also should be physically abused. These posts were seen by some of the employee's Facebook friends, including a local defense attorney and judge.

A local DHS manager brought the posts to the attention of the agency's human resources manager, who found that the posts reflected the very sort of biases that the employee should not exhibit due to her position as a caseworker. When questioned about the postings, the employee acknowledged holding some of the beliefs reflected in the posts and admitted she would have a difficult time testifying and explaining her ability to be objective.

DHS officials consulted with government attorneys who handled the agency's cases about the potential impact of the material on the employee's ability to serve as a witness. One of the attorneys, a local prosecutor, opined that the material likely would be considered discoverable and because of its content would need to be disclosed in every dependency hearing involving physical abuse in which the employee was called as a witness. Moreover, the postings would subject the employee to questioning about her views each time she was called to testify in such a case and likely could have an adverse impact on both pending and future cases. The other attorney, an assistant attorney general, noted that as a DHS social services worker, the employee often was singularly responsible for obtaining and recording statements from subjects and witnesses, as well as drafting reports of her observations in a particular case.

The employee's job was compared to that of a police officer, with all of the attendant concerns about reliability, credibility, and issues of bias while serving as a witness. The assistant attorney general concluded that "he would never be able to call her to the stand due to her credibility being terminally and irrevocably compromised."[73] The attorney added that in every case the employee "was involved with and in which she were called to the witness stand, the defense attorney would raise her Facebook postings in order to impeach her and her credibility as a DHS employee."[74] The same attorney further noted that the employee's posts would "reflect adversely and broadly on DHS in the relevant community" and that it was possible that the postings would render her incapable of performing any function for DHS.[75] The above opinions, coupled with the results of DHS' internal investigation into the employee's conduct, resulted in the agency's decision to terminate her employment.

During the course of the litigation following her dismissal from DHS, the employee acknowledged that her job was "to be a neutral appraiser of the settings in which the children live."[76] In her work evaluating dependency cases the employee was not to "consider the employment status, religious beliefs, or political beliefs of the adults in the home, or concern herself with how they chose to spend money or furnish their home."[77] Many of the parents being assessed by the employee received government assistance, such as Temporary Assistance to Needy Families (TANF), food stamps, or the Oregon Health Plan.

Following her termination from the DHS, the employee brought a First Amendment retaliation claim under 42 U.S.C.

§ 1983. In reviewing the matter pursuant to DHS' motion for summary judgment, the district court used a five-part analysis based on the balancing test set forth in *Pickering*.[78] In applying the balancing test to the facts of this case, the court assessed whether the government could demonstrate that the employee's speech "impairs discipline by superiors or harmony among coworkers, has a detrimental impact on close working relationships for which personal loyalty and confidence are necessary, or impedes the performance of the speaker's duties or interferes with the regular operation of the enterprise."[79] The court further noted that the government's interest in avoiding disruption caused by an employee's objectionable speech is greater when the employee serves in a "public contact role."[80]

In support of its position that the nature and contents of the employee's Facebook posts justified her termination, DHS argued that it was indisputable that her actions "compromised her ability to effectively perform her job and the operations of DHS and thus, the government's interest in maintaining efficient operations outweighs Plaintiff's free speech rights."[81] In rejecting the employee's argument that she should not be subject to discipline as her speech had not caused an actual disruption to the operations of the DHS, the court noted that her speech already had disrupted the working relationships she had with the government attorneys responsible for handling her cases in court. Moreover, the court noted that the government was not required to actually allow its operations to be adversely impacted before taking disciplinary action against an employee.

## Considerations in Cybervetting

As individuals' use of social media has grown exponentially, in recent years a number of law enforcement agencies have integrated a cybervetting component into the comprehensive background investigations they conduct on applicants and onboard employees. According to the December 2010 publication *Developing a Cybervetting Strategy for Law Enforcement*, "[c]ybervetting is an assessment of a person's suitability to hold a position using information found on the Internet to help make that determination."[82] Because of the substantial amount of information concerning prospective and current employees that can be located via the Internet, cybervetting can serve as a logical means to identify information about applicants that may impair their ability to serve as a public safety professional.

However, because of the risk that the cybervetting process may yield information that is either inaccurate or relates to legally protected information about the applicant, it is suggested that law enforcement agencies adopt procedures and policies that ensure they are only considering accurate and appropriate information in making employment decisions.[83] The aforementioned publication serves as an excellent introduction to this topic and offers law enforcement employers considerable guidance as to how they can incorporate cybervetting into their employment suitability review in a legally defensible manner.

Employers also should note that in what may very well signal a legislative trend in this area, a number of states recently have passed laws or are considering legislation that would restrict employers' ability to require job candidates or on-board employees to surrender their login credentials or passwords for social media sites.[84] Because these statutes do not exempt public safety agencies, government employers must ensure they are aware of the scope of the applicable statutes prior to attempting to gain access to candidates' or employees' social media accounts. Of course, information publicly available to all Internet users would remain accessible to employers and could be utilized as part of a cybervetting program subject to both federal law and other applicable state statutes.

## Conclusion

As the forgoing cases indicate, courts have provided government employers with considerable guidance as to how they can discipline employees for speech that runs afoul of departmental codes of conduct or is otherwise injurious to the employer's mission. While an objectionable text, email, or posting can be sent quickly, the fallout can be both lasting and significant for the department and the employee.

Within the last several years, many public safety agencies have proactively sought to avoid the pitfalls associated with their employees' use of social media through the adoption of clearly and concisely drafted policies.[85] A well-drafted policy, coupled with efforts to ensure employees are educated about the potential pitfalls of inappropriate use of social media, will serve to protect the agency's operational interests while recognizing the ways government employees can and do use social media responsibly and appropriately.

Agencies that have yet to adopt a social media policy may wish to review IACP's "Model Policy," available on its social media website.[86] IACP has recognized the myriad issues that can arise from public safety employees' use of social media, and its Center for Social Media can serve as an outstanding resource for law enforcement agencies interested in learning more about those issues.

Law enforcement officers of other than federal jurisdiction who are interested in this article should consult their legal advisors. Some police procedures ruled permissible under federal constitutional law are of questionable legality under state law or are not permitted at all.

## Notes

1. For purposes of this article, *social media* will be defined broadly and will encompass all Internet-based resources that integrate user-generated content and user participation. These include social networking sites (e.g., Facebook and MySpace), microblogging sites (e.g., Twitter), photo- and video-sharing sites (e.g., Flickr and YouTube), wikis, (e.g., Wikipedia), blogs, and news sites (e.g., Digg, Reddit). IACP Center for Social Media, *http://www.iacpsocialmedia.org/Resources/GlossaryTerms.aspx* (accessed October 23, 2014).

2. IACP Center for Social Media, *http://www.iacpsocialmedia.org/Resources/FunFacts.aspx* (accessed October 23, 2014).

3. *Id.*

4. Erica Goode, "Police Lesson: Social Network Tools Have Two Edges," *New York Times,* April 6, 2011, *http://www.nytimes.com/2011/04/07/us/07police.html* (accessed October 23, 2014).

5. Lauren Weber and Rachel Emma Silverman, "Workers Share Their Salary Secrets," *The Wall Street Journal,* April 16, 2013, *http://online.wsj.com/article/SB100014241278873243458045784267441685583824.htm* (accessed October 23, 2014).

6. At over 5,000 words, Facebook's privacy policy is longer than the U.S. Constitution. IACP Center for Social Media, *http://www.iacpsocialmedia.org/Resources/FunFacts.aspx* (accessed October 23, 2014).

7. *People v. Waters,* (Kings Co. NY Sup. Ct. 2009).

8. Social networking site similar to Facebook.

9. Jim Dwyer, "The Officer Who Posted Too Much on MySpace," *The New York Times,* March 10, 2009, *http://www.nytimes.com/2009/03/11/nyregion/11about.html* (accessed October 23, 2014).

10. *Id.* The movie *Training Day* depicts the actions of a police officer who engages in corrupt and improper activity while on duty.

11. *Id.*

12. *Id.*

13. *Id.*

14. *Id.*

15. *Id.*

16. Goode, "Police Lesson: Social Network Tools Have Two Edges."

17. Goode, "Police Lesson: Social Network Tools Have Two Edges."

18. Sonu Munshi, "Peoria Officer Who Posted Obama's Image on Facebook Appeals Demotion," AZ Central.com, June 11, 2012, *http://www.azcentral.com/community/peoria/articles/20120611peoria-officer-obama-image-facebook-appeals-demotion.html* (accessed October 23, 2014).

19. *Id.*

20. Upon appeal by the officer, the suspension was reduced from 80 hours to 40 hours. However, the reduction in rank from sergeant to patrol officer was upheld. See, Jennifer Thomas, "Peoria Officer's Demotion Over Obama Photo Upheld, Suspension Reduced," AZ Family.com, November 6, 2012,

*http://www.azfamily.com/news/Peoria-officers-demotion-over-Obama-photo-upheld-suspension-reduced-177503211.html* (accessed October 23, 2014).

21. Sonu Munshi, "Peoria Officer Who Posted Obama's Image on Facebook Appeals Demotion."

22. *Brady v. Maryland,* 373 U.S. 83 (1963), and *Giglio v. United States,* 405 U.S. 150 (1972).

23. IACP National Law Enforcement Policy Center, "Social Media: Concepts and Issues Paper," *http://www.iacpsocialmedia.org/Portals/1/documents/Social%20Media%20Paper.pdf* (accessed October 23, 2014).

24. *Cromer v. Lexington-Fayette Urban Co. Urban Govt.,* 2009 WL 961102 (Ky. App.).

25. *Bland v. Roberts,* 730 F.3d 368, 386 (4th Cir. 2013), in which the court of appeals held that the act of "liking" a political candidate's Facebook page constitutes speech and symbolic expression. The court of appeals characterized the act of liking a political candidate's campaign page as the Internet equivalent of displaying a political yard sign at one's home.

26. Lisa A. Baker, "Speech and the Public Employee," *FBI Law Enforcement Bulletin,* August 2008, p.23, *http://leb.fbi.gov/2008-pdfs/leb-august-2008* (accessed October 23, 2014).

27. *Connick v. Myers,* 461 U.S. 138, 143 (1983); and *Pickering v. Bd. of Educ.,* 391 U.S. 563, 568 (1968).

28. Baker, "Speech and the Public Employee."

29. Baker, "Speech and the Public Employee."

30. *City of San Diego v. Roe,* 543 U.S. 77, 83–84 (2004) (per curiam).

31. *United States v. National Treasury Employees Union,* 513 U.S. 454, 466 (1995) ("[P]rivate speech that involves nothing more than a complaint about a change in the employee's own duties may give rise to discipline without imposing any special burden of justification on the government employer.").

32. *Pickering v. Bd. of Educ.,* 391 U.S. 563, 569–71 (1968).

33. *Id.* at 564–565.

34. *Id.* at 569–570.

35. *Id.* at 570.

36. *Connick,* at 141.

37. *Id.* at 154.

38. *Id.* 151–152.

39. *Garcetti v. Ceballos,* 547 U.S. 410, 421 (2006).

40. *Id.* at 421.

41. *Id.* at 421–22.

42. *Young v. City of Providence,* 404 F.3d 4, 16 (1st Cir. 2005) (characterizing department policy as requiring officers to be in an "on duty" status at all times); *Revene v. Charles County Com'rs,* 882 F.2d 870, 873(4th Cir. 1989); *Davenport v. Bd. of Fire & Police Com'rs,* 2 Ill.App.3d 864, 278 N.E.2d 212, 216 (Ill. App. Ct. 1972) ("[t]here is no distinction between 'off duty' or 'on duty' misconduct by a police officer . . . . [B]y the very nature of his employment a police officer is in the eyes of the public and for the good of the department must exercise sound judgment and realize his responsibilities to the department and the public at all times."); and *Eubank v. Sayad,* 669 S.W. 2d 566, 568 (Mo. Ct. App. 1984) (In a very real sense a police officer is never truly off-duty.).

43. Law Enforcement Code of Ethics, *http://theiacp.org/PublicationsGuides/ResearchCenter/Publications/tabid/299/default* (accessed May 6, 2013). The IACP's Code of Ethics was adopted in the 1950s and has been incorporated into most law enforcement agencies' policies and training materials.

44. *Locurto v. Giuliani,* 447 F.3d 159, 178 (2d Cir. 2006).

45. *Garcetti* at 418.

46. 543 U.S. 77 (2004).

47. *Id.* at 78.

48. *Id.*

49. *Id.*

50. *Id.* at 79.

51. *Id.*

52. *Id.,* citing 356 F.3d 1108, 1111 (9th Cir. 2004) (internal quotations omitted.).

53. *Id.*

54. *Id.*

55. *Id.*

56. *Id.* at 79–80, citing 356 F.3d at 1110, 1113–14.

57. *Id.* at 80.

58. *Id.* at 80, quoting *United States v. National Treasury Employees Union,* 513 U.S. 454, 465, 475 (1995).

59. *Id.* at 83, quoting *Connick,* 461 U.S. at 146–147.

60. *Id.* at 84.

61. *Id.* at 81.

62. *Id.*

63. 515 F.3d 918, 922 (9th Cir. 2008).

64. *Id.* at 923.

65. *Id.*

66. *Id.*

67. *Id.*

68. *Id.* at 926. (Quoting *City of San Diego v. Roe,* 543 U.S. 77, 81 (Internal quotations omitted.)).

69. 986 F. Supp. 2d 1211(D. Or. 2013).

70. *Id.* at 1214.

71. *Id.*

72. *Id.*

73. *Id.* at 1215.

74. *Id.*

75. *Id.* at 1216.

76. *Id.* at 1214.

77. *Id.* at 1214.

78. *Id.* at 1217.

79. *Id.* at 1218 (Quoting *Rankin v. McPherson,* 483 U.S. 378, 388 (1987) (Internal quotations omitted.)).

80. *Id.* at 1218. (Quoting *Pool v. VanRheen,* 297 F.3d 899, 909 (9th Cir. 2002)).

81. *Id.*

82. *Developing a Cybervetting Strategy for Law Enforcement,* IACP, December 2010. *http:www.iacpsocialmedia.org./Portals/1/documents/CybervettingReport.pdf* (accessed October 23, 2014).

83. Criteria, such as race/color, national origin, religion, age, and genetic information, all of which are protected by one or more federal or state laws. Further information regarding the laws covering the various types of discrimination prohibited by federal law can be located at the U.S. Equal Employment Opportunity Commission's website: *http://www.eeoc.gov/laws/types/index.cfm.* Detailed information about the protections afforded under Title II of the Genetic Information Nondiscrimination Act of 2008 (GINIA) can be located at: *http://www1.eeoc.gov/laws/types/genetic.cfm* (accessed October 23, 2014).

84. For a comprehensive list of states that have either already passed or are currently considering legislation governing employer access to social media user names and passwords, the National Conference of State Legislatures' website provides up-to-date information regarding the status of pending bills. *http://www.ncsl.org/issues-research/telecom/employer-access-to-social-media-passwords2013.aspx#2014* (accessed July 23, 2014).

85. In response to a 2013 IACP survey, 69.4% of the 500 law enforcement agencies that responded indicated they have

a social media policy, and an additional 14.3% are in the process of drafting such a policy. The New York City Police Department also recently adopted social media guidelines for its employees. The guidelines were issued in the wake of several instances where officers' use of social media brought embarrassment or unwelcome publicity to the department, including the well-publicized maligning of participants in the West Indian American Day Parade in Brooklyn in 2011. William Glaberson, "N.Y.C. Police Maligned Paradegoers on Facebook," *New York Times,* December 5, 2011, *http://www.nytimes.com/2011/12/06/nyregion/on-facebook-nypd-officers-malign-west-indian-paradgoers.html* (accessed March 5, 2012).

86. IACP, *http://www.iacpsocialmedia.org/portals/1/documents/social%20media%20policy.pdf* (accessed July 25, 2014).

## Critical Thinking

1. Should a law enforcement officer be held to account for what she says or writes while off-duty?

2. Does the First Amendment protect a law enforcement officer's speech?

3. What did the court decide in Shepherd v. McGee?

## Internet References

**FBI Law Enforcement Bulletin**
https://leb.fbi.gov/2008-pdfs/leb-august-2008

**IACP Center for Social Media**
http://www.iacpsocialmedia.org

**IACP**
http://www.theiacp.org/Ethics-Toolkit

**The New York Times**
http://www.nytimes.com/2009/03/11/nyregion/11about.html

Pettry, Michael T. "Social Media: Legal Challenges and Pitfalls for Law Enforcement Agencies," *FBI Law Enforcement Bulletin*, December 9, 2014.  Federal Bureau of Investigation.

*Article*

Prepared by: Joanne Naughton

# Training Officers to Shoot First, and He Will Answer Questions Later

MATT APUZZO

## Learning Outcomes

*After reading this article, you will be able to:*

- Describe William Lewinski's work and show why it is controversial.
- Report Arien Mack's criticism of Lewinski's use of "inattentional blindness" when discussing a police shooting.

Washington—The shooting looked bad. But that is when the professor is at his best. A black motorist, pulled to the side of the road for a turn-signal violation, had stuffed his hand into his pocket. The white officer yelled for him to take it out. When the driver started to comply, the officer shot him dead.

The driver was unarmed.

Taking the stand at a public inquest, William J. Lewinski, the psychology professor, explained that the officer had no choice but to act.

"In simple terms," the district attorney in Portland, Ore., asked, "if I see the gun, I'm dead?"

"In simple terms, that's it," Dr. Lewinski replied.

When police officers shoot people under questionable circumstances, Dr. Lewinski is often there to defend their actions. Among the most influential voices on the subject, he has testified in or consulted in nearly 200 cases over the last decade or so and has helped justify countless shootings around the country.

His conclusions are consistent: The officer acted appropriately, even when shooting an unarmed person. Even when shooting someone in the back. Even when witness testimony, forensic evidence or video footage contradicts the officer's story.

He has appeared as an expert witness in criminal trials, civil cases and disciplinary hearings, and before grand juries, where such testimony is given in secret and goes unchallenged. In addition, his company, the Force Science Institute, has trained tens of thousands of police officers on how to think differently about police shootings that might appear excessive.

A string of deadly police encounters in Ferguson, Mo.; North Charleston, S.C.; and most recently in Cincinnati, have prompted a national reconsideration of how officers use force and provoked calls for them to slow down and defuse conflicts. But the debate has also left many police officers feeling unfairly maligned and suspicious of new policies that they say could put them at risk. Dr. Lewinski says his research clearly shows that officers often cannot wait to act.

"We're telling officers, 'Look for cover and then read the threat,'" he told a class of Los Angeles County deputy sheriffs recently. "Sorry, too damn late."

A former Minnesota State professor, he says his testimony and training are based on hard science, but his research has been roundly criticized by experts. An editor for *The American Journal of Psychology* called his work "pseudoscience." The Justice Department denounced his findings as "lacking in both foundation and reliability." Civil rights lawyers say he is selling dangerous ideas.

"People die because of this stuff," said John Burton, a California lawyer who specializes in police misconduct cases. "When they give these cops a pass, it just ripples through the system."

Many policing experts are for hire, but Dr. Lewinski is unique in that he conducts his own research, trains officers and internal investigators, and testifies at trial. In the protests that have followed police shootings, demonstrators have often asked why officers are so rarely punished for shootings that seem unwarranted. Dr. Lewinski is part of the answer.

# An Expert on the Stand

While his testimony at times has proved insufficient to persuade a jury, his record includes many high-profile wins.

"He won't give an inch on cross-examination," said Elden Rosenthal, a lawyer who represented the family of James Jahar Perez, the man killed in the 2004 Portland shooting. In that case, Dr. Lewinski also testified before the grand jury, which brought no charges. Defense lawyers like Dr. Lewinski, Mr. Rosenthal said. "They know that he's battle-hardened in the courtroom, so you know exactly what you're getting."

Dr. Lewinski, 70, is affable and confident in his research, but not so polished as to sound like a salesman. In testimony on the stand, for which he charges nearly $1,000 an hour, he offers winding answers to questions and seldom appears flustered. He sprinkles scientific explanations with sports analogies.

"A batter can't wait for a ball to cross home plate before deciding whether that's something to swing at," he told the Los Angeles deputy sheriffs. "Make sense? Officers have to make a prediction based on cues."

Of course, it follows that batters will sometimes swing at bad pitches, and that officers will sometimes shoot unarmed people.

Much of the criticism of his work, Dr. Lewinski said, amounts to politics. In 2012, for example, just seven months after the Justice Department excoriated him and his methods, department officials paid him $55,000 to help defend a federal drug agent who shot and killed an unarmed 18-year-old in California. Then last year, as part of a settlement over excessive force in the Seattle Police Department, the Justice Department endorsed sending officers to Mr. Lewinski for training. And in January, he was paid $15,000 to train federal marshals.

If the science is there, Dr. Lewinski said, he does not shy away from offering opinions in controversial cases. He said he was working on behalf of one of two Albuquerque officers who face murder charges in last year's shooting death of a mentally ill homeless man. He has testified in many racially charged cases involving white officers who shot black suspects, such as the 2009 case in which a Bay Area transit officer shot and killed Oscar Grant, an unarmed black man, at close range.

Dr. Lewinski said he was not trying to explain away every shooting. But when he testifies, it is almost always in defense of police shootings. Officers are his target audience—he publishes a newsletter on police use of force that he says has nearly one million subscribers—and his research was devised for them. "The science is based on trying to keep officers safe," he said.

Dr. Lewinski, who grew up in Canada, got his doctorate in 1988 from the Union for Experimenting Colleges and Universities, an accredited but alternative Cincinnati school offering accelerated programs and flexible schedules. He designed his curriculum and named his program police psychology, a specialty not available elsewhere.

# 'Invalid and Unreliable'

In 1990, a police shooting in Minneapolis changed the course of his career. Dan May, a white police officer, shot and killed Tycel Nelson, a black 17-year-old. Officer May said he fired after the teenager turned toward him and raised a handgun. But an autopsy showed he was shot in the back.

Dr. Lewinski was intrigued by the apparent contradiction. "We really need to get into the dynamics of how this unfolds," he remembers thinking. "We need a lot better research."

He began by videotaping students as they raised handguns and then quickly turned their backs. On average, that move took about half a second. By the time an officer returned fire, Dr. Lewinski concluded, a suspect could have turned his back.

He summarized his findings in 1999 in *The Police Marksman,* a popular magazine for officers. The next year, it published an expanded study, in which Dr. Lewinski timed students as they fired while turning, running or sitting with a gun at their side, as if stashed in a car's console.

Suspects, he concluded, could reach, fire and move remarkably fast. But faster than an officer could react? In 2002, a third study concluded that it takes the average officer about a second and a half to draw from a holster, aim and fire.

Together, the studies appeared to support the idea that officers were at a serious disadvantage. The studies are the foundation for much of his work over the past decade.

Because he published in a police magazine and not a scientific journal, Dr. Lewinski was not subjected to the peer-review process. But in separate cases in 2011 and 2012, the Justice Department and a private lawyer asked Lisa Fournier, a Washington State University professor and an *American Journal of Psychology* editor, to review Dr. Lewinski's studies. She said they lacked basic elements of legitimate research, such as control groups, and drew conclusions that were unsupported by the data.

"In summary, this study is invalid and unreliable," she wrote in court documents in 2012. "In my opinion, this study questions the ability of Mr. Lewinski to apply relevant and reliable data to answer a question or support an argument."

Dr. Lewinski said he chose to publish his findings in the magazine because it reached so many officers who would never read a scientific journal. If he were doing it over, he said in an interview, he would have published his early studies in academic journals and summarized them elsewhere for officers. But he said it was unfair for Dr. Fournier to criticize his research based on summaries written for a general audience. While opposing lawyers and experts found his research controversial, they were particularly frustrated by Dr. Lewinski's tendency to get inside people's heads. Time and again, his reports to defense lawyers seem to make conclusive statements about what officers saw, what they did not, and what they cannot remember.

Often, these details are hotly disputed. For example, in a 2009 case that revolved around whether a Texas sheriff's deputy felt threatened by a car coming at him, Dr. Lewinski said that the officer was so focused on firing to stop the threat, he did not immediately recognize that the car had passed him.

## Inattentional Blindness

Such gaps in observation and memory, he says, can be explained by a phenomenon called inattentional blindness, in which the brain is so focused on one task that it blocks out everything else. When an officer's version of events is disproved by video or forensic evidence, Dr. Lewinski says, inattentional blindness may be to blame. It is human nature, he says, to try to fill in the blanks.

"Whenever the cop says something that's helpful, it's as good as gold," said Mr. Burton, the California lawyer. "But when a cop says something that's inconvenient, it's a result of this memory loss."

Experts say Dr. Lewinski is too sure of himself on the subject. "I hate the fact that it's being used in this way," said Arien Mack, one of two psychologists who coined the term inattentional blindness. "When we work in a lab, we ask them if they saw something. They have no motivation to lie. A police officer involved in a shooting certainly has a reason to lie."

Dr. Lewinski acknowledged that there was no clear way to distinguish inattentional blindness from lying. He said he had tried to present it as a possibility, not a conclusion.

Almost as soon as his research was published, lawyers took notice and asked him to explain his work to juries.

In Los Angeles, he helped authorities explain the still-controversial fatal shooting of Anthony Dwain Lee, a Hollywood actor who was shot through a window by a police officer at a Halloween party in 2000. The actor carried a fake gun as part of his costume. Mr. Lee was shot several times in the back. The officer was not charged.

The city settled a lawsuit over the shooting for $225,000, but Mr. Lewinski still teaches the case as an example of a justified shooting that unfairly tarnished a good officer who "was shooting to save his own life."

In September 2001, a Cincinnati judge acquitted a police officer, Stephen Roach, in the shooting death of an unarmed black man after a chase. The officer said he believed the man, Timothy Thomas, 19, was reaching for a gun. Dr. Lewinski testified, and the judge said he found his analysis credible. The prosecutor, Stephen McIntosh, however, told *The Columbus Dispatch* that Dr. Lewinski's "radical" views could be used to justify nearly any police shooting.

"If that's the sort of direction we, as a society, are going," the prosecutor said, "I have a lot of disappointment." Since then, Dr. Lewinski has testified in many dozens of cases in state and federal court, becoming a hero to many officers who feel that politics, not science or safety, drives police policy. For example, departments often require officers to consider less-lethal options such as pepper spray, stun guns and beanbag guns before drawing their firearms.

"These have come about because of political pressure," said Les Robbins, the executive director of the Association for Los Angeles Deputy Sheriffs. In an interview, Mr. Robbins recalled how he used to keep his gun drawn and hidden behind his leg during most traffic stops. "We used to be able to use the baton and hit people where we felt necessary to get them to comply. Those days are gone."

## Positions of Authority

Dr. Lewinski and his company have provided training for dozens of departments, including in Cincinnati, Las Vegas, Milwaukee and Seattle. His messages often conflict, in both substance and tone, with the training now recommended by the Justice Department and police organizations.

The Police Executive Research Forum, a group that counts most major city police chiefs as members, has called for greater restraint from officers and slower, better decision making. Chuck Wexler, its director, said he is troubled by Dr. Lewinski's teachings. He added that even as chiefs changed their use-of-force policies, many did not know what their officers were taught in academies and private sessions.

"It's not that chiefs don't care," he said. "It's rare that a chief has time to sit at the academy and see what's being taught."

Regardless of what, if any, policy changes emerge from the current national debate, civil right lawyers say one thing will not change: Jurors want to believe police officers, and Dr. Lewinski's research tells them that they can.

On a cold night in early 2003, for instance, Robert Murtha, an officer in Hartford, Conn., shot three times at the driver of a car. He said the vehicle had sped directly at him, knocking him to the ground as he fired. Video from a nearby police cruiser told another story. The officer had not been struck. He had fired through the driver's-side window as the car passed him.

Officer Murtha's story was so obviously incorrect that he was arrested on charges of assault and fabricating evidence. If officers can get away with shooting people and lying about it, the prosecutor declared, "the system is doomed."

"There was no way around it—Murtha was dead wrong," his lawyer, Hugh F. Keefe, recalled recently. But the officer was "bright, articulate and truthful," Mr. Keefe said. Jurors needed an explanation for how the officer could be so wrong and still be innocent.

Dr. Lewinski testified at trial. The jury deliberated less than one full day. The officer was acquitted of all charges.

## Critical Thinking

1. Do you believe that it is appropriate for police chiefs not to know what their officers are being taught regarding use-of-force?

2. What effect do you think decisions like the one in *Murtha* have on the public's perception of law enforcement?

3. What's wrong with the fact that Lewinski's studies were not subject to peer-review?

## Internet References

**Force Science Institute Ltd**
http://www.forcescience.org/biomachanics.html

**Lisa Fournier**
https://s3.amazonaws.com/pacer-documents/D.%20Or.%2008-cv-00950%20dckt%20000133_011%20filed%202012-06-28.pdf

**Police Executive Research Forum**
http://www.policeforum.org/assets/reengineeringtraining1.pdf

**The Police Marksman**
http://www.forcescience.org/articles/isyourshootingclean.pdf

*Article* Prepared by: Joanne Naughton

# Defining Moments for Police Chiefs

CHUCK WEXLER

## Learning Outcomes

*After reading this article, you will be able to:*

- Understand the thinking of some police executives about critical situations.

- Show the importance of speaking to the media as soon as possible, with accurate information, after a serious police incident.

## Introduction

The position of police chief has always been a demanding job. A police chief must know how to run a complex organization, in many cases a very large organization. Chiefs must have strong leadership skills and a vision for meeting the needs of the community. And the stakes are high, because police have unique power and authority over people. The consequences of a mistake by any member of the organization can be catastrophic. As a result, police departments undergo closer scrutiny than other types of organizations.

Since PERF's (Police Executive Research Forum) creation in 1976, one of our priorities has been to work with police chiefs to identify best practices and policies for meeting the challenges of the job. Our goal is to help police departments learn from each other about the critical issues they face.

And one thing we have seen is that even in a well-run department, a department with good policies, thorough training of officers, strong leaders, and solid management systems, things can go disastrously wrong at any moment. A single officer can make a bad decision in a split-second, or a natural disaster or large-scale criminal incident can overwhelm a department's capabilities.

A police chief who responds well in a crisis can mitigate the damage, and sometimes the storyline changes as a result. Instead of focusing on the disastrous incident, the community remembers how hard the police chief and the police department worked to handle it.

Unfortunately, in other cases, a slow or ill-considered response makes the situation worse.

In the summer of 2014, PERF decided to hold a national conference to address these issues. We decided to name the conference "Defining Moments for Police Chiefs." We wanted to ask leading police officials, "In your career, what was the one critical moment when you really felt tested? What did you do that worked well? And looking back, is there anything you wish you could do over and do differently?"

As we were planning the Defining Moments conference, the fatal shooting of Michael Brown by a police officer in Ferguson, Missouri on August 9, and the large-scale protest marches and riots that followed, brought international attention to many of the issues we were addressing.

For example, a key issue for a police department in any critical incident is how effectively it shares information with the public and the news media. Traditionally, police have often held back on releasing information, believing that they should exercise caution until they are certain of all of the facts, or that they should never release information that might be used later in a criminal case or lawsuit.

At our Defining Moments conference, police chiefs told us they are finding that that approach is no longer viable, because a narrative is created within a few hours of a critical incident happening, and the narrative is written whether or not the police contribute any information to the story. Too much damage can be done if police miss their chance to explain what happened and correct wrong information that can spread in the immediate aftermath of an incident.

So today's police leaders try to get out in front of the story, rather than being dragged into it against their will. They provide preliminary information with a strong cautionary note that as more information becomes available, the story may very well change. Chief David Brown of Dallas talked about the importance of getting this preliminary information out in the first news cycle.

Another critical aspect of "defining moments" for police chiefs is whether they have a reservoir of trust in the community that can help everyone to get through the difficult situation. Police chiefs must develop personal relationships with community leaders and people from all parts of their jurisdiction, well before any incident takes place. The work of building these relationships of mutual respect must be done constantly, and especially during "non-crisis" times. A critical incident is not the time to hold your first meeting with community leaders.

Many police chiefs believe that the Ferguson incident was a defining moment for the entire policing profession. As PERF President and Philadelphia Police Commissioner Charles Ramsey said at PERF's Defining Moments conference, "All of us have been in this business for a while, and we all have had incidents that fundamentally changed how we think about things. And sometimes there are incidents that occur outside our own jurisdictions that affect all of us."

At the request of PERF's Board of Directors, we extended the Defining Moments conference from one day to two days, in order to include a full discussion of the Ferguson incident, while maintaining our original plans to discuss a wide range of other defining moments.

The bulk of this document consists of quotations from police chiefs and other leaders who participated in our conference, and who offered valuable guidance about these issues.

I'd like to highlight one key issue that seems new to me; I haven't heard this discussed in previous PERF meetings. That is the question of whether we need police officers to take on a fundamentally different role than they have had in the past.

One central theme that grew out of the conference was the importance of developing a culture of policing that recognizes when officers should step in and when they should step back from encounters with the public. For example, in active shooter situations, we now expect officers to make split-second, life-or-death decisions when lives hang in the balance. (This goes against the pre-Columbine thinking, when officers were taught not to rush in but to assess the situation and get additional help.)

On the other hand, when the stakes are not high, when police are dealing with a relatively minor situation, we want police officers to recognize that stepping back from a contentious encounter and getting assistance from other officers is a sign of strength, not weakness. In these situations, slowing down the encounter and using de-escalation and crisis intervention skills can help prevent a relatively minor incident from cascading into a bad result that no one expected or wanted.

So there are times when we expect police to "step up," and times when we expect them to "step back," and knowing the difference may be as important a lesson as we can teach officers.

I believe you will find these discussions useful and interesting. The final chapter of this report summarizes the lessons we learned in this project.

# Ferguson, Missouri: A National "Defining Moment" for Policing

The first day of PERF's conference on Defining Moments for Police Chiefs was devoted largely to a discussion of the issues raised by the August 9, 2014 shooting of Michael Brown in Ferguson, MO, and the handling of large-scale protests and riots that followed the shooting.

St. Louis County Police Chief Jon Belmar, whose department provided the bulk of the police officers responding to the incident, launched the discussion with a day-by-day summary of his thinking as he led the multi-agency response in the first few days of the protests.

Other chiefs then provided their analysis and perspectives.

## St. Louis County Chief Jon Belmar: We Had 11 Days of Serious Rioting Without a Serious Injury to a Protester

I felt like I was pretty well positioned to understand how to deal with something like Ferguson. I was in tactical operations as a commander, and I was a patrolman back in the early '90s. I have good contacts in the communities. I go to the churches; I talk to my community leaders; I am engaged. I was from North St. Louis County, where Ferguson is located.

But when this happened, you have no idea how bad it can be, and how it can spin out of control unless you have gone through something like this before.

Taking this day by day, the Michael Brown shooting was on Saturday, August 9, at 12:02 P.M., and I got a call from Ferguson Police Chief Tom Jackson at about 12:25. He said he had a fatal officer-involved shooting and asked me to investigate it. I called my chief of the Tactical Operations Unit, who was down in South County at one of our hospitals, dealing with an armed invasion. I told him we had an officer-involved shooting up in Ferguson, and that he needed to get up there. I didn't hear anything until about 4:45 or 5 that afternoon, when the captain from Tactical Operations told me, "Boss, we have had a bad afternoon up here. We almost didn't get this crime scene processed. We had a lot of gun shots and people surrounding the body." He also told me that it took 4 ½ hours to process that crime scene.

I spent seven years as a lieutenant in robbery/homicide, and I believe that doing a crime scene the right way is an absolute. I also believe that if I had this one to do over again, I would have at least thought about moving Mr. Brown faster. But I don't think we could have done it much faster. It's easy to say, "Remove the body and go." But it's also easy to imagine people asking me later, "Why didn't you do a comprehensive investigation of the crime scene?"

The next day, on Sunday, August 10, I called my TAC commander Bryan Ludwig, who asked me, "Chief, what do you want down there today?"

I said, "Let me explain what I *don't* want." I said, "I don't want any trucks, I don't want anything other than the uniform of the day. I don't want any armor; I don't want any fatigues. And I want you guys staged way offside. Perhaps we will have a problem; let's hope we don't."

I got a call about 8:25 Sunday night from Ludwig's boss, Lt. Colonel Michael Dierkes, who's in charge of special operations. He was in Ludwig's Tahoe and he said, "Boss, we got a problem down here; we may have to go to gas."

I said, "Please don't do that," and then I thought about it for a second and said, "Mike, I'm not there; use your best judgment." What I didn't know was that while he was talking to me, a piece of a cinderblock was skipping off the Tahoe and into the windshield.

In 35 minutes I stepped down onto West Florissant Avenue, and there were probably 200 police cars parked all over the place, and the crowd was angry.

We made a conscious decision not to go into the crowd with night sticks and start locking people up. There was a lot of looting going on, but there were so many people, we really didn't understand the breadth of what was happening.

I really only did two things that night. I talked to each one of my police officers and told them to maintain their bearing. And I tried to calm people down. I saw ministers I knew, government people, activists that I knew, and I was telling them, "At some point, we are going to have to insist that everybody leave." But they told me, "We have no control. These young people aren't going to listen to us."

So obviously we were thinking at this point that we had a problem.

On Monday, August 11, there was shooting going on and reports of police cars getting rocked, and we had to use tear gas in West Florissant to disperse the crowd, but we weren't making a lot of arrests. On Tuesday, August 12, there were a lot of people on the corridor, a lot of activity. We left them alone, they left us alone, and they were able to demonstrate. A woman was shot in the head at Highmont in West Florissant about 11. And there were about 200 people at West Florissant and Chambers. They started breaking out some windows, so we went down there but we decided not to use tear gas.

Wednesday, August 13, was a nightmare. At the end of the day, I went back to the command post and met with the St. Louis City police commanders, my commanders, the Highway Patrol commanders who had all been with me on this since Day One, and I said, "Ladies and gentlemen, we have got to do something different. We cannot sustain this night after night. We have to come up with a new strategy. Everybody go home tonight and I want you think about how we are going to do this differently tomorrow night."

But the next day, the Governor came in and relieved me, and put Captain Ron Johnson of the Highway Patrol in charge.

In the end, there were five shootings within the demonstration corridor over 11 days. But I would talk to the news media and ask, "Do you have any questions about the activity we are dealing with after nightfall?" But the media didn't want to talk what we were dealing with night after night. All they cared about was the criminal investigation into Mr. Brown's death, which I couldn't talk about.

I understand that the use of tear gas looks terrible on TV. My father is an 82-year-old Korean War veteran who loves his son, but on Day 4, he said to me, "Son, that tear gas didn't look good down there on West Florissant." I said, "Dad, I know, and it looks worse in person."

But I am unaware of a death attributed to CS tear gas in the United States. Police sometimes kill people with nightsticks, mace, police dogs, bullets, and everything else. But we didn't send anybody to the emergency room with a serious injury over 11 days of serious rioting.

## St. Louis Chief Sam Dotson: Our Community Relationships Helped Us When We Had an OIS After the Brown Shooting

Chief Dotson discussed a fatal officer-involved shooting in St. Louis on August 19, 10 days after the Michael Brown shooting in Ferguson and not far from where the Ferguson shooting occurred. In the St. Louis incident, officers shot Kajieme Powell, who was holding a knife and behaving erratically. The shooting was captured on video by a bystander.[1]

We received a call about a person acting erratically with a knife who has just stolen some items from a convenience store. The young man went into the store, took a couple energy drinks and got no response from the clerks. A couple minutes later he went back in, stole a package of donuts, and it almost looked like he was looking for a response. He went outside and continued to pace around, talking to himself, until the shopkeeper finally came out and asked him to pay for the donuts. The officers arrived, and all they knew when they arrived was that a larceny had occurred and there was a subject armed with a knife.

When they stepped out of the car, the suspect immediately approached them with the knife, yelling, "Shoot me, kill me now." First he moved towards the officer who had been driving, then he backed up and walked toward the officer who had been on the passenger side. By this time, the officers were out of the vehicle, had their weapons drawn, and were repeatedly giving the verbal commands, "Stop, put the knife down, police, stop, put the knife down." The suspect was closing the distance between them, and both of the officers shot him.

This happened about a mile and a half from where the Michael Brown shooting happened, 10 days after that shooting. So no one would believe me if I said I wasn't thinking about Ferguson as I drove to this scene.

One of the lessons I had learned from Ferguson was that it's important to get your story out there as soon as you can. So I made a statement to the media at the scene of the shooting. I made several mistakes through all of this, but the one I want to talk about most was that I didn't put a large enough disclaimer in front of my comments in my initial briefing. I said something like, "This is what we know at this point; we'll provide more information as soon as it's available." That statement should have been stronger, because we all know that some of the first information we get about a critical incident can later turn out to be wrong.

At the time of the news briefing, we didn't know it, but there was a cell-phone video of the shooting. We found out about the video eight or nine hours later.

We had national media as well as local reporters at the briefing, and everyone was interested in linking the shooting to Ferguson. But there also was a sense of allowing us to tell the story, because we have some very strong relationships with the community, and we had two Aldermen with me there. In fact, one of the 911 callers was an Alderwoman who happened to be at the scene and had seen Kajieme Powell with the knife, so she called the police.

I found out about the cell phone video that evening. An attorney for the person who took the video was shopping it around and wouldn't give us a copy until 9 the next morning. So we were ready the next morning, and as soon as we received it, we reviewed it and decided that nobody could tell our story better than we could. So we put together the cell phone video, which caught the entire incident, and surveillance video from the convenience store, along with the 911 calls from the Alderwoman and the store owner, and the dispatch tapes, so everyone would know exactly what the officers knew as they were arriving on the scene.

Obviously if a man is walking up and down the street and says, "Shoot me now; kill me now," there will be questions about mental illness, but I wanted the public to know that the officers arrived only with the information they were provided by the 911 callers and the dispatchers. And it was only 15 seconds from the time the first officer's foot hits the pavement to the first shot that's fired. In 15 seconds they had to make decisions about the course of action they were going to use.

One of the lessons we learned from the police shooting of Kajieme Powell was that it's important to have your narrative heard. But in our rush to push information out, there were slight misstatements that were problematic. Witnesses told us that Mr. Powell made an overhand motion with the knife, and I repeated that to the media, but the video did not show that. So in retrospect, I should have made a larger disclaimer at the briefing, and said that this was just preliminary information that we received, and sometimes the early information turns out to be incorrect.

We were not completely without protests in St. Louis about the Powell shooting, but they were smaller, they didn't last as long, and the dynamic was different. We didn't see a large group of out-of-town people, the anarchists and others like that. The protesters we saw were local people whom we knew and had relationships with. Our community out-reach and our existing relationships with the community helped us.

### Philadelphia Commissioner Chuck Ramsey: Ferguson Brought Attention to Issues That We All Should Be Addressing

Thank you both for the presentations. It was very enlightening and you made us aware of a lot of things that we didn't know about. What happened in Ferguson is the kind of incident that could have happened in many of our towns and cities in America. We can debate whether it would have had the same outcome, but it could have happened just about anywhere, I believe.

I hope we can focus on the larger issues that have surfaced as a result. For example, we've been hearing a lot about the "militarization" of police. As [Milwaukee Chief] Ed Flynn said, there is no real definition for it, but everybody visualizes for themselves what it means, and it's usually not positive as far as how policing is viewed as a profession.

So we need to talk about that, because there is a legitimate argument about the kind of equipment that we are getting into our inventory, and more importantly, the policies that we have about the circumstances under which equipment should be deployed. Do all departments need the kind of equipment that we see—MRAPs (Mine-Resistant Ambush Protected) and things of that nature? If you are going to have that kind of equipment available, especially in smaller jurisdictions, there should be a more regional approach, as opposed to individual agencies having all this equipment. I think that's a legitimate discussion that we need to have.

Another issue coming out of Ferguson—use of force—is one that we talk about all the time. We need to consider use of force not only from the standpoint of what officers deal with on an everyday basis, but also with regard to handling large demonstrations that include some violent elements. And it gets more complicated when you have multiple jurisdictions that are coming together because of a major incident. We need to discuss issues like whose authority do they fall under? Which agency's use-of-force policies control the response? What kind of equipment do you want them to bring, and what you do *not* want them to bring.

Another issue that has changed things is social media. Nearly everybody has a cell phone camera, so whenever something happens, I tend to assume there is a video somewhere. But one problem with videos is that often they don't capture the beginning of an incident—the events that started the whole thing. The camera typically is turned on sometime after the point where a situation has started to go bad, so often there is a lack of context.

We cannot ignore the fact that we have not achieved legitimacy in some of our more challenged neighborhoods. We have to go [to] back the drawing board and come up with different strategies to reach folks in these challenged neighborhoods. We can pat ourselves on the back and talk about how far we have come in reducing crime and establishing community policing, but we haven't come far enough. Ferguson isn't just about the shooting. It is about the tension and the issues that have been in existence for decades, and the reality of things that have happened to people over the years, some of which police have been very much responsible for.

So we have to recognize that and deal with it. We have got to take community policing to a different level. It's not one-size-fits-all; we must find a different way of reaching poor communities, communities of color, communities that are more challenged than others, if we really want to make progress.

It is not as simple as merely having diversity. When I was chief in DC, the MPD had 63 percent African-American police officers, but we still had tension and issues in our more challenged neighborhoods. Diversity is important, don't get me wrong, but we have to dig deeper. Having officers who look like the folks in the community in itself is not enough. We need to take a different look at community policing and what are we trying to achieve, or we will continue to have these incidents.

## Note

1. https://www.youtube.com/watch?v=sEuZiTcbGCg

## Critical Thinking

1. If a police officer steps back from a situation rather than taking immediate control, doesn't that convey weakness?
2. Chief Belmar said they had 11 days of rioting without a serious injury to a protester. What do you think about the fact that the rioting went on for 11 days?
3. What do you think about Commissioner Ramsey's comments about diversity?

## Internet References

**DOJ Report on Ferguson Police Department**
    http://www.justice.gov/sites/default/files/opa/press-releases/attachments/2015/03/04/ferguson_police_department_report.pdf

**Police Executive Research Forum**
    http://www.policeforum.org/assets/definingmoments.pdf

*Article*                                                                Prepared by: Joanne Naughton

# Understanding the Psychology of Police Misconduct

BRIAN D. FITCH

## Learning Outcomes

*After reading this article, you will be able to:*

- Express your familiarity with the rationalizations that contribute to unethical behavior by police.

- Argue in favor of the importance of ethics training for law enforcement officers.

- Describe how police officers can reduce the psychological discomfort that might accompany their misconduct.

Law enforcement is a unique profession, with officers experiencing a host of freedoms not available to the general public, including the application of deadly force, high-speed driving, and seizing personal property. While these liberties may be necessary, they also can create opportunities for wrongdoing, especially if such behavior is likely to go undetected because of poor supervision. The embarrassment caused by misconduct can damage the public trust, undermine officer morale, and expose agencies to unnecessary—and, in many cases, costly—litigation.[1] Consequently, a clear understanding of the psychology underlying unethical behavior is critical to every law enforcement supervisor and manager at every level of an organization, regardless of one's agency or mission.

Law enforcement agencies go to great lengths to recruit hire, and train only the most qualified applicants—candidates who have already demonstrated a track record of good moral values and ethical conduct. Similarly, most officers support the agency, its values, and its mission, performing their duties ethically while avoiding any misconduct or abuse of authority. Yet despite the best efforts of organizations everywhere, it seems that one does not have to look very far these days to find examples of police misconduct particularly in the popular press.[2] Even more disturbing, however, is that many of the officers engaged in immoral or unethical behavior previously demonstrated good service records, absent any of the "evil" typically associated with corruption or abuse.

While it is probably true that at least some of the officers who engage in illicit activities managed somehow to slip through the cracks in the hiring process and simply continued their unethical ways, this account fails to explain how otherwise good officers become involved in misconduct. The purpose of this article is to familiarize law enforcement managers and supervisors with the cognitive rationalizations that can contribute to unethical behavior. The article also offers strategies and suggestions intended to mitigate misconduct, before it actually occurs, by developing a culture of ethics.

## Moral Responsibility and Disengagement

Most law enforcement professionals are, at their core, good, ethical, and caring people. Despite the overuse of a popular cliché, many officers do in fact enter law enforcement because they want to make a positive difference in their communities. Officers frequently espouse strong, positive moral values while working diligently—in many cases, at great personal risk—to bring dangerous criminals to justice. Doing so provides officers with a strong sense of personal satisfaction and self-worth. As a result, most officers do not—and in many cases cannot—engage in unethical conduct unless they can somehow justify to themselves the morality of their actions.[3]

Decades of empirical research have supported the idea that whenever a person's behaviors are inconsistent with their attitudes or beliefs, the individual will experience a state of psychological tension—a phenomenon referred to as cognitive dissonance.[4] Because this tension is uncomfortable, people will modify any contradictory beliefs or behaviors in ways intended to reduce or eliminate discomfort. Officers can reduce psychological tension by changing one or more of their cognitions—that is, by modifying how they think about their actions and the consequences of those behaviors—or by adjusting their activities, attitudes, or beliefs in ways that are consistent with their values and self-image. Generally speaking, an officer will modify the cognition that is least resistant to change, which, in most cases, tends to be the officer's attitudes, not behaviors.

One of the simplest ways that officers can reduce the psychological discomfort that accompanies misconduct is to cognitively restructure unethical behaviors in ways that make them seem personally and socially acceptable, thereby allowing officers to behave immorally while preserving their self-image as ethically good people. The following is a partial list of common rationalizations that officers can use to neutralize or excuse unethical conduct.[5]

**Denial of victim.** Officers who rely on this tactic argue that because no victim exists, no real harm has been done. It is probably safe to suggest that officers do not generally regard drug dealers, thieves, and sexual predators as bona fide victims, regardless of the nature of an officer's conduct. An officer, for instance, who takes money from a suspected drug dealer during the service of a search warrant might argue that because the dealer acquired the currency illegally, the dealer was never actually entitled to the proceeds. Rather, the money belongs to whoever possesses it at the time.

**Victim of circumstance.** Officers who utilize this method convince themselves that they behaved improperly only because they had no other choice. Officers may claim that they were the victims of peer pressure, an unethical supervisor, or an environment where "everyone else is doing it," so what else could they possibly have done? Regardless of the context, these officers excuse their conduct by alleging that they had no alternative but to act unethically.

**Denial of injury.** Using this form of rationalization, officers persuade themselves that because nobody was actually hurt by their actions, their behavior was not really immoral. This explanation is especially common in cases involving drugs, stolen property, or large amounts of untraceable cash where it can be difficult, if not impossible, to identify an injured party. Officers who use this tactic may further neutralize their deviant conduct by comparing it to the harm being done by the drug dealer from whom the money was stolen.

**Advantageous comparisons.** Officers who depend on this explanation rely on selective social comparisons to defend their conduct. Officers who falsify a police report to convict a suspected drug dealer, for example, might defend their actions by minimizing their participation or the frequency of their unethical behavior, while at the same time vilifying a coworker as someone who "lies all the time on reports." In comparison to an officer who routinely falsifies reports, the first officer's conduct can seem less egregious.

**Higher cause.** Officers who practice this type of cognitive restructuring argue that sometimes, it may be necessary to break certain rules to serve a higher calling or to achieve a more important goal. An officer who conducts an unlawful search to uncover evidence against a suspected pedophile might reason that the nature of the crime justifies breaking the rules. "The ends justify the means," officers might assert—suggesting that they did what was necessary, regardless of the legality or morality of their conduct, to put a dangerous criminal behind bars. This form of rationalization can be especially disturbing because it goes beyond merely excusing or justifying deviant behavior to the point of actually glorifying certain forms of wrongdoing in the name of "justice" or "the greater good."

## Table 1  Rationalizing Misconduct

| Strategy | Description |
|---|---|
| Denial of Victim | Alleging that because there is no legitimate victim, there is no misconduct. |
| Victim of Circumstance | Behaving improperly because the officer had no other choice, either because of peer pressure or unethical supervision. |
| Denial of Injury | Because nobody was hurt by the officer's action, no misconduct actually occurred. |
| Advantageous Comparisons | Minimizing or excusing one's own wrongdoing by comparing it to the more egregious behavior of others. |
| Higher Cause | Breaking the rules because of some higher calling—that is, removing a known felon from the streets. |
| Blame the Victim | The victim invited any suffering or misconduct by breaking the law in the first place. |
| Dehumanization | Using euphemistic language to dehumanize people, thereby making them easier to victimize. |
| Diffusion of Responsibility | Relying on the diffusion of responsibility among the involved parties to excuse misconduct. |

**Blame the victim.** An officer who uses this form of justification blames the victim for any misconduct or abuse. If, for instance, officers use unreasonable force on a suspected drug dealer, they can simply argue that the victim brought on this suffering by violating the law. "If the dealer doesn't want to get beat up, the dealer should obey the law," the officer might reason. "I'm not using force on law-abiding citizens, only on drug dealers; they give up their rights when they break the rules." By assigning blame to the victim, the officer not only finds a way to excuse any wrongdoing, but also a way to feel sanctimonious about doing so.

**Dehumanization.** The amount of guilt or shame officers feel for behaving unethically depends, at least in part, on how they regard the person being abused. To avoid the feelings of self-censorship or guilt that often accompany misconduct, officers can employ euphemistic language to strip victims of their humanity. Using terms like "dirtbag" to describe law violators has the effect of dehumanizing intended targets, generally making it easier for officers to justify, ignore, or minimize the harmful effects of their actions, while at the same time reducing their personal responsibility for behaving in ways that they know are wrong.

**Diffusion of responsibility.** An officer who uses this excuse relies on the shared participation—and, by extension, the shared guilt—of everyone involved in an incident of misconduct to excuse or reduce any personal culpability. With each additional accomplice, every individual officer is seen as that much less responsible for any wrongdoing that might have occurred. If, for instance, money is stolen from an arrestee, officers might assert that there were many officers at the crime scene who could have done this, so an individual cannot be blamed. Similarly, if ten officers were involved in the service of a search warrant, then each officer is only one-tenth responsible for any misconduct that occurs.

## Misconduct's Slippery Slope

It is important to note that most officers do not jump headfirst into large-scale misconduct—instead, they weigh in gradually in a process referred to as incrementalism.[6] The strength and ease with which officers can rationalize unethical behavior also depends, at least in part, on how they view their conduct, the people harmed by their actions, and the consequences that flow from their actions. An officer's initial slide down the slippery slope of misconduct can begin with nothing more than simple policy violations that, if left unchecked, generate a mild feeling of psychological tension or discomfort. However, by learning to rationalize wrongdoing in ways that make it psychologically and morally acceptable, officers are able to relieve any feelings of distress or discomfort, effectively disengaging their moral compasses.

Officers can employ cognitive rationalizations prospectively (before the corrupt act) to forestall guilt and resistance, or retrospectively (after the misconduct) to erase any regrets. In either case, the more frequently an officer rationalizes deviant behavior, the easier each subsequent instance of misconduct becomes.[7] This is because the more frequently officers employ rationalizations, the easier it becomes to activate similar thought patterns in the future. With time and repeated experience, rationalizations can eventually become part of the habitual, automatic, effortless ways that officers think about themselves, their duties, and the consequences of their actions, eventually allowing officers to engage in increasingly egregious acts of misconduct with little, if any, of the guilt or shame commonly associated with wrongdoing.

As officers learn to pay less attention to the morality of their actions, the ways they think about misconduct—that is, their attitudes, beliefs, and values—may begin to change as well. Officers can begin defining behaviors that were once seen as unethical or immoral as necessary parts of completing their assigned duties. Even more troubling, however, is that once rationalizations become part of an agency's dominant culture, they can alter the ways officers define misconduct, particularly if wrongdoings are rewarded either informally by an officer's peer group or formally by the organization.

## Ethics Education

Law enforcement agencies throughout the United States, as well as abroad, have begun to recognize the importance of ethics training. While such attention represents a significant step in the right direction, ethical instruction is often limited to little more than the discussion and development of proper moral values—an approach commonly referred to as character education.[8] Proponents of this method suggest that officers who possess the right values—and, by extension, the right character—will always do the right thing, regardless of

the circumstances. Although few people would argue with the importance of good moral values and character, ethical decisions are not always simple.

Before officers can act ethically, they must recognize the moral nature of a situation; decide on a specific and, hopefully, ethical course of action; possess the requisite moral motivation to take action; and demonstrate the character necessary to follow through with their decisions.[9] To further complicate matters, even the best of intentions can be thwarted by peer pressure or fear of retaliation. For example, the 2003 National Business Ethics Survey found that approximately 40 percent of those surveyed would not report misconduct if they observed it because of fear of reprisal from management.[10]

This cloud does, however, contain a silver lining. Research has demonstrated that ethics education can assist officers in better navigating moral challenges by increasing ethical awareness and moral reasoning—two critical aspects of ethical decision making.[11] However, conducting meaningful ethics education requires more than lengthy philosophical lectures on the importance of character. Rather, instructors should focus on facilitating a dialogue that challenges officers on key moral issues and assumptions; tests their reasoning and decision-making skills; and allows them to share their experiences in a safe, supportive environment.[12]

For ethics education to be truly effective, organizations must make moral discussions a regular part of the agency's training program. In the same way that officers routinely train in defensive tactics, firearms, and law to better prime them for field duties, officers should prepare equally well for any ethical issues they might encounter.[13] Supervisors can stimulate ethical discussions with a video documentary, news clip, or fictional story. Regardless of the stimulus, however, the more frequently officers discuss ethics, the better able they will be to recognize a moral dilemma, make the appropriate ethical decision, and demonstrate the moral courage necessary to behave honorably.

Next, law enforcement agencies must establish a clear code of ethical conduct, including a set of core values and a mission statement. Merely establishing a code of ethical conduct is not enough, however; the department's top management must lead by example. It is important to remember that a code of conduct applies equally to employees at all levels of an organization.[14] As most leaders can confirm from experience, officers can be surprisingly quick to point out any inconsistencies between the organization's stated values and the conduct of senior management. If leaders expect officers to behave ethically, leaders must model the way.

Departments must also work to create systems that reward ethical conduct and punish unethical behavior.[15] Core values and codes of conduct are of little value if they are not supported by wider agency objectives that reward ethical actions. Not only should law enforcement organizations reward officers for behaving ethically, they must also seriously address officers' ethical concerns by thoroughly investigating any allegations, while protecting the confidentiality of those reporting such incidents. And, finally, agencies should strive to create an open environment where ethical issues can be discussed without fear of punishment or reprisal.

In the end, mitigating and, hopefully, eliminating misconduct require regular ethics training, high ethical standards, appropriate reward systems, and a culture in which ethical issues are discussed freely. While the responsibility for creating a culture of ethics rests with leadership, individual officers must do their part to behave ethically, support the moral conduct of others, and challenge misconduct in all its forms. Only by remaining vigilant to the psychology of misconduct can law enforcement professionals focus attention back on the positive aspects of their profession, while enjoying the high levels of public trust necessary to do their jobs.

## Notes

1. For a more complete discussion on the impact of police misconduct see Adam Dunn and Patrick J. Caceres, "Constructing a Better Estimate of Police Misconduct," *Policy Matters Journal* (Spring 2010): 10–16.

2. For a more complete description of police misconduct, media coverage, and public attitudes toward law enforcement see Joel Miller and Robert C. Davis, "Unpacking Public Attitudes to the Police: Contrasting Perceptions of Misconduct with Traditional Measures of Satisfaction," *International Journal of Police Science and Management* 10, no. 1 (2008): 9–22.

3. For a more complete report on the frequency of police misconduct see Mathew R. Durose, Erica L. Smith, and Patrick A. Lanan, *Contacts Between Police and the Public, 2005,* NCJ 215243, Bureau of Justice Statistics, Office of Justice Programs, Special Report (April 2007), http://bjs.ojp.usdoj.gov/content/pub/pdf/cppOS.pdf (accessed November 22, 2010).

4. For a discussion of research on cognitive dissonance, see Joel Cooper, Robert Mirabile, and Steven J. Scher, "Actions and Attitudes: The Theory of Cognitive Dissonance," in *Persuasion: Psychological Insights and Perspectives,* ed. Timothy C. Brock and Melaine C. Green (Thousand Oaks, California: Sage Publications Inc., 2005), 63–80.

5. For a more complete list of cognitive rationalizations, see Albert Bandura et al., "Mechanisms of Moral Disengagement in the Exercise of Moral Agency," *Journal of Personality and Social Psychology* 71, no. 2 (1996): 364–374; John F. Veiga, Timothy D. Golden, and Kathleen Dechant, "A Survey of the Executive's Advisory Panel: Why Managers Bend Company Rules," *Academy of Management Executive* 18, no. 2 (May 2004): 84–90; and Celia Moore, "Moral Disengagement in Processes of Organizational Corruption," *Journal of Business Ethics* 80 (June 2008): 129–139.

6. For a complete discussion of incrementalism, see Ehud Sprinzak, "The Psychopolitical Formation of the Extreme Left in Democracy: The Case of the Weathermen," in *Origins of Terrorism: Psychologies, Ideologies, Theologies, States of Mind,* ed. Walter Reich and Walter Laqueur (Cambridge, England: Cambridge University Press, 1990), 65–85.

7. For a discussion of implicit decision making, see Daniel Kahneman and Shane Frederick, "Representativeness Revisited:

Attribute Substitution in Intuitive Judgment" in *Heuristics and Biases: The Psychology of Intuitive Judgment,* ed. Thomas Gilovich, Dale Griffin, and Daniel Kahneman (New York: Cambridge University Press), 20(G), 49–81.

8. See for example, Michael Josephson, *Becoming an Examplary Peace Officer. The Guide to Ethical Decision Making* (Los Angeles: Josephson Institute, 2009).

9. For further discussion on ethical decision making, see Russell Haines, Marc D. Street, and Douglas Haines, "The Influence of Perceived Importance of an Ethical Issue on Moral Judgment, Moral Obligation, and Moral Intent" *Journal of Business Ethics* 81 (2008): 387–399.

10. Ethics Resource Center, *2003 National Business Ethics Survey (NBES)* (May 21, 2003), www.ethics.org/resource/2003-national-business-ethics-survey-nbes (accessed November 24, 2010).

11. See, for example, Cubie L. L. Lau, "A Step Forward: Ethics Education Matters," *Journal of Business Ethics* 92 (2010): 565–584.

12. For a more complete discussion on facilitation, see Peter Renner, *The Art of Teaching Adults: How to Become an Exceptional Instructor and Facilitator* (Vancouver, Canada: Training Associates, 2005).

13. For a more complete discussion of ethics training, see Brian Fitch, "Principle-Based Decision Making," *Law and Order* 56 (September 2008): 64–70.

14. See, for example, Simon Webley and Andrea Werner, "Corporate Codes of Ethics: Necessary but Not Sufficient," *Business Ethics: A European Review* 17, no. 4 (October 2008): 405–415.

15. For further discussion on ethics and supervisory influence, see James C. Wimbush and Jon M. Shepard, "Toward an Understanding of Ethical Climate: Its Relationship to Ethical Behavior and Supervisory Influence," *Journal of Business Ethics* 3, no. 8 (1994): 637–647.

## Critical Thinking

1. How can a police officer reduce the psychological discomfort that accompanies misconduct?

2. Explain the slippery slope theory regarding misconduct.

3. What can law enforcement agencies do to make ethics education truly effective?

## Create Central

www.mhhe.com/createcentral

## Internet References

**Applying Social Learning Theory to Police Misconduct**
http://ww2.odu.edu/~achappel/DB_article.pdf
**Drury University**
www.drury.edu/ess/irconf/dmangan.html

*Article*                                    Prepared by: Joanne Naughton

# Behind the Smoking Guns: Inside NYPD's 21st Century Arsenal

GREG B. SMITH

## Learning Outcomes

*After reading this article, you will be able to:*

- Describe some of the high-tech tools and massive databases of information available to the NYPD.
- Discuss some of the uses of CompStat.

## Big Brother—With a Badge

In the early morning hours of last Sept. 25, a stocky young man bolted the Bora Bora Lounge in Highbridge, the Bronx, with a gun in his hand and squeezed off seven shots.

His target fell dead on the street as the shooter fled into the darkness, leaving little behind for police save a nearly useless description: "Unknown male Hispanic in 20s."

Enter Big Brother—with a badge.

With the aid of surveillance video at the club and facial recognition technology, cops tracked down a suspect and made an arrest.

To solve a Bronx street shooting in 21st century New York—and most other crimes committed citywide—the NYPD now employs a wide variety of high-tech tools and massive databases of information culled from an incredible array of sources.

The NYPD recently provided the Daily News with an unprecedented look at its 21st century arsenal, which includes:

- Thousands of security cameras scattered throughout the city linked together in a network called the Domain Awareness System (DAS).
- Records of hundreds of thousands of license plate numbers scanned and pinned to specific locations at specific times.

- Social media posts bragging about criminal behavior.
- Facial recognition technology that matches facial characteristics of potential suspects to images in a massive NYPD database.
- Improved ballistics capability that allows cops to quickly identify the source of a bullet.
- Prosecutors in Manhattan, Brooklyn, and Staten Island have created crime strategies units, using data to identify ties between crimes. Authorities can also map the crime to spot trends, quality of life issues, or gang activity.
- A system of sensors the NYPD plans to install that would detect gunshots—even when residents don't report the shootings. Cops can then sync the sensors with cameras to capture footage of the crime.
- Last week, a select group of cops answered calls with Microsoft tablet computers in hand that can instantly tap into the criminal history at an address—including residents with outstanding warrants.

"There's nothing that technology doesn't play a huge role in today," NYPD Deputy Commissioner John Miller told *The News.*

## Harder to Get Away

The long arm of the law now spends a good amount of time with its fingers on a keyboard, downloading and Web-scraping.

The trend accelerated after the Sept. 11 attacks, with new antiterrorist tech advances morphing into all-purpose crime-fighting tools used to track down miscreants from car thieves to killers.

"So much of what has been acquired for terrorism purposes day to day, informs our crimes—with license plate scanners, the pinging capabilities we have on the phones," Police Commissioner Bill Bratton said. "And that's one of the great benefits New York gets out of being the most likely terrorist target in the world today is that the funds that come in help us on our more prevalent, consistent issue of day-to-day crime."

Of course, the nation's biggest police department continues to rely on the usual methods to crack cases—canvassing for witnesses, working informants, relying on analysis of ballistics, fingerprints, and autopsy reports.

But year by year, the NYPD has embraced the latest technology, starting perhaps most notably in 1994 with the advent of CompStat—precinct-by-precinct computerized analysis of nitty-gritty crime stats used to strategically target police activity. Bratton—who first introduced CompStat with the late Jack Maple—said current technology augments traditional police work in ways that he wouldn't have thought possible in the '90s.

"Every shell case and every piece of ballistic evidence we get, we're going to have the ability to analyze that in a very quick, timely fashion," Bratton said.

He recounted a recent CompStat session where bullet cartridges found at several crime scenes over the prior two months were matched to one gun. Surveillance cameras at multiple crime scenes revealed the same vehicle present at each scene. From there they tied the vehicle to an owner, and soon enough to a suspect.

All types of technology are now in play. In the last few years, the NYPD has discussed the introduction of infrared technology that can detect weapons on a person. They also bought two pairs of Google glasses—as yet unused.

The department also has set aside $1.5 million for a sound sensor system called Shotspot that captures gunshots at specific locations. That allows police to respond to shots even if no one calls 911.

The gunshot system has been used in Milwaukee, Oakland, Calif., and Yonkers. In 2011, the department launched a pilot program in Brownsville, Brooklyn, that was never expanded. The technology has since improved and is now considered much more reliable.

The age of social media provided police with another crime-fighting tool—tracking criminals as they brag about their misdeeds on Facebook or Twitter.

"You do a keyword search on 'capped him,' 'shot him,' 'popped him' and you bring up those pages that refer to those things that are . . . the slang words for a shooting," said Miller, the NYPD's counterterrorism chief.

Cameras, in particular, now play a huge crime-solving role. The number of NYPD and private cameras has multiplied radically over the years. Detectives now routinely track down tapes from cameras around a crime scene, and can also tap into a new $30 million network created 2 years ago with Microsoft and dubbed the Domain Awareness System.

Set up as an antiterror tool, the DAS allows the department to search images in real time from 7,000 active NYPD and private cameras, along with 400 special cameras—either at fixed locations or mounted on police cruisers that patrol the streets, collecting license plate numbers as vehicles pass by.

This puts vehicles in specific locations at specific times, useful information in corroborating a suspect's whereabouts at the time of a crime.

Cameras played a crucial role in generating an arrest in the Bora Bora shooting.

Homicide detectives started with seven bullet casings found on the street and vague witness descriptions about the shooter.

The club provided surveillance video that yielded a decent freeze frame with an image of the man witnesses believed was the shooter.

Here another crucial high-tech tool came into play—facial recognition software.

Initiated as a pilot program in Manhattan South in late 2011, the NYPD facial recognition unit works in a small windowless room at 1 Police Plaza.

Detectives there collect images of suspects and witnesses alike from Facebook, cell phones, and surveillance cameras across the city.

Since its inception, city detectives have sent more than 4,400 images to the facial recognition unit, said Inspector DeLayne Hurley, commanding officer of the NYPD's Real Time Crime Center.

Most were too blurry to be of use. But, as of last month, they'd matched more than 1,000 images to the department's database of 9 million mug shots. In the Bora Bora shooting, the club's cameras caught the alleged shooter at an angle.

Facial recognition technology requires a face-on image, so the unit used software to create a 3D, computer-generated image of the shooter's face.

With this usable image, the system brought up at least 200 mug shots deemed close matches. The unit then carefully examined each one, looking for physical similarities such as distance between the eyes, ear size, tattoos, scars, and other unique body tell-tales.

At the start of the facial recognition program, the software produced results that appeared to have misidentified five individuals. None were arrested.

"These were all in the beginning when we were all learning to use the system," Hurley said. "And people can look a lot alike."

The system has since improved dramatically, resulting in 450 arrests and the identification of 397 individuals helpful to investigators, including eyewitnesses.

The technology helped produce arrests in 11 homicides, 124 robberies, 111 larcenies, and 89 assaults or shootings.

In the Bora Bora case, detectives picked out a single likely mug shot and showed it to witnesses in the traditional photo array of similar mug shots. Witnesses all identified the same guy—Yeltsin Beltran, 22, a 5-foot-6, 150-pound Bronx man with prior arrests including false impersonation and drug possession.

Beltran was arrested Oct. 11 for second-degree murder. His lawyer, Paul Lieber, insists his client is innocent.

"My guy had nothing to do with this murder," he said, acknowledging that Beltran was identified by one eyewitness in an actual lineup.

A second witness, who identified Beltran in a photo array, picked a different man in a lineup.

## Questions of Privacy

The growing use of technology to solve crimes has triggered increased concerns about the erosion of privacy rights.

In the past few years, the courts have been asked to address concerns about everything from police warehousing data on law-abiding citizens to cops surveilling individuals without judicial permission.

Just last month, the U.S. Supreme Court ruled cops must first obtain a warrant before searching through a person's smartphone.

Four years ago the New York Civil Liberties Union took issue when it learned the NYPD was storing tens of thousands of names, addresses, and birth dates of everyone stopped and questioned on the street.

Given that 95% of those stopped broke no laws, the NYCLU argued the NYPD was wrongfully keeping tabs on citizens without probable cause to do so. In 2011, New York passed a law prohibiting this practice. This personal information is no longer stored.

The latest concern involves the NYPD's increased use of license plate scanners that result in hundreds of thousands of plate numbers being stored in a massive data file.

Cops can run a plate and see where a vehicle has been in the past few months—all without a warrant. The problem, says the NYCLU's Chris Dunn, is that 99.9% of the stored numbers belong to law-abiding citizens.

Dunn says the license plate readers allow the NYPD to "just vacuum up information about everybody regardless of suspicion. Once we're there, that's where the privacy concerns come in." Privacy rights recently triumphed regarding another high-tech device—the GPS (Global Positioning System).

In New York, police now must obtain permission from a judge before slapping a GPS device on a suspect's vehicle to track his or her whereabouts. That's because an upstate burglar named Scott Weaver objected to police secretly attaching a GPS device to his van without obtaining a warrant.

A jury found him guilty, but in 2009 the Court of Appeals—the state's highest court—reversed the conviction, finding police had violated his constitutional rights via warrantless surveillance.

## Critical Thinking

1. What are the constitutional issues to be concerned about with the use of these tools?

2. Are you confident that facial recognition software helped to correctly identify the killer in the Bora Bora case?

## Internet References

**NYPD**
   http://www.nyc.gov/html/nypd/html/home/home.shtml
**Police Foundation**
   http://www.policefoundation.org/content/compstat-practice-depth-analysis-three-cities
**The Police Chief**
   http://www.policechiefmagazine.org/magazine/index.cfm?fuseaction=display&article_id=998&issue_id=92006

## Article

Prepared by: Joanne Naughton

# Excited Delirium and the Dual Response: Preventing In-Custody Deaths

BRIAN ROACH, KELSEY ECHOLS, AND AARON BURNETT

## Learning Outcomes

*After reading this article, you will be able to:*

- Define excited delirium syndrome and show how it occurs.

- Specify the risk factors associated with ExDS.

- State the treatments to be used when the situation occurs.

Excited delirium syndrome (ExDS) is a serious and potentially deadly medical condition involving psychotic behavior, elevated temperature, and an extreme fight-or-flight response by the nervous system. Failure to recognize the symptoms and involve emergency medical services (EMS) to provide appropriate medical treatment may lead to death. Fatality rates of up to 10 percent in ExDS cases have been reported.[1] In addition to the significant morbidity and mortality associated with unrecognized ExDS, a substantial risk for litigation exists. These patients often die within 1 hour of police involvement. One study showed 75 percent of deaths from ExDS occurred at the scene or during transport.[2] Law enforcement organizations should take steps to increase officer awareness of ExDS and its symptoms and develop procedures to engage the medical community when identified. Without placing themselves or others at a greater risk for physical harm, officers must be able to rapidly detect symptoms of ExDS and immediately engage EMS for proper diagnosis and medical treatment. Failure to do so may prove fatal.

## Historical Data and Cases Reviewed

Reports of presentations consistent with ExDS have occurred for more than 150 years. In 1849 Dr. Luther Bell, a psychiatrist

in Massachusetts, described an acute exhaustive mania (Bell's Mania) in which patients developed hallucinations, profound agitation, and fever, which often were followed by death.[3] A decrease in reports occurred in the 1950s that coincided with the advent of antipsychotic medications and then an increase again in the 1980s likely secondary to widespread cocaine use. At that time, there were several reports in which an intoxicated person or an individual with mental illness exhibited aggression, hallucinations, and insensitivity to pain; was physically restrained (often in a prone position); and then died in custody.

In the last 20 years, law enforcement officers have seen this syndrome repeatedly. Several cases were outlined by a special panel review on ExDS at Penn State.[4]

**Excited delirium-associated death after handcuffing/ Hog-tying.** In October 2005 a West Palm Beach, Florida, police officer found a shirtless and distraught man stumbling on the road and attempting to stop vehicles. Told to relax, the man kept gesticulating wildly with vehicles stopping to avoid him. After a struggle the officer placed the man in a prone position and handcuffed him. Other officers arrived, helped move the man out of the street, and further restrained him by hog-tying his legs and hands. The man later became unconscious. Responding paramedics failed to resuscitate him. The chief medical examiner for Palm Beach County determined the cause of death was "sudden respiratory arrest following physical struggling restraint due to cocaine-induced ExDS."

**Excited delirium-associated death after major physical struggle.** A panel member who also serves as a Vancouver Police Department sergeant related the case of officers responding to a male subject who had a knife in a street confrontation. A foot chase ensued with police grounding the subject and multiple officers restraining him. The sergeant stated,

"The subject was so resistive and so strong that he lifted five officers off of him at one point." After a protracted struggle, the subject suddenly was quiet, went into cardiac arrest, and died at the scene. The subject suffered from mental illness and had alcohol and marijuana in his system. An autopsy concluded the subject died from choking due to the officer's restraint, and the coroner ruled the death accidental.

### Excited delirium-associated death after TASER use.

According to press reports, Dallas, Texas, police found a 23-year-old male subject in his underwear, screaming and holding a knife on a neighbor's porch on April 24, 2006. The man refused English and Spanish instructions and came at the officers with the knife. One officer fired a TASER, which failed to connect. A second shot did, causing electrical shock. A third was reportedly fired. After being handcuffed on an ambulance backboard, the subject stopped breathing and was pronounced dead at a hospital. The Dallas County medical examiner attributed the death to "excited delirium."

### Excited delirium-associated death with no police presence.

Certainly, the cases cited in the 1849 paper by Dr. Luther Bell in the *Journal of Insanity* had no police presence. Most recently, a case occurred involving an Anderson University basketball player. An Anderson County, Indiana, coroner "said [the man] had complained of cramps and vision problems just before he collapsed on a campus basketball court September 30 and had an 'extremely elevated body temperature' when he was rushed to the emergency room of AnMed Health Medical Center. The man's death days later was caused by 'acute drug toxicity with ExDS that led to multiple organ failure.'"[5]

Further, an expert panel convened by the American College of Emergency Physicians recognized ExDS as a unique clinical syndrome amenable to early therapeutic interventions.[6] This article provides a scientific background for ExDS, outlines risk factors, clarifies identification of the syndrome based on common signs and symptoms, and discusses control and sedation of affected individuals.

## Medical Background

The mechanism in which ExDS occurs is complex and not fully understood; however, recent research has provided greater insight. Although cocaine use is associated with ExDS, postmortem cocaine levels in those who have died after ExDS are similar to those of recreational cocaine users and lower than individuals who have died from heart attacks or other non-ExDS causes after cocaine use.[7] These findings suggest that cocaine intoxication alone does not cause ExDS. Further, a degree of cellular or genetic susceptibility may exist that leads some cocaine users to develop ExDS while others do not.

Researchers began to explore other mechanisms for ExDS, and the central dopamine theory emerged as a leading hypothesis.

Dopamine is a neurotransmitter with many functions. It plays a role in the brain's perception of reward and temperature regulation. Increased dopamine levels result in fast heart rates, feelings of euphoria, and hallucinations. Highly addictive drugs, specifically cocaine and methamphetamine, increase the level of dopamine in the brain. Schizophrenia also results in elevated levels of dopamine in the brain, and antipsychotics work to treat hallucinations by blocking dopamine on a cellular level. In chronic cocaine abusers who have died of ExDS, research has shown a loss of a crucial protein that eliminates dopamine from the brain. This loss results in increased dopamine levels and chaotic signaling in the brain. The elevated dopamine levels help explain some of the similarities between ExDS and schizophrenia (e.g., hallucinations, paranoia), but they do not account for the high rates of sudden cardiac arrest seen in the former but not the latter.

## Clinical Presentation

The clinical presentation of excited delirium has distinct and recognizable features. Much of what is used to identify excited delirium both on the street and in the hospital is based on case reports that have identified common clinical features, patient behaviors, and historical factors. In 2009, the American College of Emergency Physicians Task Force on Excited Delirium established that both delirium (e.g., acute confusion, hallucinations, and disorientation that is rapid in onset and may fluctuate in intensity) and an excited or agitated state must be present to consider ExDS.[8] Previously published cases identified common sequences of events, typically involving "acute drug intoxication or a history of mental illness, a struggle with law enforcement, physical or noxious chemical control measures or electrical control device (ECD) application, sudden and unexpected death, and an autopsy which fails to reveal a definite cause of death from trauma or natural disease."[9]

ExDS subjects typically are males around the age of 30, and most have a history of psychostimulant use or mental illness (see Table 1). Law enforcement agents or EMS personnel often are called to the scene because of public disturbances, agitation, or bizarre behaviors. Subjects are usually violent and combative with hallucinations, paranoia, or fear. Additionally, subjects may demonstrate profound levels of strength, resist painful stimuli or physical restraint, and seem impervious to self-inflicted injuries. This information becomes particularly important to law enforcement personnel who may use techniques intended to gain control and custody of subjects through physical means, chemical agents, or ECDs. During initial assessment patients often are noted to have elevated body temperatures, fast heart rates, rapid breathing, elevated blood pressures, and sweaty skin.

# Risk Factors Associated with Excited Delirium Syndrome

Males (average age 36)

Stimulant drug use

- Cocaine and to a lesser extent methamphetamine, PCP, and LSD

  Chronic users after an acute binge

  Preexisting psychiatric disorder

- Schizophrenia, bipolar disorder

---

Certain medical conditions have presented similarly to ExDS, including low blood sugar, thyroid abnormalities, and decompensated psychiatric illness. Methamphetamine, cocaine, PCP, and bath salt intoxication are associated with ExDS, but not every intoxicated individual develops it. Intoxication without ExDS will lack elevated body temperatures and certain laboratory abnormalities, such as metabolic acidosis. Severe sweating, a clue that a patient has an elevated temperature, combined with hallucinations always should prompt a consideration of ExDS. Differentiating ExDS from other medical causes or uncomplicated intoxication can prove difficult, but a prudent course is to assume the worst and bring patients to the hospital via EMS for evaluation by a physician.

## Treatments

When subjects are identified as potentially exhibiting excited delirium, rapid control of the situation, and timely execution of medical evaluation are important. Protocols vary by region according to local EMS policies and in many cases are driven by consensus opinions. Subjects with excited delirium often do not respond to verbal redirection. Additionally, attempts at physical control may not be as effective given extreme levels of strength and resistance to painful stimuli. Ongoing physical struggle can worsen a subject's innate fight-or-flight system, which can raise a patient's temperature, cause changes in the body's acid-base balance, and increase the risk of sudden death.

Medications are required to sedate ExDS patients to expedite the medical evaluation, decrease their fight-or-flight response, and avoid further harm to both the subject and those involved in the patient's care. Several classes of medications are available, as well as different routes of administration, including intranasal, intramuscular, and intravenous. Advanced life support EMS personnel capable of cardiac monitoring, advanced airway management, and medical resuscitation should be present

at the time of administration. Common medications include benzodiazepines (e.g., lorazepam, midazolam, and diazepam), antipsychotics (e.g., haloperidol, droperidol, olanzapine, and ziprasidone), and the dissociative agent ketamine. Benzodiazepines are very safe but are limited by varying dose requirements from patient to patient, as well as variable time until adequate sedation. Antipsychotics often are more useful in subjects presenting with acute exacerbations of psychiatric illness but are plagued by warnings about potential cardiac side effects and prolonged time until onset.

Ketamine is a unique medication that may play a larger role in the initial treatment of patients with excited delirium. It is characterized by a rapid onset of action (less than 5 minutes), stable effects on blood pressure, consistent ability to provide adequate sedation, and, in general, it maintains the subject's ability to breathe. Potential side effects include hallucinations and confusion as the medication wears off (10 to 20 percent of adults 30 to 120 minutes after administration), vocal cord spasm, and increased salivation. A recent study published by Regions Hospital EMS in St. Paul, Minnesota, reviewed 13 cases between April and December 2011 where ketamine was administered prior to hospital arrival for excited delirium.[10] This review further supports ketamine as an effective prehospital treatment of the ExDS patient. Peak sedation was achieved in less than 5 minutes in 11 of 13 cases. Moderate or deeper sedation was achieved in 12 of 13 patients. However, ketamine is a powerful medication, and ExDS is a life-threatening condition. Three patients developed low oxygen saturations. Two required endotracheal intubation, and one was assisted with a bag-valve mask. Three patients experienced emergent reactions, two of which were successfully treated with low doses of benzodiazepines. There were no deaths.

## Conclusion

In summary, excited delirium is becoming increasingly recognized as an important medical emergency encountered in the prehospital environment. Law enforcement agencies should undertake a concerted effort to increase awareness among officers of ExDS to include information to help identify symptoms and to establish protocols to engage the medical community. Armed with this information, officers will be in a better position to engage EMS for an urgent evaluation, treatment, and transport to the hospital. Using teamwork to safely and efficiently control these patients will lead to improved outcomes. Promising research is being conducted regarding the underlying mechanisms of this disease, as well as new methods of treatment, including ketamine, which may improve the ability to care for these patients.

# Notes

1. M.D. Sztajnkrycer and A.A. Baez, "Cocaine, Excited Delirium, and Sudden Unexpected Death," *EMS World,* April 2005 (updated January 11, 2011), http://www.emsworld.com/article/article.jsp?id51863 (accessed April 30, 2014).

2. D.L. Ross, "Factors Associated with Excited Delirium Deaths in Police Custody," *Modern Pathology* 11 (1998): 1127–1137.

3. L. Bell, "Acute Exhaustive Mania," *American Journal of Psychiatry* (October 1849).

4. Information regarding these cases is derived from the National Institute of Justice Weapons and Protective Systems Technologies Center, "Special Panel Review of Excited Delirium, December 2011," https://www.justnet.org/pdf/ExDS-Panel-Report-FINAL.pdf (accessed April 14, 2014).

5. As reported by N. Mayo, *Independent Mail* (November 15, 2011).

6. American College of Emergency Physicians Excited Delirium Task Force, "White Paper Report on Excited Delirium Syndrome, September, 10, 2009: Report to the Council and Board of Directors on Excited Delirium at the Direction of Amended Resolution 21(08)," http://www.fmhac.net/Assets/Documents/2012/Presentations/KrelsteinExcitedDelirium.pdf (accessed April 14, 2014).

7. D.C. Mash, L. Duque, J. Pablo, Y. Qin, N. Adi, W. Hearn, B. Hyma, S. Karch, H. Druid, and C. Wetli, "Brain Biomarkers for Identifying Excited Delirium as a Cause of Sudden Death," *Forensic Science International* 190 (2009): e13-e19.

8. American College of Emergency Physicians Excited Delirium Task Force.

9. American College of Emergency Physicians Excited Delirium Task Force.

10. A.M. Burnett, J.G. Salzman, K.R. Griffith, B. Kroeger, and R.J. Frascone, "The Emergency Department Experience with Prehospital Ketamine: A Case Series of 13 Patients," *Prehospital Emergency Care* 16 (2012):1–7.

# Critical Thinking

1. Are there other medical conditions that appear to be similar to ExDS?

2. What types of situations will often result in law enforcement or EMS being called?

3. How should law enforcement agencies treat this issue?

# Internet References

**American College of Emergency Physicians Excited Delirium Task Force**

http://www.fmhac.net/Assets/Documents/2012/Presentations/KrelsteinExcitedDelirium.pdf (accessed April 14, 2014).

**EMS World**

http://www.emsworld.com/article/10324064/cocaine-excited-delirium-and-sudden-unexpected-death

Federal Bureau of Investigation, 2014.

# Unit 4

# UNIT

Prepared by: Joanne Naughton

# The Judicial System

The courts are an equal partner in the American justice system. Just as the police have the responsibility of guarding our liberties by enforcing the laws, and prosecutors have the obligation to do justice rather than merely win cases, the courts play an important role in defending these liberties by applying and interpreting these laws, with the goal of attaining justice. The courts are the battlegrounds where civilized "wars" are fought without bloodshed, to protect individual rights and to settle disputes.

Courts must be vigilant to guard against the use of improper evidence obtained from violations of Constitutional rights, such as a suspect's right to remain silent, to be free from illegal searches; and to insure that a criminal defendant is represented by an attorney. Today, DNA testing of evidence seems almost routine, and in some cases capable of providing foolproof evidence of a suspect's guilt or innocence. But DNA testing in old cases too often highlights the tragedy of defendants having been convicted of crimes they didn't commit.

Our judicial process is an adversary system of justice, where the state is always represented by counsel, and the defendant's need for counsel is recognized in the Constitution.

*Article*                                        Prepared by: Joanne Naughton

# In Miranda Case, Supreme Court Rules on the Limits of Silence

**Justices uphold the murder conviction of a Texas man who refused to answer a question. The 5–4 ruling says suspects must invoke their legal rights.**

DAVID G. SAVAGE

## Learning Outcomes

*After reading this article, you will be able to:*

- Illustrate how the 5th Amendment didn't help Salinas.
- Discuss the Court's approach to the Miranda decision.

Crime suspects need to speak up if they want to invoke their legal right to remain silent, the Supreme Court said Monday in a ruling that highlights the limited reach of the famous Miranda decision.

The 5–4 ruling upheld the murder conviction of a Texas man who bit his lip and sat silently when a police officer asked him about the shotgun shells that were found at the scene of a double slaying. They had been traced to the suspect's shotgun.

At his trial, prosecutors pointed to the defendant's silence as evidence of his guilt. In affirming the conviction of Genovevo Salinas, the court's majority admitted that some suspects might think they had a right to say nothing.

"Popular misconceptions notwithstanding," the Constitution "does not establish an unqualified 'right to remain silent,'" said Justice Samuel A. Alito Jr.

Rather, he said, the 5th Amendment says no one may be "compelled in any criminal case to be witness against himself." Since the Miranda decision in 1966, the court has said police must warn suspects of their rights when they are taken into custody.

But the Miranda decision covers only suspects who are held in custody and are not free to leave.

In the Texas case, Salinas was asked to come to the police station, and he agreed to do so. "All agree that the interview was noncustodial," Alito said, so the police were not required to read him his rights under the Miranda decision.

And although Salinas had a qualified right to remain silent under the 5th Amendment, a suspect must invoke his rights and say he wants to remain silent, the court ruled Monday.

Salinas "alone knew why he did not answer the officer's question, and it was therefore his burden to make a timely assertion of the privilege," Alito said.

The decision is consistent with the high court's grudging approach to the Miranda decision and related 5th Amendment questions over recent decades. The court's conservative-leaning justices have not been willing to overturn the Miranda precedent, but they have repeatedly narrowed its scope.

Chief Justice John G. Roberts Jr. and Justices Antonin Scalia, Anthony M. Kennedy and Clarence Thomas voted with Alito to uphold the conviction in *Salinas vs. Texas.*

Alito noted that during a trial, defendants may refuse to testify, and prosecutors may not use their silence in court as evidence against them, citing the court's 1965 ruling in *Griffin vs. California.* In a concurring opinion, Thomas and Scalia said the Griffin case was mistaken and should be overruled.

Meanwhile, in another case, Thomas spoke for himself and four liberal justices to require a jury to find a defendant guilty of every facet of a crime that could lead to a mandatory prison term.

In *Alleyne vs. United States,* the court ruled that before a judge imposes an extra mandatory prison term on a defendant for conduct such as brandishing a firearm, a jury must find the defendant guilty of that offense. To do otherwise violates the defendant's basic right to a jury trial with his guilt proven beyond a reasonable doubt, Thomas said.

Thomas has long maintained that juries, not judges, must decide whether a defendant is guilty of all the elements of a crime that warrant extra punishment. And in a rare show of unity with the court's more liberal members, he overruled earlier decisions that left this power in the hands of a judge.

In the case before the court, Allen Alleyne was given four years in prison for helping his girlfriend rob the manager of a convenience store. Following the prosecution's recommendation, the judge gave him an extra seven years for having brandished a firearm. But Alleyne said he had not brandished a gun, and the jury had not convicted him of that extra offense.

The 5–4 ruling overturns the extra seven-year term. The dissenters faulted the majority for overruling a precedent from 2002 that allowed judges to make such decisions.

## Critical Thinking

1. How does the 5th Amendment protect us?
2. Who does the 5th Amendment protect?
3. Why didn't the 5th Amendment protect Salinas?

## Create Central

www.mhhe.com/createcentral

## Internet References

**Miranda Rights**
www.mirandarights.org/righttoremainsilent.html

**NWSidebar**
http://nwsidebar.wsba.org/2013/06/26/salinas-v-texas-miranda-rights

*Article*      Prepared by: Joanne Naughton

# US Supreme Court to Police: To Search a Cell Phone, "Get a Warrant"

**The US Supreme Court, ruling 9 to 0, invalidated the warrantless searches of cell phones, which hold "the privacies of life." Police have no right to "rummage at will," the justices said.**

WARREN RICHEY

## Learning Outcomes

*After reading this article, you will be able to:*

- State the relevant facts in *Wurie* and *Riley*.
- Present the Court's decisions in these cases.
- Explain the Court's reasoning.

Washington—In a major affirmation of privacy in the digital age, the US Supreme Court on Wednesday ruled that police must obtain a warrant before searching digital information on a cell phone seized from an individual who has been arrested.

The 9-to-0 decision marks a Fourth Amendment landmark of profound importance given the ubiquity of cell phones, tablets, and portable computers in public places throughout society.

"Modern cell phones are not just another technological convenience," Chief Justice John Roberts wrote for the court. "With all they contain and all they may reveal, they hold for many Americans the 'privacies of life,' " he said.

"The fact that technology now allows an individual to carry such information in his hand does not make the information any less worthy of the protection for which the Founders fought," the chief justice said.

"Our answer to the question of what police must do before searching a cell phone seized incident to an arrest is accordingly simple—get a warrant."

In an indication of how fundamental these protections are in the justices' view, the chief justice likened warrantless searches of cell phones to the "general warrants" and "writs of assistance" imposed during colonial America that allowed British troops to "rummage through homes in an unrestrained search for evidence of criminal activity."

"Opposition to such searches was in fact one of the driving forces behind the Revolution itself," Chief Justice Roberts said.

In reaching its decision, the justices rejected arguments by the Obama administration and the California attorney general that law enforcement officials must be able to immediately search the contents of a cell phone or other electronic device when the device was found on a person at the time of his or her lawful arrest.

The justices also rejected a suggested fallback position to allow police to conduct a limited search of a cell phone without a warrant whenever it was reasonable to believe the device contained evidence of the crime that prompted the arrest of the individual.

Roberts said that fallback position provided no practical limit because it would still give "police officers unbridled discretion to rummage at will among a person's private effects."

Instead, the court established a bright line rule that if police seize a cell phone during an arrest they must seek approval from a neutral judge before searching the phone for any evidence of crime.

Steps can be taken to secure the data on the phone to prevent destruction of potential evidence, he said. And the warrant process is becoming more efficient.

"We cannot deny that our decision today will have an impact on the ability of law enforcement to combat crime," Roberts said. "Cell phones have become important tools in facilitating coordination and communication among members of criminal enterprises, and can provide valuable incriminating information about dangerous criminals."

But the chief justice added: "Privacy comes at a cost."

Roberts said the court recognized that there might be instances when the government faces exigent circumstances that required swift and decisive action. In those cases, the courts have recognized an exception to the warrant requirement, an exception that must be later justified case by case to a judge.

The decision reflects a recognition by the high court of a growing threat to privacy in the digital age, with vast amounts of personal records, photos, video, and other intimate information readily accessible on smart phones and other electronic devices.

The government had argued that once an individual is placed under arrest, he or she has a diminished privacy interest and that diminished privacy protection does not extend to anything found in their pockets. Under this approach, searching the contents of a cell phone should be considered no different than searching inside a cigarette pack found in an arrestee's pocket, the government argued.

"This is like saying a ride on horseback is materially indistinguishable from a flight to the moon," Roberts said.

"Modern cell phones, as a category, implicate privacy concerns far beyond those implicated by the search of a cigarette pack, a wallet, or a purse," he said.

Cell phones are different, he said. Even the term cell phone doesn't accurately account for the full scope of their use.

"They could just as easily be called cameras, video players, rolodexes, calendars, tape recorders, libraries, diaries, albums, televisions, maps, or newspapers," Roberts said.

"Most people cannot lug around every piece of mail they have received for the past several months, every picture they have taken, or every book or article they have read—nor would they have reason to attempt to do so," he said.

He said to do so would require dragging a trunk around. The chief justice noted that under existing legal precedents, police would need a warrant to search such a trunk.

"Prior to the digital age, people did not typically carry a cache of sensitive personal information with them as they went about their day," he said. "Now it is the person who is not carrying a cell phone, with all that it contains, who is the exception."

Wednesday's decision stems from two cases in which police used information discovered during warrantless searches of cell phones being carried by individuals at the time of their arrest.

The phones contained images and other information that police used as evidence of criminal activity or to identify other evidence of crime.

One case involved a suspected drug dealer in Boston named Brima Wurie. Police used his cell phone to identify Mr. Wurie's home address. After obtaining a warrant they raided the home where they found drugs, cash, and a weapon.

Wurie was charged with possession with intent to distribute cocaine base, distributing cocaine base, and with being a felon in possession of a firearm.

Wurie's lawyers filed a motion to suppress the evidence that resulted from the warrantless search of his cell phone.

A federal judge denied the motion. At trial, Wurie was convicted and sentenced to nearly 22 years in prison.

On appeal, the First US Circuit Court of Appeals reversed the trial judge, ruling that the police should have obtained a warrant *before* accessing the information in Wurie's phone.

The other case involved a suspected criminal gang member in San Diego named David Riley.

Mr. Riley was pulled over in a traffic stop for driving with expired tags. After discovering that Riley's license had been suspended, the officer impounded Riley's car.

During a routine search of the car, police found two firearms under the car's hood. Riley was arrested.

As he was taken into custody, police seized Riley's smartphone. The arresting officer scrolled through the phone's text files and noticed notations that suggested that Riley was a gang member.

Two hours later, at the police department, the phone was turned over to a detective who specialized in gang crime investigations. The detective examined the contents of the phone and discovered images that allegedly linked the suspect to an earlier gang-related shooting. Police also used photos and video images found on the phone to connect the suspect to other gang-related activities.

Riley was charged with shooting at an occupied vehicle, use of a semiautomatic firearm, and attempted murder. He was also charged with involvement in a gang-related crime.

His lawyer argued that evidence obtained without a warrant from Riley's smartphone must be excluded from his trial. The judge rejected the motion, ruling that the action did not violate the Fourth Amendment.

Riley was convicted and sentenced to 15 years to life in prison. The California Court of Appeal upheld the conviction, noting that the California Supreme Court in 2011 had issued an opinion that police may search a smartphone without a warrant whenever the phone is being carried by an individual at the time of arrest.

In its ruling on Wednesday, the Supreme Court reversed the California Court of Appeal and affirmed the decision of the First Circuit in Boston.

The cases were *US v. Wurie* (13–212) and *Riley v. California* (13–132).

## Critical Thinking

1. What were the "general warrants" and "writs of assistance" referred to in the Court's decision?

2. Why is searching a cell phone different from searching inside a cigarette pack found in an arrestee's pocket?

3. Is privacy worth the cost to law enforcement?

## Internet References

**Encyclopedia.com**
http://www.encyclopedia.com/topic/Writs_of_assistance.aspx

**Findlaw**
http://criminal.findlaw.com/criminal-rights/search-and-seizure-and-the-fourth-amendment.html?DCMP=ADCCRIM_SearchSeizure-4thAmendment&&HBX_PK=fourth+amendment+regulation

**The Christian Science Monitor**
http://www.csmonitor.com/Innovation/2013/0718/FISA-101-10-key-dates-in-the-evolution-of-NSA-surveillance/Before-the-September-11-attacks

*Article*    Prepared by: Joanne Naughton

# One Simple Way to Improve How Cops and Prosecutors Do Their Jobs

Mike Riggs

## Learning Outcomes

*After reading this article, you will be able to:*

- Set forth what Byrne Grants are.
- Describe how the bulk of Byrne Grants are primarily used.

Every year, the U.S. Justice Department sends hundreds of millions of dollars to states and municipalities via the Edward Byrne Memorial Justice Assistance Grant. Named for 22-year-old NYPD Officer Edward Byrne, who was murdered in 1988 while he sat in his patrol car, the JAG program provides "critical funding necessary to support a range of program areas, including law enforcement; prosecution, courts, and indigent defense; crime prevention and education; corrections and community corrections; drug treatment and enforcement; program planning, evaluation, and technology improvement; and crime victim and witness initiatives."

Despite what that long list suggests, the bulk of JAG funding ends up going toward fighting the drug war. "Historically," the Drug Policy Alliance noted in 2010, "Byrne Grants have been used primarily to finance drug task forces, which have a record of racially disproportionate low level drug arrests and increased local and state costs with no measurable impact on public safety." At the time, the group suggested that JAG funding be reallocated in favor of more drug treatment programs, rather than enforcement.

As it stands, 60 percent of JAG funding over the last 3 years—totaling more than half a billion dollars—has gone to law enforcement activities. In a new report, titled "Reforming Funding to Reduce Mass Incarceration" [PDF], the Brennan Center for Justice explains why: Because law enforcement agencies can do whatever they want with this money, and most of them think the best way to keep that money coming is to arrest as many people as possible.

This is no accident. The annual self-evaluation JAG recipients are required to complete measures performance in a way, says the Brennan Center report, that is "roughly analogous to a hospital counting the number of emergency room admissions, instead of considering the number of lives saved." Agencies are asked how many arrests they made, and prosecutors are asked how many cases they won. Not only is that data rather useless in terms of assessing the effectiveness of a given policy, it also says to the person answering the questions that their numbers should be really big.

JAG funding is only a slice of a law enforcement agency's budget, but it can still be a lot of money. Many cities receive JAG funding directly (L.A., New York, Chicago, Houston receive millions a year), and money also goes to states to dole out as they see fit. In 2013, Texas, California, Florida, New York, and Illinois received between $10 and $30 million in JAG grants. As a result of the perception that more arrests are better, the majority of JAG funding goes toward drug and gang enforcement. Programs that arguably should receive more funding in an age of overincarceration get far less: drug treatment programs receive only 5 percent of JAG funding, while on average .004 percent goes toward indigent defense.

Former and current law enforcement officials interviewed by the Brennan Center said that the DOJ's current JAG questionnaire encourages agencies to report "accomplishments that are easy to track but meaningless." To change that, says the Brennan Center, the Justice Department could do something awfully simple: ask a better set of questions when reviewing how agencies spent their grant money.

Is a new questionnaire going to "fix" over-policing of minor crimes and overincarceration of nonviolent offenders? No. But changing incentives is a first step in changing culture. "By signaling to recipients that effectiveness, proportionality, and fairness are DOJ priorities," the Brennan report suggests, "the proposed measures can help turn off the 'automatic pilot' of more punishment—and more incarceration."

## Critical Thinking

1. What is the Brennan Center's main criticism of Byrne Grants?

2. Do you agree that too much emphasis is placed on enforcing drug and gang laws?

# Internet References

**Brennan Center for Justice**
   http://www.brennancenter.org/publication/reforming-funding-reduce-mass-incarceration

**Bureau of Justice Assistance U.S. Department of Justice**
   https://www.bja.gov/Publications/JAG_LE_Grant_Activity_03-13.pdf

**Drug Policy Alliance**
   http://www.drugpolicy.org/sites/default/files/FactSheet_ByrneJAG_Sept.%202010.pdf

*Article*

Prepared by: Joanne Naughton

# Against His Better Judgment

In the meth corridor of Iowa, a federal judge comes face to face with the reality of congressionally mandated sentencing.

ELI SASLOW

## Learning Outcomes

*After reading this article, you will be able to:*

- Explain how mandatory minimum sentences affect the ability of a judge to use discretion when imposing a sentence.

- Show that criminal defendants don't always know the sentences they are facing for their crimes.

- Discuss Judge Bennett's objections to mandatory minimum sentencing.

They filtered into the courtroom and waited for the arrival of the judge, anxious to hear what he would decide. The defendant's family knelt in the gallery to pray for a lenient sentence. A lawyer paced the entryway and rehearsed his final argument. The defendant reached into the pocket of his orange jumpsuit and pulled out a crumpled note he had written to the judge the night before: "Please, you have all the power," it read. "Just try and be merciful."

U.S. District Judge Mark Bennett entered and everyone stood. He sat and then they sat. "Another hard one," he said, and the room fell silent. He was one of 670 federal district judges in the United States, appointed for life by a president and confirmed by the Senate, and he had taken an oath to "administer justice" in each case he heard. Now he read the sentencing documents at his bench and punched numbers into an oversize calculator. When he finally looked up, he raised his hands together in the air as if his wrists were handcuffed, and then he repeated the conclusion that had come to define so much about his career.

"My hands are tied on your sentence," he said. "I'm sorry. This isn't up to me."

How many times had he issued judgments that were not his own? How often had he apologized to defendants who had come to apologize to him? For more than two decades as a federal judge, Bennett had often viewed his job as less about presiding than abiding by dozens of mandatory minimum sentences established by Congress in the late 1980s for federal offenses. Those mandatory penalties, many of which require at least a decade in prison for drug offenses, took discretion away from judges and fueled an unprecedented rise in prison populations, from 24,000 federal inmates in 1980 to more than 208,000 last year. Half of those inmates are nonviolent drug offenders. Federal prisons are overcrowded by 37 percent. The Justice Department recently called mass imprisonment a "budgetary nightmare" and a "growing and historic crisis."

Politicians as disparate as President Obama and Sen. Rand Paul (R-Ky.) are pushing new legislation in Congress to weaken mandatory minimums, but neither has persuaded Sen. Charles E. Grassley (R-Iowa), who chairs the Senate Judiciary Committee that is responsible for holding initial votes on sentencing laws. Even as Obama has begun granting clemency to a small number of drug offenders, calling their sentences "outdated," Grassley continues to credit strict sentencing with helping reduce violent crime by half in the past 25 years, and he has denounced the new proposals in a succession of speeches to Congress. "Mandatory minimum sentences play a vital role," he told Congress again last month.

But back in Grassley's home state, in Iowa's busiest federal court, the judge who has handed down so many of those sentences has concluded something else about the legacy of his work. "Unjust and ineffective," he wrote in one sentencing opinion. "Gut-wrenching," he wrote in another. "Prisons filled, families divided, communities devastated," he wrote in a third.

And now it was another Tuesday in Sioux City—five hearings listed on his docket, five more nonviolent offenders whose cases involved mandatory minimums of anywhere from 5 to 20 years without the possibility of release. Here in the methamphetamine corridor of middle America, Bennett averaged seven times as many cases each year as a federal judge in New York City or Washington. He had sentenced two convicted murderers to death and several drug cartel bosses to life in prison, but many of his defendants were addicts who had become middling dealers, people who sometimes sounded to him less like perpetrators than victims in the case reports now piled high on his bench. "History of family addiction." "Mild mental retardation." "PTSD after suffering multiple rapes." "Victim of sexual abuse." "Temporarily homeless." "Heavy user since age 14."

Bennett tried to forget the details of each case as soon as he issued a sentence. "You either drain the bathtub, or the guilt and sadness just overwhelms you," he said once, in his chambers, but what he couldn't forget was the total, more than 1,100 nonviolent offenders and counting to whom he had given mandatory minimum sentences he often considered unjust. That meant more than $200 million in taxpayer money he thought had been misspent. It meant a generation of rural Iowa drug addicts he had institutionalized. So he had begun traveling to dozens of prisons across the country to visit people he had sentenced, answering their legal questions and accompanying them to drug treatment classes, because if he couldn't always fulfill his intention of justice from the bench, then at least he could offer empathy. He could look at defendants during their sentencing hearings and give them the dignity of saying exactly what he thought.

"Congress has tied my hands," he told one defendant now.

"We are just going to be warehousing you," he told another.

"I have to uphold the law whether I agree with it or not," he said a few minutes later.

The courtroom emptied and then filled, emptied and then filled, until Bennett's back stiffened and his robe twisted around his blue jeans. He was 65 years old, with uncombed hair, a relaxed posture and a midwestern unpretentiousness. "Let's keep moving," he said, and then in came his fourth case of the day, another methamphetamine addict facing his first federal drug charge, a defendant Bennett had been thinking about all week.

His name was Mark Weller. He was 28 years old. He had pleaded guilty to two counts of distributing methamphetamine in his home town of Denison, Iowa, which meant his mandatory minimum sentence as established by Congress was 10 years in prison. His maximum sentence was life without parole. For four months, he had been awaiting his hearing while locked in a cell at the Fort Dodge Correctional Facility, where there was nothing to do but watch Fox News on TV, think over his life and write letters to people who usually didn't write back.

"I can't tell you how many times I've asked myself, 'How did I get into the situation I'm in today?'" he had written.

Marijuana starting at age 12. Whiskey at 14. Cocaine at 16, and methamphetamine a few months later. "Always hooked on something" was how some family members described him in the pre-sentencing report, but for a while he had managed to hold his life together. He graduated from high school, married, had a daughter and worked for six years at a pork slaughterhouse, becoming a union steward and earning $18 an hour. He bought a doublewide trailer and a Harley, and he tattooed the names of his wife and daughter onto his shoulder. But then his wife met a man on the Internet and moved with their daughter to Missouri, and Weller started drinking some mornings before work. Soon he had lost his job, lost custody of his daughter and, in his own accounting, lost his "morals along with all self control." He started spending as much as $200 each day on meth, selling off his Harley, his trailer and then selling meth, too. He traded meth to pay for his sister's rent, for a used car, for gas money and then for an unregistered rifle, which was still in his car when he was pulled over with 223 grams of methamphetamine last year.

He was arrested and charged with a federal offense because he had been trafficking methamphetamine across state lines. Then he met for the first time with his public defender, considered one of the state's best, Brad Hansen.

"How much is my bond?" Weller remembered asking that day.

"There is no bond in federal court," Hansen told him.

"Then how many days until I get out?" Weller asked.

"We're not just talking about days," Hansen said, and so he began to explain the severity of a criminal charge in the federal system, in which all offenders are required to serve at least 85 percent of whatever sentence they receive. Weller didn't yet know that a series of witnesses, hoping to escape their own mandatory minimum drug sentences, had informed the government that Weller had dealt 2.5 kilograms of methamphetamine over the course of eight months. He didn't yet know that 2.5 kilograms was just barely enough for a mandatory minimum of 10 years, even for a first offense. He didn't know that, after he pleaded guilty, the judge would receive a pre-sentencing report in which his case would be reduced to a series of calculations in the controversial math of federal sentencing.

"Victim impact: There is no identifiable victim."

"Criminal history: Minimal."

"Cost of imprisonment: $2,440.97 per month."

"Guideline sentence: 151 to 188 months."

What Weller knew—the only thing he knew—was the version of sentencing he had seen so many times on prime-time TV. He would have a legal right to speak in court. The court would have an obligation to listen. He asked his family to send testimonials about his character to the courthouse, believing his sentence would depend not only on Congress or on a calculator but also on another person, a judge.

The night before Weller's hearing, Bennett returned to a home overlooking Sioux City and carried the pre-sentencing report to a recliner in his living room. He already had been through it twice, but he wanted to read it again. He put on glasses, poured a glass of wine and began with the letters.

"He was doing fine with his life, it seems, until his wife met another man on-line," Weller's father had written.

"After she left, the life was sucked out of him," his sister had written.

"Broken is the only word," his brother had written. "Meth sunk its dirty little fingers into him."

"I hope this can explain how a child was set up for a fall in his life," his mother had written, in the last letter and the longest one of all. "Growing up, all he pretty much had was an alcoholic mother who was manic depressive and schizophrenic. When I wasn't cutting myself, I was getting drunk and beating the hell out of him in the middle of the night. When I wasn't doing all that I was trying to kill myself and ending up in a mental hospital. Can you imagine being a four year old and getting beat up one day and having to go visit that same person in a mental hospital the next? No heat in the house, no lights, nothing. That was his starting point."

Bennett set down the report, stood from his chair and paced across a room decorated with photos of his own daughter, in the house that had been her starting point. There were scrapbooks made to commemorate each year of her life. There were videotapes of her high school tennis matches and photos of her recent graduation from a private college near Chicago.

He had decided to become a judge just a few months after her birth, in the early 1990s. His wife had been expecting twins, a boy and a girl, and had gone into labor several months prematurely. Their daughter had survived, but their son had died when he was eight hours old, and the capriciousness of that tragedy had left him searching for order, for a life of deliberation and fairness. He had quit private practice and devoted himself to the judges' oath of providing justice, first as a magistrate judge and then as a Bill Clinton appointee to the federal bench, going into his chambers to work six days each week.

Since then he had sent more than 4,000 people to federal prison, and he thought most of them had deserved at least some time in jail. There were meth addicts who promised to seek treatment but then showed up again in court as robbers or dealers. There were rapists and child pornographers that expressed little or no remorse. He had installed chains and bolts on the courtroom floor to restrain the most violent defendants. One of those had threatened to murder his family, which meant his daughter had spent her first three months of high school being shadowed by a U.S. marshal. "It is a view of humanity that can become disillusioning," he said, and sometimes he thought that it required work to retain a sense of compassion.

Once, on the way to a family vacation, he had dropped his wife and daughter off at a shopping mall and detoured by himself to visit the prison in Marion, Ill., then the highest-security penitentiary in the country. He scheduled a tour with the warden, and at the end of the tour Bennett asked for a favor. Was there an empty cell where he could spend a few minutes alone? The warden led him to solitary confinement, where prisoners spent 23 hours each day in their cells, and he locked Bennett inside a unit about the size of a walk-in closet. Bennett sat on the concrete bed, ran his hands against the walls and listened to the hum of the fluorescent light. He imagined the minutes stretching into days and the days extending into years, and by the time the warden returned with the key Bennett's mouth was dry and his hands were clammy, and he couldn't wait to be back at the mall.

"Hell on earth," he said, explaining what just five minutes as a visitor in a federal penitentiary could feel like, and he tried to recall those minutes each time he delivered a sentence. He often gave violent offenders more prison time than the government recommended. He had a reputation for harsh sentencing on white-collar crime. But much of his docket consisted of methamphetamine cases, 87 percent of which required a mandatory minimum as established in the late 1980s by lawmakers who had hoped to send a message about being tough on crime.

By some measures, their strategy had worked: Homicides had fallen by 54 percent since the late 1980s, and property crimes had dropped by a third. Prosecutors and police officers had used the threat of mandatory sentences to entice low-level criminals into cooperating with the government, exchanging information about accomplices in order to earn a plea deal. But most mandatory sentences applied to drug charges, and according to police data, drug use had remained steady since the 1980s even as the number of drug offenders in federal prison increased by 2,200 percent.

"A draconian, ineffective policy" was how then-Attorney General Eric H. Holder Jr. had described it.

"A system that's overrun" was what Republican presidential candidate Mike Huckabee had said.

"Isn't there anything you can do?" asked Bennett's wife, joining him now in the living room. They rarely talked about his cases. But he had told her a little about Weller's, and now she wanted to know what would happen.

"Childhood trauma is a mitigating factor, right?" she said. "Shouldn't that impact his sentence?"

"Yes," he said. "Neglect and abuse are mitigating. Definitely."

"And addiction?"

"Yes."

"Remorse?"

"Yes."

"No history of violence?"

"Yes. Of course," he said, standing up. "It's all mitigating. His whole life is basically mitigating, but there still isn't much I can do."

The first people into the courtroom were Weller's mother, his sister and then his father, who had driven 600 miles from Kansas to sit in the front row, where he was having trouble catching his breath. He gasped for air and rocked in his seat until two court marshals turned to stare. "Look away," he told them. "Have a little respect on the worst day of our lives. Look the hell away."

In came Weller. In came the judge. "This is United States of America versus Mark Paul Weller," the court clerk said.

And then there was only so much left for the court to discuss. Hansen, the defense attorney, could only ask for the mandatory minimum sentence of 10 years, rather than the guideline sentence of 13 years or the maximum of life. The state prosecutor could only agree that 10 years was probably sufficient, because Weller had a "number of mitigating factors," he said. Bennett could only delay the inevitable as the court played out a script written by Congress 30 years earlier.

"This is one of those cases where I wish the court could do more," said Hansen, the defense attorney.

"He's certainly not a drug kingpin," the government prosecutor consented.

"He could use a wake-up call," Hansen said. "But, come on, I mean . . ."

"He doesn't need a 10-year wake-up call," Bennett said.

"Ten years is not a wake-up call," Hansen said. "It's more like a sledgehammer to the face."

"We talk about incremental punishment," Bennett said. "This is not incremental."

They stared at each other for a few more minutes until it was time for Weller to address the court. He leaned into a microphone and read a speech he had written in his holding cell the night before, a speech he now realized would do him no good. He apologized to his family. He apologized to the addicts who had bought his drugs. "There is no excuse for what I did," he said. "I was a hardworking family man dedicated to my family. I turned to drugs, and that was the beginning of the end for me. I hope I get the chance to better my life in the future and put this behind me."

"Thank you, Mr. Weller. Very thoughtful," Bennett said, making a point to look him in the eye. "Very, very thoughtful," he said again, and then he issued the sentence. "You are hereby committed to the custody of the bureau of prisons to be imprisoned for 120 months." He lowered his gavel and walked out, and then the court marshal took Weller to his holding cell for a five-minute visitation with his family. He looked at them through a glass wall and tried to take measure of 10 years. His grandmother would probably be dead. His daughter would be in high school. He would be nearing 40, with half of his life behind him. "It's weird to know that even the judge basically said it wasn't fair," he said.

Down the hall in his chambers, Bennett was also considering the weight of 10 years: one more nonviolent offender packed into an overcrowded prison; another $300,000 in government money spent. "I would have given him a year in rehab if I could," he told his assistant. "How does 10 years make anything better? What good are we doing?"

But already his assistant was handing him another case file, the fifth of the day, and the courtroom was beginning to fill again. "I need five minutes," he said. He went into his office, removed his robe and closed his eyes. He thought about the offer he had received a few weeks earlier from an old partner, who wanted him to return to private practice in Des Moines. No more sentencing hearings. No more bathtub of guilt to drain. "I'm going to think seriously about doing that," Bennett had said, and he was still trying to make up his mind. Now he cleared Weller's sentencing report from his desk and added it to a stack in the corner. He washed his face and changed back into his robe.

"Ready to go?" his assistant asked.

"Ready," he said.

## Critical Thinking

1. Do you believe that imprisoning drug law violators has helped alleviate the nation's drug problem?

2. Is a trial judge in a good position to have a realistic idea of the appropriate punishments that should be given to the defendants who appear before the court?

3. Does justice require that everyone who commits a crime get the same sentence, regardless of any other circumstances?

## Internet References

**The Hill**

http://thehill.com/blogs/blog-briefing-room/231775-rand-paul-revives-mandatory-sentencing-reform-bill

**The Nation**

http://www.thenation.com/article/how-mandatory-minimums-forced-me-send-more-1000-nonviolent-drug-offenders-federal-pri/

**US Sentencing Commission**

http://www.ussc.gov/news/congressional-testimony-and-reports/mandatory-minimum-penalties/report-congress-mandatory-minimum-penalties-federal-criminal-justice-system

## Article

Prepared by: Joanne Naughton

# Does an Innocent Man Have the Right to Be Exonerated?

In the 1980s, Larry Youngblood was wrongfully imprisoned for raping a 10-year-old boy. The way the Supreme Court handled his case had lasting consequences.

MARC BOOKMAN

## Learning Outcomes

*After reading this article, you will be able to:*

- Relate the facts of *Arizona v. Youngblood.*

- State the percentage of convictions that are ultimately overturned because of mistaken eyewitness identification, according to the Innocence Project.

- Explain the Supreme Court's decision in *Youngblood.*

In the early morning hours of June 16, 2004, a 31-year-old man named David Leon was killed by a train just west of Estavan Park in Tucson. The *Arizona Daily Star* ran a brief item on the accident but never mentioned Leon's background; the press seemed unaware that he had been in the middle of Tucson's biggest legal scandal for the past two decades.

There was a good reason the media hadn't recognized Leon's name: Over the years, he'd been referred to vaguely as "the victim" or under the pseudonym "Paul"; the U.S. Supreme Court had called him "David L." But concealing his identity hadn't prevented the young man from suffering untold damage. Weeks after the train accident, the autopsy revealed that he had been drunk at the time of his death, a fact that surely surprised no one who knew him. And so the story ended almost exactly where it began: within a stone's throw of Interstate 10.

By the time David Leon was in the fifth grade, he was already struggling with emotional problems. At the age of 4, he had been referred for therapy because he was acting out in his preschool and was unable to get along with the other children; a

counselor later characterized him as hyperactive. But in at least one way he was like just about every other 10-year-old boy: He preferred carnivals to church. Such was the choice he faced when he accompanied his mother to the Southgate Shopping Center on the night of October 29, 1983. His mother's church, called The Door, was hosting a music concert that night, but there was a carnival in the parking lot, and naturally David wanted to go. Toward the end of the service, when everyone stood to pray, she noticed that he had slipped out. She circled the carnival grounds a number of times, but he was nowhere to be found.

The pastor's wife called David's mother later that night. The boy had come back, shaken up, with his clothes torn and inside-out. He had been abducted, raped, and dropped back at the church. His mother took him to Kino Community Hospital and the facts of the crime began to emerge. A black man with a bad eye had asked David if he'd give him a hand transporting a tent in his car—there was $5 in it for him if he would help. David initially hesitated—he wasn't supposed to get into cars with strangers—but the man was persistent, and eventually he got the boy to follow along behind his car. One thing led to another, and eventually David was thrown into the man's car, driven out to the desert, and raped twice. Just before he was returned to the church, the man told him that he had a go-cart at home and maybe he could see David again.

The police did what police do in these situations. First one officer talked to David, then another. A composite artist worked with him to get an accurate portrait of the perpetrator. They photographed him to document any injuries and collected his clothing. Finally, the doctor at the hospital brought out a rape kit—using swabs, he collected samples from the boy's mouth and rectum, as well as samples of the boy's blood, saliva, and hair. All that was left was to catch the black man with the bad eye.

It is a common complaint that media coverage of crime spotlights the perpetrator while ignoring the victim. Certainly this was true in the Leon case, or at least partly true. As it turned out, there were two victims, and the second one, Larry Youngblood, received a great deal of unwanted attention. This is because for 17 years he was seen as the perpetrator.

Nine days after the crime, a detective in the Tucson Police Department assembled a collection of photographs, six in all, of black men—each of them had an eye randomly blotted out. When detectives make a photo lineup—instead of having the eyewitness look through books of mugshots—it means they already have a suspect in mind, what the police call a "prime." In this case, the prime was Larry Youngblood. He'd been convicted of a robbery 10 years earlier and had some subsequent minor brushes with the police—and he was a black man living in Tucson with one bad eye. As the detective put it in law-enforcement speak, "Officers had suspicions that the subject in this case may have been Mr. Youngblood."

David was in his fifth grade classroom at the Irene Erickson Elementary School when Detective Joyce Lingel came to see him with the photo spread. David held the lineup very close to his face, prompting Detective Lingel to ask if he was having trouble seeing. He said that he had left his glasses in the classroom, and she sent him back to get them. When he returned, he again looked carefully at the photos and announced with certainty that Number Three was the guy. Larry Youngblood.

That was all they needed. Youngblood was arrested a month later, and not long after that he made arrangements to use his home as equity for bail. But he was still in custody five days before Christmas, when his preliminary hearing was scheduled. David came to court that morning with a member of the Victim Witness Program, and Detective Lingel joined him on a bench outside the courtroom while they waited for the case to begin. Larry Youngblood emerged from an elevator, escorted by a deputy sheriff, wearing prison issue and with his hands cuffed behind him. It was then that David looked him over, turned to the detective, and asked, "Is that him?"

According to the Innocence Project, eyewitness misidentification is responsible for 72 percent of the convictions ultimately overturned through DNA evidence. It's easy to understand why—just think of the last time you saw an old friend reading a book in the airport, tapped him on the shoulder, and then stumbled over the apology when it turned out not to be him. And that was an old friend, not a complete stranger. But not every identification is mistaken, and as the prosecutor told the jury, David had "ample time to observe the person who did it." What she didn't say, and maybe didn't have to say, was that

Youngblood was a black man with a bad eye living in Tucson. How many could there be?

From the beginning, though, David's description wasn't a perfect match for the suspect: He'd told his mother that the car he'd been kidnapped in was a two-door, when Youngblood's was a four-door, and that the man's hair had some gray running through it, although it was confirmed at trial by a professional hair dresser that Youngblood's hair had never been dyed and had never been gray. David hadn't described a man who limped, and one of Youngblood's legs was shorter than the other. There was even the issue of musical taste: David insisted the driver of the car had been playing country music, and everyone who knew Larry Youngblood knew he hated country music.

But there is no rule that a case gets stronger for the accused when the defense begins calling its witnesses. Although Youngblood's attorney told the jury that he always wore dark glasses to hide his bad eye—a fact that had gone unmentioned by the young victim—a defense witness and neighbor testified that he only wore those glasses about half the time. An eye doctor who was called to establish David Leon's bad eyesight, and thus his inability to correctly identify the perpetrator, ended up explaining to the jury that David's eyesight was actually good enough to enable him to obtain an Arizona driver's license one day. Perhaps just as harmful were the testimonies of Youngblood himself and his on-again, off-again girlfriend. Both insisted that they remembered the specific, thoroughly uneventful details of the evening in question. That was his alibi: that he was sleeping on a couch the night of the crime.

There was one other witness for the defense, a scientist from California named Keith Inman. His testimony filled 28 pages of the transcript, but after all the evidence about left eyes and right eyes, four-door cars and hair color, and whether the rapist limped or not, it seemed almost like an afterthought. Inman discussed blood types and spermatozoa and P-30 molecules and acid phosphatase and secretors versus non-secretors, all to one end: to show that if David Leon's underwear had been refrigerated by the police, which it had not been, scientific tests of the semen stains might have exculpated Larry Youngblood. The prosecutor spent her time getting the scientist to concede that those same tests might not have exculpated Youngblood. Such were the limitations of forensic science before the era of DNA testing.

## David looked Youngblood over, turned to the detective, and asked, "Is that him?"

Although the state's failure to preserve the evidence proved critically important over the next 15 years as the case traveled up and down the appellate ladder, it turned out not to be important at all to the jurors; they took only 40 minutes to convict Young-blood of child molestation, sexual assault, and kidnapping. Right up to the moment of sentencing, Youngblood insisted on his innocence. "Any black man with a bad eye would have been found guilty," he told his pre-sentence investigator, who nonetheless recommended that he get therapy "geared toward his sexually deviant behavior" upon his eventual release. Larry Youngblood was going to prison.

To what lengths must the state go to ensure that the accused gets a fair trial? Not a perfect trial—the courts are very clear that no one is entitled to that. But the contours of a fair trial have been open to debate since the Constitution was written. For Youngblood the question was an easy one: How in the world could the police get away with not refrigerating the evidence that might have shown that he was innocent?

That is exactly how the Arizona Court of Appeals saw it. Reversing Youngblood's conviction, the opinion made clear that the court was not accusing the state of bad faith in failing to preserve the evidence; rather, the dismissal was necessary to avoid an unfair trial. Quoting a similar California case, the court held that when the police recover a semen sample of the assailant, "the authorities must take reasonable measures to adequately preserve this evidence." Youngblood had won, for the time being.

The appellate ladder had one last major rung, though. Rarely does a case get the attention of the United States Supreme Court—the Court denies 99 percent of the petitions asking for its review—but it was Larry Youngblood's continued misfortune to be in that 1 percent. In the late fall of 1988, only two years after he had won in the Arizona Court of Appeals, six justices led by Chief Justice William Rehnquist reinstated Youngblood's conviction. Seizing on the lower court's finding that the police had not acted in bad faith when they failed to refrigerate David Leon's underwear, the chief justice wrote that the state was under no obligation to preserve potentially useful evidence. In short, unless the state purposely set out to destroy evidence, you were out of luck.

The normally perspicacious Justice Stevens did not agree with the majority's opinion, but ruled against Youngblood using a different line of reasoning. He did not think that the state's good or bad faith was the deciding factor; rather, he noted that he might have voted the other way "in a case involving a closer question as to guilt or innocence . . . [T]his, however, is not such a case."

Justice Harry Blackmun, joined by the liberal lions William Brennan and Thurgood Marshall, dissented: "The Constitution requires that criminal defendants be provided with a fair trial, not merely a 'good faith' try at a fair trial," he wrote. Quoting the maxim that it's far worse to convict an innocent man than to let a guilty man go free, Blackmun drew the opposite conclusion from Stevens, stating that the evidence was "far from

conclusive," and the possibility that Youngblood might have been exonerated "was not remote." Perhaps not, but given that Blackmun was writing for the minority, it hardly mattered. The case was sent back to the Arizona courts with instructions that they proceed according to the majority opinion.

But the pendulum had not yet come to rest in the Youngblood case. While the United States Supreme Court has the last word on the meaning of the federal Constitution, each state can interpret its own constitution as it sees fit. Although the language of the Arizona Due Process Clause and the United States Due Process Clause are practically identical ("No person shall be deprived of life, liberty, or property without due process of law"), the Arizona Court of Appeals now ruled in Youngblood's favor again, finding that its constitution provided greater protection to the accused, at least under these facts, than the United States Constitution did. Once again, Youngblood's convictions were dismissed.

One can only imagine what was running through Youngblood's mind when yet another appeal was taken. The losing side never complains about endless litigation, and certainly the state of Arizona was happy to have one last chance to uphold its jury verdict—this time in the Arizona Supreme Court, which had chosen not to hear the case the first time around. Following the "bad faith" analysis set forth by Rehnquist, its opinion determined once and for all that Youngblood had not suffered a denial of due process no matter what constitution was applied; his convictions were reinstated. He had been sentenced to 10 ½ years in prison for sexually molesting David Leon, and the time had come to serve it.

As for David Leon, he never returned to the carnival. The effects of sexual assault on young victims are well-documented, and given the emotional difficulties he was already having before the night of the crime, it is not surprising that his life after it was one of struggle. The immediate impact was obvious in his mood swings—his mother testified that he had gone from being a "real tough type kid" to one who cried at the slightest thing—and his behavior at school became so violent that the administrators regularly had to send him home. David's mother told Youngblood's pre-sentence investigator that the incident had been "devastating to the family and a trauma to my son," and that David had become distant with the family, fearful, and unable to concentrate on his schoolwork. He spoke of taking revenge on his abuser, but his fear of being attacked again caused him to sleep in his mother's bed.

And it got worse from there. In 1993, the same year Youngblood finally went to prison after his long string of appeals had concluded, David was arrested for choking and kicking his girlfriend in front of her 2-year-old son. That put him behind bars, and when he came out, now a full-grown man, he started in with cocaine and alcohol. He went to live with his father, from whom he had been estranged since his parents' divorce when he was a child, but his father accused him of stealing money for drugs and threw him out. In 1999, David beat up another girlfriend, and that sent him to prison again. A probation officer wrote that David was "a very angry person. He is angry at the whole, entire world." How angry must he have been when, only a few weeks after his second incarceration, he learned that Larry Youngblood, the man at whom he had directed his rage for more than 15 years, the man he thought had altered the course of his life through the most intimate and brutal violation imaginable, was innocent?

In 1998, after serving more than five years in prison for sexually molesting David Leon, Larry Youngblood went home. But he didn't stay there. In the summer of 1999, his on-again off-again girlfriend had him removed from her house, and five months later he was arrested for failing to register a new address as a sex offender. By the late 1990s DNA testing had improved by quantum leaps, and Youngblood's new arrest prompted his lawyer to ask that the small amount of semen left unspoiled 16 years ago be tested again. The state agreed, and on August 9, 2000, prosecutors returned to court and announced that Larry Youngblood had been innocent all along. His lawyer, pointing out that it had taken 16 years to exonerate her client, proclaimed, "This is another example for the public on why we shouldn't have the death penalty."

But if Larry Youngblood was innocent, who was guilty? The crime against David Leon was reclassified as unsolved, and the DNA profile of the perpetrator was entered into a national database. The Tucson police chief announced that there were no suspects, and the case remained that way for 16 months, until the evidence was matched to Walter Calvin Cruise, who was serving time for a cocaine conviction in Texas. The prosecutors must have suspected right away that they had finally arrested the right man. Cruise was a black man who had two prior convictions for sexual abuse of children in Houston, and even an arrest for similar conduct in Tucson. And there was one other thing—he had a bad left eye.

When they brought him from a Texas prison into a Tucson courtroom in August 2002, Cruise was sentenced to 24 years in prison for sexually assaulting David Leon, who by that time was 29 years old. Cruise, for his part, said he didn't know that another man had served a prison sentence for a crime he had committed. He told the court he suffered from alcoholic blackouts, and said he was "sorry for everything I've done to hurt anybody in my life."

This was more than the state of Arizona would ever say to Larry Youngblood. Before he was even authorized to have the DNA retested, Youngblood had to sign releases agreeing not to sue the County Attorney's Office, the Police Department, or the state Department of Corrections, which ultimately assured that he would not be compensated for his years of wrongful incarceration. Indeed, the prosecution emphasized that it had done nothing wrong even when it moved to have Youngblood's conviction set aside:

> By virtue of this motion, the State is not conceding that the defendant was wrongly arrested in this matter. On the contrary, the State sought the prosecution and conviction of the defendant on these charges on the best evidence available at the time. A jury duly convicted Defendant of the charges.

But something had in fact gone very wrong. An innocent man had been convicted and gone to prison. A guilty man had avoided arrest for almost two decades even after being arrested for similar conduct in the same town, at practically the same time. Evidence that would have prevented both wrongs had been mishandled. And the courts, finding no bad faith by the government, had condoned it all.

The United States Supreme Court does not apologize for mistakes. In September 2014, Henry Lee McCollum was released from North Carolina's death row after serving 30 years there for the rape and murder of an 11-year-old girl. DNA evidence from a nearby cigarette butt had eventually implicated another man who had been overlooked by law enforcement, even though he lived only a block from where the victim's body was found and had confessed to a similar rape and murder occurring around the same time.

What made this story even more remarkable was an opinion Justice Antonin Scalia had made in 1994, when the Court refused to hear an appeal from a Texas death row prisoner. In his dissenting opinion, Justice Blackmun famously renounced capital punishment and vowed to no longer "tinker with the machinery of death." Justice Scalia, concurring with the majority, practically mocked his fellow justice, citing the awful facts of the McCollum case: "Justice Blackmun did not select as the vehicle for his announcement . . . the case of the 11-year-old girl raped by four men and then killed by stuffing her panties down her throat," wrote Scalia, describing the crime for which McCollum had been convicted. "How enviable a quiet death by lethal injection compared with that!"

## And yet, when Henry Lee McCollum walked free, Justice Scalia never said a word.

Because Larry Youngblood was ultimately vindicated by scientific evidence, the *Youngblood* decision now reads like the discarded ending to an epic story—as if the writers of *Jaws* had drafted an earlier version of the script in which the shark devoured Sheriff Brody. The Supreme Court reached its conclusion at a time when Youngblood seemed guilty and modern DNA testing wasn't yet available. Its justices were pondering purely hypothetical questions—whether the evidentiary material *could* have been subjected to tests and the results *might* have exonerated Youngblood. Today's science makes their reasoning seem quaint and anachronistic. At the very least, one would have expected Justice Stevens—who agreed with the result but never signed on to the majority's reliance on the good faith of the government—to rethink his conclusion that there was little room to wonder about Youngblood's "guilt or innocence."

## The *Youngblood* decision now reads like the discarded ending to an epic story.

And yet in the years since Youngblood's exoneration and Cruise's conviction, the United States Supreme Court has cited the opinion favorably three times. In 2009, in the case of *District Attorney's Office of the Third Judicial District v. Osborne,* a very divided Court decided that an Alaskan man named William Osborne, who was serving prison time for kidnapping and sexual assault, did not have the constitutional right to post-conviction DNA testing, even though he was willing "to test the evidence at his own expense and to thereby ascertain the truth once and for all." The majority cited the *Youngblood* opinion, arguing that DNA testing could lead down a slippery slope:

> We would soon have to decide if there is a constitutional obligation to preserve forensic evidence that might later be tested. Cf. *Arizona v. Youngblood,* 488 U. S. 51, 56–58 (1988). If so, for how long? Would it be different for different types of evidence? Would the State also have some obligation to gather such evidence in the first place? How much, and when?

These questions seemed worth pondering, especially given how Youngblood's story turned out. But Chief Justice John Roberts—writing for himself and fellow conservative Justices Scalia, Thomas, Kennedy, and Alito—determined that the Court did not want to answer them. He refused to "leap ahead" into a more scientific age, to fundamentally change the trial system by making DNA testing into a constitutional right. Even so, Roberts acknowledged that criminal justice, "like any human endeavor, cannot be perfect. DNA evidence shows that it has not been." That brief admission of fallibility was as close as the United States Supreme Court ever came to acknowledging Youngblood's innocence.

Two years later, in *Connick v. Thompson,* the Court reversed a $14 million damage reward against the New Orleans District Attorney's Office for the 14 years John Thompson wrongfully spent on death row: The state had failed to turn over test results on blood evidence that later led him to be acquitted of capital murder. The Court ruled against Thompson, refusing to set

a precedent that might open the way for wrongly convicted inmates to sue the state for misconduct by its prosecutors. Justices Scalia and Alito concurred in the result and used the *Youngblood* case to support their opinion that the state had had no obligation to provide the evidence to the defense in the first place. After that decision, Youngblood's lawyer told an *L.A. Times* reporter that she found it "astounding" that the Court was still relying on her client's case: "It was a horrible decision then, and I can't believe they are still citing it, since so many people have been cleared with DNA evidence since then."

Perhaps even more astounding was a concurring opinion in the virtually forgotten 2004 case of *Illinois v. Fisher.* Gregory Fisher had been arrested for cocaine possession, made bail, and then skipped trial for the next 10 years. By the time he was caught, the cocaine had been tested four times, found to be real, and then destroyed by the state; however, it had never been tested for his DNA. All of the justices, in an unsigned opinion, readily affirmed the *Youngblood* decision and law enforcement's right to destroy the cocaine under those circumstances. All of the justices but one, that is. Justice Stevens concurred but once again refused to join the reasoning of *Youngblood.* He maintained that there were some cases in which a piece of evidence was so critical that destroying it might make a trial fundamentally unfair, even if the state acted in good faith. Then, remarkably, he wrote: "This, like *Youngblood,* is not such a case." Was it possible he hadn't heard that Larry Youngblood was innocent?

The Supreme Court may remain attached to the *Youngblood* decision, but in academic circles the opinion has always been the subject of considerable condemnation. A 1989 article in the *Harvard Civil Rights-Civil Liberties Law Review* declared the Court's analysis "theoretically unsound and a serious erosion of protections for criminal defendants"; another, in 1990 in the *Virginia Law Review,* called the opinion "inherently flawed"; a third, in 1995 in the *Harvard Law Review* said that the bad faith test "needlessly weakened" the defendant's constitutional protection against unjust prosecution. All of this was long before Youngblood's misfortune became known. Once that truth became clear, no one captured the irony better than Peter Neufeld, co-founder of the Innocence Project, who wrote in a 2001 issue of the *New England Law Review:*

> In law school, we have been taught that, absent bad faith, the destruction of critical evidence will not be deemed prejudicial. As a result, there has been no requirement that law enforcement agencies use due diligence to preserve evidence. This doctrine rested for more than a decade on the shoulders of an innocent man.

But did the Court's decision have widespread consequences, beyond the years Youngblood himself spent in prison? Apparently so. In 2007, the *Denver Post* ran a series of articles detailing lost and destroyed evidence that left thousands of accused and victims alike without recourse to scientific testing. In 1992, the NYPD destroyed massive amounts of evidence to make room in its warehouse, which was nearing 100 percent capacity; the same space limitations caused Houston's police force to destroy rape kits through the 1990s; and between 1991 and 2001, New Orleans purged evidence for 2,500 rape cases.

In each of these purges, the lack of storage space may have seemed like a plausible rationale, but the timing was often suspect. The NYPD's decision came only a few months after New York's first DNA exoneration. In Houston, the rape kits were thrown out shortly after then-Governor George W. Bush pardoned a man based on DNA results. "If the implication is that they threw out the evidence because they thought it might produce further exonerations," then-United States Attorney General Janet Reno told the *Denver Post,* "that is cause for great concern." Yet not a single appeal concerning lost evidence in Houston, New York City, or New Orleans prompted a "bad faith" finding by a court.

---

## This doctrine rested for more than a decade on the shoulders of an innocent man.

---

Indeed, the *Youngblood* standard has even protected the state in situations where evidence was pointedly destroyed—with life-or-death consequences. In Virginia, Robin Lovitt came within a day of execution after the Fourth Circuit Court of Appeals rejected his claim that bloody scissors had been thrown out by a chief deputy clerk, even though two of the clerk's subordinates, advising him that Lovitt was on death row, urged that the scissors and other exhibits be kept. In fact, the destruction of those scissors occurred shortly after a new statute had required that such evidence be preserved until after an inmate's execution. All of this was presented in the Virginia state and federal courts, but to no avail. The clerk "made a serious error in judgment in destroying the evidence," the Fourth Circuit concluded. But "the error cannot be attributed to the police or prosecution . . . and there existed no evidence of bad faith on anyone's part."

When the courts refused to act, then-Governor Mark Warner stepped into the breach, commuting Lovitt's death sentence to life without parole. "In this case, the actions of an agent of the Commonwealth, in a manner contrary to the express direction of the law, comes at the expense of a defendant facing society's most severe and final sanction," wrote Warner. "The Commonwealth must ensure that every time this ultimate sanction is carried out, it is done fairly." Still, Robin Lovitt will spend the rest of his life in prison. Hundreds of other inmates, without recourse to lost, mishandled, or destroyed DNA evidence, will do so as well.

Victims suffer, too, when evidence goes missing. The *Denver Post* series told the story of Janette Bodden, whose daughter had been raped and murdered in 1989. No one had ever been arrested, and 14 years later, she learned that it was unlikely anyone ever would: The evidence from the case had been destroyed. "That was almost like if they had murdered her all over again, when I found out about that," she said. "You lose your child, your baby, you want justice, truth."

There was never any question David Leon would suffer permanent damage from the sexual abuse he endured at the age of 10. The prosecutor told Youngblood's jury, "Unfortunately for David, he's not going to forget. He's not going to forget. He'll never forget." After obtaining a conviction, the same prosecutor argued for an aggravated sentence for Youngblood: "There is a lifelong impact on this child as a result of this act, of this violation that was committed on him by this defendant. It's not only an impact on that child but on his entire family." David's mother, speaking to the pre-sentence investigator, said that her son needed therapy and an explanation as to why he should not feel "dirty and useless in the eyes of society."

Fifteen years later, when Youngblood turned out to be innocent and the actual perpetrator was still unknown—when the only one in jail was her own son David—Patricia Leon said that she did not accept the DNA test as proof that Youngblood was innocent. "The only infallible thing is God," she told Mark Kimble of the *Tucson Citizen.* But two years after that, when Walter Cruise pled guilty to molesting David and apologized for everything he had done, there was little choice but to believe him.

Larry Youngblood was not in the courtroom when the justice system finally got around to Walter Cruise; his lawyer invited him to the sentencing, but he decided not to come. As he told the *New York Times,* "For 17 years, I knew I was innocent. They tried to get me to plea for less time, but I would never confess, especially to something like that. I am angry. They took the best years of my life."

Youngblood spent his last years panhandling on the streets of Tucson. In a grimly ironic twist, he was arrested in 2003 for pulling a knife on a Subway employee, but only after police first detained an innocent man a block south of the sandwich shop—forcing him to his knees, pointing a gun at him, and keeping him handcuffed for 10 minutes until a Subway employee told the officer he had made a mistake. The man on his knees was Julian Kunnie, the University of Arizona's director of Africana studies. "Never before have I experienced such humiliation and degradation," he said. "My human and civil rights were violated solely on the basis of my skin color." Youngblood remained homeless until he died of a drug overdose in 2007.

---

## "I wasted most of my life hating Larry Youngblood. We've never been the same."

The other victim of the 1983 crime fared no better. Learning that he had identified the wrong man only fueled David's rage toward the true perpetrator. "I was raped repeatedly, brutally. I was 10 years old," he said. "It was bad. He should have killed me." Had the mistaken conviction of an innocent man made the pain worse? David's sister certainly thought so. "I spent most of my life and wasted most of my life hating Larry Youngblood," she told the judge at Cruise's trial. "We've never been the same. We, without option, were given life sentences . . . This is something we will deal with forever."

David Leon dealt with it for two more years. The day after he died, the local newspaper offered no explanation for the accident—the rails were straight in that area, and the night had been clear. A police sergeant speculated that he might have been attempting to cross the tracks. If so, was there a moment when he saw the glimmer of the headlight and thought that maybe, just maybe, it might be easier not to get out of the way? Or was his brain so fuzzy with alcohol that he didn't even see it coming? It's impossible to know. What we do know is that the four-mile stretch of Interstate 10, from the carnival to the train, represented a world of anguish for the young man who had been twice victimized—first by the abuser himself, and then by a justice system more committed to convictions than truth. "I figured that society wasn't fair. I give myself credit. I survived," Leon said at the Cruise sentencing. Surely he deserved more than that.

## Critical Thinking

1. What was the difference between the Arizona Court of Appeals' decision and the US Supreme Court's decision?

2. What do you think about the idea that whether someone received a fair trial could depend on whether a police officer did something wrong, but did it accidentally and not in bad faith?

## Internet References

**CaseBriefs**
http://www.casebriefs.com/blog/law/civil-procedure/civil-procedure-keyed-to-cound/trial/arizona-v-youngblood/

**FindLaw**
http://caselaw.findlaw.com/nc-court-of-appeals/1038742.html

**New England Law Review Vol. 35:3**
http://www.nesl.edu/userfiles/file/lawreview/vol35/3/neufeld.pdf

**New Republic**
http://www.newrepublic.com/article/119319/scalia-death-penalty-defense-cited-murder-case-it-was-just-overturned

# Unit 5

# UNIT

Prepared by: Joanne Naughton

# Juvenile Justice

**A**lthough there were variations within specific offense categories, the overall arrest rate for juvenile violent crime remained relatively constant for several decades. Then, in the late 1980s, something changed: more and more juveniles charged with violent offenses were brought into the justice system. The juvenile justice system is a 20th-century response to the problems of dealing with children in trouble with the law, or children who need society's protection.

Juvenile court procedure differs from the procedure in adult courts because juvenile courts are based on the philosophy that their function is to treat and help, not to punish and abandon the offender. Recently, operations of juvenile courts have received criticism, and a number of significant Supreme Court decisions have changed the way that the courts must approach the rights of children. Despite a trend toward dealing more punitively with children who commit serious crimes, by treating them as if they were adults, the major thrust of the juvenile justice system remains one of diversion and treatment, rather than adjudication and incarceration.

*Article*        Prepared by: Joanne Naughton

# Juveniles Facing Lifelong Terms Despite Rulings

Erik Eckholm

## Learning Outcomes

*After reading this article, you will be able to:*

- Relate the Supreme Court's decisions in *Miller* and *Graham.*
- Show how some states are responding to the Court's decisions regarding the use of mandatory life sentences for juveniles.

Jacksonville, FL—In decisions widely hailed as milestones, the United States Supreme Court in 2010 and 2012 acted to curtail the use of mandatory life sentences for juveniles, accepting the argument that children, even those who are convicted of murder, are less culpable than adults and usually deserve a chance at redemption.

But most states have taken half measures, at best, to carry out the rulings, which could affect more than 2,000 current inmates and countless more in years to come, according to many youth advocates and legal experts.

"States are going through the motions of compliance," said Cara H. Drinan, an associate professor of law at the Catholic University of America, "but in an anemic or hyper-technical way that flouts the spirit of the decisions."

Lawsuits now before Florida's highest court are among many across the country that demand more robust changes in juvenile justice. One of the Florida suits accuses the state of skirting the ban on life without parole in nonhomicide cases by meting out sentences so staggering that they amount to the same thing.

Other suits, such as one argued last week before the Illinois Supreme Court, ask for new sentencing hearings, at least, for inmates who received automatic life terms for murder before 2012—a retroactive application that several states have resisted.

The plaintiff in one of the Florida lawsuits, Shimeek Gridine, was 14 when he and a 12-year-old partner made a clumsy attempt to rob a man in 2009 here in Jacksonville. As the disbelieving victim turned away, Shimeek fired a shotgun, pelting the side of the man's head and shoulder.

The man was not seriously wounded, but Shimeek was prosecuted as an adult. He pleaded guilty to attempted murder and robbery, hoping for leniency as a young offender with no record of violence. The judge called his conduct "heinous" and sentenced him to 70 years without parole.

Under Florida law, he cannot be released until he turns 77, at least, several years beyond the life expectancy for a black man his age, noted his public defender, who called the sentence "de facto life without parole" in an appeal to Florida's high court.

"They sentenced him to death, that's how I see it," Shimeek's grandmother Wonona Graham said.

The Supreme Court decisions built on a 2005 ruling that banned the death penalty for juvenile offenders as cruel and unusual punishment, stating that offenders younger than 18 must be treated differently from adults.

The 2010 decision, *Graham v. Florida*, forbade sentences of life without parole for juveniles not convicted of murder and said offenders must be offered a "meaningful opportunity for release based on demonstrated maturity and rehabilitation." The ruling applied to those who had been previously sentenced.

Cases like Shimeek's aim to show that sentences of 70 years, 90 years or more violate that decision. Florida's defense was that Shimeek's sentence was not literally "life without parole" and that the life span of a young inmate could not be predicted.

Probably no more than 200 prisoners were affected nationally by the 2010 decision, and they were concentrated in Florida. So far, of 115 inmates in the state who had been sentenced to life for nonhomicide convictions, 75 have had new hearings, according to the Youth Defense Institute at the Barry University School of Law in Orlando. In 30 cases, the new sentences have been for 50 years or more. One inmate who had been convicted of gun robbery and rape has received consecutive sentences totaling 170 years.

In its 2012 decision, *Miller v. Alabama,* the Supreme Court declared that juveniles convicted of murder may not automatically be given life sentences. Life terms remain a possibility, but judges and juries must tailor the punishment to individual circumstances and consider mitigating factors.

The Supreme Court did not make it clear whether the 2012 ruling applied retroactively, and state courts have been divided, suggesting that this issue, as well as the question of de facto life sentences, may eventually return to the Supreme Court.

Advocates for victims have argued strongly against revisiting pre-2012 murder sentences or holding parole hearings for the convicts, saying it would inflict new suffering on the victims' families.

Pennsylvania has the most inmates serving automatic life sentences for murders committed when they were juveniles: more than 450, according to the Juvenile Law Center in Philadelphia. In October, the State Supreme Court found that the Miller ruling did not apply to these prior murder convictions, creating what the law center, a private advocacy group, called an "appallingly unjust situation" with radically different punishments depending on the timing of the trial.

Likewise, courts in Louisiana, with about 230 inmates serving mandatory life sentences for juvenile murders, refused to make the law retroactive. In Florida, with 198 such inmates, the issue is under consideration by the State Supreme Court, and on Wednesday it was argued before the top court of Illinois, where 100 inmates could be affected.

Misgivings about the federal Supreme Court decisions and efforts to restrict their application have come from some victim groups and legal scholars around the country.

"The Supreme Court has seriously overgeneralized about under-18 offenders," said Kent S. Scheidegger, the legal director of the Criminal Justice Legal Foundation, a conservative group in Sacramento, Calif. "There are some under 18 who are thoroughly incorrigible criminals."

Some legal experts who are otherwise sympathetic have suggested that the Supreme Court overreached, with decisions that "represent a dramatic judicial challenge to legislative authority," according to a new article in the *Missouri Law Review* by Frank O. Bowman III of the University of Missouri School of Law.

Among the handful of states with large numbers of juvenile offenders serving life terms, California is singled out by advocates for acting in the spirit of the Supreme Court rules.

"California has led the way in scaling back some of the extreme sentencing policies it imposed on children," said Jody Kent Lavy, the director of the Campaign for the Fair Sentencing of Youth, which has campaigned against juvenile life sentences and called on states to reconsider mandatory terms dispensed before the Miller ruling. Too many states, she said, are "reacting with knee-jerk, narrow efforts at compliance."

California is allowing juvenile offenders who were condemned to life without parole to seek a resentencing hearing. The State Supreme Court also addressed the issue of de facto life sentences, voiding a 110-year sentence that had been imposed for attempted murder.

Whether they alter past sentences or not, some states have adapted by imposing minimum mandatory terms for juvenile murderers of 25 or 35 years before parole can even be considered—far more flexible than mandatory life, but an approach that some experts say still fails to consider individual circumstances.

As Ms. Drinan of Catholic University wrote in a coming article in the Washington University Law Review, largely ignored is the mandate to offer young inmates a chance to "demonstrate growth and maturity," raising their chances of eventual release.

To give young offenders a real chance to mature and prepare for life outside prison, Ms. Drinan said, "states must overhaul juvenile incarceration altogether," rather than letting them languish for decades in adult prisons.

Shimeek Gridine, meanwhile, is pursuing a high school equivalency diploma in prison while awaiting a decision by the Florida Supreme Court that could alter his bleak prospects.

He has a supportive family: A dozen relatives, including his mother and grandparents and several aunts and uncles, testified at his sentencing in 2010, urging clemency for a child who played Pop Warner football and talked of becoming a merchant seaman, like his grandfather.

But the judge said the fact that Shimeek had a good family, and decent grades, only underscored that the boy knew right from wrong, and he issued a sentence 30 years longer than even the prosecution had asked for.

Now Florida's top court is pondering whether his sentence violates the federal Constitution.

"A 70-year sentence imposed upon a 14-year-old is just as cruel and unusual as a sentence of life without parole," Shimeek's public defender, Gail Anderson, argued before the Florida court in September. "Mr. Gridine will most likely die in prison."

# Critical Thinking

1. Should juveniles be prosecuted as adults, even though they aren't adults?

2. Do the advocates for victims have a valid argument against making *Miller* retroactive?

3. Do you believe Shimeek Gridine's sentence violates the Supreme Court's decision in *Graham*?

# Internet References

**Sentencing Law and Policy**
    http://sentencing.typepad.com/sentencing_law_and_policy/assessing-graham-and-its-aftermath/

**Social Science Research Network**
    http://papers.ssrn.com/sol3/papers.cfm?abstract_id=2350316

**The Campaign for the Fair Sentencing of Youth**
    http://fairsentencingofyouth.org/2014/10/01/american-correctional-association-opposes-jlwop/

*Article*

Prepared by: Joanne Naughton

# U.S. Inquiry Finds a "Culture of Violence" Against Teenage Inmates at Rikers

BENJAMIN WEISER AND MICHAEL SCHWIRTZ

## Learning Outcomes

*After reading this article, you will be able to:*

- Relate the essence of a report about conditions at Rikers Island Jail, prepared by the U.S. Attorney in Manhattan.
- Describe instances of violence against adolescent inmates by correction officers.
- Show that officers were rarely punished for violence against young inmates.

In an extraordinary rebuke of the New York City Department of Correction, the federal government said on Monday the department had systematically violated the civil rights of male teenagers at Rikers Island by failing to protect them from the rampant use of unnecessary and excessive force by correction officers.

The office of Preet Bharara, the United States attorney in Manhattan, released its findings in a graphic 79-page report that described a "deep-seated culture of violence" against youthful inmates at Rikers, perpetrated by guards who operated with little fear of punishment.

The report, addressed to Mayor Bill de Blasio and two other senior city officials, singled out for blame a "powerful code of silence" among jail staff, along with a virtually useless system for investigating attacks by guards. The result was a "staggering" number of injuries among youthful inmates, the report said.

The report also found the department relied to an "excessive and inappropriate" degree on solitary confinement to punish teenage inmates, placing them in punitive segregation, as the practice is known, for months at a time.

Although the federal investigation focused only on the three Rikers jails that house male inmates aged 16 to 18, the report said the systemic problems that were identified "may exist in equal measure at the other jails on Rikers."

Correction officers struck adolescents in the head and face at "an alarming rate" as punishment, even when inmates posed no threat; officers took inmates to isolated locations for beatings out of view of video cameras; and many inmates were so afraid of the violence that they asked, for their own protection, to be placed in solitary confinement, the report said.

Officers were rarely punished, the report said, even with strong evidence of egregious violations. Investigations, when they occurred, were often superficial, and incident reports were frequently incomplete, misleading, or intentionally falsified.

Among more than a dozen specific cases of brutality detailed in the report was one in which correction officers assaulted four inmates for several minutes, beating them with radios, batons, and broomsticks and slamming their heads against walls. Another inmate sustained a skull fracture and was left with the imprint of a boot on his back in an assault involving multiple officers. In another case, a young man was taken from a classroom after falling asleep during a lecture and beaten severely. Teachers heard him screaming and crying for his mother.

"For adolescent inmates, Rikers Island is broken," Mr. Bharara said at a news conference announcing the findings. "It is a place where brute force is the first impulse rather than the last resort, a place where verbal insults are repaid with physical injuries, where beatings are routine, while accountability is rare."

The federal investigation was not conducted as a criminal inquiry and no charges were announced against individuals. Officers involved in specific incidents were also not identified by name. But the report listed more than 10 pages of remedial measures, and it warned that if the city did not work cooperatively to develop new policies and procedures, the Justice Department could bring a federal lawsuit asking a judge to order the imposition of remedies. Mr. Bharara said the city had 49 days to respond to the findings.

Adolescents at Rikers were consigned to "a corrections crucible that seems more inspired by 'Lord of the Flies' than any legitimate philosophy of humane detention," Mr. Bharara said.

The report, which covered from 2011 through the end of 2013, touched on many of the same issues raised in an investigation by *The New York Times* into violence by guards at Rikers, particularly against inmates with mental illnesses, published last month.

The *Times* article documented 129 cases in which inmates of all ages were seriously injured last year in altercations with correction officers, including several attacks that were also singled out in the report.

New York is one of just two states in the country that automatically charges people aged 16 to 18 as adults. That population, which averages close to 500 inmates at Rikers Island, is among the most difficult at the jail complex, the report said. In the 2013 fiscal year, about 51 percent were diagnosed with a mental illness, compared with about 38 percent for the overall population. And nearly two-thirds were charged with felonies.

Even so, the report found that adolescents were overseen by the least experienced correctional staff, who, often out of frustration or malice, lashed out violently against them. In the 2013 fiscal year alone, inmates younger than 18 sustained 1,057 injuries in 565 reported uses of force by correctional staff members. In a tally of the adolescent population as of Oct. 30, 2012, nearly 44 percent had been subjected to a use of force by staff at least once. And the violence has steadily increased year by year, the report found.

Moreover, the report found, many violent episodes go unreported.

## Assaults on Young Inmates

The report included detailed narratives on more than a dozen times in which correction officers assaulted adolescent inmates. Here are three of the most egregious assaults, which occurred last year.

The investigation found officers and supervisors used coded phrases like "hold it down" to pressure inmates into not reporting beatings. "Inmates who refuse to 'hold it down' risk retaliation from officers in the form of additional physical violence and disciplinary sanctions," the report said.

One inmate said that he was continually harassed by correctional staff after reporting that he was raped by a guard and that he was warned by guards not to speak about the episode in an interview with a consultant on the investigation.

The report also found that civilian staff members, including doctors and teachers, also failed to report abuse and faced retaliation when they did.

One teacher told an investigator that when abuse occurs, civilian employees know "they should turn their head away, so that they don't witness anything."

Even when abuse is reported, the report found, the investigations typically went nowhere. The federal inquiry was highly critical of the correction department's investigative division, which is overseen by Florence Finkle. The report described the investigative division as overwhelmed, understaffed and reliant on archaic paper-based record keeping. Investigations, which are supposed to take a maximum of five months to complete, often take more than a year.

There is also a substantial bias in favor of correction officer testimony even in cases when evidence clearly indicates a guard is lying, the investigation found. And when guards are disciplined, the punishment is rarely severe. Most are sent to counseling or "retraining," the report found. Sometimes, punishments recommended by supervisors are overruled by those higher in the chain of command.

In one January 2012 episode, a correction officer became incensed after an inmate splashed her with a liquid and began punching him in the face after he had been restrained by other guards. A captain ordered her to stop, and she punched another officer who tried to pull her off the inmate. An investigating captain later concluded that the officer's use of force was "not necessary, inappropriate and excessive." But a superior, backed by the investigative division, overruled the captain, concluding that the use of force was necessary. An investigator labeled the finding "astonishing."

The investigation found one officer who had been involved in 76 uses of force over a 6-year period and had been disciplined only once.

Because the correction department fails to conduct proper investigations and hold staff accountable, the report found, "a culture of excessive force persists, where correction officers physically abuse adolescent inmates with the expectation that they will face little or no consequences for their unlawful conduct."

The report noted that the city's new correction commissioner, Joseph Ponte, had only recently assumed his position and "was not present when the misconduct" found by the investigation had occurred. It also said the department had undertaken some steps to stem the violence like providing more programs for adolescents, adding staff and requiring young inmates to wear jail-issued uniforms and shoes. But none of these measures, the report said, address the core problem: abuse by correction officers and a lack of accountability.

In one case documented in the report, a correction officer wrapped metal handcuffs around her hand and punched an inmate who had fallen asleep during a class in the ribs, according to witnesses. The inmate told investigators that when he yelled an obscenity, the officer pulled him out of class and began to beat him. She was joined by other officers who proceeded to kick him while he was sprawled on the floor. The inmate said one officer sprayed pepper stray directly in his eye from about an inch away.

In their reports, the officers offered contradictory versions of what happened, the investigations found. But all concluded that the level of force that was used was appropriate.

One of the teachers interviewed said he heard "thumping" and "screaming" during the altercation and said he heard the inmate "crying and screaming for his mother."

When he looked out the door after the episode, the teacher reported that he "saw blood and saliva on the floor."

## Critical Thinking

1. Do you believe it is necessary, in order to protect society, that 16-year-olds be considered adults under criminal law? Do you believe 16-year-olds are adults?

2. Isn't it necessary for correction officers to use force so that young inmates will respect them and obey the rules?

3. Why do you think officers were not punished for using unnecessary or excessive force?

## Internet References

**The New York Times**
http://www.nytimes.com/interactive/2014/08/05/nyregion/05rikers-report.html

**The New York Times**
http://www.nytimes.com/2014/04/05/nyregion/joseph-ponte-new-yorks-new-corrections-commissioner-faces-challenge-at-rikers.html

*Article*        Prepared by: Joanne Naughton

# Not a Lock: Youth Who Stay Closer to Home Do Better than Those in Detention, Texas Study Shows

Lynne Anderson

## Learning Outcomes

*After reading this article, you will be able to:*

- Recount some of the findings of a study of reforms in the Texas Juvenile Justice Department.

- Explain how Texas reacted after abuses within the system came to light in 2007.

A broad study of reforms in the Texas Juvenile Justice Department "puts a nail in the coffin" of the strategy of youth prisons as a public safety option, said the director of the Juvenile Justice Strategy Group of the Annie E. Casey Foundation, which funded the report.

Most strikingly, said Nate Balis of Casey, the report shows that youth released from a juvenile correction facility were 21 percent more likely to be rearrested than a youth under supervision of a local juvenile probation department. Also, youth released from a state facility who reoffended were almost three times more likely to be rearrested for a felony.

The study, called "Closer to Home," was conducted by the Council of State Governments Justice Center in conjunction with Texas A&M University. It provides a detailed look at how reforms in the Texas system actually affected youth.

"I think this is really important for the field," Balis said. "Its value will go far beyond the borders of Texas. It bolsters what academic reports already have suggested, but this looks at actual experience. This will raise serious questions about youth prisons: It is a model that is destined to fail."

## A Broken System, a Commitment to Change

Juvenile justice reform has been underway in many states for two decades. Reports and studies during that time have shown the futility of programs of youth jails, Balis said. What sets this report apart from previous studies, he said, is the breadth of its findings, collected from 165 counties in Texas over a three-year period, and the fact that the state was so transparent in sharing its numbers.

"The report and the study behind it are a huge contribution to the field," Balis said. "All parties involved deserve a huge amount of credit. . . . This isn't just an academic study but one that will lead to key actions."

After abuses within the Texas system came to light in 2007, Texas leaders moved to reduce the number of incarcerated youth. They particularly aimed to move youth closer to home.

To measure how the state was doing and how young people were affected, Texas began using an information system that let it track youth referred to the juvenile justice system, whether they were incarcerated or on probation locally.

State officials collected 1.3 million records for about 466,000 youth.

## Crime, Reincarceration Drop

A key finding was that the number of young people incarcerated between 2007 and 2012 dropped more than 60 percent, from 4,305 to 1,481. During that time, juvenile crime, as measured by arrests, dropped more than 30 percent, from 136,206 to 91,873.

While no causal connection can be established, the authors of the report cite the drop as evidence that Texans' safety was not compromised by changes in the law.

Another important finding was that the number of youth under the supervision of a local juvenile justice probation office declined 30 percent.

Youth who were under probation supervision were rearrested three years later less frequently (64 percent) than those released from a youth prison (77 percent), the report shows.

And, youth under supervision were far less likely to be reincarcerated. The three-year reincarceration rate for these youth was 13 percent for juveniles beginning probation supervision and 44 percent for juveniles released from a state-run juvenile correctional facility.

The numbers from the report are so striking, Balis said, that it "bolsters the already overwhelming evidence that confining juveniles in large correctional facilities far from their homes is a failed strategy."

The study also shows the importance of a data-driven approach to solving issues within the juvenile justice system, said Tony Fabelo of the Council of State Governments, the lead author of the report. With more detailed data, it is easier to see areas of concern, he said. That, in turn, can address where resources might need to be directed.

In Texas, for example, 80 percent of the funding for county juvenile probation offices comes from the county, while 20 percent comes from the state. The data reveal where counties might need more state resources or a rechanneling of the resources they already have, Fabelo said.

And while the report revealed good news, it also showed some areas that need continued attention, he said. Differences in outcomes between white and minority youth were apparent, and those merit deeper study. And, the study suggested that what works in the case of one youth will not necessarily work in another.

"There's a lot of room for improvement," Fabelo said. "There's no one size fits all. But hopefully, there will be conversations in the Legislature, the counties themselves and juvenile justice professionals working for their own plans in improving outcomes."

# Critical Thinking

1. Why is incarcerating juveniles in large correctional facilities far from their homes a failed strategy?

2. What are the benefits of a data-driven approach to solving issues within the juvenile justice system?

# Internet References

**Juvenile Justice Information Exchange**
http://jjie.org/hub/community-based-alternatives/

**The Council of State Governments**
http://csgjusticecenter.org

**The Council of State Governments**
http://csgjusticecenter.org/youth/publications/closer-to-home/

## *Article*

Prepared by: Joanne Naughton

# Juvenile Injustice: Truants Face Courts, Jailing without Legal Counsel to Aid Them

## Tennessee court procedures highlight national debate over minor offenders' rights.

SUSAN FERRISS

## Learning Outcomes

*After reading this article, you will be able to:*

- Describe "status offenses."

- Show the value of having legal counsel at a court appearance.

- State what the 1974 federal law provides, and what the 1980 amendment allows.

noxville, TN—She was barely 15 and scared at the prospect of being in court. She agreed to plead guilty to truancy. But when Judge Tim Irwin announced what he planned to do with her, the girl known as A.G. screamed in disbelief.

Guards forced the sobbing teen out of the Knox County Juvenile Court and clapped shackles on her legs. She had been struggling with crippling anxiety and what she said was relentless bullying at school. Now she was being led through a county juvenile detention center to a cell with a sliver of a window and a concrete slab with a mattress. For truancy.

"I cried all night long," A.G. said. "It seemed like everyone was against us in court."

Like tens of thousands of kids every year, A.G. was in court to answer for a noncriminal infraction that only a minor can commit. These infractions are called "status offenses," and they can include skipping school, running away, underage drinking or smoking or violating curfews. But since status offenses aren't technically crimes, indigent minors don't benefit from the constitutional right to the appointment of defense counsel before they plead guilty.

That meant A.G. whose family couldn't afford to hire a lawyer, was left with no trained defense counsel to argue that there might be justifiable reasons why she was having so much trouble going to school.

It also meant the girl had no counsel to object to her abrupt jailing in April 2008—a jailing that lawyers who reviewed A.G.'s file argue exceeded the court's statutory power during the teen's first appearance in court.

"A.G.'s incarceration immediately following her guilty plea for truancy, a status offense, was illegal under state and federal law," asserted Dean Rivkin, a law professor at the University of Tennessee who later represented A.G. and oversees the Knoxville campus' Education Law Practicum.

Due to litigation that's pending, Irwin declined repeated request to comment on A.G.'s case or those of other prosecuted truants, some of whom were also jailed.

A.G.'s lockup has never been investigated or reviewed on appeal. But it's the type of allegation that's put Tennessee at the center of a national debate over whether status offenders should be guaranteed immediate legal counsel once in court—to ensure minors' basic rights are respected—and under what conditions they can be incarcerated.

In late February, the nation's top juvenile justice official quietly asked the Justice Department's civil rights division to investigate whether Tennessee status offenders were wrongly deprived of legal counsel.

A.G., who was already in counseling, was so shattered by her shackling and detention that when she was released at 7 A.M. the next day her parents took her to a doctor rather than straight to school, as they said they were ordered to do. Their daughter had become suicidal, and she spent the next week in a psychiatric hospital.

## Unraveling the Rules

Forty years ago, a federal law—the Juvenile Justice and Delinquency Prevention Act—actually *barred* states that receive federal juvenile-justice funds from sending status offenders into detention, reflecting the widespread belief that incarcerating these minors exposes them to danger and bad influences. In 1980, though, Congress amended the 1974 federal Act to allow judges a significant federal exception to the lockup ban. It's called the "valid court order" exception.

The exception permits jailing as a last resort to try to control status offenders once they've pleaded guilty and gone on to violate *instructions* from the court: the valid court order. But if states want federal funds, lockup as a punitive response is only supposed to occur after courts hold multiple formal proceedings, give children time to comply with instructions, consider alternatives to jail—and take great care to ensure kids benefit from full due process rights, including right to appointment of defense counsel for indigent children.

This chance to obtain defense counsel must be afforded *before* status offenders face formal accusations that they've disobeyed valid court orders and could potentially face jailing or removal from parents' custody.

This same federal law *does* allow status offenders to be held in detention before trial for less than 24 hours or over a weekend, but only under limited circumstances—such as credible concern that minors might not appear at a scheduled hearing or because police have found kids wandering on streets and no non-jail shelter space is available, or because parents are not immediately available to pick them up.

If states don't ensure courts follow these requirements to provide legal counsel and limits on detention, they can get their federal delinquency-prevention grants pulled.

In A.G.'s case, "nobody said anything about an attorney," said A.G.'s mother, who had no idea what her daughter's rights were before A.G. pleaded guilty and was taken away and put into detention.

The Knox County District Attorney's office, which prosecutes truants, said children's privacy rights prohibit staff from commenting on specific cases like A.G.'s.

## A Continuing Controversy in Knox County

Since late last year, the Center for Public Integrity has been reviewing previously sealed documents that suggest a vigorous pattern of locking up status offenders in Knox County. Families and attorneys here have also alleged that accused truants with diagnosed mental-health and other difficulties were shackled and jailed straight from court.

Children whose only infraction was struggling with a loathing for school were pulled into the criminal-justice system, branded with permanent delinquency records and jailed with kids who had actually committed crimes, parents complained. All this happened without their kids having lawyers, some parents said, and some children dropped out rather than getting back to an education.

Patricia Puritz, executive director of the nonprofit National Juvenile Defender Center in Washington, DC, said that across the country there is a disturbing shortage of timely legal representation to ensure kids' rights are respected when they're pulled into courts for crimes and for status offenses.

"Little people, little justice," Puritz said.

In Knox County, a behind-the-scenes disagreement over providing access to counsel continues.

Judge Irwin, the county's elected and sole juvenile court judge, has refused to allow volunteer lawyers to set up a project at the courthouse to offer free counsel to accused truants as they arrive with their parents for hearings, according to Harry Ogden, a Knoxville business attorney who wants to participate in such pro bono representation.

"This project can be a 'win-win' for the court, the school system, the D.A.'s office . . . and—most of all—at-risk children and youth," wrote Rivkin, the University of Tennessee law professor, in a December 2012 letter to Judge Irwin.

Irwin did not respond to Rivkin's plea, and has also declined to speak to the Center about his decision not to endorse the pro bono idea, which remains in limbo.

On the court's behalf, Knox County Law Director Richard Armstrong sent a letter to the Center for Public Integrity that said: "Children and their families are welcomed and encouraged to retain counsel in all matters brought before the juvenile courts of this state."

But in March of last year, "know your rights" brochures that the volunteer lawyers had left in the court lobby for families of accused truants were removed, according to an email that Rivkin wrote to Irwin and sent to him via the judge's administrative assistant.

"Needless to say," Rivkin wrote, "we were surprised to learn that the brochures had been removed from the rack shortly after they were placed there." Irwin did not respond to Rivkin's email and an offer to meet to talk about the brochures.

In February, Rivkin also requested that the Tennessee Supreme Court review an appeal of one truant's conviction; for the last 2 years, as part of a series of appeals, Rivkin has also been trying, so far in vain, to convince a state court to issue an opinion that would guarantee faster appointment of defense for accused truants.

## Heavy Penalties, Confusing Courts

Whether all kids in courts, including status offenders, should automatically benefit from defense counsel is part of a broader national debate over just what legal rights children have, and whether the country's confusing patchwork of state and local regulations is enough to ensure children are treated fairly.

The National Juvenile Defender Center is leading an ongoing project that dispatches observers to juvenile courts, so they can recommend, state by state, measures to improve proceedings that are supposed to be primarily rehabilitative.

Puritz said observers have witnessed kids facing serious repercussions with no lawyers to advise them, either because they were not afforded counsel, or because they waived rights with a casual shrug that belied their confusion over what was at stake. In 2006, observers reported that half the kids they saw in Indiana courts waived counsel even though the minors were accused of misdemeanors or felonies.

Agitated parents, Puritz added, sometimes hope a rough court experience will scare a kid straight. But parents often fail to grasp, Puritz said, how pleading guilty even to a status offense can lead to penalties that could bedevil minors for years.

In Texas, teen Elizabeth Diaz spent 18 days in an adult county jail when a judge in Hidalgo County began a campaign in 2009 to collect old truancy fines. The judge issued warrants to arrest minors once they turned 17 and force them to pay—or get thrown in jail.

Elizabeth's $1,600 in fines had been imposed in a court where she had no counsel. She missed her high school exit exam while jailed, the American Civil Liberties Union said, and was traumatized by harassment in jail. A federal court in 2012 ruled that her detention for failing to pay fines she couldn't afford was an unconstitutional violation of due process.

In Knox County, A.G. was required to return to court a month after being jailed and hospitalized, but she was still not afforded an attorney. Another five months went by before, on her third court appearance, as was then the practice, A.G. was appointed a public defender, for a fee of $100. After several more months, with A.G. continuing to miss school and warned she'd be jailed again, the family was referred to Rivkin at the University of Tennessee campus in Knoxville.

Rivkin was able to put a hold on the teen's ongoing prosecution and began representing her in negotiations with her school.

A.G.'s case, her lawyers said, illustrates why they believe timely, trained counsel is in the child's best interest: In spite of increasing difficulties at school, A.G. was not tested for special needs or offered an alternative education plan before her name was turned over for truancy prosecution. Instead, A.G.'s parents said, school staff advised them to ask police to force A.G. out of the house and into the school building. Reluctantly, they followed that advice, but it only deepened the family's crisis.

School district staff said privacy rules prohibit them from discussing students' histories. But Melissa Massie, executive director of student support services for the Knox County School District, said that she had not heard of staff advising parents to call police. She did say, though, that she was critical of some past antitruancy efforts.

In 2010, approximately 137,000 status offenders like A.G. were "petitioned," or sent into courts nationwide, more than a third for truancy, according to statistics cited by the Vera Institute of Justice. In Tennessee alone in 2012, more than 9,600 minors were taken to court for truancy.

The Education Law Practicum Rivkin supervises offers pro bono help to Knoxville area families seeking special-education services. Like the Vera Institute, Rivkin favors a "counternarrative" on truancy: When counselors take the time, they find that most chronic truants are struggling with learning disabilities, emotional distress or mental-health illness, bullying, violence, or financial or other crises.

Few of these kids or their parents, Rivkin said, can be expected to understand that kids have more options than just pleading guilty in court.

In Tennessee, as in many states, statutes theoretically limit juvenile courts to initially responding to truants who plead guilty by issuing them monetary fines, ordering them to perform community service and putting them on probation, with instructions to follow, and initiating the valid court order process.

States are also expected to conduct audits to monitor how well courts are complying with the limits on putting status offenders in detention. Periodically, federal justice authorities review these state audits to look for patterns of violations.

Last November, Rivkin wrote to Robert Listenbee, the head of the Justice Department's Office of Juvenile Justice and Delinquency Prevention, suggesting a hard look at the lockups of status offenders in Knox County and the rest of Tennessee.

He suspected federal officials—while signing off on grants to the state—were not getting the full story.

In a reply to Rivkin dated Feb. 28 of this year, Listenbee explained that he had asked the Justice Department's Civil Rights Division for an "investigation."

Failure to provide counsel to kids potentially facing incarceration, Listenbee wrote to Rivkin, if true, "would be of great concern to all of us here . . . and is not in keeping with the best practices outlined by this office."

## Appealing to Higher Courts

In 2011, Rivkin began a prolonged and complex attempt to overturn convictions of four students' truancy convictions, in an attempt to clarify some of these issues.

He first lost before Irwin, then before the state's Fourth Circuit and then before a state Court of Appeals panel. He submitted a final appeal this year to the Tennessee Supreme Court on behalf of only one plaintiff. As of May, his review request was still pending.

Along the way, the battle has revealed that judges, lawyers and other officers of juvenile courts can have strikingly different interpretations of laws that can end up critical to a child's life: Do indigent status offenders have a right to appointed counsel before valid court orders are issued to them, or only after they are accused of violating orders and are thus vulnerable to judges legally jailing them or removing them from their parents' custody?

In essence, Rivkin has argued that accused truants have the constitutional right of appointment of counsel if not before pleading guilty, then before judges begin imposing court orders that could pave the way to incarceration.

"There may be compelling reasons why the [valid court order] is not warranted due to the juvenile's mental health condition, due to educational disabilities, due to family circumstances such as lack of transportation, etc.," Rivkin wrote in his appeal to the Fourth Circuit.

"Without an attorney it is unrealistic to expect a juvenile to make these arguments," he wrote. Waiting to afford children attorneys until they face imminent potential jailing, Rivkin wrote, is "too little, too late."

The four original plaintiffs were Knox County students who, like A.G., suffered from significant mental-health stress and had no legal counsel at their side when they pleaded guilty. None could afford to hire attorneys, and some parents said they didn't dream they would need legal counsel.

None were jailed the same day they pleaded guilty, but they were threatened with jailing, Rivkin's appeal alleged, if they violated any of a litany of instructions given to them under the label of probation or, in some cases, valid court orders.

The plaintiffs were admonished not to miss another day of school, unexcused, or face jail. They were also told not to get into any trouble at school, and to pay for and attend court-selected counseling programs. They were also ordered to submit to and pay for random, mandatory drug testing, although none faced drug charges.

One plaintiff, a 13-year-old middle school student identified as T.W., was jailed twice, without the benefit of legal counsel first appointed to represent him, according to the appeal.

On a February 2009 mandatory return to court after pleading guilty, T.W. was jailed overnight directly from court because his school reported he had accumulated more unexcused absences after pleading guilty. During another return to court in January 2010, T.W. was given a drug screen that registered positive for marijuana and he was immediately taken into juvenile detention again for several days.

Some kids Rivkin eventually represented at the Practicum were appointed public defenders during their third visit to court.

But Rivkin argued that there was nothing in T.W. or the other plaintiffs' files proving in writing, as required by state regulation, that they'd agreed to waive the right to defense. Like other parents, T.W.'s mother, Debbie Jones, submitted an affidavit declaring that her son was not informed of his full rights to counsel.

As his appeal moved through courts, Rivkin submitted an affidavit signed by Knox County Public Defender Mark Stephens in 2012 noting that the public defender's office had no record of a single request from the court between 2010 and fall of 2012 to represent a truant before valid court orders were imposed.

In some cases, including T.W.'s, the court assigned truants lawyers known as guardians ad litem, who advise judges on what they believe is best for children, including removal from the home. But these lawyers are distinct from defense counsel. Minors interviewed by the Center said that their guardians ad litem didn't object to them being jailed or drug tested, and didn't raise questions about their schools' responsibility to evaluate them for special needs—issues Rivkin later raised for truants after he began representing them.

## Setbacks

In 2011, in his rejection of Rivkin's appeal, Judge Irwin upheld his own convictions. In a written order, he said that the four truants entered court and after being advised of "the right to remain silent, the right to confront witnesses against them, and the right to an attorney, chose to enter a plea immediately, without the advice of counsel and offered no justification for . . . excessive absences."

But, again, while truants in Tennessee must be informed of the rights that Irwin recited, indigent status offenders don't have the right to the *appointment* of a defense attorney if they decide not to plead guilty and want a trial.

After Irwin's initial ruling, the state of Tennessee and the Knox County D.A.'s office took on the defense of the juvenile court's practices.

As part of that defense, the state argued that the juvenile court had adhered to proper procedure, including by jailing T.W., and that T.W. had missed a 10-day deadline for appealing his 2009 detention order. The state's lawyers submitted forms identified as court notes with identical language on them declaring that T.W., during each of his court appearances, was "advised of rights."

But as Rivkin noted in a filing, the state didn't challenge the argument that there were no signed waivers in the files of his plaintiffs.

In 2012, in a second rejection for Rivkin, Judge Bill Swann of the Fourth Circuit found that the juvenile court's actions were generally proper. He didn't opine on whether he thought T.W. had been appropriately afforded an opportunity for appointed counsel before he was jailed. But Swann did reject Rivkin's interpretation of federal law, arguing that existing law requires appointment of counsel only *after* indigent truants have already violated valid court orders and face possible incarceration.

"The constitutional right to counsel only attaches at that point, and not before," Swann wrote. But he added that the plaintiffs "laudably urge the advancement of a social policy" that only the state's legislators could change.

Last December, when a Court of Appeals panel also rejected Rivkin's arguments, the judges found that the plaintiffs didn't meet the burden of new evidence to justify a review of their convictions.

Knox County District Attorney Special Counsel John Gill told the Center for Public Integrity that the D.A.'s office acknowledges that state and federal law do not permit jailing truants except when valid court orders are issued and kids are informed that they have a right to the appointment of an attorney.

Asked about general allegations that kids were put into detention frequently in recent past years perhaps without understanding their rights, Gill did say: "There were some practices that hadn't been scrutinized."

"I'm not saying it hasn't happened," Gill said, referring to truants being jailed.

He said that he doesn't believe that valid court orders are currently being issued in the court to handle truants or that they are being jailed. The D.A.'s interest, he said, is "getting kids back to school, not convictions and not in locking them up."

## How Many Were Shackled, Handcuffed, and Jailed?

In his appeal filings, Rivkin noted that by Knox County's own count, more than 600 accused truants were called to the juvenile court between 2008 and 2012. But it's hard to determine who among them was locked up because the court refuses to release detailed detention data that could include reasons for jailing, and whether detention was pretrial or posttrial and if the kids had counsel.

Without transparent data, Rivkin said, "there is no way of knowing how many children and youth have suffered the consequences our clients did before we began representing them."

In 2011, Rivkin filed public record act requests asking for lockup information, with juveniles' names redacted. Irwin declined the request. The judge retained a lawyer for himself, Robert Watson of Knoxville, who has since died. Watson argued in a letter that the records were "confidential and inspection is allowed only if the judge so chooses."

A Center associate in Tennessee filed a request for redacted juvenile detention records and was told in January that she would have to provide $17,500 in processing costs to Knox County first.

In the meantime, Rivkin was able to obtain, though an unofficial channel, an internal Knox court compilation tracing status offender histories over several years; the document contains no information about whether lawyers were appointed. But it is illuminating nonetheless.

The Center reviewed the compilation, which was submitted to the Fourth Circuit Court. The review found that in 2009 alone more than 50 status offenders identified only by "client" numbers were put into detention. The only charge listed in connection with some lockups was truancy. Most followed a succession of prior appearances and prior detentions for a mix of infractions no greater than truancy, running away, cigarette possession, curfew violation and probation revocation or valid court order violations.

One minor, the records show, appeared in court twice for truancy in 2006 and 2007, and then had probation revoked in 2008 and was put into detention that same year. The same minor was back in court again for tobacco possession in 2008, followed by revocation of probation again and detention again. In 2009, the minor was in court again for revocation of probation and again put into detention.

A young woman who asked to be identified as K.P. also has a history of cycling through court in Knox County during this time frame.

In February 2008, when she was 15, she pleaded guilty to truancy, without the benefit of an attorney. She was arrested twice later that year and put into detention both times. She was accused of disobeying truancy probation, but she had no valid court order in her file, lawyers at the Practicum who later represented her said.

In September 2008, K.P. was held for several days in detention. There was nothing in her file to indicate that she was being held to ensure she would appear for a court hearing that had been scheduled. In December 2008, K.P. was arrested by police again, this time in front of classmates, while she was attending classes at the same school she was accused of failing to attend.

"Defendant was picked up at [redacted] High School on an outstanding petition for revocation of probation. She was transported to Knox County Juvenile Center," an arrest report says.

In an interview, K.P. said that being put into handcuffs, shackles and prison garb "only made me want to rebel more."

She said she originally began refusing to go to classes because of sexual harassment—she was attacked on the school bus she rode daily—and because she had developed anxiety and bladder problems at school. She said her complaints were not addressed at school, and she was not offered an alternative learning option.

"These are not all kids with chains hanging off their belts, in gangs," said attorney Brenda McGee, who is Rivkin's wife and collaborates with the Education Practicum, and much later represented K.P.

## State Proposal to Ensure Truants Get Counsel Fails

In 2012, a fledgling attempt to pass state legislation establishing an immediate right to appointment of counsel for truants quickly died.

The measure failed to get out of a subcommittee after it was estimated the state indigent defense fund would require an additional half a million dollars a year; that sounds modest, said its sponsor, former Sen. Andy Berke, now mayor of Chattanooga. But the increase was too much for some legislators, Berke said, given that less than $2 million out $37 million spent from the fund in 2010 went to juvenile defense.

Because of this failure, Rivkin believes it's more important than ever to provide pro bono counsel to accused truants.

States' rules and statutes all vary, and there's virtually no formal data on the issue, but Rivkin estimates based on his own research that 33 states now ensure a relatively early right to counsel for truants during court proceedings.

In some states, such as Pennsylvania, counsel is automatic and can only be waived after multiple steps to ensure children grasp what they are doing. Pennsylvania was rocked by a scandal a couple of years ago when two juvenile court judges in Wilkes-Barre were found guilty of taking bribes for sending kids who had waived counsel to do time at private detention camps.

Puritz of the National Juvenile Defender Center remains concerned that minors, who are being processed through crowded courts, too frequently waive rights even in states with expansive rights to counsel on paper.

The idea to offer pro bono counsel to accused truants in Knox County is modeled after a similar project in Atlanta. Judge Irwin privately confided to lawyers that he didn't think accused truants had extensive unmet legal needs, according to Harry Ogden of Knoxville's prominent Baker Donelson firm, one of those attorneys who tried to personally persuade the judge to support the project.

"He's a great guy," Ogden said of the judge, "but when you're 14 years old, and standing in front of the juvenile judge, then you are probably about as tongue-tied as I was as a third-year law student in front of a judge."

## Unnecessary Drug Rehab, Diagnoses Ignored

Irwin, 55, is a 6-foot-7 former University of Tennessee football hero who went on to a more than 14-year-pro-football career, 13 of those years as a tackle for the Minnesota Vikings. He has plenty of fans in Knoxville who admire his strong support for the local Boys and Girls Club, and gestures like passing out stuffed animals to small kids in court who could be taken from parents due to neglect.

But A.G. and other truants said that the judge, who's been on the bench since 2005, was intimidating. A.G. said that when she returned to court after her stay in a psychiatric hospital, she tried to tell him about a diagnosis she was given of "school phobia" and bipolar disorder.

"He said, 'I have a phobia, too. It's a phobia of kids not going to school,'" according to A.G.

K.P. and her mother today believe that a hostile court environment forced the family into a decision they regret and believe could have been avoided if they'd had legal counsel.

When K.P. tested positive for marijuana while on truancy probation, her mother feared the court would take her child into state custody and foster care. The mother panicked, and scrambled to find space in a secure drug and behavior rehab facility—for nine months—even though she didn't believe K.P. required such treatment. The move satisfied the court, K.P.'s mother said, but "nearly tore us apart."

"They walked all over us because we didn't have a representative," said K.P.'s mom.

K.P. said, "I lost a year of my life. Being at that rehab center didn't help at all. It was awful. I felt like I didn't belong there."

Debbie Jones, T.W.'s mom and a daycare worker, has stuck with Rivkin's appeal because she feels the court's treatment of her son made his problems worse.

Jones told the Center that T.W. loved school as a young boy. "I couldn't pay him to stay home when he was sick," she said. But at 13, he became reclusive, and struggled with classroom learning. He pretended to board his school bus and hid out instead of going to classes.

"He said he felt smothered at school," Jones said.

For all the punitive treatment he received, T.W. never graduated and now he's too old to be prosecuted. Rivkin is looking for a suitable adult school for T.W., whose phobias make it difficult for him to sit among large groups.

John Gill, the D.A.'s special counsel, said that office has been working more diligently with educators and social workers to address roots of truancy and avoid putting kids into court.

About 80 percent of initial truancy complaints the D.A. gets are resolved now, he said, after families attend the mass meetings warning them to straighten out problems. New petitions—not including ongoing petitions—to prosecute these kids declined to 65 in 2012 compared to 76 in 2011.

Knox County Assistant Public Defender Christina Kleiser said the court's reaction to truancy seems to have softened. But not long ago, when police were referring to truancy as a "gateway crime," Kleiser said many truants were getting locked up over weekends to show toughness.

Massie, who leads the school district's student support services, admits to inconsistent intervention in the past to help struggling students who were frequently absent. Educators, she said, are now required to follow an intervention checklist and convene meetings more promptly with parents so specialists can evaluate students and plan targeted support.

"I think the truancy program is much better than it was before," she said.

But she said that by statute, the district is still required to provide the D.A.'s office with names of students when they reach more than 10 unexcused absences.

Although his pro bono services remain little known, Rivkin said, two parents did contact him this year complaining that children with emotional problems were threatened at school with jailing if they missed more school. Last fall, Rivkin also met, by chance, Carla Staley, a mom who received a warning letter from the D.A. accusing her son Lowell, 13, who has cerebral palsy, with excessive absences that could land them in court.

## National Trends, Federal Teeth

Knox County isn't the only region where truancy has galvanized community crackdowns.

Communities want to increase graduation rates, boost collection of attendance-based funding schools lose when kids are absent, and keep kids off the streets. But aggressive campaigns involving prosecution are attracting scrutiny, especially when minors are not afforded counsel.

In Washington state, another lawsuit over truants' right to counsel led—briefly—to expansion of that right. In the state's Bellevue School District, a 13-year-old girl, a Bosnian refugee, appeared at an initial truancy hearing in 2006 with no counsel and signed a promise to attend school or face penalties ranging from community service to "house arrest, work crew and possibly detention," according to the American Civil Liberties Union.

The girl was appointed an attorney only when found in contempt because her absences continued and she then faced imminent punishment.

Asked to weigh in, that state's Courts of Appeals found that all accused truants had a constitutional right to counsel from the onset of hearings that could lead to penalties. The Washington State Supreme Court overturned that ruling in 2011, favoring the state's argument that truancy statutes protect a child's right to education, so no counsel is initially required.

Last December, the board of trustees of the National Council of Juvenile and Family Court Judges took another approach by urging Congress to eliminate the valid court order exception as part of a long-overdue reauthorization of the 1974 federal juvenile justice act. Back in 1980, it was this same judges' group that urged Congress to include the valid court order exception.

In 2009, Sen. Patrick Leahy, D-Vt., proposed eliminating this exception in the reauthorization of the act—which Congress has still failed to do. And in March of this year, Rep. Tony Cardenas, Democrat from California's San Fernando Valley, also introduced legislation to get rid of the valid court order.

Federal official Listenbee, a former defense attorney, is also starting to speak out more in his new role as the nation's top juvenile-justice official.

In a speech he gave last August, he warned that detention should not be taken lightly. "Research has . . . shown," Listenbee said, "that the minute a youth sets foot in detention or lock-up, he or she has a 50 percent chance of entering the criminal justice system as an adult."

In March, Listenbee responded to Center for Public Integrity's inquiries about when his office believes status offenders' right to appointment of counsel begins.

Language in the federal regulations does not specifically address whether judges must afford appointment of counsel to kids before they are issued valid court orders, Listenbee acknowledged. But he believes that this is the intent. He also said he doesn't believe states can claim they're following the rules unless they ensure that courts provide counsel before valid court orders are meted out.

"Attorneys should be appointed in advance so they can have an opportunity to meet with their clients and properly prepare for the hearings," Listenbee said. "We make this clear in our training [for state officials] and do our best to emphasize this expectation in communicating with states around compliance matters."

In January, auditors on a visit from Listenbee's office found that Tennessee must "prioritize training and technical assistance" to ensure respect for due process and the valid court order process. But auditors only examined 2012 data.

As for A.G. and K.P., they're both 20 now. It was only last summer, after both young women turned 19, that Rivkin and McGee were legally able to request that Irwin expunge delinquency records the young women said they didn't even know the judge had given them back when they were teens. The judge granted the requests to expunge the records.

Delinquency records equate status offenders with kids who've committed crimes. And they remain on file, if they aren't expunged. A delinquency record can follow a youth, surfacing to jeopardize job, college, and other applications, lawyers warn.

After the Practicum began to represent A.G., more than a year after she was jailed, A.G.'s school finally designed a learning plan that shielded her from crowds of students and bullying and enabled her to graduate in 2011.

Looking back, K.P. said the adults who ultimately helped her finish high school in 2011 were the lawyers at the Practicum, who pushed for the school district to evaluate her for special needs and provide her a special-education plan—after she was twice jailed and put into unnecessary rehab for nine months.

With lawyers' help, she said, "I actually graduated a year early. So much for being the bad kid."

## Critical Thinking

1. Should minors be able to waive their rights in court without a lawyer to advise them about what, exactly, those rights are?

2. Should Congress eliminate the "valid court order exception" to the 1974 federal juvenile justice act?

3. Does incarcerating young people have risks for their future adult lives?

## Internet References

**Center for Public Integrity**
    https://www.documentcloud.org/documents/1156538-knox-truant-found-guilty-jailed-same-day.html

**Create Central**
    www.mhhe.com/createcentral

**National Juvenile Defender Center**
    http://www.njdc.info/pdf/Indiana%20Assessment.pdf

Level 14: How a Home for Troubled Children Came Undone and What It Means for California's Chance at Reform by Joaquin Sapien

**159**

*Article*

Prepared by: Joanne Naughton

# Level 14

## *How a Home for Troubled Children Came Undone and What It Means for California's Chance at Reform*

**This story was co-published with the California Sunday Magazine.**

Joaquin Sapien

## Learning Outcomes

*After reading this article, you will be able to:*

- Describe some of the problems suffered by children entering FamiliesFirst.

- Compare group homes and wraparound care.

- Relate some of the problems faced by the staff of such facilities.

On the morning of June 6, 2013, Davis Police Department squad cars rolled up to the group home at 2100 Fifth Street. More than a dozen officers in bulletproof vests made their way past the facility's memorial planter bearing painted handprints of children. They were no strangers to the location.

For more than a year, officers had been grappling with problems at the home, one of California's largest residential facilities for emotionally damaged kids. They had repeatedly returned runaways. They had coaxed suicidal teens off rooftops. There were reports of fights, drug use, children having sex with adults. In a single week in the spring, Davis police responded to 74 calls. On May 29, though, there had been a report of a different order: An 11-year-old girl at the home claimed that boys from the facility had raped her. Two boys had been arrested. After months of unraveling, the home had come undone.

Over the next several days, the campus began to empty out as parents turned up, searching for their children and for answers about what had happened to them. Social workers scrambled to find alternate placements, sending some kids to emergency shelters. Others remained in dormitory rooms, where police tracked them down to ask a long-overdue question: Do you feel safe? State officials opened the inevitable investigation, interrogating the staff and combing through records.

In the months leading up to the raid, neither the police nor the Department of Social Services, the state agency responsible for regulating group homes, had prevented the disaster at FamiliesFirst. They didn't step in that spring when there were reports of children living in a homeless encampment in a nearby park. They didn't intervene when a 9-year-old girl, new to the home, wound up half naked on the doorstep of a house in Davis and was later detoxed in a hospital emergency room. A Department of Social Services investigator visited the campus repeatedly in the weeks before the police raid, but the agency never curbed the turmoil.

The breakdown at FamiliesFirst has helped spur California to rethink how it cares for its most troubled children, a question that for decades has confounded not just the state but the country. A panel of experts, officials, care providers, and families has generated a raft of reforms it hopes will soon become law. Over the years, the places that used to be repositories for such children—state psychiatric hospitals and juvenile detention centers—have been shuttered or scaled back, usually in the wake of their own scandals. Group homes, too, have increasingly been deemed a failed model, yet year after year vulnerable and volatile California children remain housed in them for lack of a better option.

The Davis facility, one of California's roughly 1,000 group homes, closed for good in September 2013. Spelled out in police records and Department of Social Services files, in budgets and in the recollections of staffers, is the story of negligent stewardship and a state agency's flawed oversight. It's a story that continues to haunt those it touched.

## The Child

Alex Barschat-Li spent the first days of his life in the neonatal intensive care unit at Hoag Hospital in Newport Beach, California. Born on March 12, 1999, he experienced such severe breathing difficulties that his mother, Wendy, worried that he might not survive. She was 29, supporting herself and her husband on a medical assistant's salary.

Two months after Alex came home, his parents split up. When Alex was 3, Wendy fell into such a deep depression that she checked herself into a psychiatric ward, sending him to his grandmother's. Upon her release, an aunt proposed that Wendy to marry an undocumented Chinese national in exchange for $10,000 in cash. Wendy married Peter Li on the day she met him, and ten years later, they're still together. "No one's ever treated me the way he does," she says. The family eventually moved to Roseville, half an hour north of Sacramento, where Wendy and Peter bought a floor-and-tile-installation business.

According to Wendy, Alex was an easy child the first years of his life. But after he turned 5, she became concerned about his behavior. He'd sit on the brick stoop and sing and wave at cars for hours. At 6, he would grab knives out of the kitchen cabinets and hold them against his neck. At 7, he spent hours underneath his bed, hoarding food and clothing. He obsessed over seemingly insignificant details, refusing to go to school unless his mother gave him a certain kind of pencil or allowed him to wear a particular pair of socks.

Wendy sought help from Child Protective Services, which arranged for counselors and therapists to come to the home. Alex's behavior, though, grew increasingly violent. He smashed furniture and windows. To protect themselves, Wendy and Peter installed a deadbolt on their bedroom door. Alex's food hoarding became so extreme that they secured the refrigerator and cabinets with padlocks. By the time Alex was 11, the police had come to the home at least 11 times, and he had been held for psychiatric evaluation seven times. He was diagnosed with a handful of disorders—attention deficit, anxiety, bipolar, oppositional defiant—requiring a complicated set of prescriptions, many of which had side effects.

Alex broke Wendy's resolve the afternoon he beat her bedroom door down with a kitchen chair. Peter barely managed to restrain Alex until the police arrived. "I was in a panic," she says. "I knew in my heart that if I didn't do something extreme he was going to be one of those kids I saw on TV for raping someone or making a bomb."

Wendy's options were limited. Only 11 of California's 58 counties have hospitals that provide psychiatric care, and those that do have few beds. Psychiatrists had suggested that Wendy get Alex placed in a residential treatment facility. California's system for group homes is arcane, shaped by decades of litigation and legislation. The homes are classified by levels that range from 1 through 14. The top two levels serve the most troubled children and are required by law to provide intensive psychiatric services.

A child "graduates" from a Level 14 home when it is deemed he or she can function either in a lower-level group home or a foster home, or with a relative or a biological parent. The goal is to get the child to something that most closely resembles a family.

When Alex was 11, he was sent to Compass Rose, a Level 12 group home in Loomis, California. Three months in, on a cold winter morning, he and a friend were found walking alongside the I-80 freeway in shorts and T-shirts. Alex soon ran away again, showing up at a nearby church, where he told a couple that his parents had abandoned him. After police took Alex back to Compass Rose, administrators told Wendy they'd had enough. Alex, they said, needed to be in a more restrictive group home with more intensive therapeutic services.

Alex's social worker identified two homes: Milhous Treatment Center in Nevada City and FamiliesFirst in Davis. Wendy visited both. The 6.5-acre FamiliesFirst campus, she says, was by far the more impressive. It included a school, a gym, an arts center, and eight to nine-bedroom dormitories—with names likes Pioneer House and Sapphire House—that looked out onto a large playground and an expanse of lawn.

Alex entered FamiliesFirst on April 7, 2011. He was now among the roughly 750 children in California living in a Level 14 facility.

FamiliesFirst was founded in 1974 by a 26-year-old University of California at Davis graduate named Evelyn Praul. She started with a single foster home, two employees, and three emotionally disturbed boys. Over the next two decades, Praul opened six more group homes for boys in Davis and expanded throughout Northern California. In 1994, Praul decided to build a campus at 2100 Fifth Street in the southwest corner of town. Centralizing the Davis homes, she concluded, would help the organization serve more children and make it easier for staff to respond to emergencies.

Building the campus, though, proved costly, and by the mid-2000s, the facility was running a deficit. The home's ability to meet its obligations depended on the number of children counties referred to the facility. (The current rate for Level 14 homes is $9,669 per child per month.) As a rule, group homes budget for 90 percent capacity, but the referral stream can dip and surge from month to month. If the population falls below 90 percent over an extended period of time, a home can quickly go into the red, a situation that the Davis campus found itself in.

There was an additional factor working against the facility. In the mid-1990s, just as FamiliesFirst decided to build the Davis campus, California and many other states were beginning to question the value of group homes. Concentrating troubled children in a residence, many had come to believe, tended to exacerbate their problems and make their disorders more difficult to address. Instead the state was considering a model of treatment known as wraparound care, which involves bringing therapists and counselors into the homes where children reside. Focused attention on the child within a household was viewed as a less disruptive approach that could also closely examine family dynamics.

Deciding it could not make it on its own, in 2009 FamiliesFirst merged with a larger nonprofit called Eastfield Ming Quong, or EMQ, which functioned mostly in the Bay Area and surrounding counties. The deal offered obvious advantages to both organizations. FamiliesFirst worked in regions where EMQ had almost no presence, giving the newly constituted company, EMQ FamiliesFirst, a bigger share of the social-service market. In turn, the more financially secure EMQ could provide stability to the FamiliesFirst operations it absorbed.

When Alex came to the Davis campus, the facility employed more than 130 full- and part-time staff who could look after as many as 72 children. Like many such institutions, the home accommodated a dizzying assortment of children. They ranged from 6 to 18 years old. They came from all over the state, from wealthy families as well as poor. They were white, black, Latino, and Asian. Most had passed through countless sets of foster parents and group homes. Some had been sent by school districts that lacked the resources to respond to their needs. Some had been sent by courts as part of a sentence for a minor criminal offense.

"At any given time about 20 percent of our youth have a diagnosable disorder," says Dr. Gary Blau of the U.S. Department of Health and Human Services, "and 10 percent have a serious emotional disturbance, which means their disorder impairs their ability to function at home or in the community. The rarer occasion is that they are a danger to themselves, that they warrant hospitalization or residential treatment."

The children at FamiliesFirst, as in all Level 14 homes, suffered from a spectrum of psychiatric disorders: Asperger's, autism, attention deficit, bipolar, chronic depression, obsessive compulsive, and schizophrenia. Many were suicidal, nearly all assaultive, and some self-injurious. Many were confused about their sexuality and gender orientation. Many arrived with medical problems caused by malnourishment and neglect. Some had stunted growth. Some had Type 2 diabetes. Several had spent a portion of their lives living in closets, basements, or other confined spaces. One set of twins were said to have been forced by a relative to have sex with each other inside a locked cage. A 6-year-old boy, known at the home as Cowboy Dan, was said to have stolen at least three cars by the time he arrived.

The regimen was strict: out of bed at 7:00, breakfast at 7:30, classes at 8:00. At 2:00, the children retired to the dorms, had a snack, and broke up into small groups. They'd rotate through a treatment program made up of three separate sessions: art, recreation, and life skills. In the life-skills session, children were instructed in mastering the mundane: how to clean one's feet, for example, or how to figure out what size batteries to buy, or how to board a bus. Each child was expected to have a behavioral goal, usually simple, like saying something nice to someone twice a day.

Just 12 years old when he arrived, Alex was big for his age—five foot two and 163 pounds—with short brown hair and high cheekbones. He was used to imposing himself physically and didn't take well to the structure. Early on, he got into a fight with a smaller boy and ended up in one of the campus's many "quiet rooms," which were meant to give a child in the throes of a tantrum a safe place to "de-escalate." For Alex, the experience seemed to have the opposite effect. "I got thrown in there all the time," he says. "I hated it because I would catastrophize. I thought I was being treated like an animal."

Alternately affectionate and sullen, Alex was prone to radical mood swings, speaking in a rapid staccato one minute, turning almost monosyllabic the next. According to an evaluation report sent to Wendy six months into his stay, he suffered from "an inability to build or maintain satisfactory interpersonal relationships with peers and teachers." A minor annoyance or a denial of a privilege could set him off, and he would hurl himself at whoever irked him.

In time, though, he began to show signs of progress. In the fall of 2012, he moved into a dorm called Adventurer, which was led by a group of experienced staffers who connected with him. He was still easily distracted and easily angered, but the extremes had leveled off. Where once he threw tantrums during chores, he would now take a break in his room, gather his composure, and get back to the task at hand. He was less confrontational, less violent—happier.

Toward the end of 2012, Alex noticed that there were fewer counselors on campus—he had heard there had been layoffs—and that they seemed to be under more stress than usual. They also had become more lenient. He could now walk off the campus without anyone stopping him, and whenever someone had a manic episode, the staff was less likely to employ restraints, the term for the physical holds staff are allowed to use to prevent children from harming themselves or others.

At first, Alex left campus by himself, often hanging out at a bicycle shop where the employees liked him. He went to a Dairy Queen and moped until an employee gave him an order of fries on the house. Soon he was tagging along with a group of eight to twelve children from the home who stole food and clothing from stores around Davis. They started staying out all night, drinking alcohol, smoking pot, and having sex in parks. Before long he and others were hitchhiking out of town. Alex got as far as Sacramento.

"We had different jobs for different kids," says Alex, whose task was to shoplift. "Kids who begged, kids who found bikes for us, kids who went back to campus to get blankets and stuff. We'd be gone for days."

Early in the spring of 2013, Alex and his friends took over a homeless encampment on the outskirts of a park, a tangle of blankets and mattresses, abandoned furniture and trash, all jammed into a thicket dense enough to obstruct the view of passersby. It was one of several places where the children began to sleep at night. Another favorite, which Alex calls Plan B, was behind a Comcast building alongside Interstate 80.

The staff rarely told Wendy when Alex wasn't on campus. Her most reliable way to find out his whereabouts was through his Facebook posts. Alex would go to a library and send her messages or she would see photos on his page that showed him in town. She says she drove to Davis many times looking for him. On June 3, she pleaded with him on Facebook: PLEASE ALEX PLEASE GO BACK TO THE GROUP HOME WHERE YOU ARE SAFE AND SURROUNDED BY PEOPLE THAT CARE ABOUT YOU.

He did return, but on June 6, Wendy found out he'd gone missing again, this time for two days. She drove to Davis and searched all his usual spots. Around 1:00 P.M., she called FamiliesFirst and a staffer told her Alex had turned up and was taking a shower. But when she arrived, she was told it had been a mistake: No one knew where Alex was. Furious, Wendy went looking for him again. At 3:00, staff told her that Alex had been picked up by his social worker and removed from the home. They wouldn't say where. All they said was that police and reporters had been at the campus.

## The Social Worker

After the merger in 2009, executives at EMQ FamiliesFirst faced a serious challenge: The Davis campus had lost nearly $1.5 million in the previous two years. According to a former financial officer at FamiliesFirst, making payroll every two weeks could be a "real white-knuckle" experience. In early 2010, executives turned to FamiliesFirst's longtime intake coordinator, Ron Fader, and asked if there was a population of underserved children that could keep the beds filled. Warily, Fader said yes: teenage girls.

For years, county social workers had been pleading with the Davis campus to accept girls. More recently, staffers at Community Care Licensing, the division of the Department of Social Services that oversees group homes, had pushed for the

campus to go coed; the Sacramento region, they said, desperately needed a Level 14 facility for girls. FamiliesFirst, though, had always resisted. It wasn't just that girls with mental health needs acute enough to warrant Level 14 care are difficult to treat. They demand a different approach than boys. They would require hiring new staff and retraining old.

"I said, 'Look, I can fill the beds, no problem, but these girls present some extreme challenges,'" Fader says. "They are cutters. Many have a diagnosis of borderline personality disorder. They're sexually promiscuous. They're runners. Their behaviors are very intense, and they could possibly upset the milieu here."

Despite Fader's concerns, EMQ FamiliesFirst decided to go ahead, and in the summer of 2010 the Davis home opened its first dormitory for girls. The administration, though, hadn't established a policy on what boundaries should be set. Should the boys and girls be in the same classrooms? Could they walk to school together? Should relationships be forbidden? Essentially, it was an experiment: mixing highly volatile girls and highly volatile boys, many in the grip of changing hormones.

To Andrea Guthrie, who was a social worker at the Davis campus, it was a dangerous experiment. "Since the merger happened," Guthrie says, "there was this constant need to put the plane together in the middle of the sky."

Guthrie had been on staff since June 2000, a year after she graduated from the University of California at Davis. Her first job was as a counselor, for which she was paid $8.35 an hour. She took it mostly to pay her bills while she busied herself with Peace Corps applications. She was hoping to go to West Africa. But the reward of making progress with troubled kids hooked her, and she soon dropped her plans, deciding there was no sense in traveling across the world to make a difference when she could do it 25 minutes from where she grew up. She attended graduate school, earned her master's in counseling, and, in 2005, was promoted to clinical social worker at the home. Her new salary was $37,500.

The girls filled two dorms, and Guthrie's colleague Kim Rowerdink, who had some experience counseling girls, was named supervisor of one of them. Guthrie and Rowerdink often discussed how the girls mimicked one another. Outside of a group home, this wouldn't necessarily be alarming: It could mean girls dyeing their hair the same color or wearing the same clothes. But in an institutional environment it meant an abrupt surge in cutting, running away, or violence. Rowerdink once caught three girls trying to slash their arms at the same time. As part of their daily rounds, Guthrie helped her scour the dorm for any object that could be used to inflict injury—bobby pins, broken CDs, loose screws, and cracked light fixtures. If a girl with a history of harming herself ran off the campus, they'd try to stop her.

"I can tell you that my staff had no specific training whatsoever to address self-injury, suicidality, or anything like that," Rowerdink says. "It would just be one crisis after the next.

A girl would cut herself, we'd take her to the hospital, bring her back, and then she'd do it again. It was like Groundhog Day."

Rowerdink and others say this was the daily environment for the next two years. During one psychotic episode, a girl tried eating a light bulb. During another, a girl inserted shards of glass into her vagina and anus. Unlike Guthrie and Rowerdink, the vast majority of the staff who interacted with the kids did not have degrees in education, psychology, or social work. Most had received no more than seven days of classroom training, the standard for all employees, which offered an overview of children in Level 14 facilities and instruction in how to restrain them safely.

In the fall of 2012, Audrie Meyer, the home's director, announced a change in policy. From now on, she said, physically preventing children from leaving campus should occur only when they were in "immediate danger." If that was not the case, the counselors were instructed to shadow them. The directives perplexed and angered the staff. What did "immediate danger" mean? Did a girl have to be cutting herself or merely reaching for a sharp object? Did a child need to be standing in the middle of the freeway or walking toward it? The staff had always trusted some children to leave the campus and not others. Now what were they supposed to do? Sit back and let any kid take off?

No California law directly addresses whether a child is allowed to leave the grounds of a group home. Nor is there a law that says whether a group home is responsible for the actions of the child once the child crosses the property line. Group-home administrators develop their own policies on how to handle runaways based on their interpretation of three statutes: that a group home is responsible for providing care and supervision for every child it has taken in, that a group home cannot be locked, and that restraints can't be administered unless children pose an immediate danger to themselves or others.

The act of leaving the campus doesn't constitute an immediate danger, which means that a group-home counselor is not supposed to prevent a child from leaving. "It's extremely ambiguous," says Carroll Schroeder, the executive director for a trade group called the California Alliance of Child and Family Services. "Our experience has been that folks get caught between the protection of a child's personal rights and requirements to assure a child's safety."

Michael Weston, spokesman for the Department of Social Services, says that if a child is suicidal or has a reputation for leaving the campus and inflicting harm on herself or others, it's within a group administrator's authority to prevent that child from leaving. But group-home administrators say it's not as clear-cut as that. The department can cite a home for restraining a child from leaving campus if it believes the action was unnecessary, and it can cite a home for failing to supervise children who leave the campus and harm themselves or someone else.

"It's such a Catch-22 for our kind of program," says Steven Elson, the chief executive officer of Casa Pacifica, a group-care company in Southern California. "If we knew that a child had a plan to leave the campus and drink near a park with a 25-year-old friend, we would very likely contain the child. But you don't know about those things in advance."

In late January 2013, Guthrie was given an assignment she dreaded. She would be directly responsible for the girls' care in a dorm called Jade House. To her surprise, though, Guthrie found the girls endearing. They got excited about things that held no appeal for boys. The walls of the dorm were decorated in purple and pink and covered in Hello Kitty stickers, glitter, and posters of pop stars. A trip to Walmart to buy socks sent the girls over the moon. Early on, there were indications she was making inroads. One girl, schizophrenic and violent, no longer exhibited sudden aggressive episodes. Three girls graduated, their behaviors deemed stable enough for them to move in with a relative or into a lower-level home.

As the year went on, though, the victories became less frequent. That winter, EMQ FamiliesFirst had laid off the on-call workers the home relied on to fill in for sick or injured employees, and the staff immediately felt the pinch. "It was a budgeting decision," says Ron Fader. "Everyone knew it was going to create a house of cards." When staff became injured or burnt out, no one was now available to replace them. Social workers, therapists, and sometimes management had to supervise the children, an assignment usually designated for counselors, causing paperwork, group therapy, and other duties to slip. Guthrie began putting in 60 hours or more a week. Each morning, she woke up to an email inbox filled with urgent messages requesting that she follow up with children about violent events or disappearances from campus.

"We would dread the on-call rotations," Guthrie says, "because it was sheer hell—an entire week of not sleeping on top of already being completely exhausted."

The children began to realize how much they could get away with now that the facility was understaffed and the counselors had all but stopped employing restraints. One child ripped off large pieces of a metal gutter from a dormitory roof and hurled them at the staffers beneath. Others smashed windows and vandalized staff-owned vehicles. By April, Guthrie and other staff could no longer contain their frustration. They worried that it would be only a matter of time before a child was raped, or killed, or kidnapped.

At an all-staff meeting on April 24, Guthrie and others confronted Meyer, the home's director. They told her that several girls were coming back to campus with stories of having sex, sometimes with boys from the home, sometimes with adults in the community. Meyer's response was not what the staff expected. The children, she said, were going to have to learn to avoid such trouble on their own. Guthrie remembers looking around the room and seeing aghast expressions on the faces of her colleagues. "These kids are here because they cannot think like that," Guthrie says.

That day, a wisp of a girl arrived at Jade House. She was about four and a half feet tall, 75 pounds, and wore her unwashed blond hair at shoulder length. She tried to flirt and sit in the laps of staff. She spoke often of wanting a boyfriend. She adored a pair of high heels she said her mother had given her. She was 9 years old.

"She came in right before s—hit the fan," Guthrie says. "I was livid. I was like, 'Really? We can't even handle what we have right now, and you think that's an OK environment to bring this young of a kid into a teenage-girl house?' No."

Soon the girl was leaving overnight with children several years her senior. She told the campus nurse that she hitchhiked to nearby Woodland. She told a counselor that she performed oral sex on an older boy in a park; she said the boy urinated in her mouth. Early on a Saturday morning in late May, Guthrie was asleep in her studio apartment when her phone rang. The girl had been gone since Thursday. The counselor on the line said the police had located her and she was now in the emergency room, where she was being detoxed.

When Guthrie returned to work on Monday, she learned that the girl had been found partially naked after she had banged on the door of a house in a quiet residential neighborhood in Davis, begging for help. The girl couldn't recall much. She said she'd been with a group of older kids in an abandoned freight car near the railroad tracks alongside I-80. One of the older boys panhandled for some money to buy dresses for the girls at a Rite Aid and shoplifted some liquor. The crew met a homeless man who joined them for the freight-car party. The girl described him as "really nice." She said the last thing she remembered was taking a single swig from a bottle of alcohol the kids had passed around.

Guthrie told Meyer the story later that day. Meyer tried to remain calm, but Guthrie could see she was panicked.

## The Police Officer

Jeff Beasley stood in the parking lot of Harrison Self-Storage. The facility shared a cinder-block wall with a corner of the campus. A police officer for 12 years, Beasley was the department's liaison to the group home. On this day in spring 2013, he was attempting to persuade yet another teenager from FamiliesFirst to come down off the storage roof. Beasley did what he'd always done. He asked the boy his name, where he was from, and why he was up there.

"F—you. You're a f—ing cop!" the boy shouted. "I don't have to listen to you."

Beasley took a deep breath and shook his head. "Yeah, yeah, that's fine," he replied. "But you know, we're not going

anywhere. You want to stay up there all day? You want to climb down? Or you want us to haul you down?"

"No," the boy said. "It's getting hot. I'll come down."

As he drove the boy back to campus, Beasley thought about the past two years. His fellow officers had talked the same boy off the same roof several times in the previous week. He'd talked at least three kids down off rooftops around Davis over the course of 18 months. The place was falling apart. The staff should know how to do such things on their own. Would the administration ever address the problems? Couldn't they, at a minimum, put up a barrier along the back wall to prevent children from reaching the storage facility?

For the first five months of 2013, the Davis Police Department received more than 500 calls involving FamiliesFirst. Most of the calls came from staff who were asking for assistance on campus. But many came from town: the Taco Bell on G Street, when children from the home terrorized employees and customers; the Sudwerk Brewery, around the corner from campus, where girls were often found bleeding after cutting themselves with broken bottles. Residents complained about kids harassing pedestrians. Store owners complained about kids shoplifting. Sometimes the kids themselves would call or show up at the station, demanding that the police take them to a psychiatric hospital.

For Beasley and his fellow officers, the calls raised large questions. Was defusing one more ugly and dangerous incident enough? Did the volume of problems at the facility constitute a threat to the welfare of the children and to Davis? Most of the time, in Beasley's judgment, the children weren't doing anything that warranted an arrest. They were already in the social welfare system. Some had done stints in juvenile detention. Sending them back into custody probably wasn't going to improve their situation, but bringing them back to the campus wasn't working, either.

Beasley was singularly qualified to be the department's liaison. He had graduated from Pacific Union College with a bachelor's degree in theology and had served as a pastor at an evangelical church in his 20s and 30s. He later earned a master's in counseling at the University of San Francisco, and, in 1991, accepted a job as a residential social worker in one of FamiliesFirst's three-bedroom homes in Davis. The place was special to him. It was where he met his wife—she was an office manager—and, in his four years there, he and other staffers developed a deep camaraderie, maybe because the work could be so draining.

One day, a 12-year-old boy asked for permission to spend time in a quiet room. When Beasley looked in several minutes later, the boy had smeared feces on the walls and was lying naked. He had blindfolded and gagged himself and was bleeding from his gums. He had torn his clothes and run the shreds through his teeth.

Beasley wanted to know more about where such troubled children came from, to see if he could do something at the problem's root. In 1996, he took a job as an investigator with Yolo County's Child Protective Services Department. He has no doubt that he saved lives—he removed countless children from deplorable conditions—but after four years, the job wore him out. At 47, he joined the Davis Police Department.

For a police officer, Davis is enticing. Magazines often cite the city as "one of the best places to live" in the United States. More than half of its 66,000 residents are either employees or students at the University of California, which dominates the south end of town. The violent-crime rate is less than half that of the average American city. Five murders have occurred in the past ten years. The work of police mostly involves traffic stops, burglary investigations, and breaking up the odd bar fight or raucous college party. As Beasley points out, "there is no wrong side of the tracks in Davis."

When Beasley was assigned as the department's liaison to the group home in November 2012, the two institutions were at an impasse. The home's administrators wanted officers to escort children back onto the campus when they ran away and help subdue them if they became unruly once they arrived. Beasley and another officer named Tony Dias explained that they were not private security guards. Beasley and Dias met with administrators once a month. They tried to come up with a way to handle the increase in calls to the police, a disproportionate number of which involved a group of about 12 children who routinely ran away and slept in parks around town—the group that Alex hung out with.

Beasley was well liked on campus. Fifty-eight years old, with short white hair and a neatly trimmed mustache, he still had a preacher's way, shifting easily from impassioned to contemplative. The children occasionally confided in him about another resident or staff member. He'd mentor some of the counselors in how to defuse situations or calm a disruptive child. Officers learned the backgrounds of many of the children who were leaving the campus regularly and tried to adjust their approaches when they picked them up so as not to retraumatize them. One officer played basketball with the kids on campus; another went on jogs with the kids and counselors. Still, a huge divide existed between how the home approached the children and how the police did. In general, staff thought the officers were too aggressive, and the officers thought the staff were too lenient.

By April 2013, five months after Beasley had become liaison, the relationship between officers and staff had become contentious. Police threatened to arrest staff for allowing children off campus. Counselors explained that policy prohibited them from preventing children from leaving. Beasley and Dias decided that the agency might take the department more seriously if top brass got involved. They turned to their supervisor,

Assistant Chief Darren Pytel. He had been concerned about the home since the fall of 2011, when emergency calls from the facility jumped almost threefold from the previous year. But the explosion of calls that began to occur in January 2013 had no precedent.

"Entire shifts were spent chasing around runaway kids," Pytel says. "The staff, even when they knew where the kids were, refused to come out and pick them up. They wanted us to drive them back, as if we were a taxicab service. Eventually, I couldn't walk into my office without one of my patrol officers saying, 'Hey, we've got to do something about this place.'"

In late April and then in early May, Pytel and several of his deputies met with administrators from the home. The first time was with Audrie Meyer. According to Pytel, the conversation devolved quickly. He told Meyer that the calls had exhausted his department's resources. Meyer explained that it was EMQ FamiliesFirst policy not to prevent children from leaving the campus and that doing so would constitute a violation of state guidelines. Pytel asked to meet with her superiors.

At the second meeting, EMQ FamiliesFirst regional director Gordon Richardson and a lawyer for the agency joined Meyer. They told Pytel that the home would revisit the runaway policy and consider transferring some children. Pytel came away convinced the agency's leadership was hopelessly lost.

"It was really clear that nothing was being done to change what was becoming significant criminal behavior," Pytel says. "What was so disturbing to me was that this facility was full of social workers and people whose job it was to help these minors, but that was not happening. These minors were not being protected. They were being victimized to a point that was just absolutely shocking."

Days after the second meeting, Pytel reached out to the Department of Social Services, imploring it to intervene. The department, Pytel says, didn't seem "to take great interest." (Department of Social Services spokesman Michael Weston says no record of any discussion was kept, but that the agency was "responsive to law enforcement.")

In late May, Beasley was assigned to investigate the alleged rape of an 11-year-old girl. She had been at the home just over a month and had fallen in with the children who were leaving the campus for days at a time. She came back one morning, after being out all night, and told counselors that she'd been drinking and smoking in a park with two boys, 13 and 14 years old, from the home. She said they took turns raping her while two other kids pinned her down.

After the staff reported the allegation, Beasley and a colleague spent hours talking to the alleged perpetrators and witnesses. (Another officer interviewed the victim.) The prime suspect drew diagrams for Beasley that showed who was having sex with whom on campus. He told him that adults in the community were providing them with alcohol and pot. He admitted to shoplifting. But he vehemently denied having sex with the 11-year-old. Beasley concluded that if anything sexual had occurred that night, it didn't rise to the level of criminal behavior. His partner came to the same conclusion about the second alleged perpetrator.

Beasley says he expressed his doubts, but that Pytel was adamant: He wanted an arrest. Beasley came away convinced that the assistant chief intended to use the charges to shut down the home. Beasley sympathized with Pytel's exasperation but was furious at his willingness to charge children erroneously.

Pytel denies Beasley's accusations. He notes that the local prosecutor wound up pursuing the case. One of the boys pleaded guilty to two felony counts of unlawful sexual battery, and the other was acquitted. He says his intention was never to close the home. "What we wanted," he says, "was for everything to go back to the way it was before."

To Beasley, the boys' arrest was a political move. The police could solve the problem of the home and look like saviors. "When children fleeing a dangerous environment and needing help came to Davis," he says, "Davis said, 'Get the f—out.' Whether it was the police department, FamiliesFirst, licensing, the judicial system, nobody asked, 'What can we do to help?' Instead it was, 'How fast can we get rid of them?'"

## The Director

When EMQ FamiliesFirst asked Audrie Meyer to lead the Davis home in July 2012, she was surprised. By her own admission, she was not an obvious candidate. Meyer, who is 58 years old, had spent most of her professional life working as a tech consultant. Holding a master's in business administration, she helped build information systems for Pepsi and advised the French computer firm Groupe Bull on strategic planning.

She decided to change her career, and in 2008 she earned a master's degree in counseling and took a job as a social worker at a group home northeast of Sacramento. She left to join EMQ FamiliesFirst in 2011 as an associate director for the Davis facility's day-treatment program. She had been on the job for seven months when the head of the home resigned and she was asked to serve as interim director. She had been a licensed therapist for just two years.

Meyer was taking over the home at a particularly fraught moment. EMQ FamiliesFirst was beginning to question whether the Davis campus should remain open. Despite the addition of girls, the home continued to operate at a deficit. It was essential, she was told, that expenses be brought in line. Just as worrisome, the use of restraints on campus was unacceptably high, which was arousing concerns at the Department of Social Services. In 2011, staff employed restraints more than 800 times. In the first six months of 2012, they had already employed restraints more than 500 times.

Meyer enacted policy changes at a furious pace. In November, she lowered the campus's maximum to 63 children, laying off at least six full-time employees. By December she had eliminated all the part-time workers the home had relied on to fill in for staff absences. According to Meyer, several were made full-time, ensuring adequate supervision of the children.

Meyer also quickly zeroed in on restraints. Her supervisor was Gordon Richardson, who oversaw EMQ FamiliesFirst's operations in and around Sacramento. Meyer says he asked her to reduce the use of restraints by 25 percent from the previous year. (Like all current employees of EMQ FamiliesFirst, Richardson declined to be interviewed for this story. According to an EMQ FamiliesFirst spokesperson, "Due both to privacy concerns and pending litigation, we have been advised by legal counsel not to engage in further public comments regarding this past matter.") In October 2012, a staffer broke a child's arm in a restraint, drawing more scrutiny from the Department of Social Services. During the fall, Meyer met several times with Ashley Sinclaire, the department inspector assigned to the home, who warned her that the facility was in danger of losing its license if restraints weren't decreased substantially.

"For good or bad I got restraints down by 40 percent," Meyer says. "The downside for the program was it made the staff feel unsafe. When the staff feels unsafe, the children feel unsafe. At the same time that we are dropping restraints, licensing shows up and starts hammering me to drop them further, and the Davis Police Department starts threatening to arrest staff for letting kids off the campus."

People who work in the field agree that restraints ought to be used as infrequently as possible—as a last resort. The act can be necessary to maintain safety and order but can also be emotionally unsettling and physically dangerous for both the adult and the child. Overuse of restraints, most authorities say, is almost always an indication of deeper problems at a facility.

Leslie Morrison, an attorney for the nonprofit advocacy group Disability Rights California, is an opponent of restraints and believes that they can be avoided in all but the most extreme circumstances. But she said it's common for a group home to set a hard and fast goal to reduce restraints without properly teaching staff other means of calming children. "Senior management does this thing," she says, "where they used to go hands-on quite a lot and then, suddenly, they want no hands-on. What you have to do is give your staff a lot of training on alternatives. If you don't, you are going to have problems."

Meyer acknowledges that all the policy changes were too much too fast, but she also said the staff fought every attempt to reform the campus, even her efforts to have them learn alternatives to restraints.

Staff members insist that what was happening on the ground was much different from what Meyer saw from her office—that the workforce cuts, the belated training, and the new restraint policy had dangerously reduced the quality of care. From their point of view, it was a question of trust. They didn't believe that EMQ was committed to keeping the facility open. Just look at its history, they said: This was a company that had downsized its two group homes after it had decided that wraparound care was the future. For many of the staff, every budget cut that Meyer enacted was a precursor to EMQ shuttering the place; every policy change was setting them up to fail. According to Meyer, the staff's fears were not entirely off base. EMQ's executives never said so outright, but it was clear to her they were considering closing the campus.

Some staff were sympathetic toward Meyer. "I liked her," says Vivienne Roseby, a consulting psychologist at FamiliesFirst from 2000 until November 2012. "I think she was trying hard to do what EMQ wanted her to do, which was to get it tightened up, more efficient, more coherent. I do think that the pressure that she was under and the speed that she was being asked to make these changes made it difficult, if not impossible."

Roseby's, though, was a minority view. Most of the staff came to regard Meyer as distant and negligent, and the flash point was her policy on children leaving the campus. At staff meetings, Meyer repeated the message she'd been trying to get through from almost the moment she had arrived: The children, young and vulnerable as they were, were going to have to examine their own decisions about why they were leaving and what they were doing while they were gone. What happened to the children outside its walls was not the home's responsibility. California law, she said, was clear on this. Meyer assured the staff there was a logic to her thinking. If the children came to harm, the home could document the problem and perhaps get the children placed elsewhere. "Failing up," she called it.

"There is something wrong with this woman," says Kim Rowerdink, the dorm supervisor. "The police kept asking us, 'What is Audrie doing?' And we'd say, 'They keep telling us we're not responsible for what the kids do off campus. We can let them go.'"

Meyer, for her part, came to regard the staff as too emotionally involved. "It seemed completely foreign to them," she says, "that any program would not be able to stop a child from leaving the program. But you can't. I think the staff felt like it was the program's fault if the girls put themselves in harm's way, and I just don't think that's a fair statement."

Michael Weston of the Department of Social Services says Meyer's view amounts to a misguided understanding of a home's role. "The group home," he says, "is responsible for care and supervision, regardless whether the children are on campus or not." Referring to FamiliesFirst's policy guidelines, he says, "Read it right here. It talks about when a child goes off campus, we are responsible for their care and supervision."

In truth, that's not quite what the home's guidelines say. Rather, it states that staff will shadow children who leave the campus and will try to persuade them to return, employing restraints or calling police if they begin to harm themselves or someone else. The problem for the Davis home was that if its staff shadowed all the children who were leaving in the winter and spring of 2013, there would not be enough staff to supervise the children who remained on campus.

Between October 2012 and the beginning of May 2013, records show that Sinclaire and other licensing investigators visited the facility on at least 15 occasions. In late February, Sinclaire did bring up with Meyer the number of children leaving campus and the police's involvement in returning them. But Meyer says Sinclaire told her that she couldn't prevent children from leaving the campus by restraining them. (Michael Weston says that the Department of Social Services has no record of Sinclaire giving this directive. Sinclaire declined to comment, saying that she'd been instructed not to talk.)

Every group home in California must file a report to the Department of Social Services for a range of incidents, accidental or deliberate, alleged or substantiated. The roughly 500 reports that the home filed during the first four months of 2013 paint a picture of a facility whose staff and administration were overmatched. Meyer says that by April and May there were likely hundreds more reports that were never filed, in violation of state rules. "The volume went from 300 a month to 1,000 a month," she says, "and we didn't have enough trained people to file them."

From February to May, at least six counselors, therapists, and social workers resigned. "They were quitting faster than we could fill the jobs," Meyer says. According to people who had worked at the home for years, there'd never been a time when so many staff quit or took stress leave within such a short period. In May, the police received 252 calls, five times as many as they had received in January.

When Meyer made her superiors at EMQ FamiliesFirst aware of the problems on campus, she says, they were "very slow to grasp the seriousness of what was going on." She recalls several disconcerting conversations with Gordon Richardson: "When I relayed staff concerns about not having enough people, his reflection was, 'Well, maybe that's why restraints were down, and that's a good thing.'"

By late spring, Meyer says she became convinced the situation was hopeless. "I was very, very impacted by what was going on with these kids," she says. "I was not OK. I saw that it was horrible. When I realized the police weren't going to respond, and the staff was not getting support, and the kids were getting free rein—that was a horrible situation. I couldn't see a way to recover at that point."

Meyer was right. On the morning of June 6, she was sitting in the conference room once again listening to her staff express their frustration when she took a phone call. It was the front desk. Fifteen Davis police officers in bulletproof vests were in the lobby.

# Epilogue

On January 9, 2015, California's Department of Social Services issued a 56-page report to the legislature outlining what needed to be done to care for the kinds of children who lived and suffered at the Davis home. The report called for increased minimum qualifications and training for group-care workers; more-varied therapeutic services; and better screening of children to more appropriately determine their needs and where they should be placed.

Most dramatically, the report called for group homes to be eliminated, or at least limited to offering short-term stays. "It is well-documented," the report states, "that residing long-term in group homes with shift-based care is not in the best interest of children and youth. Not only is it developmentally inappropriate, it frequently creates lifelong institutionalized behaviors and contributes to higher levels of involvement with the juvenile justice system and to poor educational outcomes."

As long as group homes exist, they will still present challenges of oversight. The Department of Social Services report says little about improving its own performance in inspecting and investigating the homes. To many, the department has long been poorly positioned or equipped to monitor Level 14 group homes. Inspections are required only once every five years, and records show they are perfunctory, mostly involving a review of physical conditions, food supplies, and water temperatures. The inspections typically do not include interviews with residents and staff or extensive examinations of records. The department employees charged with performing the inspections are not required to have backgrounds in social work, even though they are often called to look into what for an experienced police officer are the most sensitive kinds of cases—sex crimes and battery involving minors.

The state attorney general's office appears to recognize the responsibility for better protecting these children. In February, California attorney general Kamala Harris set up the Bureau of Children's Justice, a new division of the Department of Justice that will focus on holding counties and state government agencies accountable for crimes that concern child welfare.

When it comes to taking care of the state's most damaged children, the California legislature has too often been slow to act and reluctant to spend money. But Carroll Schroeder, the executive director of the California Alliance of Child and Family Services, thinks this time it could be different. "I feel much more optimistic [about it] than anything else I have seen," he says. "This is a once-in-a-generation opportunity to get it right." The report's proposals have been drafted into a formal bill that is expected to move through several legislative committees. It could be signed into law as early as July 1.

Today, the Davis campus is a ghost town. Its classrooms are empty, its hallways silent. For months food rotted in the refrigerators, bedding was piled up in the dorm rooms, and rules on restraints were still tacked on the walls.

EMQ FamiliesFirst, accused by the state of having failed to safeguard the children at the home, signed a stipulation conceding widespread violations. It continues to be one of the largest providers of social services in California. Gordon Richardson, who insisted to the state that he was not aware of the depth of the home's problems, remains a senior executive at the nonprofit.

Audrie Meyer was asked to resign in July 2013. Two months later, she signed a stipulation with the Department of Social Services. Without admitting to any of the allegations against her, she agreed never to work for another entity overseen by the department "for the balance of [her] life." She now runs a private therapy practice in Sacramento.

Andrea Guthrie was laid off in early August 2013. She now has her own family-therapy practice, working primarily with older teens, young adults, and couples. After more than 10 years working at the Davis campus, she's reluctant to work with children.

Jeff Beasley retired in August 2013, two months after the police raid.

Alex Barschat-Li was sent to another Level 14 facility after the raid. He was soon kicked out and moved to still another Level 14 residence. He graduated to a Level 12 facility. This past February, he returned home, and he now attends public high school, where he has joined the wrestling team. Wendy says she feels hopeful, but she's felt that way before.

## Critical Thinking

1. What effect did layoffs of staff seem to have on the children?
2. What changes in the way troubled children are cared for would you recommend?

## Internet References

Pro Publica
   http://www.propublica.org/documents/item/1698895-families-first-davis-program-statement
Pro Publica
   http://www.propublica.org/documents/item/1203114-2013-24-hour-ccl-reports-pbs-final-copy-redacted
Pro Publica
   http://www.propublica.org/documents/item/1698860-ccr-legislativereport
Pro Publica
   http://www.propublica.org/documents/item/1698848-ccl-familiesfirst-visits-october-2012-through

JOAQUIN SAPIEN has covered criminal justice, military healthcare, and environmental issues for ProPublica since 2008.

*Article*                                          Prepared by: Joanne Naughton

# Why Jonathan McClard Still Matters

Excerpted from a speech given by Gabrielle Horowitz-Prisco, director of the CA's Juvenile Justice Project, during the Raise the Age – NY! campaign launch press conference on July 11, 2013.

## Learning Outcomes

*After reading this article, you will be able to:*

- Explain the fears a parent might have whose child is incarcerated.
- Show the harmful effects of putting teenagers in adult facilities.

About a year ago, I was writing a piece on youth in adult jails and prisons and I wanted to write about Jonathan McClard, a seventeen year old boy in Missouri who committed suicide by hanging in an adult facility as he was awaiting transfer to a notoriously abusive adult prison.

I had met Jonathan's mother, Tracy, at a youth justice event—after Jonathan's death, she quit her job as a school teacher to devote herself to getting kids out of adult jails and prisons. Over dinner, Tracy described to me the marked changes she observed in Jonathan's appearance as he spent time in adult facilities—the hardening and shutting down, the fighting he was forced to do, and his fear. She described her powerlessness as a mother to get her son out of what she knew was a life-threatening situation. How Jonathan had been placed in solitary confinement as punishment for putting his hands in his lap during their visit. The impact of solitary on his mind and spirit.

How she believed that it was his fear of being raped in prison that led him to take his own life.

I wanted to make sure that Tracy was okay with me writing these details down, with their potential publication. So I called her at home one night and asked.

I remember this moment—she said "let me check something with my husband" and she put the phone down and I could hear through the distance. She said: "Do you think it is accurate to say that it seems like Jonathan killed himself because he was afraid of being raped?" Her husband said yes. She got back on the phone and said: "if it helps another parent not go through what we have gone through, you can talk about that—you can share whatever part of his life will help."

Do you know those moments where the world sort of stops, time slows down, and you feel things deep, deep in your belly? It was one of those moments. I felt the presence of my own partner one room away from me. We were newly engaged and our whole lives together seemed spread out before us—full of joy and promise.

I remembered that Tracy's husband and son both tried to commit suicide themselves as they grappled with the pain of losing Jonathan. Her daughter had been hospitalized with severe anxiety. And I thought about how when our conversation was over, I would go into the living room and have a light-hearted normal night at home with the person I love so much, but Tracy and her husband may never again have that kind of night.

I thought about what I want you to know: Jonathan's death is not unique—children in adult jails are 36 times more likely to commit suicide than children in adult detention facilities, and the National Prison Rape Elimination Commission stated that "more than any other group of incarcerated persons, youth incarcerated with adults are probably at the highest risk for sexual abuse."

And children in adult jails and prisons are often placed in solitary confinement for up to 23 hours a day—where they are fed through a small slot in the door so that the only contact they have is a hand coming through a slot in the door. Can you imagine that: just an arm coming through a slot to push food in to a child. Children in solitary do not leave their cells to go to school or programs, and can stay for months and even years at a time.

This all happens in New York State, and it happens because we prosecute 16- and 17-year olds as adults and confine them in adult jails and prisons. This practice causes children immeasurable physical, emotional and sexual trauma.

And it is bad for public safety—children prosecuted as adults are far more likely to commit crime and violence in the future than youth prosecuted in the youth justice system.

Finally, it is bad for taxpayers. Not only does prosecuting children as adults keep many young people from lifelong education and employment opportunities—nearby Connecticut is spending approximately 2 million dollars less on youth justice than it was 10 years ago—despite having raised the age and adding millions of dollars to community services.

Most importantly, now is the time to act, so that the next time we are here at a press conference, you do not hear from another mother who lost her son or daughter while we were waiting for the law to change.

## Critical Thinking

1. Do you believe teenagers should be considered adults in the criminal justice system?

2. Is it a good idea to prosecute children as adults when they commit very violent crimes?

3. Should the violence an inmate faces in prison be part of the punishment, or do inmates have a right to be incarcerated in a safe environment?

## Create Central

www.mhhe.com/createcentral

## Internet References

**Correctional Association of New York**
www.correctionalassociation.org/campaigns/raise-the-age

**Justice Policy Institute**
www.justicepolicy.org/images/upload/97-02_rep_riskjuvenilesface_jj.pdf

Horowitz-Prisco, Gabrielle. From *Correctional Association of New York*, July 12, 2013. Copyright © 2013 by Gabrielle Horowitz-Prisco. Reprinted by permission of the author.

# Unit 6

# UNIT

Prepared by: Joanne Naughton

# Punishment and Corrections

In the 1950s and 1960s the term *corrections* came to replace *penology*, reflecting a new philosophy that emphasized rehabilitation. But this philosophical view of offenders' treatment took an opposite turn in the 1980s when today's "get tough" policies were instituted. Corrections refers to programs and agencies that have legal authority over the custody or supervision of people who have been convicted of violating criminal law.

The correctional process begins with the sentencing of the convicted offender. The predominant sentencing pattern in the United States encourages maximum judicial discretion and offers a range of alternatives, from probation—supervised, conditional freedom within the community—through imprisonment, to the death penalty.

The current condition of the American penal system and the effects that sentencing, probation, imprisonment, and parole have on the convicted offender should receive serious consideration, because most people who have been sentenced to incarceration are eventually released back into their communities.

*Article*

Prepared by: Joanne Naughton

# Oklahoma's Botched Lethal Injection Marks New Front in Battle Over Executions

## CNN's original series "Death Row Stories" explores America's capital punishment system.

JOSH LEVS, ED PAYNE, AND GREG BOTELHO

## Learning Outcomes

*After reading this article, you will be able to:*

- Describe what happened when Oklahoma executed Clayton Lockett.

- Relate the reason states with capital punishment have been forced to find new drugs to use.

- Explain some of the issues that arise regarding the drugs that are used in executions.

- See that not every state has the death penalty.

(CNN)—A botched lethal injection in Oklahoma has catapulted the issue of U.S. capital punishment back into the international spotlight, raising new questions about the drugs being used, and the constitutional protection against cruel and unusual punishment.

"We have a fundamental standard in this country that even when the death penalty is justified, it must be carried out humanely—and I think everyone would recognize that this case fell short of that standard," White House spokesman Jay Carney said Wednesday.

What went wrong Tuesday in Oklahoma "will not only cause officials in that state to review carefully their execution procedures and methods," said Richard W. Garnett, a former Supreme Court law clerk who now teaches criminal and constitutional law at the University of Notre Dame, "it will also almost prompt many Americans across the country to rethink the wisdom, and the morality, of capital punishment."

"The Constitution allows capital punishment in some cases, and so the decision whether to use it or abandon it, and the moral responsibility for its use and misuse, are in our hands," he said.

Precisely what happened during the execution of convicted murderer and rapist Clayton Lockett remains unclear. Witnesses described the man convulsing and writhing on the gurney, as well as struggling to speak, before officials blocked the witnesses' view.

It was the state's first time using a new, three-drug cocktail for an execution.

Oklahoma halted the execution of another convicted murderer and rapist, Charles Warner, which was scheduled for later in the day.

Thirty-two U.S. states have the death penalty, as does the U.S. government and the U.S. military. Since 2009, three states—New Mexico, Connecticut, and Maryland—have voted to abolish it.

States that have capital punishment have been forced to find new drugs to use since European-based manufacturers banned U.S. prisons from using theirs for executions. One of those manufacturers is the Danish company Lundbeck, maker of pentobarbital.

Carney, speaking to reporters at a daily briefing, said he had not discussed the Oklahoma case with President Barack Obama.

"He has long said that while the evidence suggests that the death penalty does little to deter crime, he believes there are some crimes that are so heinous that the death penalty is merited." The crimes committed by the two men in Oklahoma "are indisputably horrific and heinous," Carney said.

## "There Was Chaos"

Lockett lived for 43 minutes after being administered the first drug, CNN affiliate KFOR reported. He got out the words "Man," "I'm not," and "something's wrong," reporter Courtney Francisco of KFOR said. Then the blinds were closed.

Other reporters, including Cary Aspinwall of the Tulsa World newspaper, also said Lockett was still alive and lifted his head while prison officials lowered the blinds so onlookers couldn't see what was going on.

Dean Sanderford, Lockett's attorney, said his client's body "started to twitch," and then "the convulsing got worse. It looked like his whole upper body was trying to lift off the gurney. For a minute, there was chaos."

Sanderford said guards ordered him out of the witness area, and he was never told what had happened to Lockett, who was convicted in 2000 of first-degree murder, rape, kidnapping, and robbery.

After administering the first drug, "We began pushing the second and third drugs in the protocol," said Oklahoma Department of Corrections Director Robert Patton. "There was some concern at that time that the drugs were not having the effect. So the doctor observed the line and determined that the line had blown." He said that Lockett's vein had "exploded." The execution process was halted, but Lockett died of a heart attack, Patton said.

"I notified the attorney general's office, the governor's office of my intent to stop the execution and requested a stay for 14 days," said Patton.

Gov. Mary Fallin issued a statement saying that "execution officials said Lockett remained unconscious after the lethal injection drugs were administered."

## Another State, Another Botched Execution

Earlier this year, a convicted murderer and rapist in Ohio, Dennis McGuire, appeared to gasp and convulse for at least 10 minutes before dying from the drug cocktail used in his execution.

Ohio used the sedative midazolam and the painkiller hydromorphone in McGuire's January execution, the state said.

Louisiana announced later that month that it would use the same two-drug cocktail.

Oklahoma had announced the drugs it planned to use: midazolam; vecuronium bromide to stop respiration; and potassium chloride to stop the heart. "Two intravenous lines are inserted, one in each arm. The drugs are injected by hand-held syringes simultaneously into the two intravenous lines. The sequence is in the order that the drugs are listed above. Three executioners are utilized, with each one injecting one of the drugs."

The execution was the first time Oklahoma had used midazolam as the first element in its three-drug cocktail. The drug is generally used for children "before medical procedures or before anesthesia for surgery to cause drowsiness, relieve anxiety, and prevent any memory of the event," the U.S. National Library of Medicine says. "It works by slowing activity in the brain to allow relaxation and sleep."

The drug "may cause serious or life-threatening breathing problems," so a child should only receive it "in a hospital or doctor's office that has the equipment that is needed to monitor his or her heart and lungs and to provide life-saving medical treatment quickly if his or her breathing slows or stops."

## Cruel and Unusual?

The question for courts is whether using such drugs in executions constitutes "cruel and unusual" punishment, in violation of the Eighth Amendment to the U.S. Constitution.

After his execution, McGuire's family filed a lawsuit seeking an injunction of the execution protocol the state used.

"The lawsuit alleges that when Mr. McGuire's Ohio execution was carried out on January 16th, he did endure frequent episodes of air hunger and suffocation, as predicted," the office of the family's attorney Richard Schulte said in a statement. "Following administration of the execution protocol, the decedent experienced 'repeated cycles of snorting, gurgling and arching his back, appearing to writhe in pain,' and 'looked and sounded as though he was suffocating.' This continued for 19 minutes."

In Oklahoma, attorneys for both Lockett and Warner have been engaged in a court fight over the drugs used in the state's executions.

They'd initially challenged the state Department of Corrections' unwillingness to divulge which drugs would be used. The department finally disclosed the substances.

Lockett and Warner also took issue with the state's so-called secrecy provision forbidding it from disclosing the identities of anyone involved in the execution process or suppliers of any drugs or medical equipment. The Oklahoma Supreme

Court rejected that complaint, saying such secrecy does not prevent the prisoners from challenging their executions as unconstitutional.

After Lockett's execution, Adam Leathers, cochairman of the Oklahoma Coalition to Abolish the Death Penalty, accused the state of having "tortured a human being in an unconstitutional experimental act of evil."

"Medical and legal experts from around the country had repeatedly warned Oklahoma's governor, courts and Department of Corrections about the likelihood that the protocol intended for use . . . would be highly problematic," said Deborah Denno, death penalty expert at Fordham Law School.

"This botch was foreseeable and the state (was) ill prepared to deal with the circumstances despite knowing that the entire world was watching. Lethal injection botches have existed for decades but never have they been riskier or more irresponsible than they are in 2014. This outcome is a disgrace," Denno said.

Amnesty International USA called the botched execution "one of the starkest examples yet of why the death penalty must be abolished."

"Last night the state of Oklahoma proved that justice can never be carried out from a death chamber," Executive Director Steven W. Hawkins said in a statement.

## Investigation

The Oklahoma attorney general's office is "gathering information on what happened in order to evaluate," said spokeswoman Dianne Clay.

Fallin ordered an independent review of the state's execution procedures and issued an executive order granting a two-week delay in executions.

"I believe the legal process worked. I believe the death penalty is an appropriate response and punishment to those who commit heinous crimes against their fellow men and women. However, I also believe the state needs to be certain of its protocols and its procedures for executions and that they work," she told reporters Wednesday.

Fallin gave no deadline for the review, which will be led by Department of Public Safety Commissioner Michael Thompson. If it is not done within the 14-day period, the governor said she would issue an additional stay for Warner.

Lockett's attorney slammed the announcement and called for a "truly" independent investigation.

"The DPS is a state agency, and its Commissioner reports to the Governor. As such, the review proposed by Governor Fallin would not be conducted by a neutral, independent entity.

"In order to understand exactly what went wrong in last night's horrific execution, and restore any confidence in the execution process, the death of Clayton Lockett must be investigated by a truly independent organization, not a state employee or agency," Dean Sanderford said in a statement.

Lockett was convicted in 2000 of a bevy of crimes that left Stephanie Nieman dead and two people injured.

Nieman's parents released a statement Tuesday prior to Lockett's scheduled execution.

"God blessed us with our precious daughter, Stephanie for 19 years," it read. "She was the joy of our life. We are thankful this day has finally arrived and justice will finally be served."

Warner, who now awaits execution, was convicted in 2003 for the first-degree rape and murder 6 years earlier of his then-girlfriend's 11-month-old daughter, Adrianna Waller.

His attorney, Madeline Cohen, said further legal action can be expected given that "something went horribly awry" in Lockett's execution Tuesday.

"Oklahoma cannot carry out further executions until there's transparency in this process," Cohen said. ". . . Oklahoma needs to take a step back."

In a CNN/ORC poll earlier this year, 50% of Americans said the penalty for murder in general should be death, while 45% said it should be a life sentence. The survey's sampling error made that a statistical tie. Fifty-six percent of men supported the death penalty for murder in general, while 45% of women did.

A Gallup poll last year found 62% of Americans believe the death penalty is morally acceptable, while half as many, 31%, consider it morally wrong.

## Critical Thinking

1. Was the execution of Lockett carried out humanely?
2. Does the fact that a majority of Americans believe the death penalty is morally acceptable mean the issue is settled?

## Internet References

**CNN Justice**
   http://www.cnn.com/2013/11/15/justice/states-lethal-injection-drugs/
**Oklahoma Department of Corrections**
   http://www.ok.gov/doc/Offenders/Death_Row/

*Article*            Prepared by: Joanne Naughton

# The Archipelago of Pain

DAVID BROOKS

## Learning Outcomes

*After reading this article, you will be able to:*

- Discuss studies done on the effect of isolation on animals.

- Relate what Grassian concluded from his work on the effects of solitary confinement on prisoners.

- Compare prison officials' arguments about the need for solitary confinement with what research shows.

We don't flog people in our prison system, or put them in thumbscrews or stretch them on the rack. We do, however, lock prisoners away in social isolation for 23 hours a day, often for months, years or decades at a time.

We prohibit the former and permit the latter because we make a distinction between physical and social pain. But, at the level of the brain where pain really resides, this is a distinction without a difference. Matthew Lieberman of the University of California, Los Angeles, compared the brain activities of people suffering physical pain with people suffering from social pain. As he writes in his book, "Social," "Looking at the screens side by side . . . you wouldn't have been able to tell the difference."

The brain processes both kinds of pain in similar ways. Moreover, at the level of human experience, social pain is, if anything, more traumatic, more destabilizing and inflicts more cruel and long-lasting effects than physical pain. What we're doing to prisoners in extreme isolation, in other words, is arguably more inhumane than flogging.

Yet inflicting extreme social pain is more or less standard procedure in America's prisons. Something like 80,000 prisoners are put in solitary confinement every year. Prisoners isolated in supermaximum facilities are often locked away in a 6-by-9-foot or 8-by-10-foot barren room. They may be completely isolated in that room for two days a week. For the remaining five, they may be locked away for 23 hours a day and permitted an hour of solitary exercise in a fenced-in area.

If there is communication with the prison staff, it might take place through an intercom. Communication with the world beyond is minimal. If there are visitors, conversation may be conducted through a video screen. Prisoners may go years without affectionately touching another human being. Their only physical contact will be brushing up against a guard as he puts on shackles for trips to the exercise yard.

In general, mammals do not do well in isolation. In the 1950s, Harry Harlow studied monkeys who had been isolated. The ones who were isolated for longer periods went into emotional shock, rocking back and forth. One in six refused to eat after being reintegrated and died within five days. Most of the rest were permanently withdrawn.

Studies on birds, rats and mice consistently show that isolated animals suffer from impoverished neural growth compared with socially engaged animals, especially in areas where short-term memory and threat perception are processed. Studies on Yugoslav prisoners of war in 1992 found that those who had suffered blunt blows to the head and those who had been socially isolated suffered the greatest damage to brain functioning.

Some prisoners who've been in solitary confinement are scarcely affected by it. But this is not typical. The majority of prisoners in solitary suffer severely—from headaches, an oversensitivity to stimuli, digestion problems, loss of appetite, self-mutilation, chronic dizziness, loss of the ability to concentrate, hallucinations, illusions, or paranoid ideas.

The psychiatrist Stuart Grassian conducted in-depth interviews with more than 200 prisoners in solitary and concluded that about a third developed acute psychosis with hallucinations. Many people just disintegrate. According to rough estimates, as many as half the suicides in prison take place in solitary, even though isolated prisoners make up only about 5 percent of the population.

Prison officials argue that they need isolation to preserve order. That's a view to be taken seriously because these are the people who work in the prisons. But the research on the effectiveness of solitary confinement programs is ambiguous at best. There's a fair bit of evidence to suggest that prison violence is not produced mainly by a few bad individuals who can be removed from the mainstream. Rather, violence is caused by conditions and prison culture. If there's crowding, tension, a culture of violence, and anarchic or arbitrary power, then the context itself is going to create violence no matter how many "bad seeds" are segregated away.

Fortunately, we seem to be at a moment when public opinion is turning. Last month, the executive director of the Colorado prisons, Rick Raemisch, wrote a moving first-person Op-Ed article in *The Times* about his short and voluntary stay in solitary. Colorado will no longer send prisoners with severe mental illnesses into solitary. New York officials recently agreed to new guidelines limiting the time prisoners can spend in isolation. Before long, one suspects, extreme isolation will be considered morally unacceptable.

The larger point is we need to obliterate the assumption that inflicting any amount of social pain is O.K. because it's not real pain.

When you put people in prison, you are imposing pain on them. But that doesn't mean you have to gouge out the nourishment that humans need for health, which is social, emotional and relational.

## Critical Thinking

1. Isn't a prison sentence supposed to be harsh?

2. Based on the evidence from animals and people, does solitary confinement help a prisoner become a functioning member of society upon release?

3. Is it more humane to subject prisoners to solitary confinement for rules infractions than to beat them?

## Internet References

**American Psychological Association**
   http://www.apa.org/monitor/2012/05/solitary.aspx
**The New York Times**
   http://www.nytimes.com/2014/02/21/opinion/my-night-in-solitary.html

*Article* Prepared by: Joanne Naughton

# The F.B.I. Deemed Agents Faultless in 150 Shootings

CHARLIE SAVAGE AND MICHAEL SCHMIDT

## Learning Outcomes

*After reading this article, you will be able to:*

- Discuss the process that takes place whenever an F.B.I. agent fires his weapon.

- Compare the F.B.I.'s internal review of the shooting of Joseph Schultz with independent evaluations.

After contradictory stories emerged about an F.B.I. agent's killing last month of a Chechen man in Orlando, Fla., who was being questioned over ties to the Boston Marathon bombing suspects, the bureau reassured the public that it would clear up the murky episode.

"The F.B.I. takes very seriously any shooting incidents involving our agents, and as such we have an effective, time-tested process for addressing them internally," a bureau spokesman said.

But if such internal investigations are time-tested, their outcomes are also predictable: from 1993 to early 2011, F.B.I. agents fatally shot about 70 "subjects" and wounded about 80 others—and every one of those episodes was deemed justified, according to interviews and internal F.B.I. records obtained by *The New York Times* through a Freedom of Information Act lawsuit.

The last two years have followed the same pattern: an F.B.I. spokesman said that since 2011, there had been no findings of improper intentional shootings.

In most of the shootings, the F.B.I.'s internal investigation was the only official inquiry. In the Orlando case, for example, there have been conflicting accounts about basic facts like whether the Chechen man, Ibragim Todashev, attacked an agent with a knife, was unarmed or was brandishing a metal pole. But Orlando homicide detectives are not independently investigating what happened.

"We had nothing to do with it," said Sgt. Jim Young, an Orlando police spokesman. "It's a federal matter, and we're deferring everything to the F.B.I."

Occasionally, the F.B.I. does discipline an agent. Out of 289 deliberate shootings covered by the documents, many of which left no one wounded, five were deemed to be "bad shoots," in agents' parlance—encounters that did not comply with the bureau's policy, which allows deadly force if agents fear that their lives or those of fellow agents are in danger. A typical punishment involved adding letters of censure to agents' files. But in none of the five cases did a bullet hit anyone.

Critics say the fact that for at least two decades no agent has been disciplined for any instance of deliberately shooting someone raises questions about the credibility of the bureau's internal investigations. Samuel Walker, a professor of criminal justice at the University of Nebraska Omaha who studies internal law enforcement investigations, called the bureau's conclusions about cases of improper shootings "suspiciously low."

Current and former F.B.I. officials defended the bureau's handling of shootings, arguing that the scant findings of improper behavior were attributable to several factors. Agents tend to be older, more experienced and better trained than city police officers. And they generally are involved only in planned operations and tend to go in with "overwhelming presence," minimizing the chaos that can lead to shooting the wrong people, said Tim Murphy, a former deputy director of the F.B.I. who conducted some investigations of shootings over his 23-year career.

The F.B.I.'s shootings range from episodes so obscure that they attract no news media attention to high-profile cases like the 2009 killing of an imam in a Detroit-area warehouse that is the subject of a lawsuit alleging a cover-up, and a 2002 shooting in Maryland in which the bureau paid $1.3 million to a victim and yet, the records show, deemed the shooting to have been justified.

With rare exceptions—like suicides—whenever an agent fires his weapon outside of training, a team of agents from the F.B.I.'s Inspection Division, sometimes with a liaison from the local police, compiles a report reconstructing what happened. This "shooting incident review team" interviews witnesses and studies medical, ballistics and autopsy reports, eventually producing a narrative. Such reports typically do not include whether an agent had been involved in any previous shootings, because they focus only on the episode in question, officials said.

That narrative, along with binders of supporting information, is then submitted to a "shooting incident review group"—a panel of high-level F.B.I. officials in Washington. The panel produces its own narrative as part of a report saying whether the shooting complied with bureau policy—and recommends what discipline to mete out if it did not—along with any broader observations about "lessons learned" to change training or procedures.

F.B.I. officials stressed that their shooting reviews were carried out under the oversight of both the Justice Department's inspector general and the Civil Rights Division, and that local prosecutors have the authority to bring charges.

The 2,200 pages of records obtained by *The Times* include an internal F.B.I. study that compiled shooting episode statistics over a 17-year period, as well as a collection of individual narratives of intentional shootings from 1993 to early 2011. Gunfire was exchanged in 58 such episodes; 9 law enforcement officials died, and 38 were wounded.

The five "bad shoots" included cases in which an agent fired a warning shot after feeling threatened by a group of men, an agent fired at a weapon lying on the ground to disable it during an arrest, and two agents fired their weapons while chasing fugitives but hit no one. In another case, an agent fired at a safe during a demonstration, and ricocheting material caused minor cuts in a crowd of onlookers.

Four of the cases were in the mid-1990s, and the fifth was in 2003.

In many cases, the accuracy of the F.B.I. narrative is difficult to evaluate because no independent alternative report has been produced. As part of the reporting for this article, the F.B.I. voluntarily made available a list of shootings since 2007 that gave rise to lawsuits, but it was rare for any such case to have led to a full report by an independent authority.

Occasionally, however, there were alternative reviews. One, involving a March 2002 episode in which an agent shot an innocent Maryland man in the head after mistaking him for a bank robbery suspect, offers a case study in how the nuances of an F.B.I. official narrative can come under scrutiny.

In that episode, agents thought that the suspect would be riding in a car driven by his sister and wearing a white baseball cap. An innocent man, Joseph Schultz, then 20, happened to cross their path, wearing a white cap and being driven by his girlfriend. Moments after F.B.I. agents carrying rifles pulled their car over and surrounded it, Agent Christopher Braga shot Mr. Schultz in the jaw. He later underwent facial reconstruction surgery, and in 2007 the bureau paid $1.3 million to settle a lawsuit.

The internal review, however, deemed it a good shoot. In the F.B.I.'s narrative, Agent Braga says that he shouted "show me your hands," but that Mr. Schultz instead reached toward his waist, so Agent Braga fired "to eliminate the threat." While one member of the review group said that "after reading the materials provided, he could not visualize the presence of 'imminent danger' to law enforcement officers," the rest of the group voted to find the shooting justified, citing the "totality of

the circumstances surrounding the incident," including that it involved a "high-risk stop."

But an Anne Arundel County police detective prepared an independent report about the episode, and a lawyer for Mr. Schultz, Arnold Weiner, conducted a further investigation for the lawsuit. Both raised several subtle but important differences.

For example, the F.B.I. narrative describes a lengthy chase of Mr. Schultz's car after agents turned on their siren at an intersection, bolstering an impression that it was reasonable for Agent Braga to fear that Mr. Schultz was a dangerous fugitive. The narrative spends a full page describing this moment in great detail, saying that the car "rapidly accelerated" and that one agent shouted for it to stop "over and over again." It cites another agent as estimating that the car stopped "approximately 100 yards" from the intersection.

By contrast, the police report describes this moment in a short, skeptical paragraph. Noting that agents said they had thought the car was fleeing, it points out that the car "was, however, in a merge lane and would need to accelerate to enter traffic." Moreover, a crash reconstruction specialist hired for the lawsuit estimated that the car had reached a maximum speed of 12 miles per hour, and an F.B.I. sketch, obtained in the lawsuit, put broken glass from a car window 142 feet 8 inches from the intersection.

The F.B.I. narrative does not cite Mr. Schultz's statement and omits that a crucial fact was disputed: how Mr. Schultz had moved in the car. In a 2003 sworn statement, Agent Braga said that Mr. Schultz "turned to his left, towards the middle of the car, and reached down." But Mr. Schultz insisted that he had instead reached toward the car door on his right because he had been listening to another agent who was simultaneously shouting "open the door."

A former F.B.I. agent, hired to write a report analyzing the episode for the plaintiffs, concluded that "no reasonable F.B.I. agent in Braga's position would reasonably have believed that deadly force was justified." He also noted pointedly that Agent Braga had been involved in a previous shooting episode in 2000 that he portrayed as questionable, although it had been found to be justified by the F.B.I.'s internal review process.

Asked to comment on the case, a lawyer for Agent Braga, Andrew White, noted last week that a grand jury had declined to indict his client in the shooting.

In some cases, alternative official accounts for several other shootings dovetailed with internal F.B.I. narratives.

One involved the October 2009 death of Luqman Ameen Abdullah, a prayer leader at a Detroit-area mosque who was suspected of conspiring to sell stolen goods and was shot during a raid on a warehouse. The F.B.I. report says that Mr. Abdullah got down on the ground but kept his hands hidden, so a dog was unleashed to pull his arms into view. He then pulled out a gun and shot the dog, the report says, and he was in turn shot by four agents.

The Michigan chapter of the Council on American-Islamic Relations filed a lawsuit against the F.B.I. The group was concerned in part because the handgun had no recoverable fingerprints and because of facial injuries to Mr. Abdullah. It also contends that the dog may have been shot instead by the F.B.I. agents and the gun thrown down in a cover-up.

A report by the Michigan attorney general's office, however, detailed an array of evidence that it says "corroborates the statements of the agents as to the sequence of events," including that bullet fragments in the dog's corpse were consistent with the handgun, not the rifles used by the F.B.I. agents. Such an independent account of an F.B.I. shooting is rare. After the recent killing of Mr. Todashev in Orlando, both the Florida chapter of the same group and his father have called for investigators outside the F.B.I. to scrutinize the episode.

James J. Wedick, who spent 34 years at the bureau, said the F.B.I. should change its procedures for its own good.

"At the least, it is a perception issue, and over the years the bureau has had a deaf ear to it," he said. "But if you have a shooting that has a few more complicated factors and an ethnic issue, the bureau's image goes down the toilet if it doesn't investigate itself properly."

## Critical Thinking

1. Do you believe that the F.B.I.'s internal investigation should be the only official inquiry into questionable shootings by F.B.I. personnel?

2. If the F.B.I. deems a shooting to have been justified, is paying $1.3 million to the victim also justified?

## Create Central

www.mhhe.com/createcentral

## Internet References

**Democracy Now**
www.democracynow.org/2013/6/21/the_fbis_license_to_kill_agents

**Federal Bureau of Investigation (F.B.I.)**
www.fbi.gov/news/updates-on-investigation-into-multiple-explosions-in-boston

*Article*

Prepared by: Joanne Naughton

# For Mentally Ill Inmates at Rikers Island, a Cycle of Jail and Hospitals

MICHAEL WINERIP AND MICHAEL SCHWIRTZ

## Learning Outcomes

*After reading this article, you will be able to:*

- Report what percentage of the population at Rikers has been diagnosed with mental illness.
- Relate what happened when state mental hospitals were closed in the 1960s and 1970s.
- Describe how ACT teams operate.

It was not a particularly violent crime that sent Michael Megginson to Rikers Island. He was arrested for stealing a cellphone.

But in jail, Mr. Megginson, who is 25 and has been in and out of psychiatric hospitals since the age of 6, quickly deteriorated, becoming one of the most violent inmates on the island.

In his 18 months there, he was constantly involved in some kind of disturbance, his records show. He fought with other inmates and officers; spit and threw urine at them; smashed windows and furniture and once stabbed an officer in the back of the head with a piece of glass.

At least twice, his bones were broken in beatings by guards.

He also repeatedly hurt himself, cutting his body all over, banging his head against walls and tying sheets and clothing around his neck in apparent suicide attempts.

There were times he became severely psychotic. He once stripped naked and broke the toilet in his cell, causing a flood. "I'm trying to save everybody from the devil with holy water," he said, according to jail records.

For years, Rikers has been filling with people like Mr. Megginson, who have complicated psychiatric problems that are little understood and do not get resolved elsewhere: the unwashed man passed out in a public stairwell; the 16-year-old runaway; the drug addict; the belligerent panhandler screaming in a full subway car.

It is a problem that cuts two ways. At the jail, with its harsh conditions and violent culture, the mentally ill can deteriorate, their symptoms worsening in ways Rikers is unequipped to handle. As they get sicker, they strike out at guards and other correction employees, often provoking more violence.

Judges, prosecutors, police officers and correction leaders, as well as elected officials like Mayor Bill de Blasio, have grown increasingly vocal about the damage that incarceration can do to these men and women.

By now, Mr. Megginson's Legal Aid lawyer had expected him to be freed. But his volatile behavior has kept him behind bars, and recently he was transferred to a state psychiatric prison hospital for violent criminals with no set release date.

*The New York Times* spent 10 months examining Mr. Megginson's troubled life, conducting hours of interviews with him as well as his family members, doctors and lawyers. With his permission, *The Times* also reviewed thousands of pages of medical, disciplinary and legal records from his time at Rikers and in hospitals, community programs and supervised housing.

Though there may be a consensus that Michael Megginson does not belong in jail, there is no agreement about where else he could go. At times, he was just as violent in hospitals. He once jumped over a nurses' station at Kings County Hospital Center in Brooklyn, attacking clinicians; during a stay in St. Barnabas Hospital in the Bronx, he was placed in restraints 11 times.

But unlike jail, psychiatric hospitals treated his behavior as a symptom of illness. If he was out of control, he was often given an injection to knock him out and was placed in a quiet room until he was calm.

In interviews, members of Mr. Megginson's family said they believed that longer-term hospitalization would be best for him. But that option has all but disappeared. For the last four decades, the push in the mental health field has been to close these hospitals. Since a 1970s Supreme Court ruling that was meant to protect civil liberties, only the very sickest patients can be involuntarily held for an extended period.

Mr. Megginson was repeatedly released from state hospitals against his doctors' wishes because he did not meet legal requirements for involuntary commitment.

His treatment has cost millions of dollars in public funds. Outside of hospitals, he was enrolled in some of the most successful outpatient and community programs in the mental health field.

He failed out of all of them.

Which raises the question: Is there any place for Michael Megginson?

Over the last decade, the proportion of inmates with diagnosed mental illness has climbed dramatically. Today, they make up nearly 40 percent of the population at Rikers, a total of 4,000 men and women at any given time, more than all the adult patients in New York State psychiatric hospitals combined.

Several studies have shown that they are more likely than other inmates to be the victims as well as the perpetrators of violence.

In July, *The Times* documented 129 cases from 2013 in which inmates were beaten so severely during encounters with officers that they required emergency care. Seventy-seven percent of the inmates had a mental health diagnosis.

Mr. Megginson was one of the 129. In October 2013, a nurse found him facedown on a cellblock floor, beaten unconscious. Several bones in his face were broken, and his shoulder was dislocated.

When he returned from Elmhurst Hospital in Queens, he was punished with 127 days in solitary confinement.

National penal experts have been impressed by Mr. de Blasio's efforts to make Rikers a safer and more humane place. In the last year, the mayor has appropriated tens of millions of dollars to create specialized therapeutic units that reward improvements in behavior. He has also scaled back a punitive system that had kept some inmates locked away in solitary confinement for more than a year.

But individuals like Mr. Megginson burn through resources, requiring services that jails had never been expected to provide. Each Wednesday, the department's chief, two assistant chiefs and five wardens meet with the jail's top mental health officials to discuss what to do about a small number of the most disruptive inmates—a group that included Mr. Megginson.

His problems have been a long time in the making. Psychiatrists can't even agree on what's wrong with him. He has been confined in psychiatric hospitals at least 20 times and labeled with almost every diagnosis that could be applied to a person with a history of aggressive behavior: schizophrenia, bipolar disorder, polysubstance dependence, attention deficit disorder, impulse control disorder, antisocial personality disorder and intermittent explosive disorder.

From the time he was a little boy, growing up in the Kingsbridge section of the Bronx, he had uncontrollable rages. He bit teachers, fought with classmates, urinated on hospital staff and refused to go to school for weeks at a time. At age 6, he spent nearly a month at Bronx Children's Psychiatric Center, a state hospital.

His home life was often unstable. His father, who is also mentally ill, was in and out of prison. In 1990, shortly after his mother gave birth to him at age 16, she moved to Florida, leaving him with his great-grandmother for several years.

Many members of his extended family had mental illness and substance abuse problems. His paternal grandparents were both alcoholics, and his maternal grandfather died after falling out a window—or possibly jumping.

His mother, Shakima Smith-White, acknowledged that she was not always there for her son initially. But she said she re-entered his life full-time when he started school. She has been married now for 20 years, works two jobs and is studying to be a nurse practitioner.

"We weren't perfect, but we tried with Michael," she said.

When he was 5, she said, she took him to Miami on her honeymoon, to her husband's dismay. And when Michael was going through a bad stretch in his late teens, she said, her husband took their two daughters and moved out, worried it was too dangerous to stay. "He pretty much gave me an ultimatum, that it was him or Michael," she said. "And I chose my son."

"At the time he needed me more than the girls or my husband," she said.

When Mr. Megginson was doing well, she said, he was wonderful to be around—calm, affectionate, funny.

"Normally something would happen that would be like a great disappointment," she said. "Or someone would anger him and he would lash out, and from there he would just spiral downwards."

In an interview at Rikers, Mr. Megginson said his great-grandmother had been the most important person in his life. When he was 10 and she died, he said, it was devastating. "The way my mental illness led to an outbreak of getting worse was when my great-grandmother passed," he said. "It tore my insides out and gave me a lot of darkness."

By age 12, he had been admitted to Bronx Children's Psychiatric Center four times, according to medical records, and in his teens spent time at a Manhattan group home for young people with behavioral problems. Between hospital stays he often lived with his mother, and for a while, she said, she could calm him when he was upset. When he was 19, though, they got into a vicious fight. After he started swearing at her, she said, she struck him. He punched her back, knocking out two teeth, grabbed a knife and tried to stab her, she said.

She called 911 and he was arrested, spending three months at Rikers.

When he was released, she refused to allow him back into the house, insisting that he should complete a mental health program first.

For his part, Mr. Megginson said his mother was responsible for many of his problems. He complained that she had not been there for him and blamed her for refusing to put up the $5,000 to bail him out during his most recent incarceration.

"She says a lot of hurtful things, disrespectful things," he said, "like 'Oh I wish you wasn't my son,' or 'I wish I got, you know, I almost got an abortion when you was born, I should've did it.'"

His mother disputed this, saying she was thrilled when she found out she was having a boy.

Mr. Megginson came of age at a time when the public mental health system in New York was going through a major transformation.

By the 1960s and 1970s, state psychiatric hospitals were widely considered failures, inhumane places where patients were routinely neglected and abused. New medications had been developed that allowed patients to be stabilized and discharged, leading to widespread deinstitutionalization. But as the asylums were closed, the states provided little funding for community housing programs. The discharged patients often ended up homeless and, with their illness untreated, could become a danger to themselves and at times a risk to public safety.

On Jan. 3, 1999, Andrew Goldstein, a 29-year-old man with schizophrenia, was standing on a subway platform when he pushed a young woman, Kendra Webdale, in front of an N train, killing her instantly. When asked why he did it, he told the police, "I felt a sensation like something was entering me."

Mr. Goldstein knew he was sick. He kept asking for help. But there were long waiting lists for supervised housing and case management services, and often he was only given a slip of paper with a clinic's address. He is currently at a prison upstate, serving a 23-year sentence for manslaughter.

In the aftermath, legislators passed Kendra's Law, which allows authorities to order people with a history of violence who have repeatedly rejected treatment to take their medication and report regularly to a state-designated program. The state also appropriated millions of dollars for community mental health services.

While the system still suffers from serious shortages, today there are 40,500 state-funded supervised beds where mentally ill people have regular access to clinicians, twice as many as 15 years ago.

One of the most significant innovations available to Mr. Megginson is the Assertive Community Treatment program, or ACT, which is made up of a team that includes a psychiatrist, nurses, social workers and a substance abuse counselor. It is their job to make sure that even the most troubled individuals stick with their treatment. The idea is to avoid costly hospitalizations while enabling people to live safely in the community.

The state requires an ACT team to have a caseload of no more than 68 people and to see each client at least six times a month. There are 46 such teams in New York City, 82 statewide.

On a recent Tuesday, seven members of an East Harlem-based ACT team, who work for a nonprofit agency called the Bridge, met for several hours to discuss each of their 68 clients. Among their concerns: a man with a history of suicide attempts whose cousin had recently killed himself; three people with addiction problems who needed to provide urine samples; a man who was being lewd; and a new client with a history of assault who was acting belligerent toward staff members. "He might need another mood stabilizer," said Aneeza Ali, the team leader. "Or an attitude check."

Starting when he was 18 and after numerous hospitalizations, Mr. Megginson was assigned at least twice to ACT teams including the Bridge program. After he assaulted his mother in 2009, he was mandated under Kendra's Law to enroll with an ACT team as a condition of his probation.

His mother said her son seemed happier in the program because he could live on his own. "He always wanted to feel normal," she said, adding, "It gave him a sense of 'I'm O.K., I'm like everyone else.'"

ACT teams get high marks from activists. Susan Garrison, a social worker and a member of the Harlem chapter of the National Alliance on Mental Illness, said the program had made a big difference in her son's life. At 45, despite having severe schizophrenia, he has been able to stay out of the hospital, and at times he has even held a job, including recently working seven hours a week at a Rite Aid in Harlem.

But as good as ACT is, Ms. Garrison said, her constant involvement in her son's life has been crucial. Without an anchor—a parent, a spouse, a sibling—a person will often go off treatment and deteriorate, she said.

By the time Mr. Megginson reached his 20s, he had lost almost all contact with his mother and was mostly alone.

When his father was released from prison, they made an attempt to reconnect.

At one point, the father, also named Michael, found his son a job working for a storefront tax operation in Harlem. For $100 a week, he dressed in a Statue of Liberty costume and handed out fliers.

But in the fall of 2012, the two had a falling out. The son said his father stole his savings and lost it gambling. The father said he had permission to take the money.

Either way, that November, after a heated argument, the son pulled a chicken from the oven and hurled it at his father. He was committed soon after and remained hospitalized for the next five months.

In recent years, as jails and prisons have filled with the mentally ill, academics and clinicians have suggested that long-term hospitalization could be the best option for more individuals.

Observing a person during an extended hospitalization may improve a psychiatrist's chances of establishing a reliable diagnosis. It can also provide a safe environment, in which a variety of medications and dosages can be calibrated to the patient's needs.

In a hospital, Mr. Megginson would be compelled to take his medication, which would help curtail his aggression. At Rikers, clinicians say, inmates frequently go off their medication until they become uncontrollably violent.

Under state law, patients cannot be held against their will unless they are an immediate danger to themselves or others. During several hospitalizations, Mr. Megginson appeared before judges and successfully challenged his confinement. Though doctors disagreed, they had to release him.

His final hospital stay before Rikers lasted five months and ended on a hopeful note. A psychiatrist wrote that he was taking medication and attending substance abuse programs, that his grooming and hygiene had improved and that he was "free of psychotic features."

"He was very proud of his accomplishment," an April 22, 2013, progress note said, "and anxious to move on to independent living."

But after being discharged to a housing program, Mr. Megginson deteriorated rapidly. He stopped attending treatment sessions, according to medical records, and started drinking heavily and abusing marijuana. On June 12, he hit a counselor in the face with a cellphone charger and was kicked out of the program. Two months later, he stole a woman's cellphone and was sent to Rikers.

Several prosecutors, judges, police and correction officials said in interviews that they were frustrated by the lack of options for keeping people like Mr. Megginson out of jail.

Karen Friedman Agnifilo, the chief assistant district attorney in Manhattan, said she would like to have an alternative to jail for certain convicted offenders who are seriously mentally ill, such as a voluntary confinement that would provide treatment while keeping them off the streets.

"The problem is these individuals have typically been offered every service available," Ms. Friedman Agnifilo said. "As a result, we have no choice but to continue to cycle them through the system. We wish we could do something else, but we don't know what that something else is."

At this point few, if any, alternatives exist for offenders.

The Manhattan district attorney's office has joined several other prosecutors and judges in voicing support for a treatment model being proposed by Francis J. Greenburger, a Manhattan real estate developer whose mentally ill son is currently imprisoned. Under his plan, people with serious mental illness would plead guilty to certain felonies and avoid prison by agreeing to stay in a locked treatment center for up to two years. If at some point they failed to comply, they would be sent to prison.

For the last year and a half, Mr. Greenburger has been trying to get the state to license a pilot project, with limited progress.

At Rikers, Mr. Megginson became such a problem that at times he was transported in handcuffs and leg irons. He had to wear mittens to prevent him from grabbing things, and because he had a history of spitting at officers, was made to wear a mask.

In his 18 months in jail, he had 70 physical confrontations with officers, according to records, an extraordinary number given that most inmates never have one.

In nearly half the cases, guards used pepper spray to subdue him. Eleven times he was described in records as threatening to kill himself. The trouble often started when he ignored such routine orders from guards as to return to his cell, or to get out of the shower.

In the Rikers interview, he described how enraged it would make him to have no control over his daily life. He said it could turn a minor incident like being denied telephone privileges or getting cold food into a major frustration.

"I just get agitated and, you know, you can't do anything about it because you behind a magnetically confined door," Mr. Megginson said. "Mentally ill people should not be confined inside a box; it's not healthy for the mind."

"It makes us people we're not," he said.

Last year, Mr. Megginson was among a dozen particularly volatile inmates chosen for a new program run by the city's health department. A case worker visited him three times a week for therapy sessions that included meditation, breathing exercises and conflict resolution strategies.

Martin J. Murphy, the Correction Department's top uniformed officer, said the time spent working with Mr. Megginson and the inmates like him had resulted in a significant drop in the number of use-of-force cases involving them.

Correction officers, led by union leaders, have long called solitary confinement the most effective punishment for violent inmates. But Chief Murphy said in an interview that the intensive therapy had worked better.

Mr. Megginson spoke fondly of the therapist. He said she had taught him "just to use my thinking instead of using my fists. Like, if I get in an incident with an officer, instead of resolving it in a violent manner, rather just, you know, walk away sometimes. I try to think it out, think what I'm doing first and try to alleviate the situation."

In the weeks before leaving Rikers, he sounded optimistic, saying he hoped to get a job in building maintenance. "I'm just a one-time felon," he said, "and my felony is very light. If I had two felonies on my record or three, then it would be rough. I still got a chance. I believe in opportunity."

Two months ago, Mr. Megginson pleaded guilty to stealing the cellphone as well as to the assaults on the officers. He was given a one-to-three-year prison sentence and, because of his time served at Rikers, was immediately eligible for parole.

On Feb. 18, he was transferred to Downstate Correctional Facility in Fishkill for what was supposed to be a short stay. He had a parole hearing scheduled for mid-March and his lawyer, Jane Pucher, had started looking for a therapeutic program for him in the city.

But at the prison, he was unable to hold himself together. On Feb. 26, he was disciplined for threatening to cut an officer, according to state prison records. On March 4 and 6, he got into fights with inmates, and on March 7 he was written up for smashing a table against a door.

Then on March 15, according to records, he defecated on his cell floor, smeared his feces on the window as well as a security camera and jumped on the metal bed frame until it broke off the wall. When guards arrived, he threw his feces at them.

A few days later, he was transferred to Central New York Psychiatric Center, a state maximum-security forensic hospital, located in Marcy.

In an interview there on Wednesday, Mr. Megginson said he had lost control in prison because he had stopped receiving his medication. Other inmates repeatedly picked on him, he said.

But in the last three weeks at the hospital, he said, things are going well: He is back on his medication, working out and planning to attend church on Sunday.

He said that this time, when he was released, things would be different.

"I'm not going to do nothing bad or illegal," Mr. Megginson said.

## Critical Thinking

1. Shouldn't all people who break the law be punished by the criminal justice system, regardless of their mental problems?

2. Do you think it is possible to keep people in psychiatric hospitals, against their will, without violating their Constitutional rights?

3. Do you have any suggestions for how to treat Mr. Megginson?

## Internet References

**National Alliance on Mental Illness**
    https://www.nami.org/About-NAMI/NAMI-News/Two-Major-Mental-Health-Bills-Introduced-in-US-Sen

**The New York Times**
    http://topics.nytimes.com/top/reference/timestopics/organizations/r/rikers_island_prison_complex/index.html?inline=nyt-org

**The New York Times**
    http://www.nytimes.com/2014/07/14/nyregion/rikers-study-finds-prisoners-injured-by-employees.html?_r=0

**The New York Times**
    http://www.nytimes.com/2014/11/21/nyregion/rikers-needs-culture-change-mayor-de-blasio-says.html

*Article*                                    Prepared by: Joanne Naughton

# Inside America's Toughest Federal Prison

For years, conditions inside the United States' only federal supermax facility were largely a mystery. But a landmark lawsuit is finally revealing the harsh world within.

MARK BINELLI

## Learning Outcomes

*After reading this article, you will be able to:*

- Narrate some of the history of American prisons.
- Set forth what the research on solitary confinement shows, according to David Cloud.
- Describe the lawsuit against the US Bureau of Prisons.

In prison, Rodney Jones told me, everyone had a nickname. Jones's was Saint E's, short for St. Elizabeths, the federal psychiatric hospital in Washington, best known for housing John Hinckley Jr. after he shot Ronald Reagan. Jones spent time there as well, having shown signs of mental illness from an early age; he first attempted suicide at 12, when he drank an entire bottle of Clorox. Later, he became addicted to PCP and crack and turned to robbery to support his habit.

I met Jones a few blocks from his childhood home in LeDroit Park, a D.C. neighborhood not far from Howard University. It was a warm October afternoon, but Jones, 46, was wearing a puffy black vest. The keys to his grandmother's house, where he currently lives, hung from a lanyard around his neck. His face was thin, a tightly cropped beard undergirding prominent cheekbones, and he had a lookout's gaze, drifting more than darting but always alert.

Jones had been out of prison for three years, a record for him, at least as an adult, but he still sounded a bit like Rip Van Winkle as he marveled at how gentrified his old neighborhood had become. We sat on a cafe's sun-dappled terrace, surrounded by creative-class types. A chef wandered outside to pluck some fresh rosemary from a planter. Jones was the only black patron at the cafe and probably the only person who remembered when it used to be a liquor store. "You wouldn't be sitting here," Jones said. He nodded at some toddlers playing across the street. "That park right there, that wasn't a park. That was just an open field where everybody gambled. At any given time, you would hear shots ring out."

From the age of 15, Jones found himself in and out of juvenile detention, St. Elizabeths or prison—never free for much longer than a month or so. The outside world came to feel terrifying; once, he wanted to get back inside so badly, he bought a bag of crack and called the cops on himself. "That was the world that I knew," he said.

It hadn't been easy for Jones to transition back to a life of freedom. He managed to stick it out, he said, because he was determined not to return to the place where he spent the final eight years of his last sentence: the United States Penitentiary Administrative Maximum Facility in Florence, Colo., known more colloquially as the ADX. The ADX is the highest-security prison in the country. It was designed to be escape-proof, the Alcatraz of the Rockies, a place to incarcerate the worst, most unredeemable class of criminal—"a very small subset of the inmate population who show," in the words of Norman Carlson, the former director of the Federal Bureau of Prisons, "absolutely no concern for human life." Ted Kaczynski and the Atlanta Olympics bomber Eric Rudolph call the ADX home. The 9/11 conspirator Zacarias Moussaoui is held there, too, along with the 1993 World Trade Center bombing mastermind Ramzi Yousef; the Oklahoma City bomber Terry Nichols; the underwear bomber Umar Farouk Abdulmutallab; and the former Bonanno crime-family boss Vincent Basciano. Michael Swango, a serial-killing doctor who may have poisoned 60 of his patients, is serving three consecutive life sentences; Larry Hoover, the Gangster Disciples kingpin made famous by rappers like Rick Ross, is serving six; the traitorous F.B.I. agent Robert Hanssen, a Soviet spy, 15.

Along with such notorious inmates, prisoners deemed serious behavioral or flight risks can also end up at the ADX—men like Jones, who in 2003, after racking up three assault charges in less than a year (all fights with other inmates) at a medium-security facility in Louisiana, found himself transferred to the same ADX cellblock as Kaczynski.

Inmates at the ADX spend approximately 23 hours of each day in solitary confinement. Jones had never been so isolated before. Other prisoners on his cellblock screamed and banged on their doors for hours. Jones said the staff psychiatrist stopped his prescription for Seroquel, a drug taken for bipolar disorder, telling him, "We don't give out feel-good drugs here." Jones experienced severe mood swings. To cope, he would work out in his cell until he was too tired to move. Sometimes he cut himself. In response, guards fastened his arms and legs to his bed with a medieval quartet of restraints, a process known as four-pointing.

One day in 2009, Jones was in the rec yard and spotted Michael Bacote, a friend from back home. The familiar face was welcome but also troubling. Bacote was illiterate, with an I.Q. of only 61, and suffered from acute paranoia. He had been sent to the ADX for his role as a lookout in a murder at a Texas prison, and he was not coping well. His multiple requests for transfers or psychological treatment had been denied. He was convinced that the Bureau of Prisons was trying to poison him, so he was refusing meals and medication. "You would have to be blind and crazy yourself not to see that this guy had issues," Jones said, shaking his head. "He can barely function in a normal setting. His comprehension level was pretty much at zero."

Bacote had paperwork from previous psychiatric examinations, so Jones went to the prison's law library (a room with a computer) and looked up the address of a pro bono legal-aid group he had heard about, the D.C. Prisoners' Project. Because Bacote couldn't write, Jones ghosted a query. "I suppose to have a hearing before coming to the ADX," Jones, as Bacote, wrote. "They never gave me a hearing." He continued, "I need some help cause I have facts! Please help me."

The story of the largest lawsuit ever filed against the United States Bureau of Prisons begins, improbably enough, with this letter. Deborah Golden, the director of the D.C. Prisoners' Project, fields approximately 2,000 requests each year, but Bacote's, which she received in October 2009, caught her eye. "I thought I might be missing something, because it was inconceivable

to me that the Bureau of Prisons could be operating in such a blatantly illegal and unconstitutional manner," she said. Golden was referring to Bureau of Prisons (B.O.P.) regulations that forbid the placement of inmates who "show evidence of significant mental disorder" in prisons like the ADX.

Groups like Golden's D.C. Prisoners' Project tend to focus their reform efforts on state-run prisons—in part because the Prison Litigation Reform Act, passed by Congress in 1996, made it more difficult for prisoners to file federal lawsuits, and in part because the federal government possesses, as Golden put it, "an inexhaustible supply of resources." A droll 42-year-old attorney who once considered rabbinical school, Golden has spent her entire career practicing human rights law. As she investigated Bacote's claims, she came to realize there were dozens of inmates at the ADX with comparable stories, or worse: cases of self-mutilation, obvious psychosis, suicide. Her organization had never considered filing such an enormous suit. Because it is so difficult to win cases against the federal government, challenging the B.O.P. "just didn't fit into anyone's strategic goals," Golden explained. The last major B.O.P. lawsuit to result in a settlement was in the mid 1990s (*Lucas v. White*, brought by a group of female inmates who had been sexually assaulted). But the clarity of Bacote's claims gave her pause. "A lot of cases we see involve matters of interpretation: Who knew what and when," she said. "This didn't seem to involve that kind of uncertainty. I wasn't sure if we had a chance. But it seemed like a court had to see it."

Since opening in 1994, the ADX has remained not just the only federal supermax but also the apogee of a particular strain of the American penal system, wherein abstract dreams of rehabilitation have been entirely superseded by the architecture of control. Throughout our country's history, there have been different ideas about what to do with the "worst of the worst" of our criminal offenders, ranging from the 19th-century chain gangs, who toiled in enforced silence, to the physical isolation of Alcatraz Island. The use of solitary confinement in the United States emerged as a substitute to corporal punishments popular at the end of the 18th century. The practice was first promoted in 1787, by a group of reformers called the Philadelphia Society for Alleviating the Miseries of Public Prisons. At a salon hosted by Benjamin Franklin, a pamphlet was read calling for the construction of a "house of repentance," in which solitude could work to soothe the minds of criminals—an enlightened alternative, the group believed, to inhumane "public punishments" like "the gallows, the pillory, the stocks, the whipping post, and the wheelbarrow." Inmates at Philadelphia's Eastern State Penitentiary, which opened in 1829, were completely isolated from one another in cells outfitted with skylights, toilets and access to private outdoor exercise yards, where they worked at various trades, took all meals and read the Bible. Other states tried, but quickly abandoned, the so-called Pennsylvania System, and an 1890 Supreme Court ruling against the use of solitary on Colorado's death row noted that "a considerable number of the prisoners fell, after even a short confinement, into a semifatuous condition, from which it was next to impossible to arouse them, and others became violently insane; others still, committed suicide, while those who stood the ordeal better were not generally reformed."

The concept soon fell out of favor, and beginning in the 1930s, the hardest cases in the federal system—men like Al Capone and George (Machine Gun Kelly) Barnes—were housed in the converted military prison on Alcatraz Island, until it was closed in 1963 because of the costly upkeep inherent to an island prison. By the end of the decade, many of its prisoners had been transferred to the new "control units" at a federal penitentiary in Marion, Ill., where they were kept in solitary confinement. In 1983, after the assassination of two guards in separate attacks on the same day, by members of the Aryan Brotherhood, the Marion penitentiary was converted to the first modern all-lockdown facility, the entire prison now a solitary unit. (One of the guards' killers, Tommy Silverstein, is now at the ADX. He has been in solitary confinement for the past 22 years.)

Beginning in 1989 with California's Pelican Bay, states began building their own lockdown penitentiaries, inspired by the Marion model. The renewed use of solitary coincided with the era of mass incarceration and the widespread closing of state-run mental-health facilities. The supermax became the most expedient method of controlling an increasingly overcrowded and psychologically volatile prison population. A result of this unfortunate confluence has been a network of ever more austere and utilitarian penitentiaries, built specifically to seal off a significant portion of state and federal inmates, using methods that would shock many Americans. According to a 2014 Amnesty International report, more than 40 states now operate supermax prisons. On any given day, there are 80,000 U.S. prisoners in solitary confinement.

Norman Carlson, the B.O.P. director at the time of the Marion attacks, spearheaded the construction of a federal supermax that could eventually replace Marion. Florence, a faded Colorado mining town, lobbied hard for the $60 million prison to be built within its city limits, with residents eventually donating 600 acres of land to the B.O.P.

The ADX can house up to 500 prisoners in its eight units. Inmates spend their days in 12-by-7-foot cells with thick concrete walls and double sets of sliding metal doors (with solid exteriors, so prisoners can't see one another). A single window, about three feet high but only four inches wide, offers a notched glimpse of sky and little else. Each cell has a sink-toilet combo and an automated shower, and prisoners sleep on concrete slabs topped with thin mattresses. Most cells also have

televisions (with built-in radios), and inmates have access to books and periodicals, as well as certain arts-and-craft materials. Prisoners in the general population are allotted a maximum of 10 hours of exercise a week outside their cells, alternating between solo trips to an indoor "gym" (a windowless cell with a single chin-up bar) and group visits to the outdoor rec yard (where each prisoner nonetheless remains confined to an individual cage). All meals come through slots in the interior door, as does any face-to-face human interaction (with a guard or psychiatrist, chaplain or imam). The Amnesty report said that ADX prisoners "routinely go days with only a few words spoken to them."

Robert Hood, the warden of the ADX from 2002 to 2005, told me that when he first arrived on the campus, he was struck by "the very stark environment," unlike any other prison in which he ever worked or visited—no noise, no mess, no prisoners walking the hallways. When inmates complained to him, he would tell them, "This place is not designed for humanity," he recalled. "When it's 23 hours a day in a room with a slit of a window where you can't even see the Rocky Mountains—let's be candid here. It's not designed for rehabilitation. Period. End of story."

Hood was not trying to be cruel with such frankness. The ADX was built explicitly to house men often already serving multiple life sentences and thus facing little disincentive to, say, murder a guard or another prisoner. Still, during his own tenure, Hood said he made a point of developing one-on-one relationships with as many inmates as possible—he described Salvatore (Sammy the Bull) Gravano as "a very likable guy, believe it or not," and he bonded with the Unabomber over their shared interest in running marathons—in hopes of eliciting good behavior in exchange for whatever he could do to make their sentences more bearable. But he also needed them to understand that even as warden, he lacked the authority to change the rules of their confinement. In the past, Hood has memorably described the ADX as "a clean version of hell."

Five years ago, a major lawsuit against the Federal Bureau of Prisons would have sounded quixotic. But in the present moment, the ADX case feels like the crest of a wave, as the excessive use of solitary confinement in U.S. prisons has come under intensifying scrutiny. Senator Dick Durbin, Democrat of Illinois, held the first-ever congressional hearing on the issue in 2012. Dr. Craig Haney, a psychology professor at the University of California, Santa Cruz, testified that "a shockingly high percentage" of the prisoners in solitary confinement are mentally ill, "often profoundly so"—approximately one-third of the segregated prisoners on average, though in some units the figure rises to 50 percent. The emptiness that pervades solitary-confinement units "has led some prisoners into a profound level of what might be called 'ontological insecurity,'" Haney, who worked as a principal researcher on the Stanford Prison Experiment while in graduate school, told the senators. "They are not sure that they exist and, if they do, exactly who they are."

According to David Cloud, a senior associate at the Vera Institute of Justice, a nonpartisan, nonprofit organization dedicated to the reform of the criminal-justice system, "The research is pretty conclusive: Since people started looking at this, even 200 years ago, when a guy named Francis Gray studied 4,000 people in 'silent prisons,' the studies have found that the conditions themselves can cause mental illness, stress, trauma." The devastating effects of solitary confinement, even on those who showed no previous signs of psychological problems, are now so broadly accepted by mental-health professionals that policy makers are finally taking notice. Last year the New York State attorney general approved a deal forbidding the placement of minors and mentally ill prisoners in solitary; in January, New York City banned solitary for anyone under 21. Gov. John W. Hickenlooper of Colorado signed a similar bill at the urging of the state corrections chief, Rick Raemisch, who spent a night in solitary confinement and wrote about it in a *New York Times* Op-Ed, concluding that its overuse is "counterproductive and inhumane." As Cloud told me, "Even if you tried to employ solitary confinement with the most humane intentions, people are still going to lose their minds and hurt themselves."

Golden recognized that a lawsuit against the B.O.P. would still be a long shot—and that a co-counsel with deeper pockets than her own would be necessary. So she approached Arnold & Porter, a white-shoe law firm with a history of taking on high-profile pro bono cases. Ed Aro, a partner based in Denver, was intrigued; a close family member had spent time in prison, and other relatives had suffered from mental illness. Aro himself, though, was a trial lawyer who mostly represented corporations and had never set foot in a correctional facility. The prison jargon so baffled him at first that Golden had to send him a glossary that she put together.

A Colorado native who looks the part, Aro, 50, favors cowboy boots and fleece jackets, and his cheeks have the ruddy, slightly cured quality of a man who enjoys vigorous exercise at high altitudes. "Juries are my stock in trade," he told me. "They bring me in when the story is complicated and there's not going to be a settlement and they need someone to tell a convincing narrative. With this case, I worried, How do you weave a narrative and humanize people at a prison like this?"

As he tried to get a handle on the lawsuit, he made the two-hour drive to Florence nearly every week. For years, conditions inside the ADX had remained largely a mystery; from 2002 on, the Amnesty report noted, ADX officials denied every media request for a visit or prisoner interview, aside from a restricted tour in 2007. (The B.O.P. declined to comment for this article or to allow a site visit.) Aro assumed he would find a small number of prisoners who had somehow slipped through the cracks. "The thing that shocked me most was how massive the problem was," Aro said. "The ADX is the most closely monitored and evaluated subset of the prison population in the entire country. With the extent of the problem, it's incomprehensible to me that the B.O.P. didn't notice what was going on." How, Aro wondered, did the toughest prison in the United States become a mental asylum—one incapable of controlling its own population?

He enlisted Dr. Doris Gundersen, a Denver-based forensic psychiatrist, who was allowed inside the ADX as part of his legal team. After evaluating 45 prisoners, she estimated that 70 percent met the criteria for at least one serious mental illness. She and Aro spoke to inmates who swallowed razor blades, inmates who were left for days or weeks shackled to their beds (where they were routinely allowed to soil themselves), an inmate who ate his own feces so regularly that staff psychiatrists made a special note only when he did so with unusual "voracity." A number of prisoners were taken off prescribed medications. (Until recently prison regulations forbade the placement of inmates on psychotropic medication in the Control Unit, the most restrictive section of the ADX, as, by definition, such medication implies severe mental illness.) Others claimed that they were denied treatment, aside from "therapy classes" on the prison television's educational station and workbooks with titles like "Cage Your Rage," despite repeated written requests. (The ADX lawsuit says that only two psychologists and one part-time psychiatrist serve the entire prison.)

Gunderson and Aro met one inmate, Marcellus Washington, sentenced to life for carjacking and armed robbery, who slashed his wrists in a suicide attempt and was punished for it: He lost his television and radio privileges for several weeks. They met another inmate, Herbert Perkins, also serving life for armed robbery, who, after slashing his throat with a razor and being rushed to a hospital, was returned to the same cell, given a mop and bucket and ordered to clean up the blood.

They also met David Shelby, a schizophrenic who, in 1995, became convinced that God wanted him to free Charles Manson from prison and that the best way to achieve this would be to send threatening letters to President Bill Clinton. He arrived at the ADX in 2000. Nine years later, in response to another command from God, Shelby, who just a few months earlier tried to commit suicide by slashing his arms, legs and stomach, fashioned a tourniquet around the base of his left pinkie, hacked off the top two joints with a Bic razor blade and ate his finger with a bowl of ramen. When he became agitated and summoned a guard to say he'd done a "terrible thing," he mostly meant that he'd eaten meat; for the previous few months, he had been a vegetarian.

Aro had interviewed about 25 ADX prisoners when, in October 2011, he met the man who would become the face of the lawsuit. This particular inmate, Jack Powers, who was 52, refused to take a seat during their first meeting; years in solitary had made him skittish around other humans. Still, Aro immediately found Powers striking: bright, articulate, no history of institutional violence.

"If you looked at Jack's criminal history," Aro said, "at the bizarre, unhappy confluence of circumstances that led him to the ADX and into this incredible descent into madness, it's impossible to believe what happened to him has nothing to do with his conditions of confinement." In his search for a compelling character whose story could explain the lawsuit, Aro thought as he left the prison that day, it wouldn't get much better than Jack Powers.

Jack Powers grew up in Norwich, N.Y., the son of a Vietnam veteran who beat him regularly. Powers ran away from home at 14; a few years later he was sent to prison on burglary charges. He was released in 1982, at 21, and he married and moved to Holland, Mich., where he founded a construction company and beauty salon. But by the end of the decade, both businesses had gone bankrupt, and he began robbing banks—at least 30, according to his 1990 conviction. He never armed himself; he always just slipped a note to the bank teller. He thinks his wife (now ex) turned him in.

At the U.S. penitentiary in Atlanta, where he was serving his 40-year sentence, he befriended a new inmate named Eduardo Wong, a heroin smuggler with supposed ties to Chinese organized crime. "Nice guy," Powers said in a recorded deposition. "I mean, relatively speaking." Wong and Powers liked to play chess. "But it wasn't that long, just a matter of weeks," Powers said, "before things went awry."

Wong became a target of members of the Aryan Brotherhood, who threatened to kill him if he didn't procure cash for them. Powers warned Wong about the seriousness of his situation, but Wong hesitated. One afternoon, a group of men ran onto their tier and stabbed Wong multiple times while Powers was held in the cell next door at knife point. After they ran off, Wong stumbled into Powers's arms, blood gushing from his neck. "John, help me," he said. Powers managed to carry Wong down several floors to the prison hospital, where he died.

During the murder investigation, Powers was moved to a protective custody unit. Shortly after his transfer, though, the face of an Aryan Brotherhood member appeared at the food slot of his door. "If you tell on my boys," the man warned, "I'm going to chop your head off." But Powers had a teenage son in Syracuse he wanted to reconnect with, so in exchange for what he believed would be a sentence reduction, he agreed to appear as a witness for the government. Three of the four Aryan Brotherhood members he testified against were convicted and received life sentences.

Powers had no history of mental illness before his incarceration. But after Wong's murder, he began to display symptoms of post-traumatic stress disorder, which manifested in the form of panic attacks, near-constant anxiety and nightmares in which inmates with weapons cornered Powers in an isolated area of the prison. By 1999, he had not received his sentence reduction and had become convinced that the B.O.P. was planning on transferring him out of protective custody. So he decided to escape.

He put a dummy in his bed, hid inside a grate in the rec yard and scaled the side of a building with a homemade grappling hook. From the rooftop, he jumped over a 16-foot electric fence, then climbed a second barbed-wire fence with FedEx boxes taped to his arms and legs. Once outside, he stole a car and headed to Syracuse to see his son.

When his son didn't answer his phone, he tried to visit his half sister. (She wasn't home, but when he spotted a neighbor struggling with a lawn mower, he cut her grass.) The police picked him up after two days. A reporter from *The Syracuse Post-Standard* interviewed Powers at the local jail and asked him whether he would do it again. The article reads as a light-hearted human-interest feature about a gentleman bandit, and Powers's affirmative answer became the kicker. "Without life's normal sensations and emotions and feelings," Powers said, "what have you got?"

In October 2001, Powers, now considered a flight risk, was transferred to the ADX—where all three of the Aryan Brotherhood members Powers had testified against were serving their own sentences. Powers's PTSD intensified. Tagged as a snitch and, more damaging, as an enemy of the Aryan Brotherhood, even unaffiliated prisoners avoided speaking to him. The guards, Powers said, treated him differently as well. If the whole unit is against a prisoner, he explained, "it's like, the majority prevails. If they're trying to be cool with the rest of these guys, then they can't be cool with you."

Over the next decade, Powers, by any rational accounting, lost his mind. He cut off both earlobes, chewed off a finger, sliced through his Achilles' tendon, pushed staples into his face and forehead, swallowed a toothbrush and then tried to cut open his abdomen to retrieve it and injected what he considered "a pretty fair amount of bacteria-laden fluid" into his brain cavity after smashing a hole in his forehead. In 2005, after slicing open his scrotum and removing a testicle, Powers was sent to the medical center for federal prisoners in Springfield, Mo., for treatment, where a psychiatrist determined he was "not in need of inpatient psychiatric treatment or psychotropic medication" and that his behavior "was secondary to his antisocial disorder." When he was returned to Springfield four years later, after slashing his wrists and writing "American Gulag" in blood on his bedsheets, the doctor wrote, "Considerations that [Powers] has some form of psychosis, thought disorder or mental illness are unfounded."

In 2007, an inmate named Jose Vega was placed in the cell directly below Powers. Vega had come to the ADX after attacking an associate warden with a razor blade at another prison. He had received a diagnosis of depression, and because he was sick and disruptive—flinging feces and urine at the staff—the guards came to despise him, according to Powers. But he and Vega began talking through the drains of their sinks. (Prisoners in neighboring cells could communicate through the plumbing if they used toilet-paper rolls to blow the water from the U-shaped pipes, called sink traps, that ran beneath their basins.) For the first time in years, Powers had someone he considered a friend. They would chat about the prison, their families, legal issues. Vega had lost his television privilege, so Powers would place his own headphones near the sink drain and play music loud enough so that his friend could listen, too.

At times, a guard would provoke Vega. He became convinced that staff members were sneaking into his cell at night and assaulting him. Powers knew that was impossible—the heavy cell doors could not be opened without Powers hearing—but he said that guards did withhold Vega's mail and intentionally dropped his food on the floor. One guard told Vega that he might as well kill himself, because things weren't going to get any better. "They started to break him," Powers said. "Almost like you see with pro wrestlers, like a tag-team-type thing, where one of them passes it off to the next and to the next and to the next."

On the morning of May 1, 2010, Vega was found dead in his cell. He had hanged himself with a bedsheet. After Vega's death, Powers shaved his head and began decorating his body with what he would describe as his "Avatar stripes," a reference to the striped blue aliens in the James Cameron movie. Using a razor blade to make tiny cuts in his skin and then rubbing carbon-paper dust into the wounds, Powers tattooed spiky black slashes along his arms, legs, neck, skull, under his eyes and around his Adam's apple. A photograph from 2011 presents an astounding transformation: The smirking, shaggy-haired young bank robber who entered the federal prison system in 1990 no longer existed, and the man who replaced him looked like something out of a nightmare.

Aro's team first met with members of the U.S. Justice Department in November 2011. A series of conversations with the B.O.P. followed, in which the lawyers proposed specific remedies that could head off a lawsuit. Aro described the agency as "routinely unhelpful" and said it soon became "crystal clear that they were circling the wagons. They weren't going to even admit there were problems, let alone try to fix them."

According to Golden, prisons have a history of getting lawsuits mooted by simply transferring the litigious inmate to a different facility. In anticipation of such a maneuver, Golden and Aro assembled a broad platform of plaintiffs, unwieldy enough to make the transfer strategy impractical: The initial complaint featured six primary inmates, including Powers and Shelby, and 11 backups, demonstrating a range of illnesses, races and backgrounds. (The legal team also filed a suit on behalf of the family of Jose Vega seeking damages for abuse and wrongful death.)

In 2013, Aro and a U.S. attorney representing the B.O.P. spent two days questioning Powers in a filmed deposition (the source of much of the preceding account of his time at the ADX). The video frames Powers, dressed in the standard prison uniform, seated behind a table, his hands shackled. At one point, he tells a lawyer he can't remember the last time he was in a room with so many people, probably years ago. He's thoughtful and deliberate, obviously intelligent. Despite the litany of horrors he relates, you can almost understand how people might have judged him sane.

By that fall, Judge Richard Matsch, who presided over the Oklahoma City bombing trial, had denied motions to dismiss filed by the B.O.P., and the lawsuit entered its discovery phase. And then, to Aro and Golden's genuine surprise, the government's lawyers broached the subject of a potential settlement—which, according to Golden, "is almost unheard-of" for the B.O.P. Aro added, "I don't think any of us went into this very optimistic that we'd get to a resolution without dragging them kicking and screaming across the finish line. The government routinely defends lawsuits if they think they have a snowball's chance in hell of winning."

Matsch assigned a federal magistrate judge to oversee the potential settlement, and Aro and Golden presented the B.O.P. with a list of 27 points that needed to be addressed, including specific demands for diagnosis and treatment and an oversight board to ensure that these demands were met. (The lawsuit does not include any financial settlements.) After nearly a year of negotiations, Golden told me in January, "I think we're very close to a settlement." Aro, though also increasingly optimistic, told me this month that he still couldn't predict whether there would be a settlement or a trial.

Simultaneous to the settlement negotiations, however, the B.O.P. unilaterally began effecting certain (though by no means all) of the requested changes at the ADX. New mental-health programming was added, additional psychologists were hired and a new unit for high-security mentally ill prisoners opened in Atlanta. As predicted, a number of the inmates named in the suit have been transferred out of the ADX—including Powers, who was sent to a high-security prison in Tucson last year.

Powers couldn't cope with the openness of the new facility. Aro believes the B.O.P. acted with good intentions, but it dismally failed to acclimate a man who spent much of the previous 13 years alone in a cell. Prisoners' cell doors were left unlocked for much of the day, but Powers rarely ventured out into communal areas, and his mood turned ugly. After he struck a staff member during an argument, he was put in solitary. There, with a drill bit fashioned out of a battery, he managed to bore a hole through the top of his skull in an attempted trepanation.

Aro and Golden had both grown close to Powers over the course of the lawsuit. Separately they told me how protective they felt about him and how worried they were about his continued self-destructive behavior. Changes are very likely coming at the ADX, in no small part thanks to Powers's story. But it seemed entirely possible that he might not survive to see the outcome.

David Shelby, the ADX inmate who ate his finger, was also transferred to a medium-security facility, in Butner, N.C. He is six feet tall and 300 pounds, with thick-framed prison-issue glasses and a round, clean-shaven face. (At the ADX, he had an unruly beard, suggestive of a backwoods survivalist). Before he described a violent episode from his past when I visited him this fall, he paused and said, softly: "I hope I don't make you feel uncomfortable, sir. I'm well-medicated now, so you're perfectly safe."

As a child in Mitchell, Ind., Shelby hunted squirrel and rabbit for supper and would occasionally trade the meat to old-timers for food stamps. His parents drank, and Shelby developed a taste of his own. (His favorite cocktail was a mixture of Everclear and Wild Turkey, which he called Wilder Turkey.) He went to prison in his late teens after pulling a shotgun on a man who owed him $2, and again in his 20s following a string of burglaries. He also began experiencing schizophrenic episodes in which he heard God's voice in his head. It's not difficult to imagine that Shelby's life would have followed a different trajectory had he received comprehensive psychological treatment. When officials picked him up at a post office, he was preparing to mail Clinton a package containing a pocketknife and a light bulb that was booby-trapped, Looney Tunes style, with gunpowder. "I think you are doing a good job," the note read, "and I am sending you the pocketknife as a gift and a light bulb so you won't strain your eyes." Shelby, in a deal with prosecutors, pleaded guilty and received a 24-year prison sentence. He was moved to the ADX two years later, after he took a female cook hostage with a homemade knife. Shelby told her that he wanted a warden "to order the best sniper to come in here and kill me." By all subsequent accounts, including his hostage's, he was careful not to hurt her during his suicide attempt. A staff psychiatrist eventually talked him down.

Since his move to Butner, Shelby has thrived. He shares his cell with another prisoner, and the door remains unlocked for much of the day. Shelby said his unit, Duke, was for people who are "special." (All the units at Butner are named for Southeastern college-sports powers.) "We're crazy," he cheerily explained. "We're all in the pill line in Duke. I've got three kinds of insanity: One is depression, one is bipolar, one is schizophrenia. But right now, my personal prescription is perfect." He has even had a couple of brief encounters with Butner's most famous inmate, Bernard Madoff, though, Shelby noted: "We're

from such different worlds, I don't think he'd want to know me. Unless he's interested in squirrel hunting."

Aro, who accompanied me on my visit, said this funny, personable version of Shelby was nothing like the Shelby of the ADX. The morning of my visit, I spotted other inmates tending to a vegetable garden in a pleasant central courtyard. Shelby works as a janitor. "We've got four bathrooms that stay good and clean because of me," he said, adding earnestly, "I must have done something good in a past life to deserve this. There are times in the free world where I've never had it this good."

In January, Aro and Golden told me that Powers's health also appeared to be on the upswing. He had been transferred back to Florence, to a new mental-health program the B.O.P. started in a lower-security penitentiary, part of the same complex as the ADX. The multistep program focuses on inmates' developing coping mechanisms, via individual and group-therapy sessions. During the early stages, the prisoners remain largely in solitary but are rewarded with more freedoms as they progress. Aro forwarded me a recent photograph of Powers that showed him actually smiling. Soon afterward, I began receiving letters from Powers, neatly handwritten, in all caps. He sounded upbeat at first, though subsequent correspondence expressed increasing skepticism about the program. "Traditional notions of penological care, custody and control of prisoners—and especially those who have a mental illness—differ from psychological treatment initiatives like night differs from day," he wrote, claiming the mood in the new unit had "reverted back to distrust, hostility and resistance—like a jungle reclaims an abandoned settlement."

Still, in the same letter, he acknowledged the policy changes might eventually yield results. "These programs are works in progress and must be given time to develop," he wrote. And then, without signing his name or adding any other form of valediction, he concluded with a final line: "Right now the participants are guinea pigs."

Robert Hood, the former ADX warden, thinks that changes at the supermax are long overdue. He had requested his assignment there, his last before retiring. He found the challenge appealing, especially because he considered himself a "teaching-oriented guy," rather than the "custody-oriented" type of warden you might expect to find at a supermax. Hood is proud of his time at the ADX but has also come to believe that it needs to be transformed. "Not everyone in the ADX needs to be in a supermax. I could reduce that population. I don't know what the magic number is, but a certain percentage could be put in a place that doesn't require 23-hour lockdown. The public might not like it, but I don't care if Sammy the Bull is out in the yard playing Ping-Pong with Robert Hanssen."

Hood noted that the ADX's predecessors, Alcatraz and Marion, each existed for roughly 30 years before shutting their doors. "The supermax in Colorado has been there for 20 years," Hood said, "so it's getting close to the last third of its life. I'd say the bureau is looking in the mirror and saying: 'Guess what? The world is different now than in 1994.' "

# Critical Thinking

1. Is solitary confinement an effective method for dealing with troublesome prisoners?
2. Was justice served by what happened to Jack Powers?

# Internet References

**Amnesty International**
   http://www.amnestyusa.org/research/reports/entombed-isolation-in-the-us-federal-prison-system
**The New York Times**
   http://www.nytimes.com/2014/02/21/opinion/my-night-in-solitary.html

MARK BINELLI is a contributing editor at *Rolling Stone* and the author of "Detroit City Is the Place to Be."

*Article*

Prepared by: Joanne Naughton

# The Painful Price of Aging in Prison

## Even as harsh sentences are reconsidered, the financial—and human—tolls mount.

Sari Horwitz

## Learning Outcomes

*After reading this article, you will be able to:*

- Understand some of the issues involved in incarcerating old, sick prisoners.
- Relate how six jurors felt about Bruce Harrison's case.

## Inside Coleman Prison, Fla.

Twenty-one years into his nearly 50-year sentence, the graying man steps inside his stark cell in the largest federal prison complex in America. He wears special medical boots because of a foot condition that makes walking feel as if he's "stepping on a needle." He has undergone tests for a suspected heart condition and sometimes experiences vertigo.

"I get dizzy sometimes when I'm walking," says the 63-year-old inmate, Bruce Harrison. "One time, I just couldn't get up."

In 1994, Harrison and other members of the motorcycle group he belonged to were caught up in a drug sting by undercover federal agents, who asked them to move huge volumes of cocaine and marijuana. After taking the job, making several runs and each collecting $1,000, Harrison and the others were arrested and later convicted. When their sentences were handed down, however, jurors objected.

"I am sincerely disheartened by the fact that these defendants, who participated in the staged off-loads and transports . . . are looking at life in prison or decades at best," said one of several who wrote letters to the judge and prosecutor.

In recent years, federal sentencing guidelines have been revised, resulting in less severe prison terms for low-level drug offenders. But Harrison, a decorated Vietnam War veteran,

remains one of tens of thousands of inmates who were convicted in the "war on drugs" of the 1980s and 1990s and who are still behind bars.

Harsh sentencing policies, including mandatory minimums, continue to have lasting consequences for inmates and the nation's prison system. Today, prisoners 50 and older represent the fastest-growing population in crowded federal correctional facilities, their ranks having swelled by 25 percent to nearly 31,000 from 2009 to 2013.

Some prisons have needed to set up geriatric wards, while others have effectively been turned into convalescent homes.

The aging of the prison population is driving health-care costs being borne by American taxpayers. The Bureau of Prisons saw health-care expenses for inmates increase 55 percent from 2006 to 2013, when it spent more than $1 billion. That figure is nearly equal to the entire budget of the U.S. Marshals Service or the Bureau of Alcohol, Tobacco, Firearms and Explosives, according to the Justice Department's inspector general, who is conducting a review of the impact of the aging inmate population on prison activities, housing and costs.

"Our federal prisons are starting to resemble nursing homes surrounded with razor wire," said Julie Stewart, president and founder of Families Against Mandatory Minimums. "It makes no sense fiscally, or from the perspective of human compassion, to incarcerate men and women who pose no threat to public safety and have long since paid for their crime. We need to repeal the absurd mandatory minimum sentences that keep them there."

The Obama administration is trying to overhaul the criminal justice system by allowing prisoners who meet certain criteria to be released early through clemency and urging prosecutors to reserve the most severe drug charges for serious, high-level offenders.

## America's aging federal inmates

While the younger segment of the federal inmate population has shrunk in the past 15 years, groups age 35 and older all saw increases. In 2014, inmates 55 and older accounted for 10.6 percent of the population, an increase from 6.4 percent in 2000.

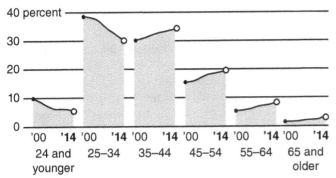

Source: Federal Bureau of Prisons

At the same time, the U.S. Sentencing Commission, an independent agency, has made tens of thousands of incarcerated drug offenders eligible for reduced sentences.

But until more elderly prisoners are discharged—either through compassionate release programs or the clemency initiative started by then-attorney general Eric H. Holder Jr. last year—the government will be forced to spend more to serve the population. Among other expenditures, that means hiring additional nurses and redesigning prisons—installing showers that can be used by the elderly, for instance, or ensuring that entryways are wheelchair-accessible.

"Prisons simply are not physically designed to accommodate the infirmities that come with age," said Jamie Fellner, a senior advisor at Human Rights Watch and an author of a report titled "Old Behind Bars."

"There are countless ways that the aging inmates, some with dementia, bump up against the prison culture," she said. "It is difficult to climb to the upper bunk, walk up stairs, wait outside for pills, take showers in facilities without bars and even hear the commands to stand up for count or sit down when you're told."

For years, state prisons followed the federal government's lead in enacting harsh sentencing laws. In 2010, there were some 246,000 prisoners age 50 and older in state and federal prisons combined, with nearly 90 percent of them held in state custody, the American Civil Liberties Union said in a report titled "At America's Expense: The Mass Incarceration of the Elderly."

On both the state and federal level, the spiraling costs are eating into funds that could be used to curtail violent crime, drug cartels, public corruption, financial fraud and human trafficking. The costs—as well as officials' concerns about racial disparities in sentencing—are also driving efforts to reduce the federal prison population.

For now, however, prison officials say there is little they can do about the costs.

Edmond Ross, a spokesman for the Bureau of Prisons, said: "We have to provide a certain level of medical care for whoever comes to us."

Except for the loud clang of heavy steel security doors that close behind a visitor, the Butner Federal Medical Center in North Carolina feels nothing like the prisons portrayed on television and in movies.

Elderly inmates dressed in khaki prison uniforms are not locked up during the day, but instead congregate with each other in their wheelchairs, wait for treatment in clinics and walk, sometimes with canes or walkers, through their living quarters.

## Federal inmate population, 1980–2014

The population is more than 93 percent male. It costs the Department of Justice $6.5 billion annually to operate the federal prison system.

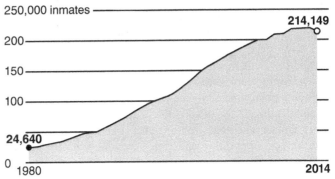

There were 208,859 federal inmates as of April 30, 2015.
Source: Federal Bureau of Prisons

Signs hang from the ceiling, directing prisoners to various units: "Urgent Care," "Mental Health," "Surgery," "Ambulatory Care, "Oncology."

"This facility mirrors a hospital more than a prison," said Kenneth McKoy, acting executive assistant to the warden at Butner, a prison about 20 minutes northeast of Durham. "We provide long-term care."

The facility is the largest medical complex in the Bureau of Prisons, which has 121 prisons, including six that have medical centers. With more than 900 inmates in need of medical care, Butner even provides hospice-like care for dying inmates.

In his "cell" on a recent day, Michael E. Hodge lay in a hospital-like bed where he spent his days mostly staring at the television. A prison official had just helped him get out of his wheelchair. A prison employee delivered his meals. He could hardly keep his eyes open.

In 2000, Hodge was convicted on charges of distribution and possession of marijuana and possessing a gun, and was sentenced to 20 years. When a *Washington Post* reporter visited Hodge in mid-April, he was dying of liver cancer. He died April 18, prison officials said.

"Tell my wife I love her," said Hodge, who said he was in great pain.

Many prisoners at Butner are as sick as Hodge was, McKoy says.

"Why are we keeping someone behind bars who is bedridden and needs assistance to get out of bed and feed and clothe himself?" asked Fellner, of Human Rights Watch. "What do we gain from keeping people behind bars at an enormous cost when they no longer pose any danger to the public if they were released?"

Hodge submitted at least four requests for compassionate release over the past few years, but none were approved by officials, according to his ex-wife Kim Hodge, whom he still referred to as his wife.

"The man is 51 and dying," Kim Hodge said in an interview last month. "He never killed nobody, he's not a child molester, he's not a bad person. Now he's going to die in there."

Taxpayers are increasingly picking up the tab for inmates who received lengthy mandatory sentences for drug offenses and have since aged and developed conditions that require around-the-clock medical care.

The average cost of housing federal inmates nearly doubles for aging prisoners. While the cost of a prisoner in the general population is $27,549 a year, the price tag associated with an older inmate who needs more medical care, including expensive prescription drugs and treatments, is $58,956, Justice Department officials say.

At Federal Medical Center Devens, a prison near Boston, 115 aging inmates with kidney failure receive treatment inside a dialysis unit.

"Renal failure is driving our costs up," said Ted Eichel, the health-services administrator for Devens. "It costs $4 million to run this unit, not counting medications, which is half our budget." Devens also employs 60 nurses, along with social workers, dietitians, psychologists, dentists and physical therapists. They look like medical workers, except for the cluster of prison keys they're carrying.

Down the hallway, inmates in wheelchairs line up to receive their daily pills and insulin shots.

Although the prison houses about 1,000 low- to high-security inmates, they are not handcuffed or shackled, except when being transferred outside the facility. A golf cart has been redesigned into a mini-ambulance.

At prisons such as Devens, younger inmates are sometimes enlisted as "companion aides," helping older inmates get out of bed, wheeling them down the halls to medical appointments and helping them take care of themselves.

"The population here is getting older and sicker," said Michael Renshaw, a Devens clinical nurse and corrections officer who noted the differences between working as a nurse there and "on the outside."

"Inmates get very good care here," Renshaw said. "But on the outside, maybe you would give a patient a hug or he would hug you. Here, you have to be able to maintain your borders. It's a prison."

As with all prisons, fights occasionally break out. At Devens, it's sometimes between patients who are in wheelchairs or, in at least one case, between an inmate who climbed out of his wheelchair and onto another prisoner's bed to assault him.

John Thompson, a patient-care technician who works with Devens's dialysis patients, said he knows a number of people who "want no part of" providing medical care to prisoners.

"But I just feel like they're good people," Thompson said. "And they're doing their time. Some guys have an attitude, but I tell them, if you show me respect, I'll show you respect."

Jesse Owens, a dialysis patient serving about 12 years for cocaine charges, said he's grateful for the care. "They're keeping us alive," he said.

Harrison's crammed cell at the Federal Correctional Complex Coleman in Florida near Orlando is devoid of the clutter of life on the outside. The space he shares with another inmate has only a sink, a toilet, a bunk bed with cots, a steel cabinet, two plastic gray chairs, a desk and a bulletin board with a postcard of a Florida waterspout.

From a tiny window, he can see Spanish moss draped over trees in the distance.

Forty-five years ago, Harrison served with the Marines in Vietnam. A machine gunner, he was shot twice and was awarded two Purple Hearts. When he came back, he felt as though he had nowhere to turn. He later joined a motorcycle group known as the Outlaws.

Harrison was approached by an undercover agent who was part of a law enforcement team trying to bring down the group, which had been suspected of illegal activity. He and fellow members of the club were offered a kilogram of cocaine to offload and transport drugs. He declined, saying none of them wanted to be paid in drugs.

"I didn't want drugs, because I really wouldn't have known what to do with them," Harrison said in an interview. "We didn't sell them."

But Harrison and the others took the job because the agents offered cash, and they needed the money. Over a period of several months, they would move what they believed to be real drugs—more than 1,400 kilos of cocaine and about 3,200 pounds of marijuana.

Harrison carried a gun for protection during two of the offloads. He didn't use it, but after authorities arrested him and fellow members of his group, he was charged with possessing a firearm while committing a drug offense.

His 1995 trial in Tampa lasted four months. His lawyer at the time argued that "this was a government operation from beginning to end. . . . Everything was orchestrated by the government. . . . He was not a leader. The only leaders in this case, the only organizers in this case was the United States government."

The jury, nonetheless, found Harrison and the others guilty of transporting the drugs.

Harrison was sentenced to roughly 24 years for possessing cocaine and marijuana with the intent to distribute. The conviction on the firearms charge carried a 25-year penalty, meaning he is effectively serving a life sentence.

"There's no doubt that that's a harsh penalty," said U.S. District Judge Susan C. Bucklew during the sentencing hearing. "But that's what the statute says, and I don't think I have any alternative but to do that."

"I don't have a whole lot of discretion here," she said at another point.

After Harrison and the others were sentenced, several of the jurors expressed shock to learn how long those convicted were to spend behind bars.

"If I would have been given the right to not only judge the facts in this case, but also the law and the actions taken by the government, the prosecutor, local and federal law enforcement officers connected in this case would be in jail and not the defendants," juror Patrick L. McNeil wrote.

Six jurors signed a letter requesting a new trial be ordered, saying that if they had been told by the court that they could have found that the government had entrapped the defendants, they would have found them not guilty.

"Bruce Harrison had never been involved in unloading drugs," said his current lawyer, Tom Dawson. "He didn't arrange for any of these drugs. The government did."

Andrea Strong, a childhood friend of Harrison, said he doesn't claim to have been a saint.

"But, in a compassionate world, this man would not be less than halfway through a sentence for a drug offense that happened 20 years ago," Strong said. "He would've done his time, paid his debt to society, and be released to his network of supportive family and friends."

Along with tens of thousands of other inmates around the country, Harrison is applying for clemency under the Obama administration's program to release drug offenders who have been in prison for at least 10 years and whose cases meet certain criteria.

"If I got out, I'd go back home and be with my three grandkids and help them out," Harrison said.

Another aging inmate at Coleman, 58-year-old Luis Anthony Rivera of Miami, has also applied for clemency. He was convicted of conspiracy to import cocaine and has so far served 30 years.

When he was sentenced in 1985, it marked his first criminal offense.

While in Coleman's maximum-security penitentiary, Rivera began painting with oil and watercolors, trying to re-create the world outside bars. When he was moved to the medium-security prison on the same grounds, he wasn't allowed to bring his art supplies, and he can't afford to buy new ones.

But the move brought a new joy. He saw a tree for the first time in 10 years.

"It was amazing to see a tree," said Rivera, a former pilot who was in the National Guard and the Army and now spends his days working in the prison commissary stocking shelves and filling orders.

"I understand the system of putting people in prison. It works. No doubt," Rivera said. "But how much time you put them in for makes a determination. For the first five years, you suffer. You really do. They keep everything away from you—food, all your basics. So you long for them, watching a commercial on TV, seeing a product that you can't touch or have."

"But after that, you start to get hardened," Rivera said, his voice cracking.

If he does not receive clemency, how much time does he have to serve before getting out?

His lips quivered and his eyes filled with tears.

"I'm not," Rivera said. "I have life, plus 140 years."

## Critical Thinking

1. Do you think harsh sentences and mandatory minimums have been successful in reducing drug use?

2. What is the purpose of a prison sentence?

3. Are old, sick prisoners likely to be a danger to society?

## Internet References

**The Clemency Report**
http://clemencyreport.org/something-doesnt-love-wall/

**Office of the Inspector General, US DOJ**
https://oig.justice.gov/challenges/2014.htm

**The Washington Post**
https://www.washingtonpost.com/world/national-security/us-clemency-effort-slow-to-start-will-rely-on-an-army-of-pro-bono-lawyers/2015/02/28/2ba8c6bc-bc42-11e4-8668-4e7ba8439ca6_story.html

JULIE TATE in Washington contributed to this report.

# Article

Prepared by: Joanne Naughton

# The Radical Humaneness of Norway's Halden Prison

The goal of the Norwegian penal system is to get inmates out of it.

JESSICA BENKO

## Learning Outcomes

*After reading this article, you will be able to:*

- Discuss the concept of "dynamic security."
- Describe the 1967 report to President Johnson, "The Challenge of Crime in a Free Society."
- Show the effects of Robert Martinson's 1974 article.

Like everything else in Norway, the two-hour drive southeast from Oslo seemed impossibly civilized. The highways were perfectly maintained and painted, the signs clear and informative and the speed-monitoring cameras primly intolerant. My destination was the town of Halden, which is on the border with Sweden, straddling a narrow fjord guarded by a 17th-century fortress. I drove down winding roads flanked in midsummer by rich green fields of young barley and dense yellow carpets of rapeseed plants in full flower. Cows clustered in woodfenced pastures next to neat farmsteads in shades of rust and ocher. On the outskirts of town, across from a road parting dark pine forest, the turnoff to Norway's newest prison was marked by a modest sign that read, simply, HALDEN FENGSEL. There were no signs warning against picking up hitchhikers, no visible fences. Only the 25-foot-tall floodlights rising along the edges hinted that something other than grazing cows lay ahead.

Smooth, featureless concrete rose on the horizon like the wall of a dam as I approached; nearly four times as tall as a man, it snaked along the crests of the hills, its top curled toward me as if under pressure. This was the outer wall of Halden Fengsel, which is often called the world's most humane maximum-security prison. I walked up the quiet driveway to the entrance and presented myself to a camera at the main door. There were no coils of razor wire in sight, no lethal electric fences, no towers manned by snipers—nothing violent, threatening or dangerous. And yet no prisoner has ever tried to escape. I rang the intercom, the lock disengaged with a click and I stepped inside.

To anyone familiar with the American correctional system, Halden seems alien. Its modern, cheerful and well-appointed facilities, the relative freedom of movement it offers, its quiet and peaceful atmosphere—these qualities are so out of sync with the forms of imprisonment found in the United States that you could be forgiven for doubting whether Halden is a prison at all. It is, of course, but it is also something more: the physical expression of an entire national philosophy about the relative merits of punishment and forgiveness.

The treatment of inmates at Halden is wholly focused on helping to prepare them for a life after they get out. Not only is there no death penalty in Norway; there are no life sentences. The maximum sentence for most crimes is 21 years—even for Anders Behring Breivik, who is responsible for probably the deadliest recorded rampage in the world, in which he killed 77 people and injured hundreds more in 2011 by detonating a bomb at a government building in Oslo and then opening fire at a nearby summer camp. Because Breivik was sentenced to "preventive detention," however, his term can be extended indefinitely for five years at a time, if he is deemed a continuing threat to society by the court. "Better out than in" is an unofficial motto of the Norwegian Correctional Service, which makes a reintegration guarantee to all released inmates. It works with other government agencies to secure a home, a job and access to a supportive social network for each inmate before release; Norway's social safety net also provides health care, education and a pension to all citizens. With one of the highest per capita gross domestic products of any country in the world, thanks to the profits from oil production in the North Sea, Norway is in a good position to provide all of this, and spending on the Halden prison runs to more than $93,000 per inmate per year, compared with just $31,000 for prisoners in the United States, according to the Vera Institute of Justice, a nonprofit research and advocacy organization.

That might sound expensive. But if the United States incarcerated its citizens at the same low rate as the Norwegians do (75 per 100,000 residents, versus roughly 700), it could spend that much per inmate and still save more than $45 billion a year. At a time when the American correctional system is under scrutiny—over the harshness of its sentences, its overreliance on solitary confinement, its racial disparities—citizens might ask themselves what all that money is getting them, besides 2.2 million incarcerated people and the hardships that fall on the families they leave behind. The extravagant brutality of the American approach to prisons is not working, and so it might just be worth looking for lessons at the opposite extreme, here in a sea of *blabaerskog,* or blueberry forest.

"This punishment, taking away their freedom—the sign of that is the wall, of course," Gudrun Molden, one of the Halden prison's architects, said on a drizzly morning a few days after I arrived. As we stood on a ridge, along with Jan Stromnes, the assistant warden, it was silent but for the chirping of birds and insects and a hoarse fluttering of birch leaves disturbed by the breeze. The prison is secluded from the surrounding farmland by the blueberry woods, which are the native forest of southeastern Norway: blue-black spruce, slender Scotch pine with red-tinged trunks and silver-skinned birches over a dense understory of blueberry bushes, ferns and mosses in deep shade. It is an ecosystem that evokes deep nostalgia in Norway, where picking wild berries is a near-universal summer pastime for families, and where the right to do so on uncultivated land is protected by law.

Norway banned capital punishment for civilians in 1902, and life sentences were abolished in 1981. But Norwegian prisons operated much like their American counterparts until 1998. That was the year Norway's Ministry of Justice reassessed the Correctional Service's goals and methods, putting the explicit focus on rehabilitating prisoners through education, job training and therapy. A second wave of change in 2007 made a priority of reintegration, with a special emphasis on helping inmates find housing and work with a steady income before they are even released. Halden was the first prison built after this overhaul, and so rehabilitation became the underpinning of its design process. Every aspect of the facility was designed to ease psychological pressures, mitigate conflict and minimize interpersonal friction. Hence the blueberry forest.

"Nature is a rehabilitation thing now," Molden said. Researchers are working to quantify the benefits of sunlight and fresh air in treating depression. But Molden viewed nature's importance for Norwegian inmates as far more personal. "We don't think of it as a rehabilitation," she said. "We think of it as a basic element in our growing up." She gestured to the knoll we stood on and the 12 acres of *blabaerskog* preserved on the prison grounds, echoing the canopy visible on the far side. Even elsewhere in Europe, most high-security prison plots are scraped completely flat and denuded of vegetation as security measures. "A lot of the staff when we started out came from other prisons in Norway," Stromnes said. "They were a little bit astonished by the trees and the number of them. Shouldn't they be taken away? And what if they climb up, the inmates? As we said, Well, if they climb up, then they can sit there until they get tired, and then they will come down." He laughed. "Never has anyone tried to hide inside. But if they should run in there, they won't get very far—they're still inside."

"Inside" meant inside the wall. The prison's defining feature, the wall is visible everywhere the inmates go, functioning as an inescapable reminder of their imprisonment. Because the prison buildings were purposely built to a human scale, with none more than two stories in height and all modest in breadth, the wall becomes an outsize presence; it looms everywhere, framed by the cell windows, shadowing the exercise yards, its pale horizontal spread emphasized by the dark vertical lines of the trees. The two primary responsibilities of the Correctional Service—detention and rehabilitation—are in perpetual tension with each other, and the architects felt that single wall could represent both. "We trusted the wall," Molden said, to serve as a symbol and an instrument of punishment.

When Molden and her collaborators visited the site in 2002, in preparing for the international competition to design the prison, they spent every minute they were allowed walking around it, trying to absorb the *genius loci,* the spirit of the place. They felt they should use as much of the site as possible, requiring inmates to walk outside to their daily commitments of school or work or therapy, over uneven ground, up and down hills, traveling to and from home, as they would in the world outside. They wound up arranging the prison's living quarters in a ring, which we could now see sloping down the hill on either side of us. In the choice of materials, the architects were inspired by the sober palette of the trees, mosses and bedrock all around; the primary building element is kiln-fired brick, blackened with some of the original red showing through. The architects used silvery galvanized-steel panels as a "hard" material to represent detention, and untreated larch wood, a low-maintenance species that weathers from taupe to soft gray, as a "soft" material associated with rehabilitation and growth.

The Correctional Service emphasizes what it calls "dynamic security," a philosophy that sees interpersonal relationships between the staff and the inmates as the primary factor in maintaining safety within the prison. They contrast this with the approach dominant in high-security prisons elsewhere in the world, which they call "static security." Static security relies on an environment designed to prevent an inmate with bad intentions from carrying them out. Inmates at those prisons are watched at a remove through cameras, contained by remote-controlled doors, prevented from vandalism or weapon-making by tamper-proof furniture, encumbered by shackles or officer escorts when moved. Corrections officers there are trained to control prisoners with as little interaction as possible, minimizing the risk of altercation.

Dynamic security focuses on preventing bad intentions from developing in the first place. Halden's officers are put in close quarters with the inmates as often as possible; the architects were instructed to make the guard stations tiny and cramped, to encourage officers to spend time in common rooms with the inmates instead. The guards socialize with the inmates every day, in casual conversation, often over tea or coffee or meals. Inmates can be monitored via surveillance cameras on the prison grounds, but they often move unaccompanied by guards, requiring a modest level of trust, which the administrators believe is crucial to their progress. Nor are there surveillance cameras in the classrooms or most of the workshops, or in the common rooms, the cell hallways or the cells themselves. The inmates have the opportunity to act out, but somehow they choose not to. In five years, the isolation cell furnished with a limb-restraining bed has never been used.

It is tempting to chalk up all this reasonableness to something peculiar in Norwegian socialization, some sort of civility driven coredeep into the inmates since birth, or perhaps attribute it to their racial and ethnic homogeneity as a group. But in actuality, only around three-fifths of the inmates are legal Norwegian citizens. The rest have come from more than 30 other countries (mostly in Eastern Europe, Africa and the Middle East) and speak little or no Norwegian; English is the lingua franca, a necessity for the officers to communicate with foreign prisoners.

Of the 251 inmates, nearly half are imprisoned for violent crimes like murder, assault or rape; a third are in for smuggling or selling drugs. Nevertheless, violent incidents and even threats are rare, and nearly all take place in Unit A. It is the prison's most restrictive unit, housing inmates who require close psychiatric or medical supervision or who committed crimes that would make them unpopular in Units B and C, the prison's more open "living" cell blocks, where the larger population of inmates mixes during the day for work, schooling and therapy programs.

I met some of the prisoners of Unit A one afternoon in the common room of an eight-man cell block. I was asked to respect the inmates' preferences for anonymity or naming, and for their choices in discussing their cases with me. The Norwegian news media does not often identify suspects or convicts by name, so confirming the details of their stories was not always possible. I sat on an orange vinyl couch next to a wooden shelving unit with a few haphazard piles of board games and magazines and legal books. On the other side of the room, near a window overlooking the unit's gravel yard, a couple of inmates were absorbed in a card game with a guard.

An inmate named Omar passed me a freshly pressed heart-shaped waffle over my shoulder on a paper plate, interrupting an intense monologue directed at me in excellent English by Chris Giske, a large man with a thick goatee and a shaved head who was wearing a heavy gold chain over a T-shirt that strained around his barrel-shaped torso.

"You have heard about the case? Sigrid?" Giske asked me. "It's one of the biggest cases in Norway."

In 2012, a 16-year-old girl named Sigrid Schjetne vanished while walking home one night, and her disappearance gripped the country. Her body was found a month later, and Giske's conviction in the case made him one of the most reviled killers in Norwegian history.

He explained to me that he asked to transfer out of Unit A, but that officials declined to move him. "They don't want me in prison," he said. "They want me in the psychiatric thing. I don't know why."

He was denied the transfer, I was later told, partly because of a desire not to outrage the other inmates, and partly because of significant concern over his mental health—and his history of unprovoked extreme violence against young women unfortunate enough to cross his path. Giske had previously spent two years in prison after attacking a woman with a crowbar. This time, there was disagreement among doctors over whether he belonged in a hospital or in prison. Until the question was settled, he was the responsibility of the staff at Halden. It was not the first, second or even third casual meal I had shared with a man convicted of murder since I arrived at the beginning of the week, but it was the first time I felt myself recoil on instinct. (After my visit, Giske was transferred to a psychiatric institution.)

Omar handed me a vacuum-sealed slice of what appeared to be flexible plastic, its wrapper decorated with a drawing of cheerful red dairy barns.

"It's fantastic!" he exclaimed. "When you are in Norway, you must try this! The first thing I learned, it was this. Brown cheese."

According to the packaging, brown cheese is one of the things that "make Norwegians Norwegians," a calorie-dense fuel of fat and sugar salvaged from whey discarded during the cheese-making process, which is cooked down for half a day until all that remains are caramelized milk sugars in a thick, sticky residue. With enthusiastic encouragement from the inmates, I peeled open the packaging and placed the glossy square on my limp waffle, following their instructions to fold the waffle as you would a taco, or a New York slice. To their great amusement, I winced as I tried to swallow what tasted to me like a paste of spray cheese mixed with fudge.

Another guard walked in and sat down next to me on the couch. "It's allowed to say you don't like it," she said.

Are Hoidal, the prison's warden, laughed from the doorway behind us and accepted his third waffle of the day. He had explained to me earlier, in response to my raised eyebrows, that in keeping with the prison's commitment to "normalcy," even the inmates in this block gather once a week to partake of waffles, which are a weekly ritual in most Norwegian homes.

At Halden, some inmates train for cooking certificates in the prison's professional-grade kitchen classroom, where I was treated to chocolate mousse presented in a wineglass, a delicate nest of orange zest curled on top. But most of the kitchen activity is more ordinary. I never entered a cell block without receiving offers of tea or coffee, an essential element of even the most basic Norwegian hospitality, and was always earnestly invited to share meals. The best meal I had in Norway—spicy lasagna, garlic bread and a salad with sun-dried tomatoes—was made by an inmate who had spent almost half of his 40 years in prison. "Every time, you make an improvement," he said of his cooking skills.

When I first met the inmates of C8, a special unit focused on addiction recovery, they were returning to their block laden with green nylon reusable bags filled with purchases from their weekly visit to the prison grocery shop, which is well stocked, carrying snacks and nonperishables but also a colorful assortment of produce, dairy products and meat. The men piled bags of food for communal suppers on the kitchen island on one side of their common room and headed back to their cells with personal items—fruit, soda, snacks, salami—to stash in their minifridges.

I met Tom, an inmate in his late 40s, as he was unpacking groceries on the counter: eggs, bacon, bread, cream, onions, tomato sauce, ground beef, lettuce, almonds, olives, frozen shrimp. Tom had a hoarse voice and a graying blond goatee, and his sleeveless basketball jersey exposed an assortment of tattoos decorating thick arms. His head was shaved smooth, with "F_____ the Police" inked in cursive along the right side of his skull; the left side said "RESPECT" in inch-tall letters. A small block of text under his right eye was blacked out, and under his left eye was "666." A long seam ran up the back of his neck and scalp, a remnant of a high-speed motorcycle accident that left him in a coma the last time he was out of prison.

"You are alone now, yeah?" Tom nodded toward the room behind me. I turned around to look.

There were maybe eight inmates around—playing a soccer video game on the modular couch, folding laundry dried on a rack in the corner by large windows overlooking the exercise yard, dealing cards at the dining table—but no guards. Tom searched my face for signs of alarm. The convictions represented among this group included murder, weapons possession and assault.

I was a little surprised, but I stayed nonchalant. I might have expected a bit more supervision—perhaps a quick briefing on safety protocol and security guidelines—but the guards could see us through the long windows of their station, sandwiched between the common rooms of C7 and C8. It was the first of many times I would be left alone with inmates in a common room or in a cell at the end of a hallway, the staff retreating to make space for candid conversation. "It's O.K.," Tom assured me, with what I thought sounded like a hint of pride.

A man named Yassin, the uncontested pastry king of C8, politely motioned for me to move aside so he could get to the baking pans in the cabinet at my feet. When Halden opened, there was a wave of foreign news reports containing snarky, florid descriptions of the "posh," "luxurious" prison, comparing its furnishings to those of a "boutique hotel." In reality, the furniture is not dissimilar from what you might find in an American college dorm. The truly striking difference is that it is *normal* furniture, not specially designed to prevent it from being turned into shivs, arson fuel or other instruments of violence. The kitchen also provides ample weapons if a prisoner were so inclined. As one inmate pointed out to me, the cabinets on the wall contained ceramic plates and glass cups, the drawers held metal silverware and there were a couple of large kitchen knives tethered by lengths of rubber-coated wire.

"If you want to ask me something, come on, no problem," Tom said, throwing open his hands in invitation. "I'm not very good in English."

Yassin stood up, laughing. "You speak very nice, Tom! It is prison English!" Yassin speaks Arabic and English and is also fluent in Norwegian, a requirement for living in the drug-treatment block, where group and individual counseling is conducted in Norwegian. Like many in the prison, Tom never finished high school. He was raised in a boys' home and has been in and out of prison, where English is common, for more than 30 years. (Yassin's first prison sentence began at 15. Now 29 and close to finishing his sentence for selling drugs, he wants to make a change and thinks he might like to run a scared-straight-style program for teenagers. Before this most recent arrest, the background photo on his Facebook profile was the Facebook logo recreated in white powder on a blue background, with a straw coming in for the snort. He immigrated to Norway as a child with his Moroccan family by way of Dubai.)

"I don't leave Norway," Tom said. "I love my country." He extended his arm with his fist clenched, showing a forearm covered in a "NORGE" tattoo shaded in the colors of the Norwegian flag. But I couldn't detect any tension between Tom and Yassin in the kitchen. Tom was adamant that overcoming his substance-abuse problem was his responsibility alone. But he conceded that the environment at Halden, and the availability of therapists, made it easier. Compared with other prisons, "it's quiet," he said. "No fighting, no drugs, no problem," he added. "You're safe."

The officers try to head off any tensions that could lead to violence. If inmates are having problems with one another, an officer or prison chaplain brings them together for a mediation session that continues until they have agreed to maintain peace and have shaken hands. Even members of rival gangs agree not to fight inside, though the promise doesn't extend to after their release. The few incidents of violence at Halden have been almost exclusively in Unit A, among the inmates with more serious psychiatric illnesses.

If an inmate does violate the rules, the consequences are swift, consistent and evenly applied. Repeated misbehavior or rule violations can result in cell confinement during regular work hours, sometimes without TV. One inmate claimed that an intrepid prisoner from Eastern Europe somehow managed to hack his TV to connect to the Internet and had it taken away for five months. ("Five months!" the inmate marveled to me. "I don't understand how he survived.")

It is perhaps hard to believe that Halden, or Norway more broadly, could hold any lessons for the United States. With its 251 inmates, Halden is one of Norway's largest prisons, in a country with only 3,800 prisoners (according to the International Center for Prison Studies); by contrast, in the United States, the average number is around 1,300 at maximum-security prisons, with a total of 2.2 million incarcerated (according to the federal Bureau of Justice Statistics). Halden's rehabilitation programs seem logistically and financially out of reach for such a system to even contemplate.

And yet there was a brief historical moment in which the United States pondered a similar approach to criminal justice. As part of his "war on crime," Lyndon B. Johnson established the President's Commission on Law Enforcement and Administration of Justice, a body of 19 advisers appointed to study, among other things, the conditions and practices of catastrophically overstretched prisons. The resulting 1967 report, "The Challenge of Crime in a Free Society," expressed concern that many correctional institutions were detrimental to rehabilitation: "Life in many institutions is at best barren and futile, at worst unspeakably brutal and degrading . . . . The conditions in which they live are the poorest possible preparation for their successful re-entry into society, and often merely reinforce in them a pattern of manipulation and destructiveness." And in its recommendations, the commission put forward a vision for prisons that would be surprisingly like Halden. "Architecturally, the model institution would resemble as much as possible a normal residential setting. Rooms, for example, would have doors rather than bars. Inmates would eat at small tables in an informal atmosphere. There would be classrooms, recreation facilities, day rooms, and perhaps a shop and library."

In the mid-1970s, the federal Bureau of Prisons completed three pretrial detention facilities that were designed to reflect those best practices. The three Metropolitan Correctional Centers, or M.C.C.s, were the first of what would come to be known as "new generation" institutions. The results, in both architecture and operation, were a radical departure from previous models. Groups of 44 prisoners populated self-contained units in which all of the single-inmate cells (with wooden doors meant to reduce both noise and cost) opened onto a day room, where they ate, socialized and met with visitors or counselors, minimizing the need for moving inmates outside the unit. All the prisoners spent the entire day outside their cells with a single unarmed correctional officer in an environment meant to diminish the sense of institutionalization and its attendant psychological stresses, with wooden and upholstered furniture, desks in the cells, porcelain toilets, exposed light fixtures, brightly colored walls, skylights and carpeted floors.

But by the time the centers opened, public and political commitment to rehabilitation programs in American prisons had shifted. Much of the backlash within penological circles can be traced to Robert Martinson, a sociology researcher at the City University of New York. In a 1974 article for the journal *Public Interest,* he summarized an analysis of data from 1945 to 1967 about the impact of rehabilitation programs on recidivism. Despite the fact that around half the individual programs did show evidence of effectiveness in reducing recidivism, Martinson's article concluded that no category of rehabilitation program (education or psychotherapy, for example) showed consistent results across prison systems. "With few and isolated exceptions," he wrote, "the rehabilitative efforts that have been reported so far have had no appreciable effect on recidivism." Martinson's paper was immediately seized upon by the news media and politicians, who latched on to the idea that "nothing works" in regard to prisoner rehabilitation. "It Doesn't Work" was the title of a "60 Minutes" segment on rehabilitation. "They don't rehabilitate, they don't deter, they don't punish and they don't protect," Jerry Brown, the governor of California, said in a 1975 speech. A top psychiatrist for the Bureau of Prisons resigned in disgust at what he perceived to be an abandonment of commitment to rehabilitation. At the dedication ceremony for the San Diego M.C.C. in 1974, one of the very structures designed with rehabilitation in mind, William Saxbe, the attorney general of the United States, declared that the ability of a correctional program to produce rehabilitation was a "myth" for all but the youngest offenders.

Martinson's paper was quickly challenged; a 1975 analysis of much of the same data by another sociologist criticized Martinson's choice to overlook the successful programs and their characteristics in favor of a broad conclusion devoid of context. By 1979, in light of new analyses, Martinson published another paper that unequivocally withdrew his previous conclusion, declaring that "contrary to my previous position, some treatment programs *do* have an appreciable effect on recidivism." But by then, the "nothing works" narrative was firmly entrenched. In 1984, a Senate report calling for more stringent sentencing guidelines cited Martinson's 1974 paper, without acknowledging his later reversal. The tough-on-crime policies that sprouted in Congress and state legislatures soon after included mandatory minimums, longer sentences, three-strikes laws, legislation allowing juveniles to be prosecuted as adults and an increase in prisoners' "maxing out," or being released without passing through reintegration programs or the parole system. Between 1975 and 2005, the rate of incarceration in the United States skyrocketed, from roughly 100 inmates per 100,000 citizens to more than 700—consistently one of the highest rates in the world. Though Americans make up about only 4.6 percent of the world's population, American prisons hold 22 percent of all incarcerated people.

Today, the M.C.C. model of incarceration, which is now known as "direct supervision," is not entirely dead. Around 350 facilities—making up less than 7 percent of the incarceration sites in the United States, mostly county-level jails, which are pretrial and short-stay institutions—have been built on the direct-supervision model and are, with greater and lesser fidelity to the ideal, run by the same principles of inmate management developed for the new-generation prisons of the 1970s. The body of data from those jails over the last 40 years has shown that they have lower levels of violence among inmates and against guards and reduced recidivism; some of these institutions, when directly compared with the older facilities they replaced, saw drops of 90 percent in violent incidents. But extrapolating from this tiny group of facilities to the entire nation, and in particular to its maximum-security prisons, is an impossible thought experiment. Much about the American culture of imprisonment today—the training of guards, the acculturation of prisoners, the incentives of politicians, the inattention of citizens—would have to change for the Norwegian approach to gain anything more than a minor foothold in the correctional system. The country has gone down a different road during the past half century, and that road does not lead to Halden Fengsel.

Even understanding how well the Norwegian approach works in Norway is a difficult business. On a Saturday afternoon in Oslo, I met Ragnar Kristoffersen, an anthropologist who teaches at the Correctional Service of Norway Staff Academy, which trains correction officers. Kristoffersen published a research paper comparing recidivism rates in the Scandinavian countries. A survey of inmates who were released in 2005 put Norway's two-year recidivism rate at 20 percent, the lowest in Scandinavia, which was widely praised in the Norwegian and international press. For comparison, a 2014 recidivism report from the United States Bureau of Justice Statistics announced that an estimated 68 percent of prisoners released in 30 states in 2005 were arrested for a new crime within three years.

I asked Kristoffersen if he had spent time at Halden. He reached into his briefcase and pulled out a handful of printed sheets. "Have you seen this?" he asked while waving them at me. "It's preposterous!" They were printouts of English-language articles about the prison, the most offensive and misleading lines highlighted. He read a few quotes about the prison's architecture and furnishings to me with disgust. I acknowledged that the hyperbolic descriptions would catch the attention of American and British readers, for whom the cost of a prison like Halden would probably need to be justified by strong evidence of a significant reduction in recidivism.

Somewhat to my surprise, Kristoffersen went into a rant about the unreliability of recidivism statistics for evaluating corrections practices. From one local, state or national justice system to another, diverse and ever-changing policies and practices in sentencing—what kinds and lengths of sentences judges impose for what types of crimes, how likely they are to reincarcerate an offender for a technical violation of parole, how much emphasis they put on community sentences over prison terms and many other factors—make it nearly impossible to know if you're comparing apples to apples. Kristoffersen pointed out that in 2005, Norway was putting people in prison for traffic offenses like speeding, something that few other countries do. Speeders are at low risk for reoffending and receiving another prison sentence for that crime or any other. Excluding traffic offenders, Norway's recidivism rate would, per that survey, be around 25 percent after two years.

Then there was the question of what qualifies as "recidivism." Some countries and states count any new arrest as recidivism, while others count only new convictions or new prison sentences; still others include parole violations. The numbers most commonly cited in news reports about recidivism, like the 20 percent celebrated by Norway or the 68 percent lamented by the United States, begin to fall apart on closer inspection. That 68 percent, for example, is a three-year number, but digging into the report shows the more comparable two-year rate to be 60 percent. And that number reflects not reincarceration (the basis for the Norwegian statistic) but rearrest, a much wider net. Fifteen pages into the Bureau of Justice Statistics report,

I found a two-year reincarceration rate, probably the best available comparison to Norway's measures. Kristoffersen's caveat in mind, that translated to a much less drastic contrast: Norway, 25 percent; the United States, 28.8 percent.

What does that mean? Is the American prison system doing a better job than conventional wisdom would suggest? It is frustratingly hard to tell. I asked Kristoffersen if that low reincarceration rate might reflect the fact that long prison sentences mean that many prisoners become naturally less likely to reoffend because of advanced age. He agreed that was possible, along with many other more and less obvious variables. It turned out that measuring the effectiveness of Halden in particular was nearly impossible; Norway's recidivism statistics are broken down by prison of release, and almost no prisoners are released directly from maximum-security prisons, so Halden doesn't have a recidivism number.

After nearly an hour of talking about the finer points of statistics, though, Kristoffersen stopped and made a point that wasn't about statistics at all.

"You have to be aware—there's a logical type of error which is common in debating these things," he said. "That is, you shouldn't mix two kinds of principles. The one is about: How do you fight crimes? How do you reduce recidivism? And the other is: What are the principles of humanity that you want to build your system on? They are two different questions."

He leaned back in his chair and went on. "We like to think that treating inmates nicely, humanely, is good for the rehabilitation. And I'm not arguing against it. I'm saying two things. There are poor evidence saying that treating people nicely will keep them from committing new crimes. Very poor evidence."

He paused. "But then again, my second point would be," he said, "if you treat people badly, it's a reflection on yourself." In officer-training school, he explained, guards are taught that treating inmates humanely is something they should do not for the inmates but for themselves. The theory is that if officers are taught to be harsh, domineering and suspicious, it will ripple outward in their lives, affecting their selfimage, their families, even Norway as a whole. Kristoffersen cited a line that is usually attributed to Dostoyevsky: "The degree of civilization in a society can be judged by entering its prisons."

I heard the same quotation from Are Hoidal, Halden's warden, not long before I left Halden. He told me proudly that people wanted to work at the prison, and officers and teachers told me that they hoped to spend their whole careers at Halden, that they were proud of making a difference.

"They make big changes in here," Hoidal said as we made our way through the succession of doors that would return us to the world outside. There was, improbably, an actual rainbow stretching from the clouds above, landing somewhere outside the wall. Hoidal was quiet for a moment, then laughed. "I have the best job in the world!" He chuckled and shook his head. He sounded surprised.

## Correction: April 26, 2015

An article on March 29 about Norway's Halden prison described incompletely the circumstances of Anders Breivik's 21-year sentence for a bombing-and-shooting attack. While the maximum sentence for most crimes is 21 years, the Norwegian penal code allows for preventive detention, which is the extension of a sentence in five-year increments if the convicted person is deemed to be a continued threat to society. Therefore, the maximum term for any crime is not 21 years.

## Critical Thinking

1. How do you think the goal of the Norwegian penal system, to get inmates out of it, compares with the goal of the American system?

2. Do you believe forgiveness should be a part of the American correctional philosophy?

3. Could a Halden-like prison be effective in the US?

## Internet References

**Bureau of Justice Statistics**
http://www.bjs.gov/index.cfm?ty=pbdetail&iid=4986

**Euro Vista**
http://euro-vista.org/wp-content/uploads/2015/01/EuroVista-vol2-no3-6-Kristofferson-edit.pdf

**International Centre for Prison Studies**
http://www.prisonstudies.org/country/norway

**The New York Times**
http://www.nytimes.com/2012/08/25/world/europe/anders-behring-breivik-murder-trial.html?_r=1

**Vera Institute for Justice**
http://www.vera.org/pubs/special/price-prisons-what-incarceration-costs-taxpayers

---

**JESSICA BENKO** is a print and radio journalist whose work has appeared in *National Geographic* and *Wired* and on "This American Life."

*Article*

Prepared by: Joanne Naughton

# Study: Pretrial Detention Creates More Crime

Erika Eichelberger

## Learning Outcomes

*After reading this article, you will be able to:*

- State what is meant by "low-risk" defendants.

- Show that many low-risk defendants who are not released from incarceration to await trial are more likely to commit new crimes later.

- Argue that judges should try to distinguish among low-, moderate-, and high-risk offenders.

Detaining certain defendants before trial makes them more likely to commit a new crime, according to a recent report.

Many pretrial detainees are low risk, meaning that if they are released before trial, they are highly unlikely to commit other crimes and very likely to return to court. When these defendants are held for two to three days before trial, as opposed to just 24 hours, they are nearly 40 percent more likely to commit new crimes before their trial, and 17 percent more likely to commit another crime within 2 years, according to a report released last month by the Laura and John Arnold Foundation, a private foundation that funds criminal justice research.

"The primary goal of the American criminal justice system is to protect the public," the authors of the report say. "But . . . the pretrial phase of the system is actually helping to create new repeat offenders."

The report—based on studies of both state and federal courts—also found that the longer low-risk detainees are held behind bars before trial, the more likely they are to commit another crime. Low-risk defendants who were detained for 31 days or more before they had their day in court offended 74 percent more frequently before trial than those detained for just one day. The study found similar results for moderate-risk defendants, though for these offenders, the rate of increase in new criminal activity is smaller. When it comes to high-risk offenders, the report found no correlation between pretrial detention time and recidivism.

The report noted that recidivism could be curbed if judges made an effort to distinguish between low-, moderate-, and high-risk offenders. "Judges, of course, do their best to sort violent, high-risk defendants from nonviolent, low-risk ones," the report says, "but they have almost no reliable, data-driven risk assessment tools at their disposal to help them make these decisions." Fewer than 10 percent of US jurisdictions do any sort of risk-assessment during the pretrial stage.

Not only does unnecessary pretrial detention create repeat offenders, it costs taxpayers a lot of money. Pretrial detainees represent more than 60 percent of the total inmate population in the country's jails. The cost of incarcerating defendants pretrial is about $9 billion.

## Critical Thinking

1. What are the costs of unnecessary pretrial detention?
2. Should risk assessment at the pretrial stage be done as a matter of course in all jurisdictions?

## Internet References

**Laura and John Arnold Foundation**
   http://arnoldfoundation.org/sites/default/files/pdf/LJAF-Pretrial-CJ-Research-brief_FNL.pdf
**LLRX.com**
   http://www.llrx.com/features/pretrialdetention.htm

*Article*

Prepared by: Joanne Naughton

# War on Drugs Failure Gives Way to Treatment in States, Cities

Saki Knafo

## Learning Outcomes

*After reading this article, you will be able to:*

- Discuss some of the new alternative ways of dealing with drug law offenders.

- Describe what has happened in Texas as a result of reforms enacted by lawmakers.

Four years ago, police officers and prosecutors in Seattle decided they'd had enough of the usual ways of fighting the war on drugs.

The police were tired of arresting the same drug users and prostitutes again and again, and the prosecutors had run out of money to keep putting people in jail. So the police department, the prosecutor's office, and the city's elected leaders decided to try something radically different.

With the approval of Seattle prosecutors and politicians, the police began directing repeat drug offenders to social-service workers who offered to help them pay for rent and school and referred them to business owners who were willing to hire people with criminal backgrounds.

The police weren't entirely hopeful that the strategy would pan out. But with a growing number of neighborhood leaders and business owners demanding safer, quieter streets, they had little choice but to try something new.

Today, their doubts are giving way to a growing confidence that they're onto something significant. "People we've dealt with over and over and over again are getting treatment and getting into housing and getting jobs," said Lt. Deanna Nollette, a supervisor in the police department. "It's a pretty big surprise."

"Law Enforcement Assisted Diversion," or LEAD, as the public-safety strategy is known in Seattle, is just one of a fast-growing number of alternatives to the traditional "tough on crime" approach that has defined America's drug war for four decades. Lawmakers throughout the country have increasingly turned to these strategies to deflect the steep costs of incarcerating the soaring population of drug offenders.

Some of these alternatives are more punitive than others, and policy experts and prison-reform advocates disagree on the best way to treat drug offenders. But taken as a whole, these alternatives represent a major shift in America's response to illegal drug use.

"As someone who has been in this now for 25 years, and thought that change was glacial, never mind incremental, what has happened recently is extraordinary," said Howard Josepher, the founder of Exponents, a 25-year-old drug-abuse treatment program in New York City.

In Texas, legislators have sharply increased investments in treatment programs and in drug courts—specialized judicial systems whose judges can order drug offenders to undergo treatment as an alternative to jail. In California, where the prisons are so crowded that the state has been ordered by a federal court to reduce the prison population by thousands of inmates, counties have been granted an expanded role in deciding whether to lock up low-level offenders or connect them with drug counselors. From New York to Arkansas to Florida, states have seen their prison populations decline after years of growth.

The burgeoning availability of these alternatives is largely born out of necessity. Since the mid-1970s, when lawmakers first began enacting tough anti-drug policies that have collectively come to be known as the "war on drugs," the number of people behind bars has increased fivefold, peaking at 2.2 million in 2010. Drug offenses accounted for much of the surge. From 1980 to 2010, the number of those incarcerated on drug charges shot up from 41,000 to more than a half-million.

Criminal justice advocates have long decried the punitive laws behind this trend, stressing the disproportionately heavy toll exacted on racial and ethnic minorities, who make up more than 60 percent of the prison population, despite using drugs and committing crimes at a rate similar to whites.

But only in recent years have lawmakers thrown their weight behind serious reform efforts. And while most of these calls for changes have come from statehouses and county headquarters, federal government officials have begun adding their voices to the chorus of reformers. In recent months, members of Congress from both parties have teamed up to introduce legislation that would reduce penalties for nonviolent drug offenders. And last week, in what has widely been hailed as a historic announcement, Attorney General Eric Holder declared that the Justice Department would do its part to cut down on severe sentences for those convicted of nonviolent drug crimes.

Some of the most striking changes have unfolded in places not always associated with progressive reforms. In Texas, for example, lawmakers have cut billions of dollars from the prison system, while investing hundreds of millions in drug courts and in counseling programs that aim to help people recover from drug addictions and get their lives under control. Proponents point out that the changes haven't reversed the state's decades of declining crime rates:

> From 2007, the first year of the shift, to 2011, the most recent year for which detailed data is available, the number of violent crimes in Texas dropped by nearly 20,000, and property crimes fell by five times as much. The state authorized the closing of one prison in 2011 and two more this year.

In Georgia, meanwhile, where 1 out of every 13 adults are either on probation, parole, or behind bars, lawmakers have passed a reform package that expands the state's treatment programs, drug courts, and the use of electronic monitoring as an substitute for prison time. States that include South Carolina and Kansas have adopted similar measures.

Not everyone is on board with these changes, however. "Probably the biggest obstacle to these reforms is what I would call establishment politicians and officeholders, and this really means on the left or on the right," said Vikrant Reddy, a policy analyst with the conservative Texas Public Policy Foundation in Austin. "I think there are still politicians who haven't broken free of the thinking of the past. They don't seem to understand that there has been a sea change among American voters, who don't always feel that incarceration is the best tack when it comes to what we do about low-level nonviolent crime."

Another obstacle to the universal adoption of these reforms is the continued scarcity of funding for programs that treat addiction. "There aren't a lot of open slots," said Doug McVay, a drug policy expert and the editor of the online book *Drug War Facts*. "And we've chosen to put money into cleaning up the mess, rather than trying to make things better so that there isn't a mess in the first place."

Yet, for those in the growing ranks of reformers—a loose alliance that spans the political spectrum from former House Speaker Newt Gingrich (R) to California Lt. Gov. Gavin Newsom (D)—the debate is no longer over whether to change the country's drug policies, but how. At the center of the conversation is the proliferation of drug courts. While conservatives and many liberals see the expansion of these courts as key to reform, libertarians and some on the left say society's response to drug abuse should take place outside the courthouse altogether.

Seattle's LEAD program, some reformers say, could prove to be a pioneering example of how police departments can help accomplish this goal. Although results from a study of the program aren't finished, cities from San Francisco to New York have already reached out to the program's supervisors for guidance.

Lisa Daugaard, a longtime public defender and one of the program's coordinators, likened LEAD to a drug court "without the stigma and costs of court involvement." Unlike most drug courts, she said, the program doesn't require participants to stay off drugs or even seek treatment. "LEAD is not only for people who are involved in drug activities because of addiction," she noted. "Some are involved for a wage."

About half the program's participants end up accepting some form of treatment, but they do so voluntarily, Daugaard said, without facing any pressure from judges or prosecutors. "It's not that we're indifferent about people moving toward sobriety," she said. "It's that requiring that is not the best way to engage people."

Levi Hoagland, a 34-year-old former high school football star who is preparing to end his year-long stay at a California rehabilitation center, can see the advantages of both the drug court system and the less punitive approach championed by the likes of Daugaard. Several years ago, while suffering from mental breakdown brought on by a methamphetamine binge, he deliberately rammed his car into a parked van and ended up in jail, where he agreed to enter a substance-abuse treatment program under the supervision of a drug court judge.

Some of the more hardened criminals in the jail scoffed at the idea, Hoagland said. But he was ready for a change.

"I couldn't listen to a guy who's got the word 'guilty' tattooed across his back," Hoagland said.

Now, as he gets ready to assimilate back into the outside world, he is wary of the obstacles faced by those who have run afoul of the criminal justice system. Like many other Californians, Hoagland is ineligible for food stamps because of the state's lifetime ban on applicants with past felony convictions, and he's concerned about how his past may look to prospective employers.

Still, it was his brush with the criminal justice system that caused him to seek treatment. And getting sober, he said, has been the "miracle of my life."

"I have two beautiful children and they used to be the most important thing in the world to me, but that's changed," Hoagland said. "The most important thing for me today is to stay clean and sober, and that allows me to be a dad to somebody."

## Critical Thinking

1. What has been the experience of Seattle with their new policy?
2. Does incarcerating drug law violators work?

## Create Central

www.mhhe.com/createcentral

## Internet References

**Drug War Facts**
   http://drugwarfacts.org/cms/Drug_Courts#sthash.1OivuGaF.dpbs

**National Association of Drug Court Professionals**
   www.nadcp.org/Drug%20Courts%20Are%20the%20Most%20Sensible%20and%20Proven%20Alternative%20to%20Incarceration

**National Institute of Justice**
   www.crimesolutions.gov/ProgramDetails.aspx?ID=89

*Article*

Prepared by: Joanne Naughton

# Portugal Cut Addiction Rates in Half by Connecting Drug Users With Communities Instead of Jailing Them

Fifteen years ago, the Portuguese had one of the worst drug problems in Europe. So they decriminalized drugs, took money out of prisons, put it into holistic rehabilitation, and found that human connection is the antidote to addiction.

JOHANN HARI

## Learning Outcomes

*After reading this article, you will be able to:*

- Describe the Rat Park experiment.

- Relate the findings of a study by the *British Journal of Criminology*.

- Explain what happened when Portugal decriminalized all drugs nearly 15 years ago.

It is now 100 years since drugs were first banned—and all through this long century of waging war on drugs, we have been told a story about addiction by our teachers and by our governments. This story is so deeply ingrained in our minds that we take it for granted: There are strong chemical hooks in these drugs, so if we stopped on day twenty-one, our bodies would need the chemical. We would have a ferocious craving. We would be addicted. That's what addiction means.

This theory was first established, in part, through rat experiments—ones that were injected into the American psyche in the 1980s, in a famous advertisement by the Partnership for a Drug-Free America. You may remember it. The experiment is simple. Put a rat in a cage, alone, with two water bottles. One is just water. The other is water laced with heroin or cocaine. Almost every time you run this experiment, the rat will become obsessed with the drugged water, and keep coming back for more and more, until it kills itself.

The ad explains: "Only one drug is so addictive, nine out of ten laboratory rats will use it. And use it. And use it. Until dead. It's called cocaine. And it can do the same thing to you."

But in the 1970s, a professor of Psychology in Vancouver called Bruce Alexander noticed something odd about this experiment. The rat is put in the cage all alone. It has nothing to do but take the drugs. What would happen, he wondered, if we tried this differently?

So Professor Alexander built Rat Park. It is a lush cage where the rats would have colored balls and the best rat-food and tunnels to scamper down and plenty of friends: everything a rat about town could want. What, Alexander wanted to know, will happen then?

In Rat Park, all the rats obviously tried both water bottles, because they didn't know what was in them. But what happened next was startling.

The rats with good lives didn't like the drugged water. They mostly shunned it, consuming less than a quarter of the drugs the isolated rats used. None of them died. While all the rats who were alone and unhappy became heavy users, none of the rats who had a happy environment did.

At first, I thought this was merely a quirk of rats, until I discovered that there was—at the same time as the Rat Park experiment—a helpful human equivalent taking place. It was called the Vietnam War. *Time* magazine reported using heroin was "as common as chewing gum" among U.S. soldiers, and there is solid evidence to back this up: some 20 percent of U.S. soldiers had become addicted to heroin there, according to a study published in the *Archives of General Psychiatry*.

Many people were understandably terrified; they believed a huge number of addicts were about to head home when the war ended.

But in fact some 95 percent of the addicted soldiers—according to the same study—simply stopped. Very few had rehab. They shifted from a terrifying cage back to a pleasant one, so didn't want the drug any more.

Professor Alexander argues this discovery is a profound challenge both to the right-wing view that addiction is a moral failing caused by too much hedonistic partying, and the liberal view that addiction is a disease taking place in a chemically hijacked brain. In fact, he argues, addiction is an adaptation. It's not you. It's your cage.

## Rats in the Park

After the first phase of Rat Park, Professor Alexander then took this test further. He reran the early experiments, where the rats were left alone, and became compulsive users of the drug. He let them use for 57 days—if anything can hook you, it's that.

Then he took them out of isolation, and placed them in Rat Park. He wanted to know, if you fall into that state of addiction, is your brain hijacked, so you can't recover? Do the drugs take you over? What happened is—again—striking. The rats seemed to have a few twitches of withdrawal, but they soon stopped their heavy use, and went back to having a normal life. The good cage saved them.

When I first learned about this, I was puzzled. How can this be? This new theory is such a radical assault on what we have been told that it felt like it could not be true. But the more scientists I interviewed, and the more I looked at their studies, the more I discovered things that don't seem to make sense—unless you take account of this new approach.

Here's one example of an experiment that is happening all around you, and may well happen to you one day. If you get run over today and you break your hip, you will probably be given diamorphine, the medical name for heroin. In the hospital around you, there will be plenty of people also given heroin for long periods, for pain relief.

The heroin you will get from the doctor will have a much higher purity and potency than the heroin being used by street-addicts, who have to buy from criminals who adulterate it. So if the old theory of addiction is right—it's the drugs that cause it; they make your body need them—then it's obvious what

should happen. Loads of people should leave the hospital and try to score smack on the streets to meet their habit.

But here's the strange thing: It virtually never happens. As the Canadian doctor Gabor Mate was the first to explain to me, medical users just stop, despite months of use. The same drug, used for the same length of time, turns street-users into desperate addicts and leaves medical patients unaffected.

If you still believe, as I used to, that chemical hooks are what cause addiction, then this makes no sense.

But if you believe Bruce Alexander's theory, the picture falls into place. The street-addict is like the rats in the first cage, isolated, alone, with only one source of solace to turn to. The medical patient is like the rats in the second cage. She is going home to a life where she is surrounded by the people she loves. The drug is the same, but the environment is different.

## The Opposite of Addiction Is Connection

This gives us an insight that goes much deeper than the need to understand addicts.

Professor Peter Cohen argues that human beings have a deep need to bond and form connections. It's how we get our satisfaction. If we can't connect with each other, we will connect with anything we can find—the whirr of a roulette wheel or the prick of a syringe. He says we should stop talking about 'addiction' altogether, and instead call it 'bonding.' A heroin addict has bonded with heroin because she couldn't bond as fully with anything else.

So the opposite of addiction is not sobriety. It is human connection.

When I learned all this, I found it slowly persuading me, but I still couldn't shake off a nagging doubt. Are these scientists saying chemical hooks make no difference? It was explained to me—you can become addicted to gambling, and nobody thinks you inject a pack of cards into your veins. You can have all the addiction, and none of the chemical hooks. I went to a Gamblers' Anonymous meeting in Las Vegas (with the permission of everyone present, who knew I was there to observe) and they were as plainly addicted as the cocaine and heroin addicts I have known in my life. Yet there are no chemical hooks on a craps table.

But still, surely, I asked, there is some role for the chemicals? It turns out there is an experiment which gives us the answer to this in quite precise terms, which I learned about in Richard DeGrandpre's book *The Cult of Pharmacology*.

Everyone agrees cigarette smoking is one of the most addictive processes around. The chemical hooks in tobacco come from a drug inside it called nicotine. So when nicotine patches were developed in the early 1990s, there was a huge surge of optimism—cigarette smokers could get all of their chemical hooks, without the other filthy (and deadly) effects of cigarette smoking. They would be freed.

But the Office of the Surgeon General has found that just 17.7 percent of cigarette smokers are able to stop using nicotine patches. That's not nothing. If the chemicals drive 17.7 percent of addiction, as this shows, that's still millions of lives ruined globally. But what it reveals again is that the story we have been taught about chemical hooks is, in fact, real, only a minor part of a much bigger picture.

This has huge implications for the 100-year-old war on drugs.

This massive war—which kills people from the malls of Mexico to the streets of Liverpool—is based on the claim that we need to physically eradicate a whole array of chemicals because they hijack people's brains and cause addiction. But if drugs aren't the driver of addiction—if, in fact, it is disconnection that drives addiction—then this makes no sense.

Ironically, the war on drugs actually increases all those larger drivers of addiction. For example, I went to a prison in Arizona—Tent City—where inmates are detained in tiny stone isolation cages ('The Hole') for weeks and weeks on end to punish them for drug use. It is as close to a human recreation of the cages that guaranteed deadly addiction in rats as I can imagine. And when those prisoners get out, they will be unemployable because of their criminal record, guaranteeing they will be cut off ever more.

# How Portugal Halved Drug Addiction Levels

There is an alternative. You can build a system that is designed to help drug addicts to reconnect with the world—and so leave behind their addictions.

This isn't theoretical. It is happening. I have seen it. Nearly 15 years ago, Portugal had one of the worst drug problems in Europe, with one percent of the population addicted to heroin. They had tried a drug war, and the problem just kept getting worse.

So they decided to do something radically different. They resolved to decriminalize all drugs, and transfer all the money they used to spend on arresting and jailing drug addicts, and spend it instead on reconnecting them—to their own feelings, and to the wider society.

The most crucial step is to get them secure housing, and subsidized jobs so they have a purpose in life, and something to get out of bed for. I watched as they are helped, in warm and welcoming clinics, to learn how to reconnect with their feelings, after years of trauma and stunning them into silence with drugs.

One group of addicts were given a loan to set up a removals firm. Suddenly, they were a group, all bonded to each other, and to the society, and responsible for each other's care.

The results of all this are now in. An independent study by the *British Journal of Criminology* found that since total decriminalization, addiction has fallen, and injecting drug use is down by 50 percent. I'll repeat that: injecting drug use is down by 50 percent.

Decriminalization has been such a manifest success that very few people in Portugal want to go back to the old system. The main campaigner against the decriminalization back in 2000 was Joao Figueira, the country's top drug cop. He offered all the dire warnings that we would expect: more crime, more addicts. But when we sat together in Lisbon, he told me that everything he predicted had not come to pass—and he now hopes the whole world will follow Portugal's example.

Happiness in "the Age of Loneliness"

This isn't only relevant to addicts. It is relevant to all of us, because it forces us to think differently about ourselves. Human beings are bonding animals. We need to connect and love. The wisest sentence of the twentieth century was E.M. Forster's: "only connect." But we have created an environment and a culture that cut us off from connection, or offer only the parody of it offered by the Internet. The rise of addiction is a symptom of a deeper sickness in the way we live—constantly directing our gaze towards the next shiny object we should buy, rather than the human beings all around us.

The writer George Monbiot has called this "the age of loneliness." We have created human societies where it is easier for people to become cut off from all human connections than ever before. Bruce Alexander, the creator of Rat Park, told me that for too long, we have talked exclusively about individual recovery from addiction. We need now to talk about social recovery—how we all recover, together, from the sickness of isolation that is sinking on us like a thick fog.

But this new evidence isn't just a challenge to us politically. It doesn't just force us to change our minds. It forces us to change our hearts.

Loving an addict is really hard. When I looked at the addicts I love, it was always tempting to follow the tough love advice doled out by reality shows like Intervention—tell the addict to shape up, or cut them off. Their message is that an addict who won't stop should be shunned. It's the logic of the drug war, imported into our private lives.

But in fact, I learned, that will only deepen their addiction—and you may lose them altogether. I came home determined to tie the addicts in my life closer to me than ever—to let them know I love them unconditionally, whether they stop, or whether they can't.

## Critical Thinking

1. Has the war on drugs worked—nationwide or worldwide?

2. Do you agree that the opposite of addiction is not sobriety, but human connection, or do you believe that drugs have a chemical "hook" which causes addiction?

3. Should all drugs be decriminalized, or should they be legalized and controlled, as tobacco and alcohol are?

## Internet References

**Bruce K. Alexander**
http://www.brucekalexander.com/articles-speeches/rat-park

**Spiegelonline international**
http://www.spiegel.de/international/europe/evaluating-drug-decriminalization-in-portugal-12-years-later-a-891060.html

**Stuart McMillen**
http://www.stuartmcmillen.com/blog/cartoon-blog/globalization-addiction-bruce-alexander/

---

**JOHANN HARI** is a British journalist whose work has appeared in the *New York Times, Le Monde, The Guardian, The New Republic,* and other publications.

This article is adapted from *Chasing the Scream: The First and Last Days of the War on Drugs* by Johann Hari.

*Article* Prepared by: Joanne Naughton

# "The Worst of the Worst" Aren't the Only Ones Who Get Executed

SIMON MCCORMACK

## Learning Outcomes

*After reading this article, you will be able to:*

- Summarize the findings of Smith's study of people who have been executed.
- State some of the criticisms of the study.
- Discuss the Eighth Amendment requirements for the death penalty.

A new study suggests that the people put to death in America are hardly the worst of the worst offenders. The study, published in *Hastings Law Journal*, looked at 100 executions between 2012 and 2013. Some of the most striking results are displayed in the graphic.

Robert Smith, the study's lead researcher and an assistant professor of law at the University of North Carolina, told *The Huffington Post* his research provides evidence that many of the people who are actually put to death are not cold, calculating, remorseless killers.

"A lot of folks even familiar with criminal justice and the death penalty system thought that, by the time you executed somebody, you're really gonna get these people that the court describes as the worst of the worst," Smith said. "It was surprising to us just how many of the people that we found had evidence in their record suggesting that there are real problems with functional deficits that you wouldn't expect to see in people being executed."

One of the people in Smith's study is Daniel Cook. Cook's mom drank and used drugs while she was pregnant with him. His mother and grandparents molested him and his dad abused him by, among other things, burning his genitals with a cigarette.

As Harvard Law Professor Charles J. Ogletree, Jr. documents in the *Washington Post*, Cook was later placed in foster care, where a "foster parent chained him nude to a bed and raped him while other adults watched from the next room through a one-way mirror."

The prosecutor who presented the death penalty case against Cook said he never would have put execution on the table if he had known about the man's brutal past. Nonetheless, Cook was put to death on Aug. 8, 2012.

In various landmark cases, the Supreme Court has found that executing people with an intellectual disability or severe mental illness can be a violation of the Eighth Amendment, which bars cruel and unusual punishment.

The court has also found that severe childhood trauma can be a mitigating factor in a defendant's case, according to a press release accompanying the report.

But Kent Scheidegger, legal director of the Criminal Justice Legal Foundation, said there are serious flaws with the study's methodology. He noted that the authors count someone as intellectually disabled if they score below a 70 on at least one IQ test. However, he said, looking at the lowest score in a series of tests can be misleading.

"How fast can you run a mile? If you run on several different days and have several different times, the speed at which you can do it is your fastest time," Scheidegger said in an email to HuffPost. "Various factors can make you perform less than your best, including simply not trying hard, but nothing can make you perform better than your best. It's the same with IQ scores. The high score is a good indication of performance. The low score means practically nothing."

Scheidegger also said mitigating factors like intellectual disability or a traumatic childhood don't matter nearly as much as the brutality of the crimes that death row inmates have committed.

"Since 1978, defendants have had carte blanche to introduce everything including the kitchen sink in mitigation," Scheidegger said. "The actions of their attorneys in finding and presenting that evidence is scrutinized repeatedly in the years after the trial. What we see in case after case is that even after years of reinvestigation and relitigation, the horrifying facts of the crime remain far more than sufficient to outweigh the minimally relevant evidence in mitigation."

But Smith said the courts have found that, independent of the heinousness of the crime, the prosecution must also show that the defendant is "morally culpable."

"The Eighth Amendment requires that the death penalty be limited in its application to only those offenders who commit the most aggravated homicides *and* who possess the most aggravated moral culpability," Smith said.

"But our research showed that of the last 100 people we executed in America, most of them had severe functional deficits. In many cases, they suffered from several mental illness and years of horrific abuse. And the problem is that there is no standard measurement for these type of functional deficits. For instance, there is no IQ score equivalent for gauging the functional deficits that mark any particular person with a severe mental illness."

Smith also said those who ended up executed did not have adequate representation at the trial level. Juries were often not informed of defendants' intellectual or mental health problems or their family history of extreme abuse.

Smith noted that the reason traumatic childhoods are brought up is not necessarily to make juries feel bad for the person on trial, but because "decades of research" has shown that these types of trauma can trigger the kinds of "functional deficits" that were present in many of the cases examined in the report.

"We're executing people who get the worst lawyers, have the least resources and are the most vulnerable," Smith said.

Sometimes these mitigating factors come out during the appeals process, but by then it may be too late, since judges often give deference to the jury's verdict.

"It's often a tale told too late," Smith said. "How many of these people would have not even come close to dying if they had had good lawyers at trial or pretrial?"

With executions either being outlawed or rarely used in many parts of the country, Smith said the punishment's days may be numbered.

"We're not talking about reform," Smith said. "We're talking about it being on its way out."

## Critical Thinking

1. In a death penalty case, should it matter to a jury that a defendant had a traumatic childhood?

2. When asking for the death penalty, isn't it enough for a prosecutor to prove that the defendant committed a heinous crime?

3. Why is it so important in capital cases that the defendant have good legal representation?

## Internet References

**Slate**
   http://www.slate.com/articles/news_and_politics/jurisprudence/2014/05 the_death_penalty_is_disappearing_in_america_except_in_the_south.html

**The Washington Post**
   http://www.washingtonpost.com/opinions/charles-ogletree-the-death-penalty-is-incompatible-with-human-dignity/2014/07/18/c0849dea-0e6b-11e4-b8e5-d0de80767fc2_story.html